TRAVELER

alaska

NATIONAL GEOGRAPHIC
TRAVELER

alaska

by Bob Devine
photography by Michael Melford

National Geographic
Washington, DC

CONTENTS

Pages 2–3: Prince William Sound   Left: Totem pole, Totem Bight State Historical Park, Ketchikan

TRAVELING WITH EYES OPEN

Alert travelers go with a purpose and leave with a benefit. If you travel responsibly, you can help support wildlife conservation, historic preservation, and cultural enrichment in the places you visit. You can enrich your own travel experience as well.

To be a geo-savvy traveler:

- Recognize that your presence has an impact on the places you visit.

- Spend your time and money in ways that sustain local character. (Besides, it's more interesting that way.)

- Value the destination's natural and cultural heritage.

- Respect the local customs and traditions.

- Express appreciation to local people about things you find interesting and unique to the place: its nature and scenery, music and food, historic villages and buildings.

- Vote with your wallet: Support the people who support the place, patronizing businesses that make an effort to celebrate and protect what's special there. Seek out shops, local restaurants, inns, and tour operators who love their home—who love taking care of it and showing it off. Avoid businesses that detract from the character of the place.

- Enrich yourself, taking home memories and stories to tell, knowing that you have contributed to the preservation and enhancement of the destination.

That is the type of travel now called geotourism, defined as "tourism that sustains or enhances the geographical character of a place—its environment, culture, aesthetics, heritage, and the well-being of its residents." To learn more, visit National Geographic's Center for Sustainable Destinations at *www.national geographic.com/travel/sustainable.*

alaska

ABOUT THE AUTHOR & THE PHOTOGRAPHER

Bob Devine writes about the environment, natural history, and outdoor travel from his home in Oregon. National Geographic has published several of his works, including the *Guide to America's Outdoors: Western Canada* and *Alien Invasion: America's Battle with Non-native Animals and Plants.* He first traveled to Alaska on assignment in 1987 and has since returned as often as possible.

Michael Melford is a renowned photographer whose assignments include both travel and editorial photography. His award-winning work has appeared in many major U.S. publications, including *National Geographic Traveler, Travel and Leisure, Life, Fortune,* and *Newsweek.* He is a contributing photographer to *National Geographic Traveler* and his work often appears in *National Geographic* magazine. He lives with his family in Mystic, Connecticut.

Charting Your Trip

The Great Land. It's an apt nickname for Alaska because in this enormous state the land is preeminent. In the rest of the United States, human development surrounds a few oases of nature, but in Alaska the untamed outdoors surrounds the few civilized enclaves.

Certainly, the state offers some notable cultural attractions—Alaska native heritage sites, historic gold rush towns, and more—but you will not have seen Alaska if you don't get out into the wilds. This doesn't necessarily mean hiking, backpacking, or camping, though those are great ways to experience the land. You also can rent a backwoods cabin, drive a lonely back road, stay in a wilderness lodge, or cruise along an undeveloped coastline on a boat. By all means, consider guided ventures and excursions. They are safer and you can learn more from the locals (see p. 29).

Getting Around

Alaska offers varied means of transportation. You can rent cars, vans, or RVs; buses are available; the Alaska Railroad (*www.alaska railroad.com*) makes regular runs north and south from Seward (on the Gulf of Alaska) to Fairbanks (in the Interior), with stops in Anchorage, Talkeetna, Denali, and other towns; bush pilots who can land on airstrips, fields, lakes, gravel beds, or inlets hire themselves out by the hour; and the Alaska Marine Highway System (AMHS; *www.dot.state.ak.us/amhs*) state ferries offer regular service to coastal communities, notably along the Inside Passage in the southeast part of the state. For details, see Travelwise, pages 234–236.

If You Have Only a Week

If you're a first-time visitor and only have a week, let's start you in **Anchorage,** where some 300,000 of Alaska's paltry population of 723,000 live. Be sure to see the **Anchorage Museum** and the **Alaska Native Heritage Center;** not only will you enjoy these facilities, but you'll be better prepared to appreciate the rest of the state. To get that first taste of the outdoors, bike the **Tony Knowles Coastal Trail** on the west side of town or venture into **Chugach State Park** on the east side of the city.

Several fine Tlingit and Haida totem poles grace Sitka National Historic Park, in Southeast Alaska.

If you want a little bit of nearly everything Alaska has to offer, head south along the scenic Seward Highway to the **Kenai Peninsula.** Throughout the peninsula you'll find opportunities to hike, fish, raft, camp, watch wildlife, canoe, and beachcomb. In **Seward**—at road's end, 125 miles (200 km) from Anchorage, on the east side of the peninsula—check out the **Alaska SeaLife Center,** an outstanding museum and research institution devoted to the state's marine ecosystems. Then explore those ecosystems by taking one of the boat tours of adjacent **Kenai Fjords National Park,** where you'll see bald eagles, sea otters, puffins, and tidewater glaciers calving huge hunks of ice into the sea.

Next, backtrack up the Seward Highway some 37 miles (59 km) to the 142-mile-long (229 km) Sterling Highway, which accesses the other side of the peninsula. Drive to this highway's end to enjoy the art galleries, museums, and other charms of **Homer.** Take a guided boat tour from the famous **Homer Spit** and poke around beautiful **Kachemak Bay,** perhaps landing on the far side for some hiking and tide-pooling in **Kachemak Bay State Park.**

To sample the vast interior of Alaska for a couple days, head north from Anchorage some 240 miles (386 km) to the immense **Denali National Park and Preserve.** Larger than Vermont, Denali encompasses broad river valleys, windswept tundra, glaciers, and the imposing Alaska Range, including 20,320-foot (6,194 m) Mount McKinley, North America's highest summit. For a treat, go on a flightseeing trip around the mountain in a bush plane. But be sure to see the land from ground level, too, by taking the park tour bus deep into the wilderness; watch for caribou, wolves, moose, Dall sheep, and the park's signature species, the grizzly bear.

NOT TO BE MISSED:

Sea kayaking along a scenic coastline **61**

An Alaska Maritime Highway System ferry trip along the Inside Passage **64–65**

Seeing a tidewater glacier calve into the sea at Glacier Bay **75**

Learning about Alaska's rich indigenous cultures at the Alaska Native Heritage Center in North Anchorage **105**

Watching brown bears foraging in the wild in Katmai National Park and Preserve **132–133**

A tour of Denali National Park and Preserve on its one backcountry road **196–197**

Watching the fiery dance of the northern lights **225**

Online Visitor Information

There's a wealth of online visitor information available at your fingertips.

General information: *www.travel alaska.com, www.alaska.com,* and *www.state.ak.us*

National Park Service: *www.nps .gov/akso*

Alaska Public Lands Information Centers: *www.alaskacenters.gov*

U.S. Fish & Wildlife Service, Alaska region: *www.r7.fws.gov*

Alaska State Parks: *www.alaskastate parks.org*

Bureau of Land Management, Alaska: *www.blm.gov/ak*

U.S. Forest Service (Chugach and Tongass NFs, Alaska region): *www.fs.usda.gov/chugach* and *www.fs.usda.gov/tongass*

Glories of the Alaska Public Lands Info Centers

Where can I go hiking in south-central Alaska? Are there poisonous snakes in the state? Can I find good salmon fishing near Anchorage?

The Alaska Public Lands Information Centers (APLIC) are the place to go for answers to such questions. They provide information about all of Alaska's public lands, which altogether constitute about 75 percent of the state.

Visitors planning a trip can glean tons of information from APLIC's website (*www.alaskacenters.gov*) or phone one of the four centers (*Anchorage, tel 907/644-3661 or 866/869-6887 toll free in U.S.; Fairbanks, tel 907/459-3780; Ketchikan, tel 907/228-6220; Tok, tel 907/883-5667*). Once in Alaska, travelers can drop by one of the APLIC for more information and for a variety of interpretive programs.

Broad Mountains & Narrow Fjords: Another fine way to spend a week in Alaska is ferrying through **Southeast Alaska** via the 900-nautical-mile-long (1,667 km) **Inside Passage.** This maze of forested islands, hidden coves, and protected waters is its own world. The splendid scenery draws flocks of cruise ships during the summer, but it's more rewarding to take an AMHS ferry (see p. 8; reserve well ahead for summer travel) and get off at various ports for a day or two before catching another ferry. Sights to see along the way include, from south to north, rain forest–cloaked **Misty Fiords National Monument, Juneau** (the state's capital), **Skagway** (once the jumping-off point for Klondike-going gold seekers), and gorgeous **Glacier Bay National Park and Preserve,** home to about a dozen tidewater glaciers.

Pros & Cons of the Shoulder Season

In Alaska there's summer (June–Aug.), winter (Oct.–April), and those spring and fall windows of opportunity that constitute the state's shoulder season: May and September. The shoulder season offers bargains, thinner crowds, fewer bugs, and certain seasonal advantages, like the brilliant fall colors in the birch forests and the wide expanse of tundra.

The shoulder season also offers a decent amount of those two desirable qualities that winter lacks: warmth and sunlight. May is one of the finest travel months; it's actually drier than summer in most of the state. September is one of the wettest months, but it still lets you avoid the winter cold. Be aware that many attractions are not open in early May or late September.

If You Have More Time

If you have more time, consider sampling some of the even more remote corners of Alaska. For example, you might spend a few days in the Prince William Sound fishing town of **Cordova,** which can only be reached by sea or air (it's a 35-minute flight from Anchorage and is served by the AMHS ferry). Stroll the friendly little downtown; savor some of the renowned Copper River red (sockeye) salmon; drive out the 50-mile (80 km) dead-end road through the amazingly wildlife-rich Copper River Delta; hang out in a hard-core fisherman's bar. After a while you'll get a feel for the local life. There are similar communities across the state: **Ketchikan** and **Haines** in the southeast, **Kodiak** on Kodiak Island, **Dillingham** in the west, and **Barrow** in the far north.

Wilderness Beyond Wilderness: Likewise, spend a few days in any of a hundred wildernesses. Take a plane, a boat, a kayak, a raft, or your own two feet and get off the road and into the backcountry (see sidebar p. 227). Maybe reserve a public use cabin in the **Tongass National Forest,** down in Southeast Alaska. Wake up each morning in the misty rain forest, a fabulously lush realm of ferns, flowers, and towering spruce trees that often are larger in diameter than you are tall. Or go for the polar opposite, almost literally: the treeless tundra north of the Arctic Circle in a place like **Gates of the Arctic National Park and Preserve,** home to sawtooth mountains, crystal clear rivers, and abundant wildlife. Or make a venture into **Chugach State Park,** where, though close to Anchorage, some mountain peaks are still unnamed. Whichever wilderness you choose to visit, you'll start to understand the true nature of the Great Land. ∎

Brown bear cubs near Brooks River, Katmai National Park and Preserve

Cell Phone Issues in Remote Places

You take a fall while hiking in the Alaska wilderness and break your ankle. It hurts like crazy but at least you're not in serious trouble because you've got your cell phone. You whip it out to call for help and . . . oops, no signal. So, can you hop 12 miles (19 km) back to the trailhead?

Don't count on cell phones in Alaska. They'll work in the state's cities, larger towns, and along parts of major highways, but coverage in the backcountry is especially bad.

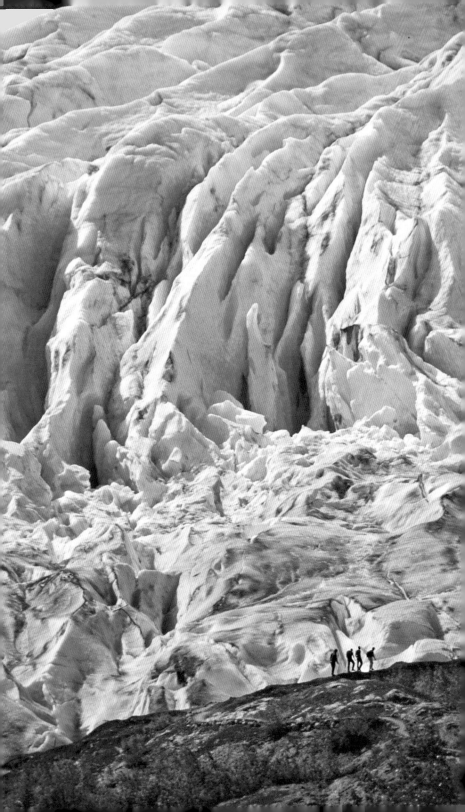

History & Culture

Above: A young dancer in
traditional dress
Opposite: The massive fissured
flank of Exit Glacier dwarfs a
group of passing hikers.

Alaska Today

Alaska. Like Tombouctou, the very name evokes a legendary remoteness. To someone from Peoria or Atlanta or London, Alaska may seem more myth than reality: a wild place inhabited by grizzly bears, moose, and wolves.

A dramatic landscape of raw-boned mountains, misty forests, windswept tundra, and glaciers that march into the sea; a realm of snow and ice and perpetual cold; a place peopled by Eskimos and pioneers living off the land. These things are part of Alaska, but the picture they paint is so incomplete that it does indeed teeter on the edge of myth. Alaska also has espresso stands, farms, Air Force bases, art galleries, suburbs, four-star restaurants, 80°F (27°C) summer days, college basketball tournaments, Internet cafés, bureaucrats, and sand dunes. The reality is that Alaska

The mural says "Alaska," but the dress of these youths in Juneau would look right at home anywhere in the United States.

is a fascinating blend of the wild and the civilized, of the traditional and the modern, and of many different landscapes and climates.

The basic reason that Alaska has so much wild left is straightforward: It is tough country and few people live there. Though Alaska is by far the biggest state in the Union—more than twice the size of number two, Texas—its population barely exceeds 700,000; more people live in metropolitan Albuquerque. This results in a population density almost a thousand times sparser than, say, New Jersey's.

Alaska does have one bona fide urban area: Anchorage. More than 280,000 people live there in a cityscape familiar to most Americans: It features skyscrapers, traffic jams, hip clubs, suburban sprawl, fine museums, and many of the other amenities and problems of a city. But even Anchorage is influenced by the proximity of the wilderness. Moose and bears often stroll through backyards. The glacier-streaked Chugach Mountains loom nearby. From the middle of town residents can drive 20 minutes and be in unspoiled forests and mountains.

Though Alaska is by far the biggest state in the Union—more than twice the size of number two, Texas—its population barely exceeds 700,000.

Living so close to the land results in people also living off the land. Whether an accountant in Fairbanks or a teacher in Juneau, it seems that most Alaskans fish or hunt for food—and many do both. When the salmon are running in summer and fall, plenty of outsiders come to Alaska to hook kings and reds and silvers, but the majority of anglers are residents of the state who are looking to pack their freezers with fillets. Likewise, it's common to hear someone in a fine restaurant in Anchorage talk about getting his moose. A day earlier this person may have been dressed in camouflage instead of a three-piece suit, and instead of carving up a rack of lamb he was carving up the moose he'd just shot.

For some Alaskans those salmon and moose are not just a supplement to food they buy in a supermarket. Thousands of residents in small towns and villages lead subsistence lifestyles, getting the bulk of their food from the land. They not only fish for those prized salmon but for grayling, tomcod, sheefish, eel, and a dozen other species, depending on the region. The list of animals they hunt is equally long, including the obvious, like moose, goose, bear, and caribou, and the surprising, such as beluga whale, seal, porcupine, and walrus. They also trap fox, beaver, marten, and other fur-bearing animals and gather berries, bird eggs, greens, and clams. What some people do for sport, these folks do to live. Many of them wouldn't have it any other way, but many also have little choice, especially given the high cost of living in Alaska (which visitors, too, will certainly notice). Those costs are even higher in the remote villages, where food often costs twice as much as it does in the lower 48.

The People's Land

Fortunately for those who use the land for subsistence, sport hunting and fishing, and recreation, the vast majority of Alaska lies in public hands, enjoying at least some protections from development. Large chunks are overseen by the state and by native organizations, and more than half of the country falls under the steward-ship of the federal government. Unlike many of their counterparts in other states, most Alaska public lands allow subsistence uses and some sport hunting and fishing. This is true even for Alaska's headliner lands, such as Denali National Park. Visitors often don't realize that its full name is Denali National Park and Preserve. The phrase "and Preserve" is found at the end of the names of most of the national parks in the state. The areas of Denali designated as preserve are open to subsistence uses and sport hunting and fishing; so, too, are large portions of the park. Only the wilderness section—which includes the main tourism area— is usually off-limits. While traveling in the backcountry, visitors may encounter fishnets, traps, and other tools employed by subsistence users. It's important to leave these items undisturbed.

Outdoor Samplers

If you want to take an outdoors-oriented guided trip in Alaska but can't decide among all the options, there are operators who have created tours with you in mind. For example, **Mountain Travel Sobek** *(www.mt sobek.com)* offers an 11-day adventure that includes flightseeing, boating, sea kayaking, rafting, biking, canoeing, wildlife-watching, and quiet nights in backcountry cabins. And that's just the basic itinerary. Gluttons for more can also go hiking, canoeing, mountain biking, and fishing. A search on the Internet reveals many more companies offering such trips.

A few of these trips require high levels of fitness and expertise, but most are designed for reasonably fit beginners with lots of energy. Some trips involve camping but many trips overnight in comfy lodges.

Alaska Natives

Many subsistence hunters and gatherers are Alaska natives. These indigenous inhabitants constitute about 19 percent of the state's population. Contrary to stereotype, not all Alaska natives are Eskimos—not even close, though they are the single most populous Native group. The term "Eskimo" is widely used for the people who live around the west and north coasts and is not considered offensive, but so-called Eskimos think of themselves as belonging to smaller cultural divisions. The two main ones are the Inupiat, who reside on the north coast and on the west coast north of Norton Sound, and the Yupik, who live on the west coast from Nor-ton Sound south to Bristol Bay. Sometimes you'll hear the terms "Inupiat Eskimo" and "Yupik Eskimo." These peoples further split into smaller groups, such as the Nunamiut, who are inland Inupiat.

The vast interior of Alaska and a few bits of the south-central coast are the realm of the Athabaskan. These people are related to some of the First Nations of Canada and the lower 48 and sometimes refer to themselves as Indians, though they generally prefer more specific names that describe the smaller groups to which they belong, such as the Dena'ina, Ahtna, and Tanana.

The Alaska Peninsula and the 1,100 miles (1,770 km) of islands in the Aleutian chain are the domain of the Aleut, who call themselves the Unangan. Closely related and still lumped together with the Aleut by some observers are the Alutiiq, who occupy the

Grand views of rugged mountain scenery around Juneau open up at the top of the steep Mount Roberts Tramway.

southeast portion of the Alaska Peninsula, the Kodiak Island Archipelago, and Prince William Sound. Finally, there are the Alaska natives of the Southeast: the Tlingit, Haida, Tsimshian, and Eyak. They share many cultural traits—though not their languages—with the Northwest Coast natives of British Columbia and Washington.

As happened with indigenous peoples around the world, the arrival of outsiders was hard on Alaska natives. The Aleut were invaded by the Russians in the mid-1700s. These acquisitive and well-armed Europeans and Asians killed most Aleut directly or via disease and starvation and enslaved most of the rest. Aleut numbers plunged from an estimated 20,000 to a tiny fraction of that, and to this day their population remains small. The Russians, as well as American and British whalers in the mid-1800s, also introduced Alaska natives to alcohol, which has had a profound impact on Native life. Though native communities have had some success fighting alcoholism, it's still a serious problem. Consequently many native communities prohibit the possession or sale of alcohol.

Despite these tribulations, many Alaska natives have improved their lot in recent times. This is largely due to the deal they worked out in 1971, codified by the passage

in Congress of the Alaska Native Claims Settlement Act (ANCSA). This secured extensive subsistence-use rights and formed 12 regional native and dozens of village corporations that together own 44 million acres (17.8 million ha) of land. These corporations
are engaged in fishing, logging, mining, oil production and exploration, health care, and
tourism and bring in billions of dollars in revenue. As this suggests, though many Alaska
natives still live close to the land, many also work regular jobs, earn college degrees, own
and manage businesses, and otherwise participate in modern society.

European Influence

Despite the impact the Russians had on Alaska, they never settled here in large
numbers. However, they left behind a sizable number of religious converts whose
descendants still attend the state's many Russian Orthodox churches. The main
exceptions are the Russian Old Believers, though they don't trace their lineage back
to the early Russians; most of the Old Believers came to Alaska in the latter half of the
20th century. Numbering only a few thousand, the majority live on the Kenai Peninsula and around Kodiak in isolated villages. However, visitors will see Old Believers
in stores or operating their fishing vessels, the women wearing ankle-length dresses
and caps or scarves and all the men sporting beards.

In the years following the transfer of Alaska from Russia
to the United States, almost all newcomers to Alaska were
of western European ancestry, particularly German and Irish.
But globalization seems to be bringing diversity to the state
in recent years, even if the 2010 census still showed only
small numbers of African, Latino, and Asian Americans in
Alaska—about 4 percent each.

> Other than government
> jobs, most Alaskans
> work in resource
> industries, notably oil,
> fishing, mining, and
> logging—and tourism,
> which in its own way
> relies on Alaska's rich
> natural assets.

Making a Living

All that salmon and moose meat in the freezer notwithstanding, most Alaskans still have to earn a paycheck.
However, due to transportation costs and the state's isolation, few large-scale manufacturers other than seafood-
processing companies locate in Alaska. The climate and
topography preclude other common industries, too, such
as agriculture, which is very limited in the state. Other than government jobs, most
Alaskans work in resource industries, notably oil, fishing, mining, and logging—and
tourism, which in its own way relies on Alaska's rich natural assets.

Nowadays, oil production is perhaps the state's most famous business, and it puts
a lot of money into state coffers. It employs thousands of Alaskans and outsiders, and
the oil support industries are some of the state's biggest companies. Oil pumped out of
Prudhoe Bay directly benefits every Alaskan: A 1976 constitutional amendment assures
that a percentage of oil goes into the Permanent Fund Dividend, which pays an annual
dividend to every person living in Alaska. In 2011 each qualified resident received $1,174.

Commercial fishing is a huge industry in Alaska. (Sportfishing also attracts big business.)
The ports of Unalaska, Dillingham, Kodiak, Cordova, and other towns near rich fishing
grounds are home to thousands of fishing vessels and a good many fish-processing
plants. At least half of the U.S. commercial fish production takes place in Alaska. The
state has one of the world's best managed fisheries and has mounted a big campaign

Floatplanes can take visitors deep into the wilds, to such places as Kulik Lake in the backcountry of Katmai National Park and Preserve, on the Alaska Peninsula.

to promote wild salmon; farming salmon is currently (and historically) illegal in Alaska.

Tourism is the state's third largest industry and seems environmentally sustainable, despite the occasional overcrowding at popular parks or the air pollution caused by RVs. However, tourism may not be culturally and economically sustainable when it's controlled by outside corporate interests, as is happening in some of the Southeast Alaska ports favored by big cruise ships. Large national and international firms are buying up retail space and hawking glitzy wares to the 5,000-plus passengers getting off the ships every day in summer, and many people feel the change is corrupting the character of those towns.

On the other hand, many Alaska towns, including some Southeast ports, offer a range of locally owned shops with an array of tour operators who sell their knowledge and love of the land. Instead of offering stuffed grizzly bears for sale, they offer real grizzly bears for viewing, boat tours to offshore wildlife refuges, meetings with noted sled-dog racers, hikes through the rain forest, plane rides over the mountains and glaciers, cultural visits to native villages, kayaking and canoeing in rivers, up fjords, and along the coast, whale-watching expeditions, and many other excursions that celebrate the essence of Alaska. That's a win-win situation for everyone. ■

Land & Landscape

Wild, unforgiving, and spectacular, nature's attributes define Alaska. In this frontier state that stretches from the Arctic Circle to the Gulf of Alaska and from near Russia to the Coast Mountains of Canada's British Columbia, the climate, the terrain, the ecosystems, and the wildlife make themselves felt at every turn. They've become the stuff of legends, humbling even the most cynical of visitors.

History of the Land

Just as Alaska is a young and dynamic state in terms of its human development, so is it a young and dynamic land in terms of its geology. Floating on the semisolid mantle of the Earth, the Pacific plate is drifting northeast into the North American plate. Being generally denser, the Pacific plate is subducting, or sliding under, the North American plate. Alaska's massive mountains are the result of this tectonic meeting. In fact, many of these mountains are still rising; Mount McKinley, the continent's highest peak at 20,320 feet (6,194 m), yet grows.

This grinding and slow-motion collision of plates also produces earthquakes and volcanic activity. More than 15 active volcanoes simmer along the Alaska Peninsula. Evidence of past eruptions is abundant. For example, the cataclysmic explosion that disintegrated the top of Aniakchak Mountain some 3,500 years ago is apparent in the 6-mile-wide (9.6 km), 2,000-foot-deep (610 m) caldera that remains. Nor are major eruptions confined to the distant past. In 1912, Novarupta Volcano shook violently for a week and then blew with a force that could be heard 1,000 miles (1,600 km) away. Its eruption cycle lasted for 60 hours, during which more rock and ash were blasted into the atmosphere than during any other volcanic event in human history, with the exception of the 1500 B.C. eruption of Thíra in Greece.

An even more recent event had a major impact on modern Alaska. At 5:36 p.m. on March 27, 1964, a fault line at the bottom of Prince William Sound spasmed and rocked south-central Alaska for three to five minutes with a magnitude 9.2 earthquake—80 times more powerful than the infamous 1906 San Francisco quake. Terra firma suddenly wasn't firm: An island in the sound rose

> **More than 15 active volcanoes simmer along the Alaska Peninsula. Evidence of past eruptions is abundant.**

33 feet (10 m). In some towns streets tilted up like drawbridges. Some coastal flatlands dropped a half dozen feet, allowing seawater to flow across them, eventually killing all the trees. In downtown Anchorage the north side of Fourth Street collapsed and restaurants and stores sank out of sight.

Then came the worst part. Tsunamis spawned by the quake washed ashore. A 70-foot (21 m) wave erased the native village of Chenega. In Seward, the quake ignited huge fires in dockside fuel tanks and a tsunami pushed that burning fuel eight blocks inland, causing a flood and a fire at the same time. In Valdez, much of the waterfront slid into the bay and the rest got pounded by a tsunami; the townspeople subsequently abandoned the site and rebuilt in a safer spot 4 miles (6.4 km) away.

Known simply as "the mountain" to many Alaskans, 20,320-foot Mount McKinley rises above Kettle Lake in Denali National Park and Preserve.

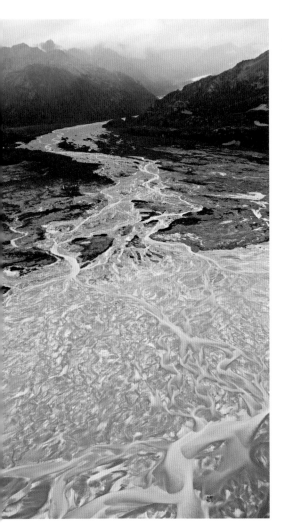

Glaciers are another geologic force in Alaska, gouging out fjords and mountain valleys and releasing meltwater to form rivers and creeks. Unlike the lower 48, where glaciers are an exotic sight in a few high mountains, Alaska's rivers of ice crop up all around from high elevations to sea level; if you count the small ones (though some are larger than Rhode Island), the state contains more than 100,000 glaciers (only 616 are named).

Surprisingly, much of Alaska remained free of ice during the ice ages. The most significant impact on the area was the result of the worldwide conversion of water into ice, which lowered sea level a few hundred feet. Several times between 10,000 and 40,000 years ago, the shallow ocean floor of the Bering Sea was exposed, creating a broad land bridge linking North America to Asia. North America's first inhabitants are thought to have walked across this land bridge from Siberia.

Climate

There are two take-home lessons about weather in Alaska. Lesson one: It can and does change quickly, so even if you're going on a two-hour outing, be prepared. Carry rain gear and extra layers of clothing almost everywhere. And if you're scheduled to go somewhere in a small plane, realize that bad weather may keep that plane on the ground. By the same token, realize that if you've been dropped off at a wilderness lodge or such by a small plane,

A river laces its way through a valley in Katmai National Park and Preserve.

you may get stranded at your destination for an extra day or two.

Lesson number two: Alaska is a big state and the weather varies tremendously depending on where you are. More than 2,000 miles (3,600 km) separate Attu, at the western tip of the Aleutians, from the Arctic National Wildlife Refuge, in the northeastern corner of the state. It's about the same distance from Ketchikan, in the southeast, to Barrow, in the northwest. Not surprisingly, their climates differ.

Ketchikan, Kodiak, and the rest of the southern coast lie in the relatively mild maritime zone, warmed by the Kuroshio (Japan Current). Not balmy, mind you, but with highs in the 50s and 60s (10°–20°C) during the summer and with winter temperatures that generally stay on the pleasant side of zero. However, that maritime weather means a lot of moisture; Ketchikan soaks up about 160 inches (4 m) of rain a year and most places get 80, 90, or 100 inches (2–2.5 m) annually. And while a lot of rain falls in winter, plenty falls in summer, too.

Shielded from the moderating influence of the ocean, the Interior experiences weather extremes. Fairbanks occasionally basks in highs of 80°F (27°C) and even 90°F (32°C), with average midsummer highs in the low 70s. And although summer is the Interior's rainy season, it is usually dry; annual rain totals are a near-desertlike 15 inches (38 cm). In winter the thermometer nose-dives. For months the temperature may not rise above zero and sometimes it sits between minus 30°F (-34°C) and minus 50°F (-45°C) for days.

Then there's the Arctic, the northern third of Alaska above the Arctic Circle. In Barrow, Alaska's northernmost point, the daily low temperature drops below freezing an average of 324 days a year. Traditional fur-lined Inupiat Eskimo parkas are more than a

Dealing With the Midnight Sun, Getting Sleep

Fishing at 3 a.m. Hiking all night long. So what's not to like about Alaska's famous midnight sun?

Well, there is the little matter of sleep, and how tough it can be to get. Trying to take advantage of all that daylight can transform travelers into sleep-deprived zombies, which in turn can lead to problems from grouchiness to car wrecks.

Self-restraint can prevent visitors from overextending themselves but the midnight sun also causes a physiological issue. Darkness is the signal for the human body to turn on melatonin, a hormone that affects sleep, so travelers may need to take extra measures, such as taping aluminum foil over windows and wearing sunglasses at night before settling in to sleep.

fashion statement here; they're a necessity. Summer highs only creep into the 30s and 40s (-1°–10°C) and it's very dry—about 5 inches (11 cm) of precipitation a year.

No matter where you are in Alaska, in summer you'll be exposed to the midnight sun. The northern part of Earth tilts toward the sun during summer, increasing the daily amount of sunlight the farther north you travel. The Arctic Circle is the line of latitude at which the sun never drops below the horizon on the summer solstice. On the shore of the Arctic Ocean, 250 miles (400 km) north of the circle, the sun will not set for maybe 80 days. In Anchorage, some 350 miles (560 km) south of the circle, the sun still hovers above the horizon for 18 or 19 hours in midsummer; even at 2 a.m. there's the glow of daylight in the sky. The reverse occurs in winter: 80 sunless days on the Arctic Ocean and just 5.5 or 6 hours of sunlight in Anchorage. On the bright side (well, not literally), all that darkness is great for viewing the aurora borealis, or northern lights.

Landscapes

As you'd expect in a land so vast, Alaska has many distinct habitats, from sand dunes to ice fields. However, the state can be broadly divided into three different vegetation zones: coastal rain forest, taiga, and tundra.

Temperate rain forest—courtesy of all the rain—blankets the islands and coast in southeastern and south-central Alaska; it also covers a little bit of the southwest.

Temperate rain forest is much less common than tropical rain forest; its rainfall is also generally well distributed across the year.

In Alaska's coastal rain forests, Sitka spruce and hemlock dominate, though other conifers, such as cedars and pines, also show up. These forests are the only ones in Alaska that have trees rivaling the 200- and 250-foot (61–76 m) old-growth denizens of British Columbia, Washington, and Oregon. The damp understory is lush with salmon-berry, devil's club, blueberry, columbine, skunk cabbage, ferns, fireweed, huckleberry, and a multitude of other plant species that thrive on moisture.

Inland from the rain forest, on the other side of the coastal mountains, the boreal forest or taiga begins. ("Taiga" comes from a Siberian word for "coniferous forest" and is the more commonly used term.) Taiga covers most of the Interior, though it grades from relatively verdant with 80- and 100-foot (24–30 m) trees in the south to sparse with 10-foot (3 m) trees at its northern edge, around the Arctic Circle. Spruce is the dominant tree; however, it's not the towering Sitka spruce so common in the rain forest but the more modest white spruce and black spruce. Birch, aspen, tamarack, alder, willow, and balsam poplar add to the mix. In the northern taiga, or where soils are poor or boggy, travelers will see seemingly endless tracts of stunted, spindly black spruce, as if a vast Christmas-tree farm had been sprayed with herbicide.

The tundra is the land above tree line, where the intense cold, short growing season, thin soil, and scouring winds make life impossible for trees. "Above" can mean two things in Alaska: higher elevation or higher latitude. In southern Alaska tree line occurs at 2,000 to 3,000 feet (610–914 m) and tundra takes over higher than that. Traveling north into ever colder climates, the harsh conditions that dictate tree line occur at increasingly lower elevations until, a bit north of the Arctic Circle, tree line is at sea level—in other words, no trees grow on the tundra-covered North Slope, which runs from the Brooks Range to the Arctic Ocean. (Consider the effects of latitude in reverse; in the Colorado Rockies tree line is at about 11,000 feet/3,353 meters.)

The tundra is the land above tree line, where the intense cold, short growing season, thin soil, and scouring winds make life impossible for trees.

At lower elevations and latitudes "moist tundra" is the norm. Hikers in Alaska curse moist tundra, a blend of thigh-high willow and birch thickets with ankle-breaking hummocks of grasses and sedges underlain by standing water and dotted with ponds. Hikers prefer the dry or alpine tundra found on higher ground. Here the hummocks are gone, there's no standing water, and the vegetation is much shorter, often just a few inches tall. At first glance alpine tundra seems barren, but look closely and you'll see a fascinating, colorful plant community working hard to make the most of a short grow-ing season. Depending on the region, alpine tundra may be alive with lupine, crowberry, arctic bell heather, bearberry, mountain saxifrage, wild geranium, moss campion, alpine azalea, cranberry, Lapland rosebay, tundra rose, and the wondrous sky blue of forget-me-not, the Alaska state flower.

Almost anywhere in Alaska, whether rain forest, taiga, or tundra, mountains are part of the picture. Only the extreme north has a sizable expanse flat enough to really qualify

The trans-Alaska pipeline delivers oil some 800 miles (1,280 km) from the edge of the Arctic Ocean to the port at Valdez, on Prince William Sound.

as a plain. Even many of the islands in the southeast and the Aleutians feature jagged peaks—natural enough given that those islands are the tops of much bigger mountains whose bottoms are submerged.

The king of Alaska's peaks, and the highest peak in North America, 20,320-foot (6,194 m) Mount McKinley crowns the Alaska Range, which curves through the southern interior of the state. However, McKinley notwithstanding, the most impressive mountains in Alaska are the craggy, snowcapped Wrangell and St. Elias Mountains, neighbors in southern Alaska. In this fastness of lofty summits and mammoth glaciers lie 12 of the 15 highest mountains in Alaska and 10 of the 15 highest on the continent.

The nation's northernmost mountain chain, the Brooks Range, is an older uplift and sports only one peak above 9,000 feet (2,743 m)—9,239-foot (2,816 m) Mount Michelson—yet the length and width of this range is truly Alaska sized. More than 100 miles (160 km) broad, the Brooks Range forms a great wall 600 miles (960 km) long, stretching across the state from the Canadian border in the east to the Chukchi Sea in the west. Lying just north of the Arctic Circle, the Brooks Range marks the Arctic Divide, sending rivers off its southern slopes to the Bering Sea and rivers off its northern slopes to the Arctic Ocean.

Moose Dangers

Seriously, you don't want to get stomped by a moose. Alaskans and visitors get killed and injured every year by these 1,000-pound (454 kg) beasts, even near Anchorage, yet nearly all these attacks are avoidable.

Exercise common sense, like not walking up to have your picture taken with Bullwinkle. Cows with calves are probably the most dangerous (though bulls in the fall rut are ornery), so don't get near them and especially don't get between them. If the hairs on a moose's hump are standing up and its ears are laid back, stomping may be imminent, so get into your car, climb a tree, or otherwise seek safety.

For information, contact the Alaska Department of Fish and Game, Division of Wildlife Conservation (tel 907/465-4190, www.adfg.alaska.gov).

Wildlife

Any discussion of Alaska wildlife must begin with bears. Some visitors to Alaska hardly go outdoors due to a fear of bear attacks, while other people blithely romp through the woods without giving bears much thought. Both of these extremes are irrational and underscore the importance of getting accurate information about bears in Alaska. The details of dealing with bears can be learned at public lands throughout Alaska (for information visit the National Park Service "Bear Safety" Web page, www.alaskacenters.gov/bear-safety.cfm). If you take sensible precautions, both you and the bears will survive your encounters unscathed.

That last statement would not be true if more polar bears lived in the heavily visited parts of Alaska. These cream-furred giants are seriously dangerous and will hunt people. Fortunately, Alaska's polar bears live along the remote western and northern Arctic coasts and spend most of their time out on the sea ice.

Grizzly/brown and black bears also live in Alaska, making it the only state that has all of the North American bear species. (Another bear, the Kodiak bear, is actually a subspecies of the grizzly/brown; it is genetically and physically isolated and has a slightly differently shaped skull.) Visitors often get confused because they hear locals referring to "brown bears," but that's just the common name for grizzlies that live within 100 miles

Though visitors seldom see them, polar bears roam Alaska's Arctic coastlines. They are found most abundantly near the edge of the pack ice, moving seasonally.

(160 km) of the coast. Due to their salmon-rich diet, coastal brown bears grow to almost twice the size of their inland brethren, with big males reaching heights of 9-plus feet (2.7 m) and weights of 1,200 pounds (544 kg). Grizzlies, whether brown bears or not, are found throughout almost all of Alaska—on the beaches, in the forests, in the tundra, up in the mountains, and even on many islands. Understandably, the size of grizzlies/brownies scares people, but black bears, though only about a third as large, are at least as dangerous. They generally stick to forested areas. Visitors who want to safely observe either grizzly/brown or black bears will find numerous organized opportunities in Alaska.

Some Alaskans worry more about moose attacks than bears. It's hard for the uniniti- ated to be concerned about an herbivore, but moose are as big as brown bears, just as fast, more commonly seen, and more temperamental, especially cows with calves. However, moose are easily dealt with compared to bears: Keep your distance and don't get between cows and their calves; then relax and enjoy watching them munch on willows or stilt around in ponds on those long legs.

Assuming you don't feed or mistreat them, the rest of Alaska's wildlife generally present no cause for concern. On the contrary, watching the many fascinating and beautiful animals that call Alaska home is a highlight for many visitors. From rain forest to Arctic tundra, listen for the thrilling howls of wolves. On steep slopes in the high country look for the brilliant white of Dall sheep, closely related to the bighorns of the lower 48; the males sport curled horns that serve as battering rams during battles over females. On even higher and steeper slopes, scan for the cream color of mountain goats, the champion climbers among hoofed animals. In the Interior and way up north, watch for caribou; if you plan carefully, you may be able to see one of the great caribou herds, which number in the tens of thousands.

> **Alaska has the nation's biggest national park, the biggest national wildlife refuge, and the biggest state park.**

Not all animals of interest in Alaska wear fur. More than 400 bird species inhabit or migrate through Alaska, including some Asiatic species. Bald eagles are common in coastal Alaska; their cousins, the golden eagles, soar above the Interior tundra looking for marmot and hare. Other avian favorites include trumpeter swans, sandhill cranes, and peregrine falcons.

Take a boat out on the open waters to see puffins, auklets, and huge, raucous nesting colonies of seabirds. Tour boats also allow visitors to explore nearshore environments, which host a dazzling array of marine mammals, including humpback whales, orcas, beluga whales, sea lions, walrus, harbor seals, and the perennial crowd favorite, sea otters.

And one last category of wildlife must be mentioned: biting bugs. Led by Alaska's notorious mosquitoes (and a variety of biting flies), these pests can spoil outings if you're not prepared—and sometimes even when you are. Learn how to handle them, or find out when their numbers peak in the places you want to visit and time your travels accordingly.

Public Lands

Visiting the rain forest, taiga, and tundra to see wildlife is made easier by the fact that most of Alaska is public land. Alaska has the nation's biggest national park, the biggest national wildlife refuge, and the biggest state park. However, be aware that many of these public lands bear little resemblance to their lower 48 counterparts, where visitors often enjoy flush toilets, elaborate visitor centers, extensive trail systems, well-tended campgrounds, and other amenities. Many of Alaska's public lands are raw wildernesses, with perhaps one visitor center or ranger station on the boundary. For information contact the specific site or the excellent Alaska Public Lands Information Centers (*www.alaskacenters .gov;* see sidebar p. 10).

Guided Tours

Because of the remoteness, the fickle weather, the bears, and all the other rigors of travel in Alaska's outdoors, guided excursions provide a nice complement to independent outings. A wide array of qualified outfitters and individuals can take you kayaking, fishing, bear viewing, hiking, boating, birding, and flying, whether on a one-hour tour or a two-week expedition. Not only is going with a guide safer, you can learn from these local experts. To choose a good guide, use common sense and recommendations from convention and visitor bureaus and chambers of commerce. Some public lands have lists of authorized outfitters. ■

Caribou inhabit much of Alaska. The largest herd, the Western Arctic in northwestern Alaska, numbers close to 325,000 caribou.

History of Alaska

Much of Alaska's history has revolved around natural resources. When humans first entered the Western Hemisphere by crossing the Bering land bridge, they probably were hunting mammoths and other animals. When Europeans first sailed into Alaska waters, they came seeking the pelts of sea otters and seals. When Americans first came to Alaska in significant numbers, they searched for gold, and later for black gold in the oil fields.

Yet along with the fortune hunters came people who settled in Alaska, people looking to establish a new home. Whether native peoples that have been around for almost 500 generations or recent arrivals, these resident Alaskans are a major part of the state's history, too. They're the ones who build the clan houses, fly the bush planes, populate villages and towns, and skipper small fishing boats.

Coming to America

The majority view holds that America's first inhabitants came between 10,000 and 30,000 years ago, when Ice Age glaciers bound up so much water that sea level dropped about 250 feet (76 m), exposing the shallow ocean shelf in the Bering Strait, where Russia and Alaska are only some 56 miles (90 km) apart. This created the Bering land bridge, though the word "bridge" presents a misleading image because at low water levels the exposed landmass was actually hundreds of miles wide. This bridge may have been exposed for thousands of years and perhaps more than once. Having been available for so long, it's natural that the hunting tribes in Siberia would have followed their prey across the bridge to Alaska.

Alaska's First Inhabitants

Much debate clouds the original arrival of humans in the Americas (see sidebar this page). Whether some of these first North Americans stayed in Alaska or whether all of them moved south through the Americas and later back to Alaska has been lost in the mists of time. Anthropologists and archaeologists do know that the ancestors of today's Alaska natives have lived in Alaska for thousands of years. During that time—and perhaps to some degree before arriving in Alaska—they split into a rich variety of linguistic and cultural groups. Some remained nomadic while others settled into permanent villages. They developed increasingly sophisticated techniques for making a living from hunting caribou, catching salmon, harpooning bowhead and beluga whales, and gathering plants from the forest and tundra. Many arts flourished, including sculpting ivory and stone, weaving baskets, storytelling, carving totem poles, dancing, and fashioning elaborate masks.

The Russians Are Coming

In the early 1700s the European powers—mainly Great Britain, France, and Spain—were busy colonizing the world, including North America. They were vaguely aware of the big hole on their maps to the east of Siberia, but they were at war and ignored the area. But Tsar Peter the Great of Russia showed interest. Shortly before his death he sent Vitus Bering to sail east from Siberia's Kamchatka Peninsula. It took a couple of tries and a lot of years, but in 1741 both of the ships in Bering's expedition, after getting separated in foul weather, encountered what is now southern Alaska.

Bering's expedition brought back many pelts, including those of sea otters, which wealthy clients, especially among the Chinese, prized above all others because of the unmatched density of the warm fur. A nice sea otter pelt fetched a price equal to three year's pay for a regular working man. The reports of abundant sea otters attracted *promyshlenniki*—trappers and fur traders who typically took local hostages and forced their fellow tribesmen to buy back the hostages with furs. The promyshlenniki inflicted this cruel system on the Aleut, along with European diseases, and wiped out most of the population. Equally acquisitive but less barbaric Russian fur companies followed and set up operations in Southeast and south-central Alaska.

For several decades the Russians kept the secret of the Alaska sea otters to themselves, but in the 1770s British and Spanish ships explored Alaska and the word spread. Chasing sea otters, the mythical Northwest Passage (an ice-free shipping route between the Pacific and the Atlantic), political advantage, and scientific information, Europeans made some 200 voyages to Alaska waters by 1805. Still, under the iron hand of Alexander Baranov (1746–1819), the manager of Alaska operations for the ruling fur-trading Russian-American Company (he came to be called the "Lord of Alaska"), the Russians consolidated and extended their sway in Alaska.

Peter the Great sent Vitus Bering on his first voyage to Alaska.

But overhunting caused sea otters and other furbearers to become scarce by the 1820s and 1830s. Coupled with wars and political setbacks at home, the decline in furs caused Russia to gradually lose interest in Alaska. By the 1850s the Russians were ready to sell. (This being the era of colonialism, no one with any power ever questioned the right of the Russians to sell Alaska.) However, they did not want the region to fall into the hands of the British or any of Russia's other European rivals, so, once the U.S. Civil War ended, in 1865, the Russians approached the Americans.

Seward's Folly

U.S. Secretary of State William H. Seward and other American political leaders were as eager to acquire Alaska as the Russians were to unload it. Seward was a zealous believer in America's "manifest destiny" to rule over all of North America, even Canada. Other Americans, even those who likewise believed in manifest destiny, disagreed with Seward, pointing to Alaska's remoteness and brutal climate. These critics panned Alaska as "Seward's icebox," "Walrussia," and "Icebergia." And in 1867, when Seward signed the deal with the Russians and paid them $7.2 million, the critics labeled the agreement as "Seward's Folly."

Having closed the deal, the Americans started wondering just what they'd bought. Neither the Russians nor anyone else had explored much beyond the coastline.

(The native peoples who lived beyond the coast knew a little something about what lay in the Interior, but no one asked them.) The new owners didn't even know what to call their new property. Seward chose "Alaska," the Aleut word for "great land." The Aleut had used the term only for what is now the Alaska Peninsula, but Seward adopted it for the entire . . . the entire what?

The federal government refused to make the land a territory, as happened with lands acquired by previous international treaties, like the Louisiana Purchase. Territorial status would have conferred citizenship upon all the inhabitants and put Alaska on a trajectory toward eventual statehood, and Congress didn't think Alaska rated such treatment. Instead, Alaska's status was left somewhat vague, though clearly it was not bound for statehood and Russians and Alaska natives were specifically denied citizenship. More than anything the arrangement made Alaska resemble a colony.

For the next few decades, members of the federal government, like the Russians before them, largely ceded day-to-day administration to a fur-trading company: the Alaska Commercial Company, which mainly wanted fur seal pelts (since sea otters were nearly extinct). With fur seal populations in steep decline, the company and the government agreed upon the taking of 100,000 fur seals a year while leaving females and pups. Even with these limitations the company raked in enormous profits.

John Muir & Other Visitors: During those early years of American tenure, Alaska got a visit from someone who couldn't be more different from the seal hunters. Fascinated by glaciers, along with everything else wild, John Muir came north to Alaska, where he knew there were many glaciers. In 1879, he took a ship to Wrangell, in southeastern Alaska, and headed out from there with four Tlingit paddlers and a Presbyterian missionary on what turned into an 800-mile (1,280 km) canoe trip. Among the many grand places they explored was Glacier Bay, where today visitors will find Muir Glacier (not named that by Muir). John Muir's glowing stories about his visit to Glacier Bay and an 1880 return trip are said to have launched Alaska tourism. Within a decade thousands of people had cruised up the Inside Passage to witness for themselves the grandeur of Glacier Bay.

> John Muir's glowing stories about his visit to Glacier Bay . . . are said to have launched Alaska tourism.

Numerous others, including missionaries and military men, also were exploring Alaska during the 1870s and 1880s, slowly figuring out whether Seward's purchase of Alaska had been folly or not. They found a diversity of intriguing Alaska natives, prolific fisheries, ample wildlife, and spectacular landscapes—but of course all of that was overshadowed by the discovery of gold.

A painting by Edward Leutze depicts the signing of the 1867 treaty that transferred ownership of Alaska from Russia to the United States.

Gold Rush

When Alaskans talk about the "gold rush," they're referring to the stampede of miners to the Klondike that started in 1898. However, there were many other significant discoveries of gold, too. Joe Juneau and Richard Harris hit it big at Gold Creek in 1880, at the site of the city that now bears Joe's name. (The town that grew along Gold Creek was first named Harrisburg, but with his earnings Juneau bribed citizens to name it after him in an 1881 contest of less than a hundred votes.) However, independent miners faced a problem: that gold required hard-rock mining. Big companies with expensive equipment to drill tunnels into mountainsides and money to build stamp mills and other facilities to extract the gold from the ore were needed at these types of gold strikes. Generally, gold rushes, where thousands upon thousands of people converge on an area, occurred in places where gold had filtered out into streams and could be found by individual miners panning for the yellow metal.

One classic rush took place in Nome, where three prospectors struck gold in 1898 and in 1899 people found gold flakes amid the beach sands on the Bering Sea near town. By the summer of 1900 some 20,000 fortune hunters were camped out on the beach. One prospector found a gold nugget that weighed 107 ounces—the largest one ever recorded in Alaska.

Klondike Gold Rush: And then there was the Klondike gold rush. Perhaps the strangest thing about this most extravagant of all Alaska gold rushes is that the Klondike isn't in Alaska. The Klondike River and its tributary creeks where the gold was discovered lie fully 60 miles (96 km) east of Alaska in Canada's Yukon Territory. This rush became an Alaska legend because the most popular routes to the Klondike started in and passed through Alaska, and because this rush was *huge*.

Having rested at The Scales, the last camp on the trail in Alaska, miners bound for Canada's Klondike goldfields labor up the "Golden Stairs" cut into the snow of Chilkoot Pass.

Ships carrying news of the Klondike strike—and carrying a ton of gold to drive the point home—arrived in Seattle in July 1897. Because the Klondike was remote and a challenge to reach, July was too late to start out without getting trapped by winter, so people waited until 1898. Come spring some 50,000 gold seekers headed north, with another 50,000 leaving later that year or in 1899. Of those 100,000, only about 30,000 to 50,000 made it to the goldfields. Most of the 70,000 to 50,000 who came up short managed to straggle back to civilization, but a terrible number died trying.

Some of those deaths occurred because there was no obvious best route, so people tried all sorts of ways. One party of 18 New Yorkers decided to cross the Malaspina Glacier, in Southeast Alaska, apparently unaware that it is the largest piedmont glacier in North America, larger than Rhode Island. For an agonizing three months they struggled atop the glacier. One man fell into a crevasse and died; three died in an avalanche. The rest got off the glacier but were utterly lost when winter caught them. They threw together a rickety shelter to wait for spring. Some men went insane with cabin fever and struck out into the teeth of winter to reach the Klondike; they were never heard from again. The seven who survived until spring recrossed the glacier back to where they started, in Yakutat Bay. Only four were alive when a ship found them, and two suffered snow blindness. When the four broken men were dropped in Seattle, an example of irresponsible journalism transformed what should have been a cautionary tale into an inducement to head for the Klondike: The *Seattle Times* incorrectly reported that the men had returned with half a million dollars worth of gold.

Most stampeders sailed to Skagway or Dyea, neighboring Southeast Alaska towns that competed to be the gateway to the Klondike. From there they made for the goldfields via Chilkoot Pass, a route the Tlingit had been using for centuries to trade with Interior peoples. It required 33 miles (53 km) of steep, difficult hiking to Lake Lindemann or Lake Bennett, where the gold seekers had to build crude boats and float 550 miles (880 km) to the goldfields. Tough, but not as bad as the Malaspina Glacier or some other routes. However, when the tired stampeders topped the 3,739-foot (1,140 m) pass, inside Canadian territory, they were confronted by the Northwest Mounted Police. Originally sent to keep order and make sure customs duties were paid, the Mounties heard that supplies were running low in the Klondike. As a result, they began requiring that each person headed for the goldfields bring enough food to last for a year—about a ton. That meant the gold seekers had to go up and down the pass a dozen, maybe two dozen times.

Although the Klondike fields yielded some $300 million in gold, the vast majority of stampeders didn't strike it rich. Some moved on to Nome or some other gold strike. Most went home. But many stayed and made Alaska home; from 1890 to 1900 the state's year-round population doubled from 30,000 to 60,000. This mass migration jump-started the 20th century in Alaska, boosting the building of the railroads, the founding of cities and towns, and the growth of resource industries like fishing and logging. Alaska continued growing steadily, but it didn't experience another great leap forward until World War II.

The Storied Gold Rush

The gold may have given out, but the old drama and characters made money year after year for storytellers. Twenty-year-old Klondike gold-rusher Jack London turned his adventures into such stories as *Call of the Wild* and *To Build a Fire*; part one of his novel *Burning Daylight* centers on the gold rush. Jules Verne wrote *Volcano of Gold* about the Klondike. Filmmaker Charlie Chaplin struck gold with his 1925 movie *The Gold Rush*. Mae West made her own attempt in 1936 with *Klondike Annie*. A 1955 Jimmy Stewart movie called *The Far Country* is set in Skagway and Dawson City during the gold rush. James Michener's *Alaska* devotes a chapter to the era. A good history of the gold rush is by Canadian Pierre Berton called *Klondike Fever*; he also narrated the 1957 documentary *City of Gold* about Dawson City.

World War II

Few people know that the Japanese invaded Alaska during World War II. Unlike the bombing of Pearl Harbor, the Japanese military actually put troops on the ground and flew the flag of the rising sun over American soil for nearly a year in the Aleutians. The invasion did not come as a total surprise. U.S. military planners knew that the westernmost Aleutian Islands lay closer to Japan than they did to Anchorage, and that San Francisco was 1,000 miles (1,600 km) closer to Tokyo via the Aleutians than via Hawaii.

The invasion began as a diversion. In early June of 1942 the Battle of Midway was about to begin some 1,500 miles (2,414 km) south of the Aleutians, and the Japanese hoped an attack here would draw some American forces away from Midway. So on June 3 they bombed Unalaska/Dutch Harbor. They caused some damage and created confusion in the Aleutians, but the tactic didn't work: The Japanese suffered a stunning defeat at Midway.

Partly to save face, the Japanese forces at Alaska's door then invaded two far-western Aleutian Islands, Attu and Kiska, which were undefended and nearly unpopulated. The Japanese built an airfield and bunkers and brought in several thousand soldiers. In response, the Americans island-hopped out to the Aleutians, setting up bases ever closer to Attu and Kiska. American planes repeatedly bombed the two islands and the supply ships coming from Japan, and American ships fought a major engagement with a big Japanese supply convoy in March 1943. But the main battle occurred in May of that year.

> **World War II rapidly transformed Alaska from a frontier backwater into part of modern America, albeit a part that remained a frontier in most ways.**

On May 11 some 11,000 American troops landed on Attu, which was defended by 2,600 Japanese soldiers. One of the war's most brutal battles ensued, lasting several weeks. In the end all but 28 Japanese were dead and American casualties reached nearly 4,000. An equally bloody battle seemed inevitable on Kiska, but the Japanese evacuated the island under cover of fog. When American and Canadian troops stormed ashore, they didn't find anyone to fight.

No more combat occurred in Alaska, but war-related development continued apace, notably the construction of airfields and the Alaska Highway, which finally connected Alaska to the lower 48 by road. Even more significantly, the war brought tens of thousands of American troops to Alaska, many of whom fell in love with the Great Land and returned to live and work and raise families there after the war. World War II rapidly transformed Alaska from a frontier backwater into part of modern America, albeit a part that remained a frontier in most ways.

Modern Times

The end of World War II was soon followed by the beginning of the Cold War. With the Soviet Union looming just miles from Alaska, the military presence in Alaska expanded in the decades following World War II. Mostly due to the influx of military personnel and their families, the population of Anchorage jumped from 3,000 in 1940 to about 47,000 residents only 11 years later. By 1950 one in six Alaska residents served in the military. All the new residents plus massive military construction and spending gave the Alaska economy a huge shot in the arm. As

Workers endeavor to clean a cormorant befouled by the 1989 *Exxon Valdez* oil spill.

a rapidly modernizing region and a vital link in America's national defense, Alaska was declared the United States' 49th state in 1959.

Statehood notwithstanding, Alaska had one more frontier-like boom up its sleeve. In 1968, oil company geologists found a huge oil field on the North Slope, the vast Arctic Ocean coastal plain north of the Brooks Range. Environmental concerns and native land rights raised serious questions about the development of this field, particularly the construction of the 800-mile (1,280 km) pipeline to Valdez and the subsequent shipping of oil through pristine waters, but the Arab oil embargo in 1973 gave oil advocates just enough of a boost. Buoyed by the resulting oil shortages, Congress authorized the pipeline in a 50 to 49 vote in the Senate on the key legislation. Oil money soon poured into Alaska and into the coffers of the big oil companies—and oil poured into the waters of Prince William Sound when the *Exxon Valdez* ran aground, in 1989. This episode epitomizes the issues that Alaska faces in the 21st century as it continues to try to balance the use and conservation of its natural resources. ∎

EXPERIENCE:
Disaster Strikes

You can get a feeling for both the immense resources and fragile ecology of Alaska by learning about two recent disasters—the 1964 earthquake and the 1989 *Exxon Valdez* oil spill—at the **Valdez Museum** (tel 907/835-2764, www.valdezmuseum.org, closed a.m. & Mon. mid-Sept.–mid-May, $$). The first demonstrates Alaska's vulnerability to the immense plate tectonic forces beneath it; the second how one of its richest natural resources can travel 800 miles (1,280 km) only to foul 1,500 miles (2,414 km) of shoreline. The museum—Valdez was close to ground zero for both disasters—has large collections on the quake and the spill.

The Arts

For a state populated by only 700,000 or so people, Alaska has a varied and vibrant arts scene. The visual arts are especially robust—with wood-carvers taking center stage—but lovers of music, theater, dance, and literature also will find much to enjoy.

Not surprisingly, given the powerful presence of the surrounding landscape, many Alaska artists pursue themes related to wilderness, wildlife, and the relationship between human beings and the land. Some express these themes through traditional methods; others use cutting-edge contemporary styles. A few leading artists are mentioned below, but they form just a small sampling of the many who have done or are doing fine work.

Visual Arts

The earliest visual artists were the Alaska natives from past centuries whose names have been lost to time. Most of their work also has been lost, but a few pieces survive in museum collections. The University of Alaska Museum of the North displays several walrus-ivory toys unearthed in an archaeological dig on St. Lawrence Island. Coastal Eskimos have been carving ivory figures since at least 500 B.C.

A new wave of art washed into Alaska when European explorers arrived. Typically an expedition would bring along an artist the way today's travelers bring along a camera, though some of their drawings and sketches have artistic merit and rise above being mere visual recordings. One well-known officially appointed artist was John Webber, who sailed with Capt. James Cook, the renowned British seafarer, on his third and last voyage, from 1776 to 1780. Webber drew and painted landscapes, wildlife, and some of the Alaska natives he encountered. On that same trip, William Ellis, the surgeon's mate, also painted some of the sights they encountered.

The first professionally trained artist to live in Alaska was Sydney Laurence (1865–1940), who went on to become the state's most famous and influential painter. Born in Brooklyn, he roamed the world as a young man, studying painting in Paris and London. Later he used his talents as an illustrator and photographer to capture such conflicts as the Boxer Rebellion in China, the South African Zulu War, and the Spanish-American War.

In 1904 Laurence headed north to Alaska but for several years he eschewed painting in favor of prospecting—even artists can catch gold fever. Necessity rather than artistic passion forced him back to his brushes; as he

frankly put it, "I was broke and couldn't get away. So I resumed my painting."
Laurence generally painted traditional, even iconic Alaska subjects, such as Mount
McKinley and trappers. His specialty was large canvases that glorified Alaska's wild
landscapes. Today his major works sell for sums well into six figures. Most of his paintings hang in private collections, but the Anchorage Museum and the Alaska Heritage
Museum (also in Anchorage) have good selections; the former devotes an entire
gallery to him.

A contemporary of Laurence's who became nearly as famous was Eustace Ziegler
(1881–1969), born in Detroit. He began painting at age 7 and by the time he turned 20
he was selling his work professionally. He had plenty to sell, too; from age 20 until just a
few months before his death, at age 87, Ziegler produced about 40 paintings a year. The
son of an Episcopal minister, Ziegler came to Cordova, on Prince William Sound, at the
request of the Episcopal bishop of Alaska to run the Red Dragon, a nonalcoholic social
center and mission. Ziegler later went to divinity school and became a priest, returning
to Cordova to preside at St. George's Church.

**World-renowned Tlingit master carver Nathan Jackson adds his own creative flair to
traditional totem pole motifs.**

Totem poles, such as this one at Totem Bight State Historical Park in Ketchikan, convey stories via their intricate details.

Like Laurence, Ziegler was fascinated by the Alaska outdoors, but unlike Laurence, Ziegler was equally fascinated by the people of Alaska. He traveled all over via packhorse, canoe, riverboat, and dogsled, meeting folks from all walks of life. In an honest, sympathetic style he painted fishermen, prospectors, native mothers, gamblers, priests, and prostitutes. He also continued his work as a priest until 1924, when a mural commission in Seattle from the Alaska Steamship Company convinced him to commit

full-time to painting.
Ziegler eventually moved
to Seattle, but he returned to
Alaska almost every summer to find
renewed inspiration.

Fast-forward now to the 21st century
and a major solo exhibition at the Alaska State
Museum, in Juneau. Museumgoers wander through
a dazzling and befuddling series of works fashioned
from tape, light, water, space, and video projections,
works that invite viewers to interact with and become
part of the pieces. The artist is professor Kat Tomka
of the University of Alaska, Anchorage, whose mixed-
media work has been shown around the world. She is
representative of an active contemporary art scene in

**Ivory carving of a caribou, late 19th or
early 20th century, Alaska's west coast**

Alaska that lies at the opposite end of the artistic spectrum
from Laurence and Ziegler. Yet even Tomka notes that her love of translucent tape
derives at least in part from the waterproof seal-gut parkas used historically by the
Aleut, so some connection to the land and people of the Great Land appears even in
her avant-garde work.

Native Artists Today: Anolic Unneengnuzinna Aalughuk, also known as Ted
Mayac, Sr., is an Inupiat Eskimo from King Island, a pinpoint of land about 30 miles
(48 km) off the coast of the remote Seward Peninsula. The Inupiat have been
carving walrus ivory for thousands of years and Mayac carries on this tradition, with
a few innovations in the way he paints his works. After
being employed by the Alaska Department of Transportation for 25 years, Mayac retired; he now carves and
does traditional drumming at community events. Inspired
by the migrating birds that pass through the island, he
shapes incredibly intricate and lifelike figures of some 70
different species, often shown engaged in behaviors that
reveal Mayac's intimate knowledge of these birds.

James Schoppert, a Tlingit, deeply respected traditional
Alaska native art, yet in his work he liked to use tradition as
a departure point and take off in new, sometimes surreal
directions. After studying the history of Alaska native art,
Schoppert decided that innovation was itself a tradition
among the indigenous peoples of Alaska. His pieces became
a bridge between the past and the future.

> The Inupiat have been
> carving walrus ivory for
> thousands of years and
> Ted Mayac carries on
> this tradition, with a few
> innovations in the way
> he paints his works.

A multitalented man, Schoppert painted, carved, taught, wrote poetry, and became
a leader among Alaska native artists. He shared his knowledge widely, teaching in places
as disparate as the University of Alaska, Fairbanks, and the Fairbanks Correctional Center.
He liked to make elaborate masks, which often reflect his sense of humor. One called
"Walrus Goes to Dinner" is a walrus face with a fork and spoon for tusks. Another,
based on an old Chugach mask with one ear, Schoppert entitled "Art Is a One-eared
Madman" as a tribute to Vincent van Gogh. Schoppert died in 1992 at the age of 45.

A young Alaska native woman performs a traditional Yupik dance at Anchorage's Alaska Native Heritage Center, one of the state's major cultural institutions.

Sonya Kelliher-Combs, born in Bethel in 1969, is an innovative Alaska native artist whose methods and media at first glance bear little resemblance to anything in her Inupiat Eskimo or Athabaskan heritage. (She also is part German and part Irish.) Yet a closer look reveals certain materials and symbols that hark back to her childhood in Nome, where in the summer she labored at a subsistence lifestyle. For example, in her layers of acrylic polymer—the foundation of much of her work—she sometimes implants walrus stomach, a substance used as a window covering in traditional homes because it lets light in and smoke out. She also implants string, beadwork, seal and pig intestines, net, paper, human hair, and other objects. Kelliher-Combs's work is displayed in Alaska's major museums and galleries and has been shown across the United States and in Canada.

Totem Poles: One of the most celebrated and unusual media used by Alaska native artists is the totem pole—a carved log, usually cedar, that often stands 20 or 30 feet (6 or 9 m) high. (The tallest in Alaska towers 132 feet/40.2 meters above the village of Kake, on Kupreanof Island.) Totem poles are part of the Northwest Coast native culture, which includes the peoples of Southeast Alaska: the Tlingit, Haida, Eyak, and Tsimshian. These traditional works of art got their name because they generally include at least one carved figure representing the totem of a clan or other social group, usually an animal such as a raven, wolf, or orca.

Though often quite artistic, totem poles traditionally are not simply works of art. Some are memorial poles, created as a tribute to an important member of the clan

upon his death. Others commemorate major events and tell stories and
There even are "ridicule" or "shame" poles, erected to shame someone
down after that person atones for his errant ways. Historically, in a gen
poles often were used to display the wealth and power of a clan. Incic
"low man on the totem pole" is based on a mistaken idea; the lowes
pole often is the most important one.

Perhaps the most famous carver of totem poles today is master carver Nai
Jackson (1938–), a Tlingit who for several decades has deftly used his adze to shape
beautiful poles that are firmly rooted in tradition yet show a creative flair. His poles
stand outside in public places, in Alaska's major museums, and in museums in the lower
48, England, and Japan. He represented Alaska at the Smithsonian Festival of American
Folklife. Jackson also is known for carving other objects—masks, canoes, and doors—and
for his painting and metalworking. Yet his greatest accomplishment may be that he
helped revive the once languishing tradition of
totem pole carving by motivating a new generation
of young Southeast Alaska natives to learn the art.

Performing Arts

Alaska has little of the urban critical mass typically needed to support high-level performing
arts programs, but Anchorage and certain
individual groups do provide excellent music,
theater, and dance experiences.

It comes as no surprise that Anchorage occupies
center stage in Alaska's performing arts scene,
being the only municipality in the state that can
lay claim to being a big city. Anchorage also has an
advantage over other cities: oil money. Through
taxes and direct contributions; the oil companies
that loom so large in the Alaska economy have put
millions into the performing arts in Alaska, particularly in Anchorage. The city's Alaska Center for the
Performing Arts is an outstanding facility that hosts
major traveling shows as well as the highly regarded
Anchorage Symphony Orchestra (which almost
always sells out its 2,000-plus-seat theater) and the
Anchorage Opera.

Independent performing artists and groups also
thrive in Anchorage, epitomized by the group Pamyua (pronounced BUM-yo-ah). A
high-energy foursome of young Yupik and Inuit performers who got together in 1996,
Pamyua has blossomed into one of Alaska's most beloved groups. They're enjoying
success beyond the state, too, appearing at world music festivals and winning record-of-
the-year honors at the Native American Music Awards in 2003—the first Alaska artists
to win it. But labeling their work as "world music" or "Alaska native music" doesn't fully
capture their diversity and creativity. They blend traditional song, drumming, and dancing in an eclectic style that has hints of jazz, gospel, rhythm and blues, funk, hip-hop,
and doo-wop. They even include comedy and Yupik storytelling.

Master Artist

Widely heralded as the father of
contemporary Alaska art, Ron Senungetuk is famed for his unique
wood paintings. Using vibrant
colored oils, he brings to life such
majestic Alaska icons as whales,
seabirds, seals, reindeer, even
the aurora borealis, in intriguing
abstract forms. An Inupiat born
in 1933 in Wales, on the Seward
Peninsula, Senungetuk sold his
ivory carvings to tourists when he
was a boy. He went on to obtain
advanced art degrees, and he
launched the University of Alaska's
Native Arts Center, which, to this
day, provides young Alaska natives
with a chance to pursue their own
artistic dreams. You can see Senungetuk's work at museums, gallery
shows, and solo exhibitions.

For proof that Anchorage doesn't have a monopoly on performing arts in Alaska, one need look no further than the Perseverance Theatre in Juneau. Considered one of the finest regional theaters in the nation, PT, as locals call it, likes to mix challenging classics with innovative and often edgy lesser-known works. Even the classics range widely, from *Death of a Salesman* to *Hair* to a rendition of *MacBeth* set in Tlingit culture and featuring an all-Alaska native cast. Nonclassics have included a play about the Columbine High School shootings and a musical about the lives of Filipino Alaskans. PT also aggressively premieres new works, such as Paula Vogel's Pulitzer Prize–winning *How I Learned to Drive,* which she wrote and developed while an artist-in-residence at PT.

Literature

More than most, Alaska is the kind of place that inspires people to write, to grope for the words to capture what they see and to express what they feel. Alaska's authors also have used fiction and poetry to examine life in the Great Land. Certainly this is true for Seth Kantner, whose work reflects the untamed landscape that surrounds his home in remote northwest Alaska. Kantner was born and raised in a sod house on the tundra, fishing, trapping, and hunting as part of his family's subsistence lifestyle. Today he still engages in those traditional pursuits but he has added "famous author" and "wildlife photographer" to his resume. In 2004, Kantner's debut novel, *Ordinary Wolves,* was published to rave reviews ("An astounding book" wrote Barbara Kingsolver; "a magnificently realized story," said the *New York Times*). Kantner followed up in 2008 with a well-received nonfiction title, *Shopping for Porcupine,* richly illustrated with his own photographs. Its essay topics range from hunting to odd Alaska characters to the vanishing wilderness.

> **More than most, Alaska is the kind of place that inspires people to write, to grope for the words to capture what they see and to express what they feel.**

These themes also are explored in the fascinating chronicles of recent and contemporary life found in the excellent collection of writings in *Authentic Alaska: Voices of Its Native Writers* (1998), edited by Susan B. Andrews and John Creed. Also of note, award-winning author Sherry Simpson gazes deeply at issues facing America's last frontier in *The Way Winter Comes* (1998).

Other notable Alaska writers include Richard Nelson, a former Alaska State Writer Laureate and the author of many books on Alaska life, most famously *Make Prayers to the Raven: A Koyukon View of the Northern Forest,* which was made into an award-winning public television series; and Jo-Ann Mapson, who has written eight novels, three of them national best sellers.

And finally, Linda McCarriston and Robert Service, both poets, deserve attention for their compositions. McCarriston, a National Book Award finalist and university professor, pursues complex truths about family life, friendship, and children. Service, on the other hand, came to the Yukon around the Klondike gold rush era. Writing poems for the people and not the critics, Service was beloved in his time. Some of his works, such as "The Cremation of Sam McGee" and "The Shooting of Dan McGrew" (both first published in his 1907 book of verse *Songs of a Sourdough*), are still memorized by Alaska schoolchildren to this day. ■

A remote realm of islands, forests, fjords, mountains, and wildlife, but also of appealing towns and a rich human history

Southeast Alaska

The bald eagle, ubiquitous along Alaska's southern coastlines

Map labels:

WRANGELL-ST. ELIAS
NATIONAL PARK
AND PRESERVE

RUSSELL
FIORD
WILDERNESS

Yakutat
Bay

Russell
Fiord

Tatshenshini

Yakutat

ALASKA MARINE HIGHWAY

BRABAZON RANGE

Dry Bay

Alsek

Tarr Inlet

Mount
Fairweather
15,320 ft

FAIRWEATHER RANGE

Gulf of Alaska

ALASKA MARITI...

Southeast Alaska

Alaska's panhandle, southeast Alaska consists of a narrow strip of mainland and thousands of islands bounded by British Columbia and the Coast Mountains to the east and the Pacific Ocean to the west. Only three towns—Skagway, Haines, and Hyder—connect to the rest of Alaska by road, but motorists must drive hundreds of miles through Canada to get to them.

The rest of the Southeast is only accessible by air or water, but the plane service is decent and the opportunities to travel by boat are legendary. This is the home of the renowned Inside Passage: the route through protected waters that slaloms among islands almost the whole length of the Southeast. Every year hundreds of thousands of visitors, and many locals, board cruise ships and ferries to travel all or part of this scenic waterway.

Mountains, some rising thousands of feet out of the sea, seem to tower everywhere. This cool, wet region is covered by temperate rain forest, designated as Tongass National Forest (the nation's largest at 17 million acres/ 7 million ha). With up to 150 inches (4 m) of precipitation a year, the forest of spruce and hemlock stands shrouded in mist and teeming with life—grizzly (inland), brown (coastal), and black bears, mountain goats, wolves, deer, and eagles. Five species of salmon swim up the rivers and creeks to spawn. The ocean waters also are full of wildlife, including humpback whales, sea lions, porpoises, orcas, and sea otters.

Its natural assets would more than suffice, but the Southeast, home to only about 70,000 people, also possesses a rich historical and cultural heritage—from the indigenous peoples to the later Europeans and gold seekers—that is richly exhibited in excellent museums, art galleries, music, and festivals. ∎

CHILKOOT TRAIL

Klondike Gold Rush Nat. Hist. Park

Taiya River

98 White Pass Summit 3,292 ft

SOUTH KLONDIKE HWY.

Dyea
Skagway

Chilkoot Lake State Recreation Site

7

HAINES HWY.

Chilkat Lake

LUTAK ROAD

Haines

Alaska color-coded by region

Anchorage

Juneau

Area of map detail

Alaska Chilkat Bald Eagle Preserve

GLACIER BAY NATIONAL PARK & PRESERVE

Echo Cove

Eagle Beach State Recreation Area

GLACIER / JUNEAU VETERANS' MEMORIAL HWY.

Bartlett Cove

Beardslee Islands

Point Gustavus

Gustavus

Mansfield Peninsula

7 **Mendenhall Glacier Visitor Center**

★ **JUNEAU**

Auke Bay

Douglas Island

Gastineau Channel

CANADA

60 kilometers

30 miles

0

0

Glacier Bay

Icy Strait

Hoonah

Pelican

Chichagof Island

ADMIRALTY ISLAND NATIONAL MONUMENT

Chatham Strait

Stephens Passage

Pack Creek

Admiralty Island

Angoon

KOOTZNOOWOO WILDERNESS

Frederick Sound

Kruzof Island

Mount Edgecumbe 3,201 ft

St. Lazaria Island

Starrigavan Recreation Area

Sitka

Sitka Sound

TONGASS NATIONAL FOREST

Kake

LeConte Glacier

Petersburg

Baranof Island

Kuiu Island

Chatham Strait

Kupreanof Island

Wrangell Narrows

Mitkof Island

7

To Telegraph Creek

Petroglyph Beach State Historic Site

Point Baker

Wrangell

Rainbow Falls Trail

Wrangell Island

Etolin Island

Blind Slough

Anan Wildlife Observatory

Coffman Cove

MISTY FIORDS

NATIONAL

Stewart

Hyder

Port Alexander

Summer Strait

Naukati Bay

Prince of Wales Island

Thorne Bay

MONUMENT

WILDERNESS

Revillagigedo Island

Rudyerd Bay

Iphigenia Bay

Klawock

Hollis

Kasaan

New Eddystone Rock

MISTY FIORDS NATIONAL MONUMENT

Craig

Behm Canal

Totem Bight State Historical Park

★ **Ketchikan**

Herring Cove

Point Alava

Rudyerd Island

PEABODY MOUNTAINS

Hydaburg

TONGASS HWY.

Annette Island

Metlakatla

Dall Island

Cordova Bay

ALASKA MARINE HIGHWAY

Dixon Entrance

NATIONAL ALEXANDER ARCHIPELAGO WILDLIFE REFUGE

PACIFIC OCEAN

Revillagigedo Channel

Ketchikan

Rain often greets people as they arrive in this famously soggy town, where an average of about 160 inches (406 cm) of rain falls every year. But the sportfishing and wealth of other natural and urban attractions more than compensate for any weather inconveniences.

Waterfront diners relish a sunny day in Ketchikan.

Ketchikan

🗺 Map p. 47

Visitor Information

✉ Ketchikan
Visitors
Information
Center, 131
Front St.

☎ 907/225-6166
or
800/770-3300

**www.visit-ketchikan
.com**

Many visitors come to chase salmon and halibut. The abundance of salmon and timber led to the founding of the town in the 1880s. By the 1930s more than a dozen canneries annually produced 1.5 million cases of salmon, giving Ketchikan its reputation as the salmon capital of the world. Those numbers have declined, but the industry remains an economic mainstay in the region. These days, tourism is a major employer, mostly catering to the approximately 850,000 cruise-ship visitors who arrive each year.

The Waterfront

Ships tie up at the docks beside the **Waterfront Promenade** along Front Street. (The promenade wraps around the **Thomas Basin Boat Harbor,** where the commercial fishing fleet docks.) This is the perfect place to begin a tour of Ketchikan.

Among the first things you'll notice is that dozens of galleries and shops line the streets. Most galleries feature a wealth of local art. Many Tlingit, Eyak, Haida, and Tsimshian artists, both traditional and contemporary, work here. World-renowned master carver Nathan Jackson has striking totem poles and other carvings on

INSIDER TIP:

Totem pole sites are particularly plentiful around Ketchikan on Revillagigedo Island.

—ROWLAND SHELLEY
National Geographic field researcher

display in galleries, museums, and outdoor public spaces. (For information on galleries, ask in stores and galleries for the "Ketchikan Arts Guide.") A good place to start exploring is the historic **Star Building** (5 Creek St., closed Sun. Oct.–April), which houses two galleries that carry the work of many locals: **Soho Coho** (tel 907/225-5954) and **Alaska Eagle Arts** (tel 907/225-8365).

The **Southeast Alaska Discovery Center** on the promenade displays a fine collection of native art. The lobby features three sumptuous totems, one Tlingit style, one Haida, and one Tsimshian. The center presents other aspects of native life, too; one exhibit re-creates a traditional fish camp and another allows visitors to listen to recordings of Native elders discussing their ways of life. However, the majority of the space is devoted to the natural

world and the use of natural resources. The rain forest exhibit comes complete with running water and birdcalls. Interactive exhibits detail all seven of the main ecosystems in the Southeast, from tide pools to alpine tundra.

If in the mood for something lighter, stroll across the street to the **Great Alaskan Lumberjack Show** (420 Spruce Mill Way, tel 907/225-9050 or 888/320-9049, www.lumberjackshows.com, $$$$$).

Fishing

Fishing is popular across Alaska, but Ketchikan, the "salmon capital of the world," is especially popular with sport fishermen. Salmon swarm from the open ocean to the protected waters of the Inside Passage. Tlingit made fishing camps near Ketchikan and commercial fishermen founded the modern town in 1900. Halibut, trout, red snapper, and cod also abound in the region.

Fishermen can sign into lodges and resorts that shepherd their whole experience. They can also venture to wilderness cabins accessible only by floatplane, boat, or hike, but reservations are needed far in advance—for one source, see www.dnr.alaska.gov/parks/cabins.

Part show, part contest, these programs feature highly skilled individuals who compete against each other in such events, as sawing, chopping, logrolling, and

Southeast Alaska Discovery Center

- ✉ 50 Main St.
- ☎ 907/228-6220
- 🕐 Closed Sun.–Wed. Oct.–April
- 💲 $ May–Sept. Free rest of year

www.alaskacenters.gov/ketchikan.cfm

the astounding speed climb, in which the contestants ascend very tall poles with monkey-like quickness.

Along Ketchikan Creek

Ketchikan's past is conjured up at the **Tongass Historical Museum** (629 Dock St.,

Lush vegetation along the trail to Punchbowl Cove in Misty Fiords bears testament to the area's rainfall.

Saxman Totem Park
☎ 907/225-4166

Saxman Native Village Tours
☎ 907/225-4421
💲 $$$$. Tickets at gift shop across street from Saxman Totem Park

www.capefox tours.com

907/225-5600, closed Sat.–Sun. Oct.–April, $), which occupies a large building along the bank of Ketchikan Creek. Visitors can progress from the town's early incarnation as a Tlingit fish camp through the mining, timber, and fishing eras to the present. A shadier past, of which Ketchikan seems quite proud, can be explored by following the creek downstream for a block

and crossing the bridge to Creek Street. The red-light district until the 1950s, **Creek Street** was the place where "both fish and fishermen went upstream to spawn," as the local joke goes. Built on boardwalks above the creek, the district now houses shops, galleries, and restaurants.

A ways up Ketchikan Creek, appropriately on Salmon Street, sits the **Deer Mountain Tribal Hatchery and Eagle Center** (1158 Salmon Rd., 907/228-5530, closed Oct.–April, $$$). The hatchery supplements the natural salmon and trout runs in the creek where they have spawned for ages. The coho salmon come up in the fall and winter; the kings surge upstream in August. The hatchery tour gives information about salmon and takes visitors to see the raptors at the adjoining eagle center.

Facing the hatchery from across the creek is the **Totem Heritage Center** (601 Deermount St., 907/225-5900, closed Sat.–Sun. Oct.–April, $$). The beautiful contemporary totem pole "Raven-Fog Woman," created by Nathan Jackson, stands outside; however, the center focuses on rescuing old, unrestored poles from abandoned native villages. The center also contains displays of native beadwork and basket weaving, and sometimes visitors can see artists at work.

Tongass Highway

If the beauty and mythology of totem poles capture your imagination, drive 2.5 miles (4 km) south on the shore-hugging South Tongass Highway, and then go left one block on Totem Row to the **Saxman Totem Park,** which boasts one of the largest collections of standing poles in the world. Note the plain-shafted pole topped by the figure of former Secretary of State William H. Seward—the man who acquired Alaska for the United States. Rumor has it

INSIDER TIP:

Take a ferry ride from Ketchikan to explore hundreds of miles of Forest Service and abandoned logging roads in the mountainous Tongass rain forest on northern Prince of Wales Island.

—DAVID ROHR
National Geographic field researcher

that this is a ridicule pole carved because Seward visited a Tlingit village in 1869 and didn't reciprocate the gifts and hospitality shown him by the villagers. You may look around for free on your own or you can go on a two-hour tour (offered by

Saxman Native Village Tours), which includes watching a traditional dance performance, observing artists at work, hearing stories about the totems, and visiting the tribal house.

About 6 miles (9.6 km) farther south on the highway, turn left on Wood Road to the **Alaska Rainforest Sanctuary.** The 1.75-hour tour leads through a second-growth rain forest and the Eagle Creek Estuary; watch for black bears, bald eagles, seals, and the spawning salmon that entice these birds and animals. The tour also takes in a historic sawmill, resident reindeer, and the working studio of a master carver. The sanctuary has numerous zip lines, which enable securely harnessed customers to slide slowly through the treetops 130 feet (40 m) above the forest floor.

More totem poles are on display at the **Totem Bight State Historical Park,** 10 miles (16 km) north of Ketchikan on the North Tongass Highway. A short trail leads through a lovely seaside forest to 14 totem poles and a copy of a clan house. A brochure reveals the complexities of the art and culture represented. ■

Alaska Rainforest Sanctuary

- 116 Wood Rd.
- 907/225-5503
- Closed Oct.–April
- $$$$$

www.alaskarainforest.com

Totem Bight State Historical Park

- Map p. 47
- 9883 N. Tongass Hwy.
- 907/247-8574

www.dnr.alaska.gov/parks/units/totembgh.htm

Tsimshian of Annette Island

Unlike the Tlingit, Eyak, and Haida, the Tsimshian people are relative newcomers to Alaska. Their ancestral homeland is in British Columbia, but in the late 1800s a group of Tsimshian led by Church of England missionary William Duncan applied to the U.S. for religious asylum. Granted permission to settle on Annette Island, a few miles south of Ketchikan, some 800 Tsimshian moved there from Old Metlakatla and founded New Metlakatla in 1887. Today the community is just called Metlakatla. In 1891, the U.S. government formally recognized the community and established the Annette Islands Reserve, the only federal Indian reserve in Alaska.

Cruising Through Misty Fiords

Misty Fiords National Monument is as striking and mysterious as its name suggests. A vista of lofty waterfalls, bald eagles, volcanic plugs, harbor seals, rugged mountains, and lush rain forest unfolds before you as your tour boat delves deep into Misty's 2.2 million acres (0.9 million ha), almost all of it wilderness. You'll also likely see bears and salmon and perhaps humpback whales, deer, and otters. Some people cruise round-trip, but most fly back on a floatplane, a wonderful experience in itself.

After weighing anchor in Ketchikan, the boat cruises *(for a list of tour operators contact Ketchikan Visitors Information Center; see p. 48)* east down Tongass Narrows and out into Revillagigedo Channel. To the south lies Annette Island, Alaska's lone Native American reservation (see sidebar p. 51). At Point Alava the boat turns north into the monument via **Behm Canal ❶**. Handsome Behm Canal is a nearly straight, 100-mile-long (160 km), 2-to-4-mile-wide (3.2–6.4 km) natural waterway, framed at this end by low mountains and curtains of hemlock, spruce, and cedar. Scan the tall trees along the shore for bald eagles and their nests.

After about 8 miles (12.8 km), the boat steers for the western shore and squeezes through the narrows between Revillagigedo (the big island that is home to Ketchikan) and little **Rudyerd Island ❷**. Back in the 1920s, a local established a fox farm here—a common enterprise in Alaska at that time, when fox furs were popular. Abundant fish made feeding the foxes easy. The Great Depression and the fact that southeastern Alaska is a little too warm for foxes brought this and other fox farms to an end. However, their remote locations appealed to bootleggers, who during Prohibition smuggled liquor into the United States from Canada through places like Rudyerd Island.

About 15 miles (24 km) up Behm Canal from Rudyerd Island, **New Eddystone Rock ❸** juts 237 feet (72 m) above the water. A six-million-year-old volcanic plug, the remains of an eroded volcano, this landmark was named in

NOT TO BE MISSED:

New Eddystone Rock • Punchbowl Cove • Nooya Creek Wildlife • Rudyerd Bay waterfalls

1793 by Capt. George Vancouver—on his four-year-plus voyage of exploration for Britain—for its resemblance to the lighthouse on Eddystone Rock in the English Channel.

Into Rudyerd Bay

A couple of miles north of New Eddystone the tour turns east into **Rudyerd Bay ❹**, one of the gorgeous fjords for which the monument is named. Waterfalls pour off burly granite cliffs, which shoulder in close around this half-mile-wide (0.8 km) waterway. A few miles along the boat stops in **Punchbowl Cove ❺**, facing a sheer, 3,000-foot (914 m) cliff that only a handful of climbers have conquered. Nearby is a pictograph (rock carving) thought to mark the grave of a Tlingit shaman. Several miles deeper into the fjord, **Nooya Creek ❻** tumbles into the bay; look for salmon mid-July through September and for the bears, seals, and eagles that come for a fish feed. From way back here in Rudyerd Bay, most boat passengers opt to catch a 30-minute flight back to Ketchikan aboard a floatplane for a uniquely different perspective of the misty fjords.

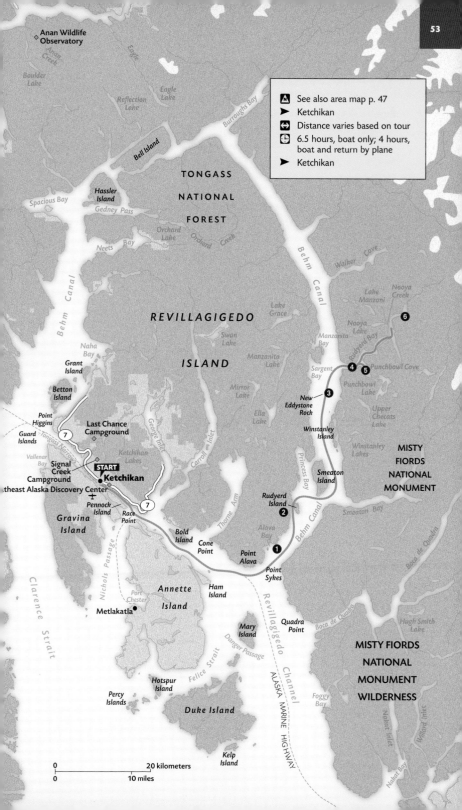

Anan Wildlife
Observatory

Anan Creek

Boulder
Lake

Eagle

Eagle
Lake

Reflection
Lake

Burroughs Bay

Bell Island

TONGASS

NATIONAL

FOREST

Spacious Bay

Hassler
Island

Gedney Pass

Neets Bay

Orchard
Lake

Orchard Creek

Walker Cove

Behm Canal

Lake
Manzoni

Nooya
Creek

Nooya
Lake

6

Behm Canal

REVILLAGIGEDO

Lake
Grace

Manzanita
Bay

Manzanita
Lake

Sargent
Bay

Punchbowl Cove

4
5

Rudyerd Bay

Naha
Bay

ISLAND

Swan
Lake

Punchbowl
Lake

Upper
Checats
Lake

Grant
Island

Mirror
Lake

New
Eddystone
Rock

3

Betton
Island

Point
Higgins

Guard
Islands

7

Last Chance
Campground

Ketchikan
Lakes

Ella
Lake

Winstanley
Island

Winstanley
Bay

MISTY
FIORDS

NATIONAL

MONUMENT

Vallenar
Bay

Signal
Creek
Campground

Southeast Alaska Discovery Center

START

Ketchikan

George Inlet

Carroll Inlet

Thorne Arm

Smeaton
Island

Winstanley
Lakes

Princess Bay

Pennock
Island

7

Race
Point

Gravina
Island

Bold
Island

Cone
Point

Point
Alava

Rudyerd
Island

2

Alava
Bay

1

Smeaton Bay

Behm Canal

Boca de Quadra

Nichols Passage

Port
Chester

Annette
Island

Ham
Island

Point
Sykes

Metlakatla

Clarence Strait

Danger Passage

Mary
Island

Quadra
Point

Boca de Quadra

Hugh Smith
Lake

Felice Strait

Revillagigedo Channel

MISTY FIORDS

NATIONAL

MONUMENT

WILDERNESS

Hotspur
Island

Percy
Islands

Duke Island

ALASKA MARINE HIGHWAY

Foggy
Bay

Nakat Bay

Winstanley Inlet

Kelp
Island

0   20 kilometers
0   10 miles

☐ See also area map p. 47
▶ Ketchikan
↔ Distance varies based on tour
⊕ 6.5 hours, boat only; 4 hours,
   boat and return by plane
▶ Ketchikan

Wrangell

Travelers seeking authentic Southeast Alaska should head for Wrangell. Situated on the northern tip of Wrangell Island, this friendly town of 2,400 is the kind of place where visitors can easily strike up a conversation with someone sitting at a café or watching the fishing boats from the pier. Wrangell also serves as a jumping-off point to the LeConte Glacier, Anan Wildlife Observatory, and the Stikine River—all Southeast treasures.

The ferry from Petersburg to Wrangell offers travelers scenic vistas of the Inside Passage.

Wrangell

⚑ Map p. 47

Visitor Information

✉ Wrangell Visitor Center, 296 Campbell Dr.

☎ 907/874-3699

www.wrangell.com

The Wrangell Visitor Center is housed in the James and Elsie Nolan Center, most of which is devoted to the **Wrangell Museum.** This museum is much larger and finer than one would expect in a town of this size. It covers the town's unique history; it's the only town that was governed by four sovereigns—the Tlingit, Russians, British, and Americans. Just inside the museum's entrance stand four of Alaska's oldest carved house

posts, fine Tlingit work dating from the late 1700s. The museum also displays photos from the rowdy decades following the 1861 gold rush on the Stikine. One exhibit tells how Wyatt Earp once filled in as a marshal and had to disarm a man whom he realized he'd arrested 20 years earlier in Dodge City.

Connected to the south end of downtown by a narrow footbridge is **Chief Shakes Island** *(end of Shakes St.).* In the bustling harbor this small island is an oasis of calm and reflection as you walk around the **Shakes Tribal House;** contemplate the totem poles that encircle the latter. Scattered about the beach a mile (1.6 km) north of town at **Petroglyph Beach State Historic Site** are artifacts from even older native inhabitants. Even native elders don't know their origins, some of which may be 8,000 years old. Search the boulders and exposed bedrock near the interpretive platform and you may discover mysterious rock carvings, including representative figures such as killer whales.

South of town, thousands of square miles of Wrangell Island await exploration on foot. One of the finest trails, the **Rainbow Falls Trail** *(Tongass National Forest, Wrangell Ranger District, tel 907/874-2323),* starts just 4.5 miles (7.2 km) south of Wrangell on the Zimovia Highway. It winds 0.7 mile (1.1 km) through old-growth forest to 100-foot-tall (30.5 m) Rainbow Falls.

Nearby Attractions

Thirty-five miles (56 km) away, **Anan Creek** enjoys one of the largest pink salmon runs in the Southeast. The abundance of fish attracts both brown and black bears to the creek. Visitors can safely view bears snagging salmon from the **Anan Wildlife Observatory** *(Tongass National Forest, tel 907/874-2323, www .usda.gov/tongass, reservations required July–Aug.).*

Many people are equally thrilled by **LeConte Glacier,** a tidewater glacier located in a snowcap-ringed fjord about 25 miles (40 km) north of Wrangell. An extremely active glacier, it routinely calves icebergs. The area is also home to a seal nursery.

The closest natural wonder to Wrangell is the **Stikine River,** a swift, 400-mile-long (643 km) river that drains a vast chunk of British Columbia. A number of tour boats operating out of Wrangell *(for information contact Wrangell Visitor Center)* offer day

trips that pass through country studded with stunning glaciers, icebergs, brown and black bears, moose, spawning salmon, bald eagles, and even hot springs. Hardy travelers can go on an overnight journey 130 miles upriver to **Telegraph Creek,** the only settlement on the Stikine. ∎

Wrangell Museum

✉ 296 Campbell Dr.

☎ 907/874-3770

🕐 Closed Sun. May–Sept., Sat.–Sun. Oct.–April

EXPERIENCE:
Scuba Diving

Scuba diving in Alaska? Sounds as likely as skiing in the Sahara. Yet a surprising number of divers brave icy Alaska coastal waters and are rewarded with views of a rich underwater world. Though we humans flinch when we touch a toe to the 50°F (10°C) sea, many marine species find it cozy. As you flipper around the kelp you'll encounter lion's mane jellies, 3-foot-high (1 m) sea anemones, wolf eels, orange sea cucumbers, and other intriguing ocean denizens. Clearly, you'll need some serious gear to withstand the cold, but a smattering of scuba shops and tour operators provide the requisite equipment, plus lessons and outings (a website to start with is www.akscuba.com). Southeast Alaska and, to a lesser degree, the Kenai Peninsula and Prince William Sound are Alaska's scuba hot spots, so to speak.

Petersburg

Proud of its Norwegian ties, Petersburg bills itself as Alaska's "Little Norway." Indeed, this heritage is displayed in numerous ways, such as the frequent use of the word "Velkommen" by local businesses, the annual Little Norway Festival, the reproduction Viking ship that sits downtown, and the house and building exteriors that feature rosemaling—the colorful, flowing floral painting that developed as a folk art in Norway in the mid-18th century.

Petersburg

△ Map p. 47

Visitor Information

✉ Petersburg Visitor Information Center, 1st & Fram Sts.

☎ 907/772-4636

🕐 Closed Sat.–Sun. in winter

www.petersburg.org

However, this little town and its splendid setting on the northern tip of Mitkof Island (the mountains and narrow waterways reminded Petersburg's founders of the fjord country back home in Norway) offer far more than Norwegian flavors.

The town's major industry is readily apparent along the waterfront. Three adjacent harbors sheltering hundreds of trollers, gillnetters, long-liners, and other fishing boats make Petersburg a top fishing port. Some of the big seafood-processing plants offer tours *(for more information try the Petersburg visitor center).*

A block off Middle and South Harbors is **Sing Lee Alley,** the town's historical heart and a pleasant shopping district. Within its few blocks visitors will find **Sing Lee Alley Books** *(11 Sing Lee Alley, tel 907/772-4440),* which sells many Alaska titles and maps; **The Party House** *(14 Sing Lee Alley, tel 907/772-2717),* for souvenirs brightened by beautiful rosemaling; **Tonka Seafoods** *(22 Sing Lee Alley, tel 907/772-3662 or 888/560-3662),* where you can pick out gift boxes of salmon and other seafood to take back home; and the **Sons of Norway Hall** *(23 Sing Lee Alley,*

Petersburg's Norwegian roots and fishing heritage are evident throughout town.

About two hours north of Petersburg headed toward Juneau is a place where humpback whales tend to mass—they can be seen from ferries spouting in all directions.

—ROWLAND SHELLEY
National Geographic field researcher

tel 907/772-4575), a national historic site built in 1912 on pilings over Hammer Slough. This lovely building and others hanging over the slough offer some of the finest examples of rosemaling in the town of Petersburg.

To learn about the history and culture of Petersburg and vicinity, visit the **Clausen Memorial Museum.** It houses Tlingit artifacts, a massive lighthouse lens, a dugout canoe, and a stuffed salmon so big that it brings fishermen to their knees in awe; this unbelievable 126.5-pound (57.4 kg) chinook behemoth is thought to be the world's largest salmon ever caught.

Mitkof Highway

The Mitkof Highway heads south from Petersburg along the scenic Wrangell Narrows and affords easy exploration of some of the outlying parts of Mitkof Island. Most of the highway is paved, but close to the end it turns to gravel. Near Mile 14 the road intersects the **Blind River Rapids Boardwalk.** This quarter-mile (0.4 km) trail crosses muskeg bogs, which cover much of the island, to a favorite fishing spot with the locals. The highway turns inland shortly after the boardwalk and heads southeast. At Mile 16.2, the **Blind Slough Swan Observatory** hosts migrating trumpeter swans in late fall; some 50 to 75 stay the winter. In summer, visitors may spy salmon a little downriver—and bears fishing for those spawners. For its last few lovely miles, the highway hugs the island's eastern shore and looks across at the mouth of the glorious Stikine River (see p. 55). Boat trips can be arranged by way of one of the tour operators located in Wrangell and Petersburg; contract the local visitor centers for information. ■

Public Use Cabins

If you want to experience the wilderness surrounding Petersburg and want a roof over your head, consider renting a public use cabin. These basic accommodations—usually just bunks for four to six people, a table, chairs, and maybe a wood- or oil-burning stove—are generally in remote and scenic places, accessible only by small plane or boat, though a few are along trails or roads. They are very popular and can be reserved up to six months in advance. The Southeast's **Tongass National Forest** *(tel 907/228-6220, www.fs.usda.gov/tongass)* has more than 170 public use cabins and shelters.

Clausen Memorial Museum

✉ 203 Fram St.

☎ 907/772-3598

🕐 Closed Sun. in summer, Sun.–Mon. (most weeks) rest of year

💲 $

www.clausen museum.net

Sitka

Even by Inside Passage standards Sitka is remote because, technically speaking, it's not in the Inside Passage. Of all the southeastern Alaska ports served by the Alaska Marine Highway and visited by cruise ships, only Sitka lies on the outside, facing the open Pacific. This means the town occasionally gets hammered by winter storms, but the summer weather is about average for the region.

The Russian Orthodox St. Michael's Cathedral sits at the head of Sitka's main drag, Lincoln Street.

Sitka

🏕 Map p. 47

Visitor Information

✉ Sitka Convention & Visitors Bureau, Box 1226, 303 Lincoln St., Sitka, AK 99835

☎ 907/747-5940

www.sitka.org

Sitka was a busy port during the first half of the 19th century, when Novo Arkhangelsk (New Archangel, the early Russian name for what is now Sitka) was the capital of Russian Alaska. The ships coming for sea otter pelts brought merchandise from around the globe and Sitka became, for a New World outpost, a large and sophisticated town by the mid-1830s. One admittedly overheated but not entirely irrational visitor dubbed it the "Paris of the Pacific."

Contemporary Sitka retains many of its past characteristics. This town of 8,900 (the fifth most populous city in Alaska) still features a frenetic port, with a large commercial fishing fleet, hundreds of charter fishing boats, and cruise ships that visit constantly throughout the summer. And the spice of Tlingit and Russian culture still seasons the town.

Castle Hill

Baranof Castle Hill State Historic Site (*between foot of John*

O'Connell Bridge & back of Harry Race Pharmacy on Lincoln St.) makes a fine starting point for three reasons: Though not even 100 feet (30.5 m) high, Castle Hill provides a fabulous 360-degree view; it lies between the terrestrial attractions and the marine activities; and it served as the starting point of American Alaska. On October 18, 1867, the Russians lowered their flag here and the Americans raised theirs, signaling the change in ownership of Alaska.

As you stroll around the perimeter, brace yourself for the staggering beauty of Sitka's setting: mountains and forest to the north and east and islands and ocean to the south and west. Drinking in the scenery will occupy you for a while, but when you eventually set your sights a little lower, you can see the layout of the town. Downtown lies immediately below Castle Hill and consists of just a few square blocks. The clustered part of town fans out a little beyond downtown, but the rest of Sitka, mostly residential, stretches out along the shore for several miles both east and west.

Note the John O'Connell Bridge visitor landing to the south. Because Sitka lacks a downtown dock that can accommodate large cruise ships, during the summer a fleet of tenders is busy ferrying passengers from the ships anchored in the harbor to the landing area. You may notice a bumper sticker battle between locals who support expanding the port facilities and those who oppose the expansion. One clever anti sticker reads "Resist Pier Pressure."

To RV or Not to RV?

Though not as numerous as mosquitoes, RVs proliferate on Alaska roads in summer. Some travelers seek the freedom to stop wherever they please rather than being tied to reservations. Others want to avoid paying for lodging. Many like to have metal instead of nylon between them and the grizzlies. Most of Alaska's RV rental outfits are in Anchorage and charge about $250 a day. A few offer minimalist camper shells on small pickups for $150 a day. Whatever RV you rent, please take pity on motorists bunching up behind you and let them pass.

Lincoln Street & Around

Walking from Castle Hill up Lincoln Street, Sitka's main drag downtown, the first street to the left is Katlian Street. Look down and you'll see a building with a striking carved-and-painted entryway, the **Sheet'ka Kwaan Naa Kahidi Tribal Community House** *(200 Katlian St., tel 907/747-7290 or 888/270-8687, www.sitkatours.com)*—a modern version of a traditional clan house. The Tlingit name roughly translates to "the clan house for all the people of Sitka." During the summer, visitors can watch a 30-minute song-and-dance performance by the renowned Naa Kahidi Native Dancers,

Ten-mile-distant (16 km) snowcapped Mount Edgecumbe looms majestically above Sitka's harbor.

Sitka National Historical Park

- ✉ 106 Monastery St.
- ☎ 907/747-0110
- 🕐 Visitor center: closed Sun. in winter; Russian Bishop's House: closed Oct.– mid-May except by appt.
- 💲 $ (guided tour of Russian Bishop's House)

www.nps.gov/sitk

a performance that the local Tlingit say has changed little in thousands of years. The elaborately costumed dancers stage one to three performances daily when large cruise ships are in port. Alternatively, private shows can be arranged (contact the community house).

The blocks of Lincoln Street that are nearest to the John O'Connell Bridge visitor landing contain many souvenir and luxury shops, but sprinkled among them are some estimable local stores and galleries. The **Artist Cove Gallery** (241 Lincoln St., tel 907/747-6990) features the work of local artists and of Northwest Coast and Southeast native and Inupiat Eskimo artists.

Four blocks from the waterfront, at the confluence with Cathedral Way, Lincoln Street splits like a river meeting a rock and flows around **St. Michael's Cathedral** (tel 907-747-8120, open for tours, days vary, donation).

A national historic landmark, this beautiful Russian Orthodox church dates from the 1840s. The original building burned down in 1966, but residents gathered to save many of the artifacts from the flames. In 1967, a near replica of the original was erected on the site and filled with the rescued treasures.

The secular history of Sitka can be explored at the **Sitka Historical Museum** (330 Harbor Dr., tel 907/747-6455, www.sitkahistory .org, closed Sun. May–Sept., Sun.– Mon. rest of year, $), located in Harrigan Centennial Hall near the entrance to Crescent Harbor. The centerpiece of this modest-but-interesting museum is a sprawling detailed model of 1867 Sitka. The old photographs are worth a closer look; check out the grinning woman in the pioneer-style full-length dress leading the sprint in an old Fourth of July race down main street. Harrigan Centennial Hall also hosts the esteemed **New Archangel Dancers** (tel 907/747-5516, www.newarchangeldancers.com, summer shows, $), women who perform authentic folk dances from Russia.

Sitka National Historical Park

The town's premier historic attraction, Sitka National Historical Park was established to commemorate the Battle of Sitka, an 1804 conflict between the Tlingit and the Russians. The park consists of two separate sites. The **Russian Bishop's House,** on Lincoln Street between Monastery and Baranof Streets, dates back to

the year 1842 and is one of only four original Russian structures remaining in the entire Western Hemisphere. Constructed from Sitka spruce, this restored original housed bishops from its completion until 1969. These bishops oversaw an enormous Russian Orthodox diocese that encompassed part of Alaska, Siberia, and reached all the way down the Pacific coast into California. Displays on the ground floor of the house include elaborate clerical garments and a large brass samovar.

The **Tlingit Fort Site** begins a few blocks from the Russian Bishop's House, at the end of Lincoln Street. The **Visitor Center and Southeast Alaska Indian Cultural Center** contains artifacts that tell the stories of both cultures before and after the battle. Though few in number, the objects are of high quality;

note the ceremonial bone dagger inlaid with abalone and the bib made from red, yellow, white, black, blue, and turquoise beads. Native artists work at the center, where visitors are encouraged to watch them carve and weave and to talk with them about their art. Outside, miles of easy walking trails cut through the park's beautiful forests that border Sitka Sound and the estuary of the Indian River. The area south of the estuary features totem poles and the 1804 battle site; the northern area contains picnic areas and the Russian Memorial.

Along the northern boundary of the park perches the **Alaska Raptor Center.** The center rehabilitates and, whenever possible, releases back into the wild raptors and other birds. To educate people about the various birds of prey in the area, the center makes presentations using its

Alaska Raptor Center

- ✉ 1000 Raptor Way
- ☎ 907/747-8662 or 800/643-9425
- 🕐 Closed Sat.–Sun. mid-Sept.– mid-May
- 💲 $$. Free in winter

www.alaska raptor.org

EXPERIENCE: Sea Kayaking Lessons

Sea kayaking dates back to the misty past, when Eskimo and Aleut hunted in animal-hide umiaks and baidarkas, the ancestors of today's sea kayaks. Modern materials have replaced seal skin, but the experience remains largely unchanged: skimming along scenic shorelines in the company of mountains, killer whales, bald eagles, glaciers, and sea otters.

Alaska entices paddlers with some 6,600 miles (10,600 km) of coastline, though most kayaking takes place in Southeast Alaska and Prince William Sound, due to the beauty, the wildlife, and the abundance of protected waters. Given the rigors of the Alaska outdoors, the specialized equipment required, and

the skills and knowledge needed, most visitors opt for guided tours. In the towns of the Southeast and the sound you can hardly swing a paddle without hitting a kayak tour operator, so you'll have plenty of outfitters from which to choose. As a start, contact the **Alaska Sea Kayaking Symposium** (*www.aksks.org; click on "kayak resources"*).

Tours often include lessons for beginners and can last from an hour to weeks. The level of pampering likewise varies, from trips in which participants do the chores with the guides to operations that have gourmet dinners and tents waiting when you paddle into camp. Some outfits offer tours with a particular focus, such as whale-watching or glacier visiting.

Sheldon Jackson Museum

✉ 104 College Dr.

☎ 907/747-8991

🕐 Closed Sun.–Mon. in winter & holidays

💲 $

www.museums.state.ak.us

permanent residents, including bald and golden eagles, a peregrine falcon, and a snowy owl.

Just west of the park, the airy confines of the **Sheldon Jackson Museum** house one of the finest native art collections in southeastern Alaska. During the late 1800s teacher and missionary Rev. Sheldon Jackson accumulated a vast collection of native artifacts from all over Alaska—ranging from scary shaman masks and food dishes carved to look like bears to armor made from walrus ivory and mukluks (boots) fashioned from fish skins. Informational panels make the native way of life emerge from these objects. The Eskimo whaling

The architectural setting of the Sheldon Jackson Museum complements the collections.

outfit, for example, a bearded-sealskin creation that looks like a space suit, is waterproof and airtight. It was worn while butchering whales, which required wading in icy water because the dead whales were floated to the shallows. The dozens of drawers to rummage through inside this building are a

treasure trove of smaller bits and pieces of bygone days.

Starrigavan Recreation Area

The Tongass National Forest embraces Sitka. Starrigavan Recreation Area, 7 miles (11 km) north of town on Halibut Point Road, offers an excellent and easily accessible introduction to the land. The area's three trails provide a glimpse of most of the region's main ecosystems; to learn about them, take one of the guided hikes offered by Sitka tour operators and by the nonprofit Sitka Trail Works *(801 Halibut Point Rd., tel 907/747-7244, www.sitkatrailworks.org)*, which established much of the trail network around Sitka. To hike Starrigavan or other trails with Trail Works guides, it is best to contact them at least a week ahead. Participants must pay $20 and join the organization.

The **Forest and Muskeg Trail,** an easy, 0.75-mile (1.2 km) jaunt, winds through spruce-hemlock forest and along a boardwalk through muskeg (peat bog) populated by a diverse array of tiny mosses and tiny but voracious sundews—carnivorous plants smaller than a dime. At the east end of the trail you can cross the bridge over Starrigavan Creek and start right into the **Estuary Life Trail,** a 0.25-mile (0.4 km) boardwalk through the marshes of the creek's estuary. If you visit the estuary in the early morning, you'll likely spot a variety of birds and maybe a brown bear or a Sitka black-tailed deer.

Walk about 200 yards (183 m) north from the bird-viewing shelter at the end of the estuary trail and you come to the recreation area's campground. Continue a little farther north to the far end and you'll come to the finest of the three hikes: the **Mosquito Cove Trail.** This 1.25-mile (2 km) loop hugs the beautiful shores of Starrigavan Bay and Mosquito Cove for about 0.75 mile (1.2 km) and then circles back through the coastal rain forest.

INSIDER TIP:

Sitka organizes a fantastic WhaleFest each November, providing guided boat excursions, natural history talks, and an opportunity to experience the community in the off-season.

—VOLKER DEECKE
National Geographic field researcher

Sitka Sound

The sound nurtures a rich marine ecosystem. In addition to the charismatic megafauna—whales, seals, sea otters—vast numbers of other creatures favor Alaska's chilly waters, which are among the most productive in the world. A few hardy souls go scuba diving to check out this small-scale realm of sea cucumbers, pipefish, abalones, wolf eels, and rock crabs, but most visitors prefer to glimpse this watery world on terra firma by touring the **Sitka**

Sound Science Center. Tours include the salmon hatchery and touch tanks.

Hundreds of boats ply Sitka Sound and more distant coastal waters. A large majority of them cater to anglers, but tour operators flourish as well. Offerings vary greatly—from small boats to large cruisers, from one-hour tours to all-day excursions—with something for everyone *(for information contact the Sitka visitors bureau; see p. 58).*

Whichever you choose, no doubt you'll see sea otters floating on their backs, munching shellfish or cuddling their pups. Maybe you'll cruise through the immense shadow of **Mount Edgecumbe,** the 3,201-foot (975.7 m) volcano that looms 10 miles (16 km) west of Sitka on Kruzof Island. (Hardy trekkers can hike and scramble the 7 miles/11.2 km to its summit; the trail starts at Fred Creek's Cabin.) You'll typically see at least one humpback whale; the boat captain may cut the engines so you can hear the humpback's blow.

If the seas aren't rough, the boat may head to **St. Lazaria Island** *(landing not allowed),* which forms part of the immense **Alaska Maritime National Wildlife Refuge** (see pp. 162–163), a conglomerate of 2,500 coastal islands, spires, rocks, and headlands stretching all along Alaska's outskirts. The island's 65 acres (26 ha) teem with hundreds of thousands of nesting seabirds in summer. You'll see kittiwakes wheeling boisterously around the steep cliffs, cormorants spreading their wings to dry, and the lovable puffins diving for food. ∎

Starrigavan Recreation Area

- 🗺 Map p. 47
- ✉ Tongass National Forest, Sitka Ranger District, 204 Siginaka Way, Suite 109, Sitka, AK 99835
- ☎ 907-747-6671

www.fs.usda.gov/tongass

Sitka Sound Science Center

- ✉ 834 Lincoln St.
- ☎ 907/747-8878
- 🕐 Closed Sun. mid-May–mid-Sept., Sun.–Mon. rest of year
- 💲 $

www.sitkasoundsciencecenter.org

WhaleFest

www.sitkasoundsciencecenter.org

Traveling the Inside Passage

Southeast Alaska is a water world. To experience it fully, one must meet it on its own terms, and that means traveling by ship on the Inside Passage. This virtual marine highway stretches some 900 nautical miles (1,667 km) from Vancouver, British Columbia, to Skagway, Alaska, connecting villages, towns, and cities. (See map inside back cover.)

The spectacular snowcapped mountains of the Inside Passage tower over the biggest cruise ships.

The Inside Passage snakes through hundreds of islands, squeezing into straits, narrows, and sounds. The islands buffer these inside waters from the fierce winds and storms of the Pacific Ocean, but navigational challenges abound: summer fog, swift currents, tidal rips, whirlpools, icebergs, sandbars, and suckholes, to name but a few. Despite these hazards, traveling the Inside Passage is one of the great scenic adventures of a lifetime. Travelers instinctively realize this. A mere 20,000 visitors fly into a typical mainline Southeast Alaska port in a year, while hundreds of thousands arrive by cruise ship.

Some people navigate through the Inside Passage on their own vessels. Others charter a yacht or a cabin cruiser. But those are the notable exceptions. Nearly everyone else travels either by large or small cruise ship or aboard the ferries of the Alaska Marine Highway System.

Big Cruise Ships

More than 95 percent of travelers choose to travel the passage aboard large cruisers—some carry more than 2,500 passengers plus crew. Now a premier destination, the Southeast attracts ships that are not only large but elaborate. They feature health spas, towering atriums, Vegas-style musical shows, pools, cabarets, casinos, and those legendary buffets of finely prepared food in quantities that would sink smaller ships.

In addition to all the shipboard activities, most cruise ships offer a smorgasbord of shore excursions, from shopping and bus tours to kayaking and helicopter landings on glaciers. These trips range from a few hours to most of the day, depending on port time, but passengers almost always return to the ship for the night.

Small Cruise Ships

Small cruise ships get passengers closer to land—literally and figuratively. Depending on the operator, these ships hold anywhere from 10 to 250 people, their smaller size and shallower draft allow them to slip into little spaces closer to shore, making wildlife and glacier viewing better.

More important, the focus on these ships is on Southeast Alaska, not shipboard entertainment. The smaller ships frequently offer talks by expert naturalists or Alaska natives, and they'll stop overnight in ports inaccessible to the big ships. The shore excursions tend to visit less traveled places, too. The drawbacks? These boats don't have as many amenities as the big ships, and they're often more expensive.

Alaska Marine Highway

Designated an "All-American Road" by the U.S. Department of Transportation, the Alaska Marine Highway System (AMHS) is the state ferry service. The AMHS takes vehicles and passengers on its 11 vessels. Visiting dozens of towns (ten along the Inside Passage), the marine highway is how the locals travel; when a high school basketball team plays an away game, it takes the ferry.

The mainline ships hold nearly 500 people, while those that serve smaller towns hold 150 to 250. Enough ferries ply these waters that people get off in one of the major ports and catch another ferry in a day or two—or a month. Many people set up lodging in several port towns and spend a few days in each, tying this sampler itinerary together with the ferries.

The marine highway is inexpensive compared to the cruise ships, well run, and generally reliable. The ferries even offer a few amenities, such as staterooms, restaurants, movies, and showers. At night some of the passengers who don't have staterooms pitch tents on covered decks. In summer, reservations are required for travelers with vehicles, and are advised for people on foot. Book early for vehicles and cabins.

See Travelwise (p. 235) for more information on the AMHS.

EXPERIENCE: Choosing Your Cruise

Dozens of companies make voyages through the Inside Passage every year. Here is a variety pack that ranges from intimate yachts to town-size ships.

Holland America Line (tel 877/932-4259, www.hollandamerica.com) This venerable line provides dozens of cruises aboard ships of up to 2,000 passengers. Entertainment abounds and the enrichment lectures are considered first-rate. The traditional flavor extends to occasional formal "tuxedo" nights.

Pacific Catalyst II, Inc. (tel 800/378-1708 or 360/378-7123, www.pacificcatalyst.com) The 75-foot wooden Catalyst was built in 1932 as an oceanographic research ship for the University of Washington. Now it takes up to 12 passengers on voyages up and down the Inside Passage. It moves slowly through backwaters and pokes into remote coves; the pace and route are designed to provide an intimate and leisurely communion with Alaska's natural wonders.

Un-Cruise Adventures (tel 888/862-8881, www.un-cruise.com) This line offers a combination of R&R and adventure on its seven motor yachts, whose capacities range from 22 to 88 passengers. The options range from vigorous itineraries packed with hiking, kayaking, and glacier trekking to trips that balance close encounters with Alaska scenery and wildlife with gourmet meals, yoga, and massage.

Juneau

Juneau is not your ordinary state capital: No roads connect it to the outside world, bears sometimes wander through town, and its setting is drop-dead gorgeous. Built along the shore of Gastineau Channel, the city backs up against heavily forested mountains that elevate abruptly to heights of several thousand feet—more like the backdrop for a Swiss resort than a state capital.

Settled during the gold-rush era, Juneau's downtown is a cornucopia of historic buildings.

Juneau

 Map p. 47

Visitor Information

✉ Centennial Hall Visitor Center, 101 Egan Dr.

☎ 907/586-2201 or 888/581-2201

www.travel juneau.com

The third largest city in Alaska, Juneau (population 32,000), offers good lodgings, fine restaurants and lively cafés, plenty of cultural activities, and access to a wealth of scenery.

Historic Downtown

History surrounds visitors as they stroll Juneau's downtown. Thanks to good luck and the heroic work of the Volunteer Fire Department, this city never suffered a major fire, as many Alaska towns have. In the

seven-block radius of the original downtown, 143 buildings dating from before 1914 still stand—60 of them go back earlier than 1904. As you wander around, note the more than 20 totem poles and other public art in the form of sculptures and murals. And take the time to walk through the adjacent old residential areas up the steep hills, some half dozen blocks above the shore.

Given the importance of government here in Alaska's

capital—nearly half of the locals work for the public—it would be appropriate to begin a tour of Juneau at the **Alaska State Capitol.** Completed in 1931, this unassuming brick-faced building originally housed the territorial legislature, governor, the post office, courts, and numerous other federal and territorial agencies. The second floor displays historical photos.

Delve deeper into Juneau's past at the **Juneau-Douglas City Museum** across Main Street from the capitol. Learn how two prospectors and a Tlingit chief together in 1880 touched off one of the quickest gold rushes ever, with the first boatloads of would-be millionaires arriving about a

INSIDER TIP:

Use the trails around Juneau, or around the Mendenhall Glacier Visitor Center to take in a view of the glacier, the lake at its base, and a nearby waterfall.

—ROWLAND SHELLEY
National Geographic field researcher

month after Chief Kowee directed Joe Juneau and Richard Harris to the mother lode above Gold Creek (now Silver Bow Basin). Millions of ounces of gold came out of the ground, but it had to be painstakingly extracted from low-grade ore, which required the efforts of big mining companies rather than independent miners. The mining heritage carries over into exhibits and activities in the

Rainproof Gear

Alaska can be cold and wet any time of the year, especially along the southern and southwestern coasts, where in many places annual rainfall averages more than 150 inches (4 m). Most travelers know this and bring a rain jacket, a rain hat, and perhaps even rain pants. So far, so good. But are they really waterproof? Before you go to Alaska make sure that your gear will truly repel rain and not just slow it down. (A hose can provide a robust test.) Too often the clothing you thought was waterproof is actually just water resistant, which could lead to discomfort or even danger if you get wet in the wilds.

children's area. Displays cover many other aspects of Juneau's history, too, from shipwrecks to 19th-century domestic life. And don't overlook the 45-foot (13.7 m) Haida-style totem pole in front of the museum.

Another key element of Juneau's history is evoked a couple of blocks up the hill, on Seventh Street, at the **House of Wickersham,** a state and national historic site. Built in 1898 for a mine superintendent, this handsome house was bought in 1928 by Judge James Wickersham, a prominent Alaska lawyer, politician, judge, author, and historian. Wickersham was instrumental in the effort to make Alaska a

Alaska State Capitol

- ✉ 4th & Main Sts.
- ☎ 907/465-3853
- 🕐 Tours daily early May–late Sept.

Juneau-Douglas City Museum

- ✉ 155 S. Seward St.
- ☎ 907/586-3572
- 🕐 Closed Sun.–Mon. late Sept.–May
- 💲 $
- www.juneau.org/parksrec/museum

Wickersham State Historic Site

- ✉ 213 7th St.
- ☎ 907/586-9001
- 🕐 Call for hours
- 💲 $
- www.dnr.alaska.gov/parks/units/wickrshm.htm

Alaska State Museum

✉ 395 Whittier St.
☎ 907/465-2901
🕐 Closed Sun.–Mon. late Sept.–mid-May & holidays
💲 $

www.museums.state.ak.us

territory, which finally succeeded in 1912. Soon after that victory, Wickersham began the drive to make Alaska a state, though he died 20 years before that happened in 1959. The tour of his house details the judge's illustrious past and displays some of his vast collection of Alaska artifacts plus his personal mementos.

Alaska State Museum

The Alaska State Museum is a 32,000-object-strong treasure trove of interesting native artifacts, fine art, and natural history specimens.

Capital Contest

Sitka was the capital of Russian Alaska, but by 1900 much of the region's commerce had shifted to the area around Joe Juneau's former mining camp. Officials established Juneau as the capital; it remained so when Alaska became a territory in 1912 and a state in 1959. After World War II, the population and much commerce of Alaska shifted northwest, in part because of government work. There arose an effort to move the state capital from Juneau to Anchorage, and the debate reached a peak in the 1970s when a commission earmarked unused land at Willow north of Anchorage for the new city. But voters were repelled by the price tag of building a new capital and the movement collapsed.

The ground floor explores the rich past and present of Alaska's diverse native peoples. The galleries exhibit rarities such as a belt fashioned from some 200 caribou mandibles and baskets thousands of years old, as well as artifacts of exceptional quality. Consider a contemporary artist's rendition of an Aleut hunting hat, its thin, steam-bent wood tapered like an Olympic cyclist's helmet, the outer surface replete with intricate designs, colorful beads, ivory carvings, and a fringe of sea lion whiskers. Look at the exquisitely fine weaving and elaborate painting on the historical hat on the Kaagwaantaan dancer; experts proclaim it one of the finest spruce-root hats in existence.

The ramp to the second floor circles around a two-story model of a tree topped by an immense bald eagle nest, complete with piped-in eagle calls. Added to over the reproductive lifetime of a pair of eagles, baldies' nests can end up the size of a pickup truck.

The second floor houses some natural history exhibits, but mostly it is devoted to the state's post-European-contact human history, particularly the Russian era. Look for the samovar the size of a potbellied stove and the imperial crest of a double-headed eagle— the symbol of Russian Alaska. The American period galleries examine in great detail the development of the state's natural resources through exhibits on mining, logging, fishing, and oil exploration.

South Franklin & Around

Near the waterfront, numerous shops, restaurants, galleries, bars,

EXPERIENCE: Watching the Whales

Even if you're not the type to get carried away and holler "Thar she blows," you would be a rare person indeed if the sight of a whale didn't quicken your pulse. Alaska offers many opportunities to get your heart rate up by watching these leviathans, some of which inhabit Alaska coastal waters year-round and some of which migrate north to summer feeding grounds in the Gulf of Alaska, the Bering Sea, and the Arctic Ocean.

Whales—notably large numbers of humpbacks—frequent the waters of Frederick Sound, near Petersburg, in summer.

also make appearances, but less often. The belugas in Cook Inlet, near Anchorage, used to be easily seen, but in recent years the population of these small whales has crashed due to human development.

Consider one of the following whale-watching outfits:

Kenai Fjords Tours *(Small Boat Harbor, Seward, AK, tel 877/777-4051, www.kenaifjords .com)* See gray, humpback, and killer whales in Resurrection Bay and Kenai Fjords from large tour vessels.

Rainbow Tours *(P.O. Box 1526, Homer, AK 99603, tel 907/235-7272, www.rainbowtours.net)* Watch humpbacks spouting and breaching in scenic Kachemak Bay and in the mouth of Cook Inlet.

TAZ Whale Watching Tours *(Gustavus, AK, tel 888/698-2726, www.taz.gustavus.com)* This 45-foot (13.5 m) observation boat not only lets people watch humpbacks, but uses hydrophones so you can hear their haunting songs.

Whale Song Cruises *(P.O. Box 930, Petersburg, AK 99833, tel 907/772-9393, www.whalesong cruises.com)* Visit humpback summer feeding grounds in Frederick Sound. Look for orcas, porpoises, and sea lions, too.

Occasionally you'll spot whales from land, but most whale-watching takes place from the water. Alert passengers on cruise ships and ferries often glimpse whales; sometimes ship's officers will announce sightings. (Yes, they have been known to shout "Thar she blows.") But serious cetacean fans will want to go out on smaller boats dedicated to finding whales and other marine wildlife.

Dozens of Alaska ports offer whale-watching/ natural history boat trips. Hot spots include Icy Strait, Frederick Sound, and Sitka Sound in Southeast Alaska; Prince William Sound; and Resurrection Bay out of Seward on the Kenai Peninsula. Depending on when and where you go, you're likely to see humpbacks, orcas, and gray whales. Other species, such as blue and sperm whales,

Mount Roberts Tramway

- 490 S. Franklin St.
- ☎ 907/463-3412 or 888/461-8726
- 🕐 Closed late Sept.–early May
- 💲 $$$$

www.mountroberts
tramway.com

and theaters compete for the patronage of visitors. The closer you get to the busy docks along South Franklin Street, the more you'll see the influence of the many cruise ships that stop here. On any given summer day three to five ships moor dockside to unload their thousands of

Exhibits at the Alaska State Museum tell the story of the Great Land.

passengers. Tourist dollars are encouraging the growth of new shops and luxury stores; still, many local, distinctly Alaska businesses remain, some even on South Franklin.

Stop in the old **Senate Building** and view the art and crafts in the **Juneau Artists Gallery** (*175 S. Franklin St., tel 907/586-9891, www.juneauartistsgallery.com*). A block down try the **Decker Gallery** (*233 S. Franklin St., tel 907/463-5536, www.riemunoz.com*), which carries work by one of the state's most renowned artists, Rie Muñoz. Fine arts and crafts by Alaska artists can be found just off South Franklin Street at **Annie Kaill's** (*244 Front St., tel 907/586-2880, www.annie kaills.com*).

Mount Roberts

Just down the street from Raven's Journey is the **Mount Roberts Tramway,** which hauls passengers up one of Juneau's finest attractions. The tram climbs steeply to the 1,800-foot (548 m) level of the 3,819-foot-high (1,164 m) eponymous mountain that looms over South Franklin Street and Marine Way.

As the tram rises, the views grow from fine to fantastic. The urban Alaska Native Corporation owns the tram, so many employees are Alaska natives. The tram operator will talk about the area's history and culture as he takes visitors up or down the mountain. The native influence continues up top at the tram's terminus: A theater shows a film about Tlingit culture and a gift shop serves somewhat as a museum, where artisans at work are frequently on view. There's also a restaurant with an amazing view and a nature center. But this complex isn't the best thing about the Mount Roberts Tram. The best thing is Mount Roberts itself.

When your cruise ship docks, get out of town. Many towns offer bike excursions, and within five minutes, you can find yourself in untamed countryside on a multihour adventure.

—EVERETT POTTER
Writer, National Geographic Traveler *magazine*

Beyond the nature center sprawls a network of easy, well-marked trails that lead up the mountain through increasingly sparse forest to a stunning expanse of subalpine and alpine habitat. It only takes 10 to 15 minutes to hike above tree line, where marvelous vistas open up: mountains, waterfalls, and the bodies of water far to the west and south of Juneau. During summer wildflowers blaze from the meadows, where hoary marmots graze. Porcupines lumber through the undergrowth, bears occasionally pass through, and mountain goats occupy the highest slopes. If you feel energetic and have proper gear, you can roam for miles—even choosing to return to the city via the 4.5-mile (7.2 km) **Mount Roberts Trail,** which has its trailhead at the end of Sixth Street.

Glacier/Juneau Veterans' Memorial Highway

Juneau's one highway, the Glacier/Juneau Veterans' Memorial Highway, may be a dead end, but there are so many worthy sites along the road that motorists won't mind driving up and back. The road starts in downtown as Egan Drive and goes north along Gastineau and Favorite Channels. At Mile 9.3

EXPERIENCE: Flying High on Zip Lines

When it comes to zip lines in Alaska, there are two distinct flavors. One is a brief, intense, pulse-pounding ride that emphasizes the "zip" in zip line. The operator takes you and other thrill seekers up to a cliff about 1,300 feet (400 m) above sea level, straps you into a chairlift-like seat, and sends you screaming (literally) down a heavy cable toward the shore more than a mile (1.6 km) away. At times you are 300 feet (91 m) above the forest floor and hurtling along at speeds of 60 mph (97 kph). Ninety seconds after launch you'll come to a stop at the beach and wobble away on shaky legs to boast of your adventure. As of this writing, the only place in Alaska offering such rides is **Icy Strait Point** (tel 907/945-3141, *www .icystraitpoint.com*), a remote attraction near the Tlingit village of Hoonah, about 30 miles (48 km) west of Juneau.

While hardly sedate, the other style of zip lines emphasizes an exploration of the canopy of the rain forest. Strung platform to platform, the cables enable you to don a harness and glide through the treetops, observing wildlife and seeing the forest from the perspective of a bird flying 100 feet (30 m) above the ground. One company, with courses in Juneau and Ketchikan, is **Alaska Canopy Adventures** (*www.alaskacanopy.com*).

Glacier Gardens Rainforest Adventure

- 7600 Glacier Hwy.
- ☎ 907/790-3377
- ⊕ Closed Oct.–April
- 💲 $$$

www.glacier
gardens.com

Mendenhall Glacier

- ⧄ Map p. 47
- ✉ Mendenhall Loop Rd.
- ☎ 907/789-0097
- ⊕ Visitor center closed Mon.–Thurs. Oct.–April
- 💲 $ in summer, free in winter

www.fs.usda.gov/
tongass

(as measured from the cruise-ship terminal on South Franklin Street) it officially becomes the Glacier Highway. At Mile 12.1 it technically becomes the Juneau Veterans' Memorial Highway, but most locals still call it the Glacier Highway. By whatever name, the road continues on or near the shore of Favorite Channel and Lynn Canal until it ends 40 miles (64 km) from town at Echo Cove.

The first quarter of this route passes through the Mendenhall Valley, home to Juneau's version of

---

Glacier Adventures

A good way to see the Mendenhall Glacier and the icefield that feeds it is by plane or helicopter, which can whisk you the dozen miles (19 km) from Juneau. Helicopters can set you down for a walk on the glacier with a guide. For the more hardy, there are treks and ice-climbing packages, for which you will be fitted with an ice ax and crampons. Or you can merely view the glacier from nearby trails of from 0.5 to 3 miles (0.8 to 4.8 km) long.

---

suburbia. At Mile 8, near the Fred Meyer store, there is the **Glacier Gardens Rainforest Adventure.** You can explore 51.5 acres (21 ha) of rain forest with a guide along a 2-mile (3.2 km) loop, but among the big draws here are the acres of flower-intensive gardens. Big

conifer trees cut down to maybe 20 feet (6 m) and then rammed upside down into the ground so the root masses stick up, forming

INSIDER TIP:

The Mendenhall trail on the west side of Mendenhall Glacier gives relatively easy access to the ice caves and terrain in front of the glacier. Touch the glacier and examine the sole of the ice where it interacts with surface rock and sediments.

—GREGORY WILES
National Geographic field researcher

a platform for scads of colorful hanging plants, are the most eye-catching displays.

Mendenhall Glacier: At Mile 9.3 the south junction of the Mendenhall Loop Road intersects the highway. This road leads 3.4 miles (5.5 km) inland to dead-end at the visitor center at Mendenhall Glacier, one of the most popular attractions in all of Alaska. *(To avoid crowds, go before late morning, when tour buses start arriving.)* Spawned high in the mountains by the vast Juneau Icefield, this 12-mile-long (19.3 km), mile-wide (1.6 km) ribbon of blue-and-white ice rumbles to its present terminus—a mile or more across Mendenhall Lake from the visitor center. The glacier has been melting

Nugget Falls gushes down rocky slopes into the lake that has formed below Mendenhall Glacier.

rapidly in recent years. In a typical year in the 1940s it might have retreated 10 feet (3 m). Now the glacier shrinks back about 500 feet (152 m) a year.

At the **visitor center,** exhibits and a film educate visitors on the mechanics of glaciers, discussing in depth the Juneau Icefield and Mendenhall Glacier. Large panoramic windows allow warm viewing of the glacier. For a closer look, stroll along the easy 0.3-mile-long (0.5 km) **Photo Point Trail** that winds out to the edge of the lake. To get closer still, take a kayak tour on the lake; there's even an outfit that takes people around the lake in a traditional Tlingit canoe. For the closest look of all, take a helicopter tour and land on the glacier for a guided walk. The copters land well back from the terminus, but the buzz of so many helicopters still annoys many Juneau residents and nature lovers, fueling an ongoing debate

about imposing limitations on the ever present whirlybirds.

The area around the glacier is well worth exploring. Right at the end of the parking lot farthest from the visitor center is a platform for watching the sockeye and coho salmon that spawn in Steep Creek in the summer. But be alert, because black bears also are drawn by the fish. Beavers favor the creek as well; look for their dams and lodges.

Along with the path from the visitor center to the lake, several trails provide access to the surrounding landscape. The easy half-mile (0.8 km) **Trail of Time,** a self-guided nature trail, leaves from the center and provides a glimpse of the rain forest. One of the prettiest routes is the 3.5-mile (5.6 km), moderately difficult **East Glacier Loop,** which branches off from the Trail of Time. The loop passes through rain forest and at various points offers views of the glacier,

Nugget Falls, and alpine slopes frequented by mountain goats.

Beyond the Mendenhall Glacier: Back on the Glacier Highway, at Mile 12.4 you will encounter **Auke Bay,** a harbor that has kayak tours, whale-watching trips, and sportfishing charters. Nearby are the University of Alaska Southeast

---

Glacier Bear

Look closely at every bear you see in the rain forests of Southeast Alaska, because one of them might just be the state's rarest: the glacier (or blue) bear. Both names are, in fact, misnomers. The glacier bear does not live on glaciers or ice fields, for it could not find anything to eat there. This seldom seen creature does live near glaciers, however; it is most often spotted wandering forest trails, ambling along beaches, or grazing in flower-filled meadows. Finally, the blue bear is anything but blue. Its fur is black at the roots but silver at the tips, lending it an overall bluish appearance.

Campus and the terminal for the state ferry. After skirting the bay, the highway turns north and curves along Favorite Channel. At times the lofty peaks of the Chilkat Range stab the horizon, 25 to 30 miles (40 to 48 km) to the west. **Inspiration Point** at Mile 18.8 features a great view of these peaks.

A sanctuary of peace and quiet awaits at Mile 22.5: the **Shrine of St. Therese** (tel 907/780-6112, www.shrineofsainttherese.org). A retreat for the Diocese of Juneau, the complex of cabins, gardens, walking paths, lodge, and a shrine is open to day-trippers and any "who respect the spirit of the shrine." Walk across the 400-foot (122 m) causeway to tiny Shrine Island for a view of the beautiful stone chapel.

At Mile 29 pull into the main parking lot of the **Eagle Beach State Recreation Area** (tel 907/465-2482, $), which includes a ranger station, several trails, some cabins, wetlands, a sizable chunk of old-growth forest, and a campground. This area lay beneath thousands of feet of glacial ice until just 250 years ago, so this landscape is quite young. Use the spotting scopes by the interpretive signs to pull in the Chilkats from far across the waters of Lynn Canal or the bald eagles swooping above the estuary fed by Eagle River.

A quarter mile (0.4 km) farther on the highway, look for the dirt road to the **Eagle Beach picnic area.** This less developed area offers great views across Lynn Canal, and many bird species favor the nearby tidal flats, including great blue herons, bald eagles, and squawking flocks of gulls.

At Mile 34 a sign warns "Travel Beyond This Point Not Recommended. If You Must Use This Road, Carry Cold Weather Survival Gear." If it's summer and you've got some cool-weather clothing with you, proceed to the end of the highway in Echo Cove, a lovely picnicking spot. ∎

Glacier Bay National Park & Preserve

The heart of Glacier Bay National Park and Preserve is a new land. When Capt. James Cook, the famed British explorer, sailed down this stretch of coastline, in 1778, he encountered a sheet of glacial ice thousands of feet thick and several miles wide. But the little ice age was fading fast, and by 1794, when Capt. George Vancouver passed this way, a 5-mile-long (8 km) bay had appeared—Glacier Bay. The ice continues to melt away: Today the deep, double-armed bay cuts 65 miles (105 km) back into the Alaska mainland.

Calving ice from the Johns Hopkins Glacier belly flops into the waters of a remote inlet of Glacier Bay.

Near the mouth of Glacier Bay, where the ice melted some 250 years ago, mature forest has grown up. At the far end of the bay, where the ice did not recede until much more recently, the early stages of recovery are evident, with colonizing plants like alder and the brilliantly colored fire-weed predominating the area. Scientists and visitors alike are able to witness the rebirth of a landscape.

The glaciers may have receded, but they hardly have gone away. With about a dozen tidewater glaciers (glaciers that reach the ocean), most of them actively calving slabs of ice into the water, the park has one of the highest concentrations of such glaciers in the world. These glaciers are the park's biggest draw. Numerous

Glacier Bay National Park & Preserve

Maps pp. 47 & 79

✉ P.O. Box 140, Gustavus, AK 99826; visitor center at Bartlett Cove

☎ 907/697-2230

🕓 Closed early Sept.–late May

www.nps.gov/glba

Gustavus

Maps pp. 47 & 79

Visitor Information

Gustavus Visitors Assoc., P.O. Box 167, Gustavus, AK 99826

907/697-2454

www.gustavus ak.com

cruise ships make this bay part of their Inside Passage itineraries. Of course, the overall scenery and the abundance of wildlife certainly share in the spotlight.

Visitors who want to give this 3.3-million-acre (1.3 million ha) park its due should spend a few days here. **Gustavus,** a small settlement, serves as gateway to the park. Oddly, Gustavus has one of the best airstrips in the Southeast; it was built as a refueling site during World War II. The airstrip allows Alaska Airlines to make daily summer flights from Juneau. Visitors who prefer a more leisurely approach can reach Gustavus via the Alaska Marine Highway; a ferry arrives

golf course. However, this charming town does not have a main street or a city center. Instead, it lies scattered about the landscape, so visitors need to walk, rent a bike, take a taxi, catch the bus, or rent a car. The town's one paved (mostly) road runs from Gustavus into the park, dead-ending in Bartlett Cove, the national park's main point of entry.

Bartlett Cove

Wedged into the rain forest on the eastern shore of Glacier Bay, Bartlett Cove is home to **Glacier Bay Lodge,** the only lodging inside the park. The 56-room timber lodge provides kayak and fishing-pole rentals and includes

A boardwalk takes hikers above the rain forest floor of Bartlett Cove.

at the town's new dock twice a week in summer.

Gustavus provides about 15 choices of lodging, ranging from nice but simple cabins to pleasant bed-and-breakfasts to one of the finest country inns in Alaska. Amenities include galleries, restaurants, tour operators, and a nine-hole

a small natural history museum. Most important, it's the headquarters and visitor center of the Glacier Bay National Park and Preserve. This is the place to find out about taking ranger-led hikes and boat tours, finding a campsite, or noting the schedule of evening talks in the auditorium. Near the lodge, the backcountry office dispenses invaluable information for backpackers, kayakers, glacier trekkers, and mountaineers.

There are only three maintained trails in the park. The 1-mile (1.6 km) **Forest Loop Trail** begins at the lodge, swings through a young spruce-hemlock forest dotted with ponds, and then circles back to parallel the beach. Wildflowers bloom in profusion in June and July. Bears and coyotes sometimes wander the beach; red squirrels and porcupines comb the forest. The same animals may cross your path on the more challenging **Bartlett River Trail,** which starts a little ways up the road from the lodge. This 5-mile-out-and-back (8 km) path passes an intertidal lagoon, forest, and river estuary habitats; it has some muddy spots if rain has fallen, so allow half a day for tromping and savoring. Look for salmon running the river in the late summer, and ducks, geese, and waterbirds bobbing their heads in the estuary. Fewer people use the **Bartlett Lake Trail,** whose 6 miles (9.6 km) round-trip are more primitive and demanding, but it's a beautiful and tranquil hike to the lake. The trail branches off the Bartlett River Trail.

Hikers can always strike out cross-country, but that requires route-finding skills and a lot more effort. The forest undergrowth and the dreaded alder thickets that clog many unforested areas can turn a cheerful outing into an accursed slog. By far the best off-trail opportunity is to go down to the Bartlett Cove dock and walk south along the beach for 6 miles (9.6 km) to lovely **Point Gustavus.** The scenery is delightful and you may spot both marine and terrestrial wildlife.

Identifying Icebergs

Icebergs are massive floating chunks of ice that have broken off glaciers. In olden days, sailors had names that conveyed their size. For example, if the berg showed about 3 feet (1 m) of ice above water, it was "growler ice," and if it showed 3 to 15 feet (1 to 5 m), it was a "bergy bit." The nature of an iceberg can be discerned by its color. The bluer a berg is, the denser and more compressed the ice; a white berg has large numbers of air bubbles trapped inside it; a greenish black berg is one that calved off the bottom of a glacier.

The Bay & Glaciers

Rewarding as the hikes and views around Bartlett Cove can be, venture farther afield to fully experience the park's grandeur and majesty: the glaciers and bay. **Flightseeing** opportunities are available out of Gustavus or from distant Southeast towns, and while thrilling, they do not provide as intimate viewing experience as boats.

Visitors who want to see Glacier Bay from the water have two main options: kayaks and boats. Kayak rentals are available from the park concessionaire Glacier Bay Sea Kayaks *(tel 907/697-2257, www.glacierbaysea kayaks.com)* for day or multiday trips. A limited number of companies are authorized to provide **guided kayak excursions** within the park. A popular six-hour trip includes instruction before setting off into Bartlett Cove and on to the nearby **Beardslee Entrance,** an enchanting maze of small islands and narrow channels with enticing names, such as Spider Island and Secret Bay.

The tour boat *(tel 888/229-8687, www.visitglacierbay.com, $$$$$, advance reservations recommended)* doesn't offer as close a commu-

nion as do kayaks, but it is much easier on your backside, it delves far deeper into the bay than a kayak day trip, and a naturalist provides a running commentary. By venturing into the backcountry of Glacier Bay, you enter a world of notable distinction. When the park's acres are combined with the undeveloped expanses of its neighbors, **Wrangell–St. Elias** (see pp. 178–181) and Canada's **Tatshenshini-Alsek Provincial Park** and **Kluane National Park,** they form the biggest parkland wilderness in the world.

The glories of that wilderness become apparent during the boat tour: Colonies of cormorants, murres, and puffins throng jagged islands; hulking brown bears fish for salmon at the mouth of creeks; humpback whales spout, slapping the surface with their 15-foot (4.5 m) flippers and leaping halfway out of the water. Looming to the northwest is the snowcapped Fairweather Range, crowned by 15,300-foot (4,663 m) Mount

EXPERIENCE:
Glacier Bay's Muir Inlet

The eastern arm of upper Glacier Bay is called Muir Inlet, a 25-mile (40 km) fjord into wild and glacier country. Kayakers love Muir Inlet because cruise ships, tour boats, and fishing boats generally avoid it. In one of Muir Inlet's branches called Adams Inlet motorboats are prohibited from May to mid-September, but you have to time your entry and exit with the strong tides that rush in and out. The hiking and camping along Muir Inlet is good also. Rewarding hikes are up White Thunder Ridge or McConnell Ridge. The views from the top are spectacular, but the rise is 1,500 feet (457 m) and passes through difficult alder thickets.

This is bear country, so if you are spending time ashore, be cautious. In addition, the mosquitoes are notorious, so bring lots of repellent. Ask for hiking and kayaking information at the park visitor center in Glacier Bay Lodge *(tel 888/229-8687, www.visitglacierbay.com).*

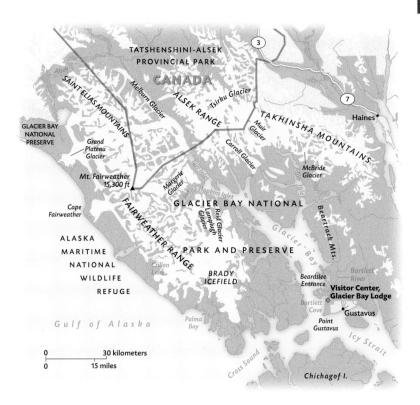

Fairweather. As the boat slaloms slowly among icebergs of infinite shapes and sizes, you can hear the bergs' air pockets pop and their melting surfaces drip.

West Arm: Sailing up the West Arm of the bay, you'll soon reach the **Reid Glacier.** It moves an average of 8 feet (2.4 m) a day, making it one of Glacier Bay's fastest-moving glaciers. Next comes **Lamplugh Glacier,** with its castle-like turrets and spires of blue ice. Scores of ice floes carrying seals litter **John Hopkins Inlet.** The boat will eventually head into **Tarr Inlet,** to the far reaches of the West Arm, and come to rest a quarter of a mile from the furrowed **Margerie Glacier.** This active

glacier, some 250 feet (76 m) tall above the surface of the water, commonly calves chunks of ice into the bay, often every few minutes.

Standing on the boat's deck, you'll occasionally hear what sounds like a loud rifle shot followed by the sight of a car-size hunk of ice splitting from the glacier face and splashing headlong into the water. This event might repeat numerous times, with the dimensions of the falling ice ranging from dishwasher size to as big as an RV. If you're lucky, an ice hunk more massive than a large house will slide into the sea, creating a gigantic splash and a thunderous echo that reverberates throughout the inlet. You'll long for more of this spectacle! ■

Haines

Haines is like a favorite flannel shirt: familiar, comfy, unassuming. Yet surrounding the town's cozy cafés and little harbor is a landscape of surpassing beauty: snowy mountains, waterfalls, forest, fjords, broad rivers, glaciers, lakes, and wildlife galore. And this landscape gets a mere 60 inches (406 cm) of precipitation a year on average, a relative desert in Southeast Alaska.

Under the right conditions, Lynn Canal assumes the look of a subtle landscape painting.

Haines
- Map p. 47

Visitor Information
- ✉ Haines Convention & Visitors Bureau, 122 2nd Ave.
- ☎ 970/766-2234 or 800/458-3579
- 🕐 Closed Sat.–Sun. in winter

www.haines.ak.us

The big cruise ships rarely stop here, and it's a long drive from Fairbanks (653 miles/1,051 km) and Anchorage (775 miles/ 1,247 km), so this friendly town of 2,200 people is a delight to explore. The town had its origins as a trading post for the Chilkat and Interior Indians; the first non-natives settled here in 1880. The town grew as it became a mining supply town, and later the only Alaska site of a U.S. Army post. **Lookout Park,** at the foot of Mission Street, overlooking the harbor and Chilkoot Inlet, makes a good starting point for a walk

through historic Haines. From the viewing platforms you can make a 360-degree scan of the area; use the topographic sign to identify the natural features encircling you.

Head north to Main Street and the **Sheldon Museum and Cultural Center.** The core of the 3,000-item collection comes from Steve Sheldon, who began acquiring things in the early 1900s at age eight. The array of native artifacts stands out, especially those from the local Tlingit, such as the carved ceremonial hat. But the collection ranges all over, from a lighthouse lens to Chinese camphorwood

INSIDER TIP:

Sea kayaking outfitters operate from every port community up and down Alaska's scenic Inside Passage. They offer the absolute best way to see the state from the water.

—EVERETT POTTER
Writer, National Geographic
Traveler *magazine*

trunks brought to Alaska by early traders to a whole corner devoted to Jack Dalton. Dalton was an early resident of Haines; he is most remembered for his unscrupulous dealings with travelers who needed to use the Dalton Trail—a toll road to the Interior. Later he built a hotel and saloon in town. The museum displays the sawed-off shotgun that he kept loaded with rock salt behind the bar in his saloon.

A very different sort of museum sits a block up Main Street from the Sheldon. The entertaining **Hammer Museum** contains 1,400 hammers and counting. You'll soon realize how much history can be discovered in a hammer. The Tlingit Warrior's Pick "Slave Killer," an 800-year-old hammer found in the ground right under the museum, was used to sacrifice slaves to bury under the corner posts of new longhouses. Patrons at Harlem's Cotton Club rapped "drink" hammers on the tables as a form of applause. And then there's the autopsy hammer, the Waterford crystal hammer,

the Chinese war and Roman battle hammers, and so on.

A few blocks from downtown, on the southwest side of Chilkoot Inlet, sprawls the gleaming white, well-kept frame buildings of **Fort William H. Seward National Historic Landmark.** Fort Seward was an active Army outpost from 1904 to 1947. After it was decommissioned, it was turned into the community of Port Chilkoot, which later merged with Haines. Many of the former officers' houses are private homes, but a variety of businesses occupy other buildings in the complex, including the Hotel Hälsingland; **Alaska Indian Arts,** where visitors can watch Tlingit artists at work; and the **Chilkat Center for the Arts.**

Thirty miles (48 km) north of Haines sprawl the naturalistic enclosures of the **Kroschel Wildlife Center.** Visitors get up close with wolves, grizzlies, lynx, and other native critters.

Alaska Bald Eagle Festival

Haines celebrates the return of eagles to the Chilkat Bald Eagle Preserve each year with the Alaska Bald Eagle Festival (www.baldeagles.org/ festival), usually held during the second weekend in November. Local artists and musicians abound. There may also be photography workshops and excursions to watch the bald eagles, which seem to occupy every treetop that time of year.

Sheldon Museum and Cultural Center

- ✉ 11 Main St.
- ☎ 907/766-2366
- 🕐 Closed Sun.
- 💲 $

www.sheldon
museum.org

Hammer Museum

- ✉ 108 Main St.
- ☎ 907/766-2374
- 🕐 Open Mon.–Fri. May–Sept.
- 💲 $

www.hammer
museum.org

Kroschel Wildlife Center

- ✉ Mile 1.8 Mosquito Lake Rd., off Haines Hwy. (about 30 miles/48 km N of Haines)
- ☎ 907/767-5464
- 🕐 Open May–Oct.; at other times of year, call to see if possible to visit
- 💲 $$$$

www.kroschel
films.com

Alaska Chilkat Bald Eagle Preserve

✉ Haines Ranger Station, Alaska State Parks, 259 Main St., Haines

☎ 907/766-2292

www.dnr.alaska .gov/parks/units/ eagleprv.htm

Alaska Chilkat Bald Eagle Preserve

Haines' biggest claim to fame lies northwest up the Haines Highway on the Chilkat River: the 48,000-acre (19,000 ha) Alaska Chilkat Bald Eagle Preserve. An upwelling of warm water and an exceptionally late salmon run entices more than 3,000 bald eagles to overwinter along the river, primarily between Miles 10 and 26, an area aptly known as the **Valley of the Eagles.** They begin gathering in early October and taper off by February; the best viewing is from October through December.

During the summer, you can take a boat trip and explore the endless maze of waterways that wind through the bottomlands. You likely will see countless moose, often the cows with their spindly-legged calves. You'll also glimpse trumpeter swans; and some of the nature preserve's resident 200 to 400 eagles.

Lutak Road

Nature lovers may wish to explore 11-mile (17.7 km) Lutak Road, which leads north out of Haines to **Chilkoot Lake State Recreation Site.** The first few miles on this shore road yield pretty views of Chilkoot

Chilkat State Park

Chilkat State Park outside Haines offers good hiking. One trail scales 1, 760-foot (536 m) Mount Riley, the highest on the Chilkat Peninsula; at the top you'll have fine views of the mountains, glaciers, and Lynn Canal. Even more strenuous is the climb up Mount Ripinski directly behind Haines. From the campground of the park begins the 6.8-mile (11 km) one-way Seduction Point Trail, skirting Seduction Point, which divides the Chilkat and Chilkoot Inlets. Allow about nine hours for this hike, along which you may see bears, moose, whales, seals, sea lions, and blue herons. Contact the park (*P. O. Box 430, Haines, AK 99827, tel 907/766-2292*).

The highest concentrations of bald eagles are found on the **Eagle Council Grounds,** a stretch of river flats that parallels the highway between Miles 18 and 24. Here, well-developed road turnouts with interpretive signs allow easy viewing of these iconic predators catching and eating the spawning chum salmon. The bountiful banquet also attracts bears, wolves, and other animals. Numerous operators offer tours *(contact visitors bureau; see p. 80)* to this natural phenomenon.

Inlet and rafts of sea ducks bobbing on the water, including handsome harlequin ducks and orange-billed surf scoters. The scenery and the wildlife sightings get even better after the route rounds **Tanani Point** and heads up narrow **Lutak Inlet,** which ends at the outlet stream from **Chilkoot Lake.** Bald eagles, harbor seals, bears feeding on salmon, mountain goats on the slopes—it's hard to know where to point your binoculars first. ∎

Skagway

Skagway is an unabashed tourist town—the daily summer flood of some 6,000 to 12,000 visitors, most of them from cruise ships, totally swamps the town's summer population of about 1,800—though with good reason: The town boasts an impressive array of buildings from the turn-of-the-20th-century Klondike gold-rush era. Much of downtown Skagway is preserved and maintained as part of the Klondike Gold Rush National Historical Park.

Historic downtown Skagway has become a shoppers' paradise and a magnet for cruise ships.

After word of the 1896 gold strike reached Seattle, in the summer of 1897, hordes of prospectors and adventurers looking for a gateway to the Yukon raced to Skagway, swelling its population from 1 in 1896 up to 10,000 by the end of 1897. In a few years the gold played out and Skagway's population plunged to about 500 by 1902, but many of the buildings survived. You can now shop and explore a flamboyant historical era at the same time.

As nearly every visitor to Skagway arrives via water—either from a cruise ship, the state ferry, or the fast ferry from Haines—it makes sense to start your wander near the docks. Walk up Congress Way to the corner of Second Avenue and Spring Street; the **White Pass & Yukon Route railroad depot** (see pp. 86–87) is here. Continue on Second Avenue to Broadway, Skagway's main street. At the corner is the railroad's old depot, which now houses the visitor center of the **Klondike Gold Rush National Historical Park.** The park service staff answers questions, shows a 30-minute film, and offers 45-minute interpretive tours. Note the reproduction of the *Seattle Post-Intelligencer* for July 19, 1897, that announces the discovery of that seductive yellow metal.

Skagway

🔺 Map p. 47

Visitor Information

✉ Skagway Convention & Visitors Bureau, 245 Broadway

☎ 907/983-2854 or 888/762-1898

www.skagway.com

Klondike Gold Rush National Historical Park

✉ 2nd Ave. & Broadway

☎ 907/983-9200

🕐 Open daily May–Sept., Mon.–Fri. rest of year (only museum and office open)

www.nps.gov/klgo

In huge bold letters the headline reads "Gold! Gold! Gold! Gold!"

An adjacent part of the visitor center showcases exhibits on the gold rush. Evocative photographs reveal the hardship of the gold rush. One shows dozens of gold seekers on the beach at nearby Dyea with their mountains of gear—gear that needed to be hauled up and over the daunting Chilkoot Trail. The center displays some of that gear, too, such as dog packs, snowshoes, and, of course, gold pans.

A few steps up Broadway stands the **Arctic Brotherhood Hall** (*245 Broadway*)—reputedly the most photographed building in Alaska. The Brotherhood, a fraternal organization of pioneers, fashioned the facade from thousands of pieces of driftwood. The hall now houses the Skagway

Convention and Visitors Bureau; the staff is friendly and you can pick up the excellent and detailed walking-tour map and brochure.

A stroll up Broadway reveals one restored historic edifice after another, including old wooden sidewalks, cabins, and renovated saloons. Many now contain the diamond stores, gift shops, and art galleries aimed at the cruise-ship passengers, but others have interiors that re-create the buildings' historic use. For instance, the **Mascot Saloon,** at the corner of Third Avenue and Broadway, looks much like it did in 1898, when hard-drinking men bellied up to the bar and downed whiskey—as one of the interpretive signs notes, whiskey was a drink, beer a mere chaser. The Mascot was one of some 70 or 80 saloons catering to the thousands of gold

Part of Klondike Gold Rush National Historical Park, the Red Onion Saloon—first opened in 1898—remains a popular watering hole in the 21st century.

INSIDER TIP:

If you cruise the Inside Passage in southeast Alaska, try to take a ship of less than 100 passengers; you'll have a more intimate experience.

—MICHAEL MELFORD
National Geographic photographer

seekers. Lawlessness was rampant; Skagway was reputed to be the roughest place around. "Skagway was little better than a hell on earth," recalled Samuel Steele, superintendent of the North West Mounted Police, after he visited the town in 1898.

After wandering up Broadway, turn right at Seventh Avenue and walk one block to the corner of Spring Street, site of the nicely restored 1899 granite-faced Mc-Cabe College building, which now houses city hall and the **Skagway Museum.** Check out the eclectic collection, ranging from a Tlingit canoe to a stuffed brown bear to the July 15, 1898, edition of the *Skagway News,* which reports the gunfight that resulted in the death of notorious Skagway crime boss Jefferson Randolph "Soapy" Smith. (A marker near the corner of First Avenue and State Street commemorates this pivotal event.)

Outside Skagway

Skagway is set against a backdrop of comely mountains, forest, and rivers. The easiest way to enjoy the scenery is to drive some or all of the **South**

Klondike Highway. It's 99 miles (159 km) to the junction with the Alaska Highway, in the Yukon, but within just a few miles the highway climbs into stirring alpine country blessed with waterfalls, lakes, and deep gorges. The British Columbia border and Canada customs await about 15 miles (24 km) from Skagway, just past the 3,292-foot (1,003 m) **White Pass Summit.**

If you'd like to experience what the gold seekers had to face to reach the goldfields, the historic 33-mile (53 km) **Chilkoot Trail** challenges trekkers with a lot of elevation gain. You can get a small taste of the trail by hiking just the first few miles, which are fairly flat and lead through a pretty rain forest along the **Taiya River.** The trailhead is by the bridge over the

Skagway Museum
- ✉ 700 Spring St.
- ☎ 907/983-2420
- 🕐 Open daily May–Sept.
- 💲 $

Skagway Excursions

Skagway offers numerous excursions, the Chilkoot Trail in Klondike Gold Rush National Historical Park being one and a stirring railroad trip being another. But note some other treks also. There's the Lower Dewey Lake Trail, which is only 0.7 mile (1 km) long, rising 600 feet (183 m) to its namesake; it begins on Spring Street between Third and Fourth Streets. Those wanting to stride farther can take the 7-mile (11 km) hike to Upper Dewey Lake, beyond the lower lake and skirting the border of Denver Glacier.

river, 9.5 miles (15.3 km) out the Dyea Road from Skagway. Also, local outfits guide hikers 2 miles (3.2 km) on the Chilkoot Trail and then take them back to the trailhead by rafting the gentle Taiya. ∎

White Pass & Yukon Route

During the Klondike gold rush, the narrow-gauge White Pass & Yukon Route was blasted and chiseled 110 miles (177 km) through the mountains to connect Skagway (which had access to the ocean) to Whitehorse, Yukon (which had access to rivers to the interior goldfields). Today passengers board vintage railcars and travel 20 miles (32 km) to White Pass Summit and back, a stunningly scenic three-hour journey.

The White Pass & Yukon Route runs through the high country above Skagway.

This trip is very popular, so book well in advance of your departure *(tel 800/343-7373, www.wpyr.com, 2–3 times daily May–Sept., $$$$$).* The journey starts at the **depot ❶** on the corner of Second Avenue and Spring Street. For the best views, sit on the left going up and the right coming back. You can also stand on the outside platforms at either end of the cars; they are great for taking photos and for feeling even closer to the landscape, but be careful—and bring a coat, it gets cold out there.

The train eases out along the east side of town, passing the **Gold Rush Cemetery ❷** at railroad Mile 2.5. Here rest the bones of gold-rush gangster Soapy Smith and Frank Reid, the man who shot him, as the interpreter will explain over the speakers. (There are also

NOT TO BE MISSED:

Rocky Point •Bridal Veil Falls • Inspiration Point

roving interpreters, who move through the cars answering questions.)

Continuing above the Skagway River, steadily gaining elevation, the train chugs up to **Denver ❸** at Mile 5.8. On morning runs hikers often get off here to head up the **Denver Glacier Trail.** Hikers and backpackers can flag down the train to get a ride back to town in the afternoon. At Denver you'll see an old red caboose that can be rented through the Forest Service for overnight stays. The train crosses the Skagway East Fork River and then about a mile later reaches **Rocky Point ④**, which yields tremendous views down the valley to Skagway, the harbor, and beyond.

The hardship of gouging this route out of these rugged mountains is grimly memorialized at Mile 10.4 at Black Cross Rock. A blasting accident buried two workers under the 100-ton (90.7 tonnes) hunk of black granite by the tracks; altogether 35 laborers died during the two years of construction. Hundreds of horses used to haul equipment also perished, earning one area along the route the nickname "Dead Horse Gulch." On the brighter side, a profusion of waterfalls decorates the route as it proceeds, topped at Mile 11.5 by the spectacular **Bridal Veil Falls ⑤**, fed by nearby glaciers.

At Mile 16, just before entering **Tunnel Mountain ⑥**, the train crawls across a bridge 1,000 feet (305 m) above Glacier Gorge; anyone afraid of heights should not look down. Shortly after the long tunnel, at Mile 17, arguably the finest vista of the route appears: **Inspiration Point ⑦**. The views down the valley stretch to Skagway, to the Lynn Canal, and to the Chilkat Range, some 20 miles (32 km) farther south. Finally, after much huffing and puffing, the engines pull the railcars up to their destination, **White Pass Summit ⑧**, 2,865 vertical feet (873.3 m) higher than sea level, where the train started.

- ⬛ See also area map p. 47
- ▶ Skagway
- ⬌ 40 miles (64 km) round-trip
- 🕒 3 hours round-trip
- ▶ Skagway

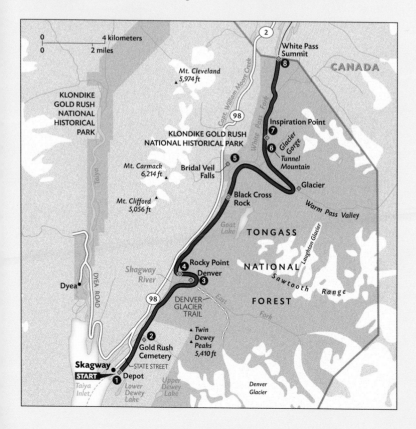

More Places to Visit in Southeast Alaska

Putting in for a paddle to Admiralty Island to watch the brown bears at Pack Creek

Admiralty Island National Monument

The Tlingit call Admiralty Island Kootznoowoo, which means "fortress of the bears," for good reason: More than 1,500 brown bears call this island home, about one per square mile (1 per 2.6 sq km). The population remains high due to the lush habitat and the abundant supply of food protected by the **Kootznoowoo Wilderness,** part of Admiralty Island National Monument.

The monument's most famous attraction is **Pack Creek,** where many of the 1,000-pound (453 kg) bears congregate during summer to feast on salmon. This is one of Alaska's most renowned bear-viewing sites and a permit system is in place to protect people and bears. Make plans well ahead, as these permits get snapped up quickly. Many visitors go on organized tours, most of which are run out of Juneau, only 15 miles (24 km) north of the monument.

The monument also features soaring rain forest, one of Southeast Alaska's greatest concentrations of nesting bald eagles, and coastal waters favored by humpback whales. A number of Juneau companies run sea-kayaking trips along Admiralty's shores. The famous freshwater Cross-Admiralty Canoe Trail also allows people to canoe and kayak across the island.

www.fs.usda.gov/tongass Map p. 47 **Visitor Information** ✉ 8510 Mendenhall Loop Rd., Juneau, AK 99801 ☎ 907/586-8790

Tatshenshini & Alsek Rivers

The Tatshenshini and Alsek Rivers meander through the largest designated wilderness area on the planet: the combined acreages of **Tatshenshini-Alsek Provincial Park, Kluane National Park, Wrangell–St. Elias National Park and Preserve** (see pp. 178–181), and **Glacier Bay National Park and Preserve** (see pp. 75–79). The only practical way to venture across this pristine expanse is by river.

The put-ins for rafts and kayakers are along the Haines Highway. A few hardy souls take on the Alsek River; its upper stretch has challenging white water and one set of rapids that requires a helicopter portage. Most people start on the Tatshenshini River, which has some rapids but nothing too bad. The Tat joins the lower Alsek below the rapids, and flows through Glacier Bay National Park to Dry Bay. Trips generally run 11 to 12 days and take rafters past 14,000-foot (4,267 m) peaks and prime grizzly country. Unless you're a wilderness vet, go with a tour.

Map p. 46

Yakutat

This out-of-the-way coastal town of 680 is flanked by the **Russell Fiord Wilderness** and the southern end of **Wrangell–St. Elias National Park and Preserve** (see pp. 178–181). Visitors come for the legendary sportfishing (salmon and halibut but also Situk River steelhead), the surfing (Yakutat's big waves and miles of sandy beaches have made it the state's surfing capital), and the magnificent beaches, mountains, glaciers, lakes, and wildlife.

www.ptialaska.net/~gycc Map p. 46 **Visitor Information** ✉ Yakutat Chamber of Commerce, P.O. Box 510, Yakutat, AK 99689

Urban and fast-growing, with the feel of the lower 48, but steeped in an abundance of natural attractions

Anchorage & Mat-Su

Atop Flattop, a popular hiking destination just east of Anchorage

Anchorage & Mat-Su

Of all the places in this distinctive state, Anchorage and the Matanuska-Susitna Borough will feel most familiar to travelers from the lower 48. An old one-liner quips that "Anchorage is only 20 minutes from Alaska." While that's a bit harsh, it's true that most of Anchorage consists of subdivisions, office buildings, fast-food restaurants, parks, and all the other development typical of 21st-century America.

This is increasingly true of the Mat-Su Borough, too, where sprawling cities like Wasilla are looking more like California suburbs every day and outlying areas are turning into bedroom communities from which people commute to Anchorage.

Yet these urban outposts have their attractions, and travelers would be wise to sample them. For a city still visited by bears, Anchorage offers plenty of civilized amenities, from excellent museums to trendy bars, music festivals to innovative restaurants, fine art galleries to scenic bike paths. The pretty downtown is largely free of chain stores and strip malls and

is an appealing place to stroll while shopping and sightseeing. Up in the Mat-Su Borough, whose heart lies about 40 miles (64 km) north of Anchorage, civilization has taken a different form. The Mat-Su emerged in the 1930s as an

NOT TO BE MISSED:

agricultural region, the only one of any size in Alaska. This heritage remains strong today, as visitors will notice when driving the back roads past ranches, red barns, and gardens that boast those famously large midnight-sun veggies.

Those curious about what came before the ranches, art galleries, and, yes, fast-food joints will find a rich human history. It began with the Dena'ina, an Athabaskan people, who inhabited the Anchorage area and most of the Mat-Su core. Captain Cook sailed by in 1778, and Russian settlers drifted in before the end of the 18th century. Various gold rushes, including minor ones near Anchorage and in the Mat-Su

Borough, brought more people during the late 1800s and early 1900s. After that the railroad, pioneering aviators, the military buildup sparked by World War II, and the oil boom of the 1970s took Anchorage and the Mat-Su into modern times.

And, despite that old joke, Anchorage and the Mat-Su are indeed part of Alaska. The region teems with outdoor activities and outstanding natural features. Visitors will find wilderness hikes, fishing, boating, glaciers, whales, wetlands busy with birds, lofty mountains, glorious alpine meadows, moose on the loose, and scenery galore. ■

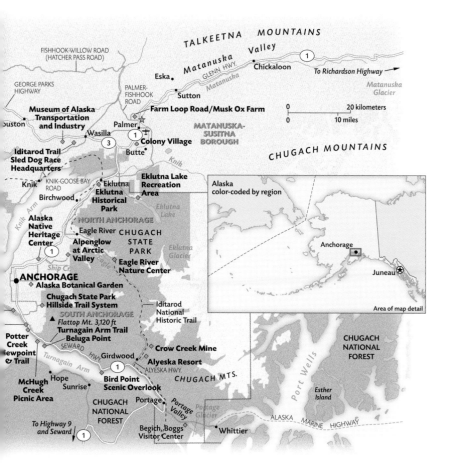

orage

rly 300,000 people, Anchorage is by far Alaska's largest city. Travelers out in the wilds may experience culture shock when they encounter its trendy bars. Certainly, after cooking over a campfire for a week, visitors can find it disorienting to sit down in an elegant restaurant and dine on free-range chicken stuffed with prosciutto, spinach, caramelized onions, and Romano cheese.

Downtown Anchorage represents Alaska's only big-city skyline.

Anchorage

 Map p. 91

Visitor Information

✉ 524 W. 4th Ave.

☎ 907/276-4118
or
800/446-5352

www.anchorage.net

Bewildered as they may be, however, travelers who have been roughing it are often ready to indulge in urban pleasures. Anyone who has been camping in Alaska's wet and cold regions will also appreciate the mild and often dry summer weather in this city that gets only about 16 inches (41 cm) of precipitation a year. The relatively gentle climate is one of the factors that have led so many people to settle here.

Civilized amenities notwithstanding, the great outdoors

is never far away. For example, nearly every city resident has a tale to tell of his or her encounter with a bear or a moose here in town. (Happily, nearly 100 percent of these meetings end without any harm.) Visitors and residents alike also appreciate the fact that even when they're stuck in a traffic jam or coming out of shopping malls, the views of the mountains that ring the city provide relief from the visual nightmare of urban sprawl. Of note, here salmon enter city streams to spawn. At lunchtime downtown workers, some dressed in suits, take their fishing rods to Ship Creek's renowned fishing hole and, amid tall office buildings and the port's industrial zone, reel in 30-pound (14 kg) kings before returning to their desks.

Ship Creek curves along the northern edge of downtown from Knik Arm up through the port. The fishing hole, near the railroad depot, is a good place to start your city tour. Those visitors eager to see spawning salmon simply need to walk about half a mile (0.8 km) east along Ship Creek Avenue to a bridge at the **Salmon Viewing Area.** Downtown lies on higher ground, a couple of blocks south up Port

INSIDER TIP:

It's a good idea to confirm reservations for boat trips, sightseeing ventures, hotels, and such a day or so in advance so service providers know you are really coming.

—ROWLAND SHELLEY
National Geographic field researcher

Access Road. The area of most interest to travelers is bordered by Second Avenue on the north, Ninth Avenue on the south, M Street on the west, and Gambell Street on the east.

Historic Anchorage

Anchorage is fairly new as cities go. Many of its older buildings were destroyed by the 1964

Saturday Market

On a Saturday or Sunday in the summertime, stop by the **Anchorage Market & Festival,** better known by the locals as the Saturday Market. This is not a farmers market so much as an outdoor bazaar where more than 300 local merchants sell an amazing array of goods, including jams and jellies, smoked salmon, ivory jewelry, carved wooden moose heads, pottery, fur coats, coonskin (and skunkskin) caps, and duct-tape wallets. Street performers add a festive air; occasionally a phalanx of bagpipers will march up one of the walkways, noisily parting the enthusiastic crowds. Most of the food stalls sell such Alaska treats as halibut fritters, salmon quesadillas, and Kachemak Bay oysters.

earthquake, but visitors still find remnants of the past scattered around downtown. At the corner of Fourth Avenue and D Street is the **Wendler Building,** distinguished by a sidewalk statue of Balto, a famous sled dog that led the heroic Serum Run to Nome; each March mushers start the Iditarod here. Among the city's oldest buildings, it's the only one with a corner turret. At 420 M Street, the **Oscar Anderson House,** built in 1915, is the first proper frame house in Anchorage. Now a museum, it displays many of the Anderson family's original belongings.

Saturday Market

- ✉ 3rd Ave. between E & C Sts.
- ☎ 907/272-5634
- 🕐 Open 10 a.m.–6 p.m. Sat.–Sun. mid-May–mid-Sept.

www.anchoragemarkets.com

Oscar Anderson House

- ✉ 420 M St.
- ☎ 907/274-2336
- 🕐 Closed mid-Sept.–May
- 💲 $

Anglers line Ship Creek, in the shadow of downtown Anchorage.

Another cluster of homes from the early 1900s graces the neighborhood bounded by First and Third Avenues and F and Christensen Streets.

Just west of the historic neighborhood, on Second Avenue, the **Tony Knowles Coastal Trail** (see sidebar p. 96) begins its 11-mile (17 km) meander along Knik Arm and Cook Inlet. Runners, cyclists, in-line skaters, and people just out for a stroll flock to this scenic path that largely follows the shoreline on the western edge of town to **Kincaid Park.** Look carefully for whales, particularly just outside downtown, and also watch for other wildlife, including moose, as you head farther south from Point Woronzof around Kincaid Park. On a clear day you will be able to spot majestic Mount McKinley to the far north and Mount Susitna (the "sleeping lady") to the west.

Galleries & Museums

Art lovers will find plenty to browse in the dozens of downtown galleries. Try to attend a **First Friday Art Walk,** held between 5:30 and 7:30 p.m. on the first Friday of the month, when dozens of galleries, shops, and restaurants offer an endless variety of food, drink, live music, and appearances by exhibited artists (the Anchorage Daily News prints a map/guide).

For outstanding photos and paintings of traditional Alaska subjects, try **Stephan Fine Arts Gallery** (939 W. 5th Ave., tel 907/ 274-5009, www.stephanfinearts .com), which carries a variety of Alaska artists.

At the other end of the art spectrum is the nonprofit **International Gallery of Contemporary Art** (427 D St., tel 907/ 279-1116, www.igcaalaska.org). Past displays included a video installation of a lady applying red lipstick to herself and a collection that chronicled an artist's hip-replacement surgery, making art of his blood, x-rays, bone fragments, and related paraphernalia.

Aurora Fine Art Gallery *(737 W. 5th Ave., tel 907/274-0234, www.aurorafineart-alaska.com)* offers the browser an eclectic blend of traditional and contemporary styles, epitomized by the "totemic design" art pieces by Marilyn Miller sometimes carried by the art gallery. Miller takes classic native subjects and nature scenes and renders them in a funky, imaginative form via copper, aluminum, and raku-fired clay.

Anchorage Museum: For a generous helping of art, history, and culture, visit the Anchorage Museum. Though the official state museum is in Juneau, the capital, this museum also covers all of Alaska, serving as a de facto second state museum. Vastly expanded in 2009, it has added a focus on the sciences to its portfolio. To this end, the new spaces include a **planetarium,** an **Arctic Studies Center,** and the Imaginarium, a longtime downtown attraction beloved by schoolchildren for its interactive hands-on science exhibits that has relocated to the museum. In the **Imaginarium** kids—and adults who like to learn by playing—can fire an air cannon, touch intertidal critters, and trigger an earthquake. Many of the exhibits focus on science of special interest in Alaska, such as the northern lights and volcanoes.

Several galleries exhibit works from the time of European contact to modern days. This collection reaches back to an engraving of a Prince William Sound man done in 1784 by Captain Cook's expedition artist and up to contemporary art. It devotes considerable wall space to massive landscapes, many by one of the state's most celebrated painters, Sydney Laurence.

In the **Alaska Gallery** a mix of art and artifacts depicts the long history of Alaska from ancient times to the 21st century. Much

INSIDER TIP:

Learn about the 1964 earthquake by visiting Anchorage's Earthquake Park, located on the spot where a landslide that day destroyed 75 homes.

—SARAH ROESKE
National Geographic field researcher

of this gallery features the past lives of the state's indigenous peoples, such as the cutaway diorama of a traditional Aleut house. You should try to seek out the little things, too, such as the photo taken in 1908 in Nome of men in white top hats herding reindeer through town during a parade.

Uniquely Alaska: Near the Town Square fountains and flowers are three venues that showcase what Alaska has to offer. "Aurora—Alaska's Great Northern Lights" *(Sydney Laurence Theatre, Alaska Center for the Performing Arts, 621 W. 6th Ave., tel 907/263-2993, www .thealaskacollection.com, closed early Sept.–late May, $$)* is a

Anchorage Museum

✉ 1625 C St.
☎ 907/929-9200
🕐 Closed Mon. Oct.–April
💲 $$

www.anchorage museum.org

Earthquake Park

✉ 4306 W. Northern Lights Blvd.

Alaska Experience Theatre

✉ 333 W. 4th Ave.

☎ 907/272-9076

$ $$

www.alaskaexper
iencetheatre.com

40-minute show of aurora borealis photos set to music. The **Alaska Experience Theatre** wows visitors with Alaska-themed movies projected onto a huge, wraparound screen. Whether it's a looming grizzly, a racing river peppered with icebergs, a breaching humpback whale, or mountaineers crunching across a vast glacier, you'll feel like you're right there with them. There also are exhibits and a short film about the massive 1964 Alaska earthquake.

A store as unusual as its name, **Oomingmak** (604 H St., tel 907/272-9225 or 888/360-9665, www.qiviut.com) is a co-op that sells sweaters, hats, baby booties, and other clothing hand-knitted by native craftspeople using qiviut, the ultrawarm inner hair of musk oxen.

Beyond downtown there are places worth exploring. Inside a Wells Fargo Bank building, the **Alaska Heritage Museum** (301 W. Northern Lights Blvd., tel 907/265-2834, closed Sat.–Sun.) boasts a large collection of native artifacts and artwork by several Alaska masters. The museum centers on the first floor, but look for other items in elevator lobbies and entrances throughout the building.

To understand how important aviation is to Alaska, visit the **Alaska Aviation Heritage**

EXPERIENCE: Cycling in the Wilderness

What with its mountains, bears, cold, and all-around wildness, Alaska is not exactly a natural when it comes to bicycling. That said, cyclists can find ways.

Beginning in downtown Anchorage at 2nd Avenue, the 11-mile (17 km) **Tony Knowles Coastal Trail** hugs the coastline of Knik Arm and Cook Inlet in what may be one of the world's most stunning urban bike trails. Mileposts tick off the miles, and there are access points along the way. The thing is, you really have to be on your guard—encounters with moose, and even bears, can happen. The trail ends at Kincaid Park. The paved trail is also popular for hiking, running, and, in winter, cross-country skiing and sledding.

If you're seeking something a little more adventurous, there's the **Dalton Highway:** 414 miles (666 km) one way. Most of it is gravel; three-quarters is north of the Arctic Circle; and one stretch of more than 200 miles (320 km) lacks roadside services. Not bike-friendly, yet even nonmaniacal cyclists can enjoy the splendid views and wildlife with a little help. Tour operators offer many options, such as driving you one way or carrying your gear in an accompanying van. Try **Dalton Highway Express** (tel 904/474-3555, www.daltonhighwayexpress.com).

Of course, not all routes are as challenging as the Dalton Highway. Paved highways with ample services do exist, and they're quite scenic. With or without guides, you can pedal skinny-tire road bikes along the shoulders of these main roads every summer.

However, Alaska is more of a fat-tire kind of state, and it presents abundant opportunities to mountain bikers. Some people opt for treks on rough but pretty roads, such as the one that winds deep into **Denali National Park** (see pp. 193–199). Other skilled bikers will go for single-track trails that lead through forests and meadows.

Museum *(4721 Aircraft Dr., tel 907/248-5325, www.alaskaair museum.org, closed Mon.–Tues. mid-Sept.–mid-May, $$).* The museum's collection of 27 aircraft includes such rarities as a 1944 Grumman Widgeon amphibious plane and a Stinson L-1 Army reconnaissance plane, the only one of its kind still fit to fly. An observation platform

Chugach State Park: A couple of miles east of the botanical garden lies Chugach State Park, Anchorage's immense backyard playground. Locals make about a million visits a year to hike, ski, fish, pick berries, and otherwise enjoy this wild sanctuary. You could spend a week here or simply drive 20 minutes from

Chugach State Park

🗺 Map p. 91

✉ Potter Section House, Mile 115.2, Seward Hwy.

☎ 907/345-5014

www.dnr.alaska.gov/ parks/units/chugach

Cyclists pause at an overlook along the 11-mile (17 km) Tony Knowles Coastal Trail to admire views of icy Cook Inlet.

overlooks the huge floatplane base on nearby Lake Hood, constantly abuzz with small aircraft.

Gardens & Parks

To spy native flora, stroll the **Alaska Botanical Garden** *(4601 Campbell Airstrip Rd., tel 907/770-3692, www.alaska bg.org, $),* especially the **Wild-flower Trail** and **Lowenfels Family Nature Trail.** Along the former you'll see bluebell, fool's huckleberry, and other blooms. The latter leads to a creek that hosts spawning king salmon in summer. Watch for moose and bears in this 110-acre (44 ha) woodland.

downtown, walk a short trail, and be treated to a 360-degree panorama of the city, Cook Inlet, and mountains.

The park boasts astounding wilderness. Parts have never been explored; some peaks have never been climbed and many are nameless. The park is home to a host of mammals: wolves, bears, moose, ermines, lynx, flying squirrels, beaver, coyotes, mountain goats and mountain sheep. Anchorage is nearest the western boundary, where good hiking abounds. Another popular entrance is south of the city along the Seward Highway flanking the shore of Turnagain Arm (see pp. 101–103). ■

Buying Alaska Native Art

All over Alaska, even in remote locations, visitors will encounter shops selling traditional Alaska native art. The variety is wonderfully overwhelming, reflecting the different styles, themes, traditions, and media that have developed in different regions. Travelers will see the fine beadwork on moose hide characteristic of Athabaskan tribes, the etched walrus ivory produced by Eskimos, and the intricately carved and brightly painted headdresses of the Tlingit, to name a few.

A Tlingit ornamental visor; the Tlingit Nation is spread across much of Alaska's southeast.

Along with the variety, the high-quality craftsmanship and natural materials that go into native art will delight visitors. These diverse cultures have spent thousands of years refining their traditional arts, and genuine native art is dazzling. However, not all the items advertised in shops as "native" art are genuine. Each year collectors spend millions of dollars on native art, and the temptation to cash in on that hot market has given rise to unscrupulous imitators, such as carvers who substitute resin for soapstone. The authenticity of a pair of $15 earrings may not matter to a buyer (then again, it may), but travelers paying hundreds or thousands of dollars for a work of native art likely want to ensure it's the real McCoy.

How to know? Perhaps the easiest way is to look for the "silver hand" sticker, which bears a hand symbol and the words "Authentic Alaska Native Art from Alaska." While intended to guarantee that items for sale were made by an Alaska native, it does not, of course, guarantee quality. The method also isn't foolproof, as stickers can be transferred and not all genuine pieces bear the silver hand.

Probably the surest approach, short of personally knowing the artist, is to buy from a reputable shop. This isn't intuitive if you're an outsider, but one good bet is to patronize gift shops at museums and cultural centers. For example, shops at the Alaska Native Heritage Center, in Anchorage, and the Alaska State Museum, in Juneau, are well known for native artwork. A less obvious choice, but one re-nowned for both authenticity and good value, is the gift shop at the Alaska Native Medical Center, in Anchorage. For advice regarding reputable shops at other museums and cultural centers, contact the Alaska State Council on the Arts *(161 Klevin St., Ste. 102, Anchorage, AK 99508, tel 907/269-6610, www.eed.state.ak.us/aksca)*.

When visiting an unfamiliar shop, ask about an item's origins or request written proof of its authenticity. If the salesperson claims a seal figurine has been made of walrus ivory by a Yupik on St. Lawrence, ask the clerk to write that claim on your receipt. Carefully inspect the material from which artwork is made. For example, genuine soapstone can be distinguished from resin by its cool feel (resin is warmer) and its weight (soapstone is heavier). A brochure outlining such identification methods is available from the Federal Trade Commission *(www.consumer.ftc.gov/articles/pdf -0055-alaska-native-art.pdf)*.

If worse comes to worst and you are scammed, lodge a complaint with the Federal

Dorica Jackson colors a totem pole made by her Tlingit husband, Nathan Jackson.

Trade Commission *(tel 877/382-4357, www.ftc .gov)* or the Alaska Attorney General's Office *(tel 907/269-5100, www.law.state.ak.us/consumer)*.

EXPERIENCE: Native Arts & Culture Courses

Travelers can easily see evidence of Alaska's native cultures. Totem poles outside city offices, salmon being dried in backyards, hand-crafted jewelry on display in shops; the rich heritage of one-fifth of the state's population is all around.

If you want to explore these traditions, consider the tours that provide a glimpse inside the life of Alaska natives. For example, one of the trips offered by **Northern Alaska Tour Company** *(tel 907/474-8600, www.northernalaska.com)* takes visitors up to the remote village of Anaktuvuk Pass, an inholding in the Gates of the Arctic National Park and Preserve, whose population of some 300 Nunamiut Eskimos still lead a largely subsistence lifestyle. Or you can visit the even smaller village of Klukwan, near Haines in Southeast Alaska. For information, see **Chilkat**

Indian Village *(tel 907/767-5505, http:// chilkatindianvillage.org)*.

Alternatively, you can learn traditional crafts at the **Morris Thompson Cultural and Visitors Center** *(Tanana Chiefs Conference Cultural Programs, tel 907/459-3741, www.morristhompsoncenter.org)*. In one- to three-day workshops, expert native artists will teach you how to make moose skin bags, suncatchers, or birchbark baskets. You'll learn how to use exotic materials, such as caribou hair and porcupine quills.

Interested in diving really deep into native culture? Take a four- to six-week summer course at the **University of Alaska, Fairbanks** *(tel 907/474-7021, www.uaf.edu/summer)*. Try Native Cultures of Alaska or Archaeological Field School, which involves excavating a prehistoric human site that dates back 14,000 years.

Turnagain Arm

The official boundaries of the Municipality of Anchorage extend far south and southeast of the city proper, encompassing small towns, rural areas, and vast wilderness expanses. The sprawl continues to roll southward down the Seward Highway, along the northeast shore of Turnagain Arm, the southern branch of Cook Inlet.

The highway twists and turns for some 50 miles (80 km) south of downtown to where Turnagain Arm ends and the Kenai Peninsula begins.

Birders and other nature lovers visit Potter Marsh and scan the wetlands for the birds and spawning salmon that frequent the area.

The Seward Highway forms the backbone of south Anchorage. All attractions lie along this shore-hugging highway, either off the handful of short side roads or along trails that start from the side roads or highway. This guide covers the 43 miles (70 km) between urban Anchorage and the tip of Turnagain Arm—named for Capt. James Cook's 1778 need to once again turn his ship around when he discovered the passage did not go through.

Potter Marsh, as residents call it, is the most scenic and accessible part of the **Anchorage Coastal Wildlife Refuge.** Officially named the Potter Point State Game Refuge (*Alaska Department of Fish & Game, tel 907/267-2556, www.adfg .state.ak.us*), the marsh lies at Mile 117.4, less than 10 miles (16 km) south of downtown. Watch for moose amid willows along the drive leading to the trailhead parking lot—they'll sometimes feed in the marsh, too.

Bring binoculars to scout for birds along the quarter-mile interpretive boardwalk. During spring migration—roughly late April to mid-May—large flocks of waterfowl throng the marsh. Though early summer sees fewer birds, a number of species do come to nest on the refuge, including bald eagle, arctic tern, and, most conspicuous, lesser Canada geese. Seeing a dozen fuzzy goslings

Ice Worms

Thanks to Robert Service's humorous poem "The Ballad of the Ice Worm Cocktail," many people think the ice worm is about as real as the unicorn or the jackalope. But ice worms do exist, though not typically in cocktails. About half an inch (1.3 cm) long and as husky as a piece of thread, ice worms came by their common name because they do, indeed, inhabit ice, living just beneath the surface of glaciers. Scientists have yet to understand how these creatures thrive in the extraordinary cold.

paddling along behind mama goose is always a highlight for visitors. In late July and August, masses of migrating shorebirds pause here on their way south.

Chugach State Park

As one drives south from Potter Marsh, the sheer scenic power of this stretch of the Seward Highway hits home. Immediately to the right are the waters of Turnagain Arm. Here, at the wide base of this ever narrowing wedge of water, it's about 10 miles (16 km) across to the majestic Kenai Peninsula. To the left are the peaks and forests of Chugach State Park, punctuated by rocky cliffs, creeks, and waterfalls. For information about the state park's many offerings, pull in at Mile 115.2 and visit its headquarters, housed in the

historic **Potter Section House** *(closed weekends),* home to a crew of railroad workers in the old days.

A few hundred feet down the highway is the turnoff to **Potter Creek Viewpoint & Trail.** (The state park administers this pullout and other turnouts, viewpoints, and trails down to Girdwood.) Stroll over to the platform here for fine views, enhanced by spotting scopes and informational signs. Travelers looking for a short hike will enjoy the 0.4-mile (0.8 km) **nature trail.** That said, those looking for a longer hike have also come to the right place,

INSIDER TIP:

Alaska is a state of characters. Try to "get off the bus." Outside the touristy places, most local people are really interested in meeting visitors.

—SARAH ROESKE
National Geographic field researcher

as this is the northernmost trailhead for the **Turnagain Arm Trail** (formerly the Old Johnson Trail).

This is among the state's most beloved trails, used heavily by locals. For 9.4 miles (15 km) it parallels the highway, offering grand vistas across Turnagain Arm, slipping through thick spruce forests, and crossing cool creeks. Due to its south-facing slope and sun exposure it's also one of the first places in the area where snow melts and wildflowers erupt in

**Chugach
State Park**

Map p. 91

Potter Section House, Mile 115.2, Seward Hwy.

907/345-5014

**www.dnr.alaska.gov/
parks/units/chugach**

The Seward Highway skirts the shore of Turnagain Arm, offering stunning views of the surrounding mountains.

viewing platform, wildlife interpretive signs, and spotting scopes. Survey the mountains beyond Turnagain Arm or swivel the scopes around and scan steep slopes to the east for Dall sheep—mountainsides above this stretch of highway are among the best places in Alaska to spot these snow-white relatives of bighorn sheep. Interpretive signs cover subjects ranging from moose stomachs to the history of the railroad.

A mile and a half (2.4 km) farther, off the west side of the highway, is **Beluga Point,** another pullout with great views of the arm and scopes with which to watch Dall sheep. As its name suggests, the point is also a great spot to observe the beluga whales that cruise these waters following coho salmon runs in mid- to late August. Though their numbers have dropped, these small white whales that always seem to be grinning still swim by on occasion. *(Warning: Never walk out onto mudflats that are uncovered at low tide—neither here at Beluga Point nor anywhere along Turnagain Arm. What looks like solid ground may turn out to be quicksand; people have gotten stuck and drowned as the tide rapidly rolled back in.)*

Watching a rising tide may sound as exciting as watching paint dry, but when observed from a safe distance, the tide at Turnagain Arm can be a thrilling sight. The arm experiences one of the world's broadest tidal fluctuations—up to 35 feet (11 m) between low and high tides. As that enormous mass of incoming water squeezes into the narrowing confines of the arm, it creates a tidal bore—a rush of water some

the spring. After a modest initial climb, the route remains fairly level and easy until the last 2 miles (3.2 km), which are moderately difficult. Hikers short on time or who want to start somewhere besides Potter Creek can choose from two entry points on the way to trail's end at Windy Corner.

One of those intermediate entry points is at **McHugh Creek Picnic Area** (Mile 111.9), but trail access isn't the only reason to stop here. The picnic area offers three successively higher parking lots *(fee)* with increasingly expansive views. The second lot features a

six feet (2 m) high. The arm is one of only two places in the U.S. where this phenomenon occurs—the other is Knik Arm, the branch of Cook Inlet that lies north of Anchorage.

Perhaps the best site from which to behold the tidal bore is **Bird Point Scenic Overlook,** (Mile 96.5), where interpretive signs explain the tide changes, and a handsome network of stone paths and platforms overlooks the arm. About 45 minutes after low tide in Anchorage, plus or minus 30 minutes, the growling wall of water will sweep past the point. (Of course, depending on conditions, the wave may be as puny as six inches and that growl may be more of a purr.) The tidal bore stretches all the way across the arm and travels 10 to 15 miles

wave reshaped Turnagain Arm, and the method used by local Dena'ina Athabaskan to hunt belugas. (At low tide hunters would place an upside-down tree trunk in the mudflats, hide atop it as the tide rolled back in, then harpoon a passing beluga. The men attached the harpoon point to air-filled bladders that would slow the beluga until fellow hunters in kayaks could catch it.)

Alyeska Highway

At Mile 90 motorists reach Girdwood Junction, though Girdwood is nowhere in sight. The reason is that the town was so damaged by the 1964 earthquake and tidal wave that its citizens decided to rebuild it 2 miles (3.2 km) up the Alyeska Highway—the spur road running

Cold Water Shock

Cold water can kill you. When someone falls into water as cold as Alaska's, he will experience responses known as cold water shock. The first is the involuntary gasp reflex, which is gasping for air and an inability to hold one's breath. Someone who plunges in deep may suck in water before he can resurface.

To avoid drowning, a person must avoid panic, gain control of his breathing, and get out of the water in minutes, even if it's only getting atop a capsized canoe. Trying to swim to safety is risky; authorities recommend staying with one's boat.

Prevention is best. Wear a flotation device, never go out alone, and stick close to shore if you're not an expert or with an expert. For more information contact the Alaska Marine Safety Education Association (*tel 907/747-3287, www.amsea.org*).

(16 to 24 km) an hour. Sometimes locals actually surf the wave.

Between Miles 95.3 and 92.5, on the west side of the highway, you'll encounter five scenic turnouts that feature enough interpretive panels to constitute a museum. Stop and learn about the area's prehistory, the abandoned gold rush town of Sunrise, ways in which the 1964 earthquake and tidal

northeast from the junction.

Up the Alyeska Highway, just shy of the new Girdwood, Crow Creek Road forks off to the left. Three miles (5 km) up this deeply rutted gravel road is the **Crow Creek Mine.** From the 1890s to the 1940s, this productive mine yielded tons of gold. Eight original buildings filled with mining artifacts are open. Though fairly ramshackle,

Crow Creek Mine

Map p. 91

Crow Creek Rd.

907/229-3105

Closed mid-Sept.–mid-May

 $

www.crowcreek mine.com

Portage Glacier & Portage Valley

 Map p. 91

✉ Begich, Boggs Visitor Center

☎ 907/783-2326, (off-season: 907/783-3242)

🕐 Closed Sept.– Mem. Day

www.fs.usda.gov/ chugach

the site is an accurate reflection of the mine's rough-hewn past. Gold still flows down Crow Creek, and visitors can rent a pan and bucket, get instructions, then try their luck.

INSIDER TIP:

Byron Glacier, near the Begich, Boggs Visitor Center, is perhaps the last readily accessible place to view glacier ice worms in the wild. It's a 20-minute hike; arrive after dark to see worms in their glory.

—DAN SHAIN
National Geographic field researcher

Bird Point Scenic Overlook on Turnagain Arm

A mile (1.6 km) farther the highway ends at **Alyeska Resort** *(tel 907/754-1111 or 800/880-3880, www.alyeskaresort .com)*, a ski area, with offerings for summer and winter fun. Turn left on Arlberg Road and continue past the condos and vacation homes about a mile (1.6 km) to

the resort's Alyeska Prince Hotel. Behind this luxurious hotel, you can catch a tram to the 2,300-foot level of Mount Alyeska. From here you can enjoy the fantastic views over basic food at a cafeteria or indulge in fine, four-diamond dining and the incredible setting at the Seven Glaciers Restaurant. Visitors who have made prior arrangements can paraglide down instead of taking the tram. Other summer activities include hiking, mountain biking, and berry picking.

Mileposts

Milepost references correspond to actual mileage signs along the road, which are calculated from Seward—the town that gives the highway its name.

Portage

At Mile 78.9 on the Seward Highway travelers arrive at the **Portage Glacier** and **Portage Valley.** Turn onto the spur road that heads east toward the glacier and Whittier. As you drive along Portage Creek through this valley framed by mountains and glaciers, you'll pass a number of campgrounds and trails. Just past the 5-mile (8 km) mark, turn right to the **Begich, Boggs Visitor Center,** a facility with ample exhibits. From the glassed-in viewing room you can admire icebergs in Portage Lake, though the glacier itself has receded out of sight. Try taking a boat tour to its face. ■

North Anchorage

Once motorists headed north on the Glenn Highway clear the urban core of Anch speed up to 65 miles an hour (105 kph) and don't slow down until they reach the and enter the Mat-Su Borough, about 30 miles (48 km) up the road. That's fine if you're late for a wedding, but travelers should tarry a bit. North Anchorage harbors several intriguing cultural and historical sites and offers a wealth of natural beauty and outdoor activities. The Glenn Highway ties the area together.

Alaska Native Heritage Center

On the city outskirts, at Mile 4.4, take the Muldoon Road exit north and follow signs to the Alaska Native Heritage Center. *(Free shuttles also available from several locations.)* The center is an excellent place to learn about Alaska native culture and history. Although it displays wonderful artwork and historical artifacts, the center is emphatically not a museum of static display. People representing 11 native cultures gather here to preserve their traditions and educate others about them.

Staff greet visitors at the Welcome House. From there a half-mile (0.8 km) trail leads around a small lake to several "village" sites, each depicting a particular culture or a group of similar cultures. Tours are conducted frequently. One village features an underground community house built in Inupiat and St. Lawrence Yupik styles.

The **Hall of Cultures** brims with art and crafts, both historic and contemporary. Stop by the tables at which native artists from around the state create their works while chatting with visitors. They offer many of

A Tlingit dancer dresses in traditional garb for a performance at the Alaska Native Heritage Center.

The Alaska Native Heritage Center serves as a doorway to the region's rich cultural legacy.

Alaska Native Heritage Center

- Map p. 91
- 8800 Heritage Center Dr.
- 907/330-8000 or 800/315-6608
- Closed early Sept.–mid-May
- $$$$

www.alaskanative.net

their works for ready sale. The **Gathering Place** hosts native storytellers, dancers, athletes, and other performers.

Exit the Glenn at Mile 6.1 and head east on Arctic Valley Road, which climbs a steep, gravelly route for 7 miles (11 km) to **Alpenglow at Arctic Valley** *(tel 907/428-1208, www.skiarctic.net).* This is a ski resort favored among many of the locals for blueberry picking in late summer and fall, as well as for excellent hiking. Strong hikers can likely make the 3.5-mile (5.6 km) round-trip climb of **Rendezvous Peak** in two to three hours, but should allow an extra hour to loll atop the 4,050-foot (1,234 m) summit and feast on the scenery.

Eagle River Nature Center

Those who crave hiking with a dose of education should take the Eagle River exit (Mile 13.4) and turn right on Eagle River Road. Follow it east through a bedroom community for a few miles until you're alongside a river hugged by burly mountains. At the end of the road, 12.5 miles (20 km) from the Glenn, you'll find the Eagle River Nature Center.

INSIDER TIP:

The best way to see the wilderness is to stay at any number of remote camps or lodges, but they can be expensive.

—SARAH ROESKE
National Geographic field researcher

This small nature center features nice displays and helpful, friendly staff that conduct nature walks during the summer. The picnic area provides a pleasant setting from which to watch wildlife and savor the incredible natural setting. Choose from among several excellent hikes.

The **Iditarod National Historic Trail** (aka Crow Pass Trail), one of Alaska's most storied multiday routes, winds 27 miles (43.5 km) from the center to the end of Crow Creek Road, above Girdwood. Watch for grizzlies, glaciers, moose, beavers, Dall sheep, mine ruins, peaks, and pristine forest. The first 4.5 miles (7 km) from the center are easy to moderate.

At the other end of the scale is the center's **Rodak Nature Trail,** a gentle, 0.75-mile (1.2 km) interpretive loop. It passes beaver- and salmon-viewing decks. From this trail hikers can follow the Eagle River along the 3-mile (5 km) **Albert Loop Trail** *(except when portions are closed to allow bears to fish for salmon).*

Eklutna

In this Athabaskan village, just west of Mile 26.5, you'll find

Eklutna Historical Park, a blend of native and Russian Orthodox spiritual traditions. Filled with about 80 brightly colored spirit houses, the Athabaskan cemetery dates to at least 1652, and probably has been in use for a thousand years. Also on the grounds is the 1870 **St. Nicholas Russian Orthodox Church.** Native touches in the building's design speak to its largely Athabaskan parish.

Head east from Eklutna and follow signs 10 miles (16 km) up a slow, curving road to the campground and day-use area at **Eklutna Lake Recreation Area** *(tel 907/688-0908).* The lake there is a favorite for canoeing, kayaking, and fishing for Dolly Varden. ■

**Eagle River
Nature Center**
🏔 Map p. 91
✉ 32750 Eagle
 River Rd.
☎ 907/694-2108
🕐 Open Wed.–
 Sun. May–Sept.,
 Fri.–Sun.
 Oct.–April
💲 $$
www.ernc.org

**Eklutna
Historical Park**
🏔 Map p. 91
☎ 907/688-6026
🕐 Open Mon.–Sat.
 mid-May–Sept.
💲 $

Watch Out! Mosquitoes & Bugs

You've heard the stories. Mosquitoes the size of stealth bombers. Black flies as stealthy as Ninjas. No-see-ums that can slip through the eye of a needle. Swarms of buzzing biting bugs that number in the tens of millions.

Well, don't believe everything you hear. The mosquitoes aren't the size of stealth bombers. However, they are pretty big, and everything else in the first paragraph is true, so make bugs part of your planning for a trip to Alaska.

First, avoid them if possible. January is marvelously pest-free. But if you like sunlight and temperatures above zero, try early May to mid-June or mid-August to early September. However, get specific information about the place you're visiting; different parts of Alaska have different bug timetables—and many areas are relatively bug-free. Hiking and camping in

breezy spots or at higher elevations also can help you escape biting insects.

In case you can't avoid the little buggers, come prepared. Repellent is de rigueur; high deet concentrations work best, but you'll have to decide if it's worth using this strong chemical. Wear long sleeves and long pants with a weave tight enough to repel mozzie proboscises. Don't forget to tighten those sleeves and tuck your pant legs into your socks or the black flies will crawl right up them. And, for those special occasions when there are ten mosquitoes per square inch (ten per 6 sq cm; you wish I was exaggerating), bring a head net.

One last tip. To keep bugs out of your car, stand about 20 feet (6 m) from the door, jump around like a demented person to shake the beasties off, sprint to the door, jump in, and slam it shut.

Mat-Su Borough

The Matanuska-Susitna Borough is Alaska's breadbasket—not that that's saying much in this state of unforgiving weather and equally harsh soil. The Mat-Su Borough, as Alaskans call it, does have a relatively mild climate and some flat land suitable for farming, but the region also contains huge mountains, glaciers, broad braided rivers, and vast expanses of bear- and wolf-laden wilderness.

Fall colors illuminate the view along the Glenn Highway, which winds through the Matanuska Valley.

Palmer

⬛ Map p. 91

Visitor Information

✉ Palmer Chamber of Commerce, 723 S. Valley Way

☎ 907/745-2880

🕐 Closed Sun.–Tues. Oct.–April

www.palmer chamber.org

The Mat-Su's reputation as an agricultural region stems largely from a decision made by the Roosevelt Administration during the Great Depression, when Midwestern farms were failing by the bushel. The government recruited 203 families whose farms had gone under and in 1935 transplanted them to the Mat-Su. They struggled terribly at first, but enough of these hardy colonists (the project was called the Matanuska Colony) persevered,

eventually developing a viable farming community. Today the Mat-Su is better known as an outdoor-activity destination and the site of burgeoning bedroom communities for Anchorage, less than an hour's drive south.

The vast Mat-Su's geographic boundaries are wildly arbitrary. The borough covers a 24,683 square mile (63,930 sq. km) area that reaches north even into Denali National Park—more than 200 miles (322 km) from Mat-Su's southern boundary, defined by Cook Inlet and Knik Arm. For the purposes of this book the three other margins are Matanuska Glacier to the east, the Susitna River to the west, and Hatcher Pass Road (see pp. 112–113) to the north. At about 30 by 100 miles (48 by 160 km) in size, that is plenty big enough.

Palmer

The 1935 colonists set down roots in Palmer, so it's an appropriate place to begin a journey through the Mat-Su Borough. Start at the **Palmer Chamber of Commerce,** which serves as a fount of tourist information and houses a small history museum dedicated to the Matanuska Colony. Whipsaws, scythes, and clothes wringers all testify to the colonists' backbreaking work.

INSIDER TIP:

Matanuska Glacier, east of Anchorage, is the largest Alaska glacier accessible by car. Guided hikes on the glacier are possible.

—DAN SHAIN
National Geographic field researcher

The collection's dogsled and ice chisel remind visitors that these farmers also had to cope with very unfamiliar conditions. And don't miss the gorgeous community garden.

A short walk from the visitor center is the **Colony House Museum,** former home of Oscar and Irene Beylund; it has been

restored to look as it did between 1935 and 1945. The Beylunds' furnishings and personal possessions evoke the early days of the colony, but what really animates this museum are its guides. Most are descendants of original colonists and a few are original colonists who came here as children.

Across the street is the **Colony Inn.** Built in 1935, the building was a teacher dormitory through the 1960s. Today it's an elegant small inn and restaurant. A block east, at the corner of East Elmwood Avenue and South Denali Street, is **United Protestant Church,** otherwise known as the "Church of a Thousand Trees" or "Church of a Thousand Logs." Colonists built this church between 1935 and 1937, using logs even for the striking altar. The church is still in use, so visit it respectfully.

Back roads lace the valley, crossing farmland established by the early colonists. Where better to loop among the farms than on **Farm Loop Road?** From Palmer, head north on the Glenn a few miles and turn west onto Palmer-Fishhook Road, the turnoff to Hatcher Pass, at Mile 49.5. Drive 1.4 miles, turn right onto the Farm Loop, and follow it for 3 miles (4.8 km) past fields dotted with horses and traditional barns, ending at Mile 50.7 of the Glenn.

Musk Ox Farm: Half a mile south off the Glenn, a spur road leads west to the Musk Ox Farm *(watch for signs).* Musk oxen are fascinating creatures, though they neither have musk glands nor belong to the ox family. At a half ton (454 kg), their most

Mat-Su Borough
- Map p. 91

Visitor Information
- Mile 35.5, Parks Hwy.
- 907/746-5000
- Visitor center closed mid-Sept.–mid-May

www.alaskavisit.com

Colony House Museum
- 316 E. Elmwood Ave.
- 907/745-1935
- Open Tues.–Sat. May–Aug. (by appt. rest of year)
- $

www.palmer historicalsociety.org

Musk Ox Farm
- Map p. 91
- Mile 50 Glenn Hwy.
- 907/745-4151
- Closed mid-Sept.–Mother's Day
- $$

www.muskox farm.org

Matanuska Glacier
- Map p. 91
- Glacier Park Resort, Mile 102 Glenn Hwy. (60 miles/96 km N of Palmer)
- $$$ (incl. self-guided tour). $$$$$ guided tours

Visitors to the Musk Ox Farm can get a close look at these quintessential shaggy Arctic beasts *(Ovibos moschatus)*—and vice versa.

noticeable feature is their shaggy coat. The farm's animals are descendants of 34 oxen brought from Greenland in the 1930s to replace the Alaska musk oxen, which had been hunted out by the 1860s. Today several thousand musk oxen roam wild in Alaska.

The replacement musk oxen weren't brought over primarily for conservation reasons, though. They were intended to provide Alaska natives with a cottage industry. Beneath a musk ox's guard hairs is a woolly undercoat called qiviut, said to be eight times warmer than sheep's wool yet very silky and lightweight. Farm staff comb out the qiviut once a year and send it to native weavers, who in turn make scarves, hats, and other garments from this marvelous hair.

The gift shop sells a variety of qiviut products; even if you don't buy anything, at least feel the

material. Nearby is a small musk oxen museum, a place to browse while waiting for tours, which leave every 45 minutes.

Each tour includes a close look at these cute critters. In the springtime you'll see the 20-pound (9 kg) calves elicit baby-talk from visitors, especially when the furry youngsters suckle from their moms or get fed from a bottle. Later in the year, you may witness ferocious 800-pound rutting bulls charge each other at 35 miles an hour (56 kph) and thunderously butt heads.

Wasilla

Centered 10 miles (16 km) west of Palmer via the Palmer-Wasilla or Parks Highway is Wasilla. Resist the urge to hit the gas and put this town in your rearview mirror, as there are a few worthwhile sights. Start on Main Street at the **Dorothy Page Museum** *(323 N. Main*

St., tel 907/373-9071, www.cityof
wasilla.com/museum, closed Sat.–
Mon., $), amid the remnants of
old town Wasilla, a block north
of the Parks Highway. This small
facility offers rotating exhibits
and interpretive displays about
early pioneer life.

Turn off the Parks at Neuser
Drive (Mile 47), and follow the
signs about a mile to the **Museum of Alaska Transportation
& Industry** (3800 W. Museum Dr.,
Mile 47, Parks Hwy., tel 907/376-
1211, www.museumofalaska.org,
closed early Sept.–mid-May, $$), a
large facility with a split personal-
ity. Inside the main building are
orderly exhibits on bush pilots,
cherry vintage cars, and the hang
glider one Robert Burns used
to sail down from the summit

of Mount McKinley. Outside,
however, looks like a junkyard,
though visitors enjoy wandering
amid the jumble of boats, police
cars, helicopters, ambulances,
and military jets.

INSIDER TIP:

**Visit a bush checkpoint
in March during the
Iditarod Trail Sled Dog
Race to learn about
mushing and how
important it is to the
villages. You can vol-
unteer at checkpoints
(www.iditarod.com/
resources/volunteer).**

—PAM GROVES
Professor, University of Alaska

Wasilla is a center for dog
mushing and the Iditarod. On
Knik-Goose Bay Road you'll find
the **Iditarod Trail Sled Dog
Race Headquarters** (Mile 2.2,
tel 907/376-5155, www.iditarod
.com, closed Sat.–Sun. in winter)
and the **Knik Museum & Sled
Dog Mushers' Hall of Fame**
(Mile 13.9, Knik-Goose Bay Rd., tel
907/376-2005, open Thurs.–Sun.
June–Aug.). Both present exhibits
and artifacts related to mushing
and that most venerable of all the
sled dog races, the Iditarod. Some
Wasilla-area mushers, including
four-time Iditarod champion
Martin Buser, offer tours of their
kennels. You can chat with these
mushers about their sport, but
best of all, you can pet the sled
dogs and cuddle puppies. ∎

Wasilla

 Map p. 91

Visitor Information

415 E. Railroad
Ave.

907/376-1299

Closed Sat.–Sun.

**www.wasilla
chamber.org**

Giant Veggies

Veggies love the land
of the midnight sun.
With TLC and 18 to 20
hours a day of energiz-
ing sunshine, vegetables
in the Mat-Su Borough
balloon to preposterous
sizes. Backs strain to lift
60-pound (27 kg) zucchini.
Pulling 20-pound (9 kg)
carrots from the ground
qualifies as an upper-body
workout. One bunch of
Swiss chard topped out at
9 feet (3 m)—tall enough
to qualify as a tree. The
Olympics of big produce is
the Giant Cabbage Weigh-
Off at the Alaska State Fair,
where the winner harvests
$2,000. The current record
cabbage tipped the scales
at 138.35 pounds (62.7 kg).

Hatcher Pass Drive

Hatcher Pass Road runs from the low country by the Matanuska River to the low country by the Susitna River, along the way winding through the handsome high country of the Talkeetna Mountains.

Historic buildings and tundra-covered slopes grace the route through Hatcher Pass.

The route's higher elevations receive lots of snow, which often closes the midsection of this route from October through early July. In summer the road is suitable for most vehicles, although the middle 25 miles (40 km) are gravel and sometimes narrow and bumpy, so slow down and enjoy the views. For general info, contact the **Mat-Su Convention & Visitors Bureau** *(tel 907/746-5000)* or **Alaska State Parks** *(tel 907/745-3975).*

The route begins 7.5 miles (12 km) north of downtown **Palmer** at Mile 49.5 (as measured from Anchorage) on the Glenn Highway. Turn west on Palmer-Fishhook Road (aka Fishhook-Willow Road) and follow it north through farm country. At Mile 8.5 take the turnout for the **Little Susitna River ❶**, a frothy waterway that rushes down from Mint Glacier.

The next 5 miles (8 km) feature half a dozen turnouts from which you can savor the

---

NOT TO BE MISSED:

Little Susitna River • Independence Mine • Hatcher Pass Summit

---

Little Susitna and tundra-covered mountains in every direction. This beautiful stretch of road ends at a parking area for the **Gold Mint Trail ❷**. Here the road parts ways with the Little Susitna. To see more of the river, hike this gently sloping trail through the waterway's striking alpine valley. The hike is about 8 miles (12.9 km) to **Mint Glacier.**

After a sharp turn at the Gold Mint parking area, the road climbs steeply west. At Mile 14.6, **Archangel Road,** a rough spur best left to 4WD vehicles and mountain goats, leads north to a trailhead for **Reed Lakes.**

Parking for the **Fishhook Trail** is right off the main road at Mile 16.4.

Independence Mine & Beyond

At Mile 17 visitors approach the spur to **Independence Mine State Historical Park** ❸ (*tel 907/745-2827 or 907/745-3975, www .dnr.alaska.gov/parks/units/indmine.htm, closed early Sept.–mid-June, $*). While individual prospectors panned for gold flakes down in the creeks, the big outfits opted for hard-rock mining in the mountains, searching for the mother lodes that spawned those flakes. At its peak, in the early 1940s, the Independence Mine employed more than 200 workers, an easy number to imagine when you tour the mess hall, bunkhouses, commissary, assay office, and other build-ings that compose this sprawling complex. Visitors can wander around on their own, peer through a few windows, and peruse the interpretive signs, but it's better to take one of the informative guided tours, which take you inside several of the buildings.

At Mile 18.9 the road peaks at 3,886-foot (12,870 m) **Hatcher Pass Summit.** Trails fan out from the parking lot, letting you roam the alpine slopes and soak up the views. Similar landscapes and views await at Mile 19.3; park at **Summit Lake State Recreation Site** ❹ and stroll around the lake or up to the bluff.

From the summit the road narrows and winds steeply down for about 7 miles (11.2 km) before running flat. Despite a few good views, the odd beaver pond, and glimpses of Willow Creek, this section of road, particularly the last 10 or 15 miles (16 to 24 km), is just a pretty drive.

> 🗺 See also area map pp. 90–91
> ▶ Palmer
> ↔ 49 miles (78 km) one way
> 🕐 2–3 hours plus stops
> ▶ Junction of Parks Hwy., 70 miles (112.7 km) north of Anchorage

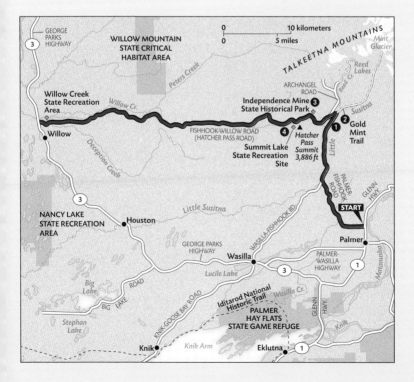

Just outside Anchorage in Chugach State Park, en route to Flattop Mountain's apex

More Places to Visit in Anchorage & Mat-Su

Chilkoot Charlie's

Known affectionately as Koot's, this huge bar/restaurant/nightclub features three stages and 11 bars. While largely a loud, raucous, hormone-charged anarchy of young singles, it's stranger than that. Many of the bars are themed, such as the **Swing Bar,** a 1940s send-up complete with big band music, martinis, and black-and-white TVs. Other themes are truly bizarre, such as the **Russia Room** and the **Soviet Walk,** which, respectively, go for an opulent tsarist ambience and the feel of a Soviet subway. On **The Deck** patrons sit on old patio furniture and get drinks from an ice cream truck. Somehow, over the years it's been in business, Koot's has landed such big-name bands as the Beach Boys, Metallica, and Bon Jovi to play here. What's more, it was named America's best bar in 2000 by none other than *Playboy* magazine—not exactly a Nobel Prize, but hey, it's a bar.
www.koots.com ✉ 2435 Spenard Rd., Anchorage ☎ 907/272-1010

Chugach State Park Hillside Trail System

Hikers rave about this deservedly popular network of trails in Chugach State Park, on the east side of Anchorage just 20 minutes from downtown. Perhaps nowhere else in the United States can you travel from skyscrapers to wilderness in less time. Short spur roads off Hillside Drive lead to major access points where visitors can park and start tromping: **Prospect Heights,** off O'Malley, and **Glen Alps,** off Upper Huffman. From Glen Alps, for example, you can take a 3.5-mile (5.6 km) round-trip trail (1,550-foot/4,724 meter elevation gain) to the top of **Flattop Mountain**—a relatively moderate climb except for a slippery scramble up the steep last stretch. Your rewards are considerable, including panoramic views of Anchorage, Cook Inlet, the Kenai Peninsula, and even the distant Alaska Range. Pick up a copy of the park's Hillside Trail System map/brochure.
www.dnr.alaska.gov/parks/units/chugach
🗺 Map p. 91 ✉ Chugach State Park
☎ 907/345-5014 💲 $ (parking)

Ulu Factory

A knife that looks nothing like a typical knife, the ulu has been used by Eskimos for thousands of years. In ancient times ulus were fashioned from natural materials—perhaps a slate blade and an ivory handle—and were used for tasks such as skinning seals and preparing walrus hides to make an umiak (skin boat). Today they're usually made of steel and wood and they're used for everything from filleting salmon to slicing pizza. At this factory in downtown Anchorage visitors can watch a demonstration showing how to use an ulu and see ulus being shaped, sharpened, polished, and fitted with handles. All sorts of ulus are for sale at the factory store.
http://theulufactory.com ✉ 211 W. Ship Creek Ave., Anchorage ☎ 907/276-3119 or 800/488-5592 🕐 Closed Sun. & Jan 1–late Feb.

A microcosm of Alaska, from native cultures and abundant
to coastal activities and urban amenities

Kenai Peninsula

An array of colorful flies reveals
the fishing frenzy that grips the
Kenai Peninsula.

Kenai Peninsula

Kenai Peninsula's diverse attractions include the dramatic Kenai Fjords National Park, first-rate canoeing, world-class museums, islands thick with seabirds, intriguing reminders of Russian Alaska, a vast national wildlife refuge, luxurious wilderness lodges, hundreds of miles of beautiful coastline, and world-renowned fishing.

Just outside Seward, Fox Island straddles the broad mouth of Resurrection Bay.

The Kenai, as Alaskans call it, is a roughly oval peninsula that juts southwest into Cook Inlet. About 55,000 people live here, 7,200 in Kenai, the peninsula's largest town. The peninsula's northern boundary is just 52 miles (84 km) from Anchorage, connected by the pretty Seward Highway, and residents of the state's biggest city often head to the Kenai for recreation. It's about the size of West Virginia, although some 40 percent is covered by lakes, rivers, and vast wetlands. All that fresh water near the salt water that virtually surrounds the peninsula largely accounts for the fishing mania you'll find here.

The first peoples to settle the peninsula were Athabaskan in the north and west and Alutiiq, or Aleut, in the south and east. Next came the Russians, whose influence has been particularly strong. The town of Kenai was founded in 1791 by Russian fur traders, and many place-names (for example, Kasilof and Kalifornsky) speak to the peninsula's Russian past. Still living in small pockets around the Kenai are Old Believers, a traditional Russian Orthodox people who dress in old-fashioned garb and speak Russian as well as English.

As in much of the state, the Kenai's modern growth was boosted by the discovery of gold (around 1850) and oil and gas (around 1960). Today the oil and gas industry (offshore in Cook Inlet), commercial fishing, and tourism are the economic mainstays.

NOT TO BE MISSED:

The Seward Highway leads to Seward and Resurrection Bay. The peninsula is otherwise accessible along the 143 miles of the Sterling Highway, which branches west off the Seward through Kenai National Wildlife Refuge, threads the towns of Kenai and Soldotna, and continues south along the Cook Inlet to the end of the road at Homer and the land across Kachemak Bay. ■

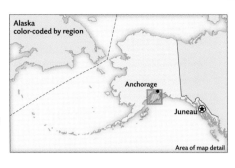

Alaska color-coded by region

Anchorage

Juneau

Area of map detail

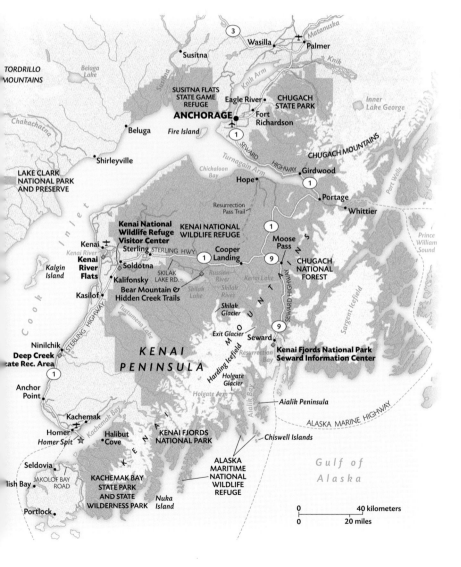

TORDRILLO MOUNTAINS

Beluga Lake

3

Susitna

Wasilla   Palmer

Matanuska

Knik

SUSITNA FLATS STATE GAME REFUGE

Eagle River

CHUGACH STATE PARK

Knik Arm

Inner Lake George

Chakachatna

Beluga

Fire Island

ANCHORAGE

Fort Richardson

1

SEWARD HIGHWAY

CHUGACH MOUNTAINS

Port Wells

Shirleyville

Turnagain Arm

Chickaloon Bay

Hope

Girdwood

1

LAKE CLARK NATIONAL PARK AND PRESERVE

Portage

Whittier

Prince William Sound

Resurrection Pass Trail

Kenai

Kenai River

Kenai River Flats

Kenai National Wildlife Refuge Visitor Center

Sterling STERLING HWY.

KENAI NATIONAL WILDLIFE REFUGE

Cooper Landing

1

Moose Pass

9

Kalgin Island

Soldotna

Kalifonsky

SKILAK LAKE RD.

Russian River

Kenai River

CHUGACH NATIONAL FOREST

Kasilof

Bear Mountain & Hidden Creek Trails

Skilak Lake

Skilak River

Seward Highway

Sargent Icefield

Skilak Glacier

MOUNTAINS

Tustumena Lake

Exit Glacier

Harding Icefield

Seward

9

Ninilchik

Deep Creek State Rec. Area

STERLING HIGHWAY

KENAI PENINSULA

Resurrection Bay

Kenai Fjords National Park Seward Information Center

1

Anchor Point

Holgate Glacier

Aialik Bay

Holgate Arm

Aialik Peninsula

ALASKA MARINE HIGHWAY

Kachemak

Homer

Homer Spit

Halibut Cove

KENAI FJORDS NATIONAL PARK

Chiswell Islands

Gulf of Alaska

Seldovia

JAKOLOF BAY ROAD

KACHEMAK BAY STATE PARK AND STATE WILDERNESS PARK

ALASKA MARITIME NATIONAL WILDLIFE REFUGE

lish Bay

Nuka Island

Portlock

0   40 kilometers

0   20 miles

Cook Inlet

Seward

The Seward Highway is a hard act to follow. Heading south through the Kenai Peninsula, this All-American Road, Alaska Scenic Byway, and USFS Scenic Byway slips through the dramatic forest and mountains of Chugach National Forest, passing white-water creeks, hanging glaciers, and moose stilting through beaver ponds.

Downtown Seward is a pleasant mix of shops and historic buildings.

Seward

⊠ Map p. 117

Visitor Information

✉ Seward Chamber of Commerce–Convention & Visitors Bureau, 2001 Seward Hwy.

☎ 907/224-8051

🕐 Closed Sat.–Sun. Labor Day–Mem. Day

www.seward.com

When motorists reach the end of the road, in the city that gave the highway its name, they'll find that Seward and environs more than live up to the scenic byway's promise.

Seward overlooks Resurrection Bay, a svelte finger of the Gulf of Alaska. Framed by rugged peaks and dark spruce forest, the town comprises a pleasantly rustic port of about 2,700 residents, roughly divided into two parts: the relaxed, older downtown and a busy cluster of new development around the small boat harbor a mile (1.6 km) north.

Alaska SeaLife Center

One fairly recent development has taken center stage in Seward: the Alaska SeaLife Center, one of the state's top museums and research institutions, located on Resurrection Bay at Mile 0 of the Seward Highway. The center is devoted to wildlife rehabilitation, Alaska's marine ecosystems, and communicating that understanding to the public. The museum presents plenty of serious information about research on the Bering Sea and ongoing ramifications of the

Exxon Valdez oil spill. But the center also knows how to elicit a "gee whiz."

Large underwater viewing galleries let visitors press their faces against the glass to watch harbor seals and sea lions zip by with astounding speed and grace. In the Discovery Pool, kids can run their fingers over sticky sea anemone tentacles or a sea star's smooth arms. In the aviary, watch as seabirds stand atop the rocks and flap vigorously. Kneel for an underwater view of tufted puffins and pigeon guillemots stroking around beneath the surface.

While you're there, listen for special announcements, such as a sea lion training session that visitors can watch from an over-head viewing deck. Don't worry, these sessions foster safe handling when the pinnipeds are moved

or vets care for them. As trainers approach, the sea lions whack their flippers against the fence and frolic like excited puppies.

Take a **behind-the-scenes tour** *(reservations recommended, extra fee)* to learn even more fascinating facts. For example, did you know that octopuses crave stimulation and contact? In the labs, staffers tell visitors all about these intelligent animals while feeding them by hand. On daily **Encounter Tours** *(reservations recommended, extra fee)*, you can confirm staffers' claims that octopus suckers feel soft, like a baby sucking a thumb—albeit a hundred times stronger.

Video monitors offer a closer look of the creatures. Since the center is the state's primary marine mammal and seabird rehabilitation facility, the cast

Alaska SeaLife Center

✉ 301 Railway Ave.
☎ 907/224-6300
 or
 800/224-2525
$ $$$$
www.alaskasea
life.org

EXPERIENCE: Take a Boat Trip

Small tour boats are the keys that unlock many of the treasures of coastal Alaska. Cruise ships introduce visitors to this realm of sea and shore, but the little watercraft that carry 50 or 20 or maybe just a handful of passengers allow you to explore the nooks and crannies

Perhaps you'll take a cabin cruiser through Sitka Sound to circle St. Lazaria Island, summer home to hundreds of thousands of nesting storm-petrels, puffins, auklets, and murres. If you're in Homer, hop aboard the old fishing boat that takes a few dozen passengers to Halibut Cove. For a combination of mountain scenery, wildlife viewing, and thrill ride, head up the Stikine River in a jet boat.

Some tours are wonderfully exotic. How about going out of Ketchikan aboard

one of the crab boats that was featured on the Discovery Channel's *Deadliest Catch*? Don't worry; they won't take passengers out into the storms that make it hard to even watch the TV show without getting scared and seasick. The captain keeps the boat in protected waters and lets you watch the crew haul in the catch of the day, including crabs, cod, prawns, and other seafood.

If none of the established tours strikes your fancy, you can always charter a boat and go wherever on the waters you like. In some calm regions you can even hire landing craft that can run you up on a beach and drop you off in the middle of nowhere.

For a list of boat tour companies, search the Internet, starting with *www.alaskatia.org* or *www.travelalaska.com*.

of animal characters continually changes. One day you may witness blood being drawn from a puffin, another day anesthesia being administered to a sea otter.

Downtown

Immediately north of the Alaska SeaLife Center is downtown Seward, a compact district that measures about half a dozen by three blocks. Fourth Avenue serves as the main drag. You'll find a few gift shops, but downtown is not a tourist mecca; many of its restaurants, clothing stores, and the like are geared toward locals, making them all the more appealing to travelers eager to sample a slice of Alaska life.

Mount Marathon Race

Most people wouldn't look at a 3,000-foot-plus (915 m) peak and think, *Let's run up and down that mountain as fast as we can!* Then again, most people aren't from Seward. Every Fourth of July since 1915, runners starting at sea level in downtown Seward have raced 1.5 miles (2.4 km) up Mount Marathon and 1.5 miles back down. The slopes are so steep in spots that contestants must use their hands to haul themselves up. Add to that gullies, loose shale, ice, and snow, and it's no wonder that bloodied knees are par for the course. The record is 43 minutes 23 seconds. The race has become a major event that draws 900 participants (the maximum allowed) and thousands of onlookers from Alaska and beyond (*www.sewardchamber.org*).

Stop in at the new **Seward Community Library Museum** (*238 6th Ave., tel 907/224-4082, www.cityofseward.net/library, call for hours*) to check out books and

local history. The cultural combo features paintings by leading Alaska artists, a collection of Russian icons, and the original Alaska flag, designed in 1927 by a boy from a local orphanage. Don't miss the harrowing video of the 1964 Good Friday earthquake, which hit Seward hard.

Delve further into local history by respectfully wandering the corridors of the historic **Van Gilder Hotel** (*308 Adams St., tel 800/204-6835, www.van gilderhotel.com*), which boasts an extensive collection of photographs. Be sure to read the captions. For example, the text beside a photo of the 1941 downtown fire reveals that soldiers stationed in town took a military approach to extinguishing the blaze. Unfortunately, when they dynamited the building in which the fire started, the explosion blew flaming debris all over town.

For a taste of contemporary life in Seward, stop in at **Resurrect Art Coffee House Gallery** (*320 3rd Ave., tel 907/224-7161, www.resurrectart.com*), run out of a historic former Lutheran church. A favorite local hangout, it offers espresso, tasty pastries, and a healthy helping of local art, ranging from simple crafts to expensive paintings.

Seward Small Boat Harbor

A mile north of downtown is the Seward Small Boat Harbor, its west side flanked by relatively new development—upscale restaurants, galleries, and shops. The docks are thick with sportfishing charter outfits. Stroll through here as the boats return at day's end to watch anglers string up their catch. The docks also house the Kenai Fjords National Park Seward Information Center (see p. 122), and several outfitters offering boat tours.

From the small boat harbor, a paved **shoreline path** runs south along the bay about a mile (1.6 km) then strikes west along the waterfront to the Alaska SeaLife Center, passing through a couple of parks on the way. Scattered along the trail are interpretive displays on a variety of topics, such as rain forest flora, commercial fishing, and the history of the Alaska Railroad (whose southern terminus is in Seward, near the north end of the path).

Outside Seward

A couple of miles south on the shore road is **Lowell Point State Recreation Site.** This 20-acre (8 ha) spread offers beach access to Resurrection Bay, but it is better known as a jumping-off point for kayak trips. It's also the trailhead for a 4.5-mile (7.2 km) hike to **Caines Head State Recreation Area.** The scenic route follows the western shore along a beach framed by mountains. Check with park staff to time the hike properly, as portions are only passable at low tide.

At the recreation area you can explore **Fort McGilvray,** an abandoned strategic command center built during World War II to protect Seward at a

A playful Steller sea lion swooshes past delighted visitors at Seward's Alaska SeaLife Center.

time when Japanese had landed on the Aleutian Islands. Take a flashlight and wander the subterranean maze of passageways or enjoy views from former artillery batteries atop the 650-foot (198 m) promontory.

About 12 miles (19 km) south of Seward, the cliffs and bird-thronged sea stacks (look for puffins and cormorants) of **Fox Island** jut from Resurrection Bay. The only way to visit this private isle is via native-owned Kenai Fjords Tours *(tel 877/777-4051, www.kenaifjords.com),* which offers 3- to 4.5-hour-long cruises of Resurrection Bay that include lunch or dinner at the attractive Fox Island Lodge. ∎

Caines Head State Recreation Area

✉ Alaska State Parks, Kenai/ PWS Area Office

☎ 907/262-5581

www.dnr.alaska .gov/parks/units/ caineshd.htm

Kenai Fjords National Park

Kenai Fjords is a primordial place. Nature in the raw. A world where you can witness fundamental geological processes in action. Except for a fringe of temperate rain forest, the park is a rugged land of rock and ice—especially ice, which sheathes a large majority of its 607,805 acres (245,970 ha). The Harding Icefield alone buries more than half the park beneath hundreds and thousands of feet of ice. Tour the park to be transported back to the ice ages.

Tour boat passengers hope for a glimpse of calving ice from one of the park's grand glaciers.

Kenai Fjords National Park

⛰ Map p. 117

✉ Kenai Fjords NP Seward Information Center, 1212 4th Ave., Seward

☎ 907/224-7500

🕐 Closed Oct.–April

www.nps.gov/kefj

Visiting Kenai Fjords is no walk in the park, so to speak. With the exception of those visiting Exit Glacier, few people venture into this unforgiving landscape on their own—nor should they, unless they know what they are doing. Fortunately, a cadre of experienced tour operators have set up shop in the gateway town of Seward. The Park Service also offers a handful of guided tours.

Start your visit at the **Kenai Fjords National Park Seward Information Center,** at the Seward Small Boat Harbor. Though it's small and lacks the museum-like displays of some national park visitor centers, it does screen several good films about the park in its small auditorium. Stop by to learn about the park's scenic wonders and abundant wildlife. Also pick up a list of authorized tour operators; many boat trips provide Park Service interpreters.

Dozens of these operations are run out of a row of buildings adjacent to the information center. Stroll the district for brochures and ask staff for tour specifics. Decide if you want a flightseeing trip, a scenic boat tour, a fishing trip, a kayaking expedition, a glacier trek,

KENAI
NATIONAL
WILDLIFE
REFUGE

Tustumena Lake

Skilak Glacier

CHUGACH
NATIONAL
FOREST

HARDING ICEFIELD TRAIL

Resurrection R.

EXIT GLACIER ROAD

Exit Glacier

Nature Center

Seward

Kenai Fjords National Park
Seward Information Center

Resurrection Bay

COASTAL TRAIL

CAINES HEAD S.R.A.

Killey Glacier

Indian Glacier

Tustumena Glacier

ICEFIELD

KENAI

HARDING

Aialik Glacier

Bear Glacier

Bulldog Cove

Fox

Truuli Peak
6,612 ft

FJORDS

Holgate Glacier

Aialik Bay

Aialik Peninsula

Chernof Glacier

Northwestern Glacier

MOUNTAINS

McCarty Gl.

NATIONAL

Harris Peninsula

Holgate Arm

Fox

Sheep Creek

Dinglestadt Glacier

Kachemak Glacier

Northwestern Lagoon

PARK

McCarty Fjord

Harris Bay

emak

Bradley Lake

KENAI

Nuka

North Arm

Storm Mountain
3,793 ft

Granite Island

Chiswell Islands

ALASKA
MARITIME NATIONAL
WILDLIFE REFUGE

Iceworm Peak
5,800 ft

Palisade Peak
3,442 ft

Two Arm Bay

Cloudy Mountain
1,810 ft

West Arm

Yalik Glacier

Petrof Glacier

Thunder Bay

Gulf
of
Alaska

Yalik Point

Ragged Island

Nuka Bay

Pye Islands

ALASKA
MARITIME
NATIONAL
WILDLIFE
REFUGE

KACHEMAK BAY
STATE PARK AND
TE WILDERNESS PARK

Nuka Island

0   20 kilometers
0   10 miles

or something else. Do you want to explore for three hours or three days? Do you want minimal guidance—say, a charter boat that will drop you off in a wilderness cove and come back for you in a week—or a full-service tour in a heated boat with lunch and drinks?

The quickest means to a literal overview of Kenai Fjords

EXPERIENCE: Mountain Rock & Ice Climbing

Want to spend your vacation dangling from a rope on a mountainside? Or learning how to use an ice ax to stop an uncontrolled slide down a glacier? Admittedly, such pursuits aren't for every visitor, but if you do want to climb or learn how to, Alaska is rich in possibility.

The diversity extends from Arctic crags in the Brooks Range to bouldering on the bizarre rock formations of the Granite Tors near Fairbanks to ice climbing on frozen waterfalls along the Richardson Highway to precipices in the Kenai Peninsula and tackling North America's highest summit, Mount McKinley.

Given that climbing involves, well, climbing, inexperienced visitors should not attempt any technical climbing (efforts that require ropes and other protective gear) without guidance.

Fortunately, Alaska has almost as many climbing guides as mountains. Ask for guide info at public lands offices (see sidebar p. 10), especially those at climbing hot spots such as Denali and Wrangell–St. Elias National Parks.

Some of these climbing companies offer instruction for novices, ranging from lessons that last a few hours to trips that last several days. More challenging courses for climbers last up to two weeks. You should be aware that even short classes usually require a fairly high level of fitness. Perhaps the easiest entry into Alaska climbing you'll find is at the **Alaska Rock Gym** (4840 Fairbanks St., Anchorage, tel 907/562-7265, www.alaskarockgym.com), where prospective climbers as young as six can learn the ropes.

---

is in a small plane or helicopter. Though you won't see things up close—unless you arrange a glacier landing—you will see remote spots that boat tours can't reach. Within minutes you'll be buzzing above the 300-square-mile (483 km) **Harding Icefield,** skimming over blinding snowfields and aqua crevasses. Watch for the stony tips of mountains that just peek above the ice; the Eskimos call these *nunataks,* or lonely peaks.

Here, hundreds of inches of annual snowfall compact into dense ice that fuels 32 distinct glaciers. However, these rivers of ice are retreating faster than they're being replenished, as happened in the last ice age, when withdrawing glaciers left behind the deep, narrow, U-shaped fjords that give the park its name.

These sublime fjords are best approached from the sea. Most visitors choose a powerboat tour, whether aboard a smaller vessel with 20 passengers or a multideck cruiser. Others opt for guided kayak trips, boating out to a drop-off point for a day trip rather than paddling all the way out from Seward—a rigorous, multiday adventure.

The boat tours range from three-hour loops of Resurrection Bay to day trips lasting nearly ten hours. To fully appreciate the park, choose at least an eight-hour voyage. Those with deep pockets and the desire to roam the park's far reaches can arrange multiday charters. Whichever tour you choose, dress warmly. It'd be a shame to spend your tour holed up belowdecks.

Typical full-day trips start along the western shore of **Resurrection Bay,** where you'll spot eagles, sea otters, and perhaps a passing orca (killer whale). At the mouth of the bay, take note of the murky water—a mix of glacial

silt and abundant phytoplankton, the base of a rich food chain that produces krill and attracts humpback whales.

Farther out lie the **Chiswell Islands,** among the few easily accessible areas of the **Alaska Maritime National Wildlife Refuge** (see pp. 162–163). These grassy sea stacks host a sea lion rookery, as well as kittiwakes, murres, and tufted and horned puffins.

At the far end of the route, boats head up Aialik Bay and Holgate Arm, stopping near the towering face of **Holgate Glacier.** Drifting amid icebergs may seem reward enough for the trek, but everyone is waiting for one more treat. They want to see and hear this tidewater giant calve an ice chunk, sometimes as big as a

house, accompanied by a loud report and huge splash.

The Park by Land

Exit Glacier, the only part of the park accessible by road, is a 12-mile (19 km) drive from Seward. Stop at the Nature Center to learn about the glacier. An easy, half-mile (0.8 km) trail leads to the face of the glacier, but admire it from behind the warning signs—in 1987 a visitor was killed by calving ice.

Consider slogging up the steep **Overlook Loop Trail** a half mile (0.8 km) for a close-up view of the glacier's crevassed north side.

Up close and personal with a glacier at Kenai Fjords National Park

A side trail, on the return trip, follows Exit Creek back to the center. Hardier hikers might tackle the challenging **Harding Icefield Trail,** a 6-mile (10 km) round-trip that gains 3,000 vertical feet (914 m). *(Check with rangers; trail can be snowbound into summer.)* Watch for black bears and mountain goats, and feast on incredible views. ■

Fishing Tales

One summer afternoon, Nevadan Don Hanks was on a charter fishing boat in Kachemak Bay when he felt a powerful tug on his line. When he was done reeling in, he'd landed a behemoth of a halibut. Back on the dock in Homer, the monster weighed in at a whopping 352.6 pounds (159.9 kg).

Anglers fishing for salmon work the upper Kenai River, near Cooper Landing.

That was a happy day for Hanks, and not just because he had a big fish to brag on. It turned out that his halibut was worth $51,298. Even a fish as tasty as halibut isn't normally worth $146 a pound, but Hanks's catch of the day also happened to be the winning entry in Homer's celebrated Jackpot Halibut Derby.

The Homer Jackpot Halibut Derby is just one symptom of the sportfishing madness that grips this state. Residents and visitors alike fish until they drop, from the banks of wilderness rivers above the Arctic Circle to Ship Creek in downtown Anchorage. They fish out of swanky $500-a-day lodges and they fish out of old canvas tents. They fish for grayling, Pacific cod, steelhead, rockfish, Dolly Varden, lake trout, lingcod, whitefish, northern pike, and rainbow trout. But most of all, they fish for halibut and salmon.

The obsession with halibut and salmon is most pronounced on the Kenai Peninsula. Consider that Homer, a gem of a town that had plenty of fine choices for a municipal motto, proudly branded itself "The Halibut Fishing Capital of the World." As you drive along the Homer Spit, you run a gauntlet of charter-fishing offices, each wallpapered with photos of grinning anglers standing beside considerably larger halibut.

The Seward Silver Salmon Derby—one of several on the peninsula and dozens state-wide—epitomizes the lust for Alaska salmon, especially king (chinook), red (sockeye), and silver (coho). The latter is the focal point of the derby, which got started in 1955. Thousands of anglers come to town, jamming the hotels and camping out on the waterfront. They wouldn't think of throwing back the biggest silver salmon—worth $10,000—but $50,000 goes to whomever lands the silver that bears the grand-prize tag. Tags on other released fish correlate to prizes such as a new Ford Explorer and a Hawaiian vacation.

Extensive regulations govern the Seward derby. The last line of the weigh-in rules warns contestants that "any evidence of fish tampering will result in permanent disqualification."

Alaska may be a laissez-faire state, but fish tampering . . . now, that's a serious matter requiring strict regulation.

The most egregious example of Alaska's over-the-top fishing culture is "combat" fishing, which occurs during major salmon runs along easily accessible rivers, most notably the Kenai. Battling for position, plagues of anglers crowd the riverbanks, sometimes literally elbow to elbow. If you're an angler yourself, morbidly curious, or just bored, this is a phenomenon well worth watching. Just don't stand too close to all those folks casting into the river or you may get hooked for real.

EXPERIENCE: Fishing in Great Fish Country

Hundreds of Alaska fishing outfitters will help you hook dinner or a trophy, be you looking for salmon or trout. Some simply take you out in a boat, others are based in lodges and offer packages that include food, shelter, and non-fishing activities. Though these outfitters can be found all over the state, they're especially numerous on the Kenai Peninsula. Here's a sampling of what's on offer:

Afognak Wilderness Lodge *(P.O. Box SYB, Seal Bay, Kodiak, AK 99697, tel 360/799-3250, www.afognaklodge.com)* A classic remote fishing lodge tucked into an island of the Kodiak Archipelago. In addition to the outstanding fresh- and saltwater fishing, guests can look for whales, watch brown bears, and take guided wildlife photography excursions.

Alaska River Adventures *(P.O. Box 725, Cooper Landing, AK 99572, tel 907/595-2000 or 888/836-9027, www.alaskariver adventures.com)* These veteran guides take people down the scenic waters of the upper Kenai and Kasilof Rivers, prime salmon country thronged by kings, reds, and silvers.

Alaska Wilderness Outfitting Co. *(P.O. Box 1516, Cordova, AK 99574, tel 907/424-5552, www.alaskawilderness.com)* Variety is this outfit's hallmark. Guests can chase game fish, and they can do it from a fully staffed fishing camp or lodge, a remote camp or a floating cabin.

The Fish House *(P.O. Box 1209, Seward, AK 99664, tel 907/224-3674 or 800/257-7760, www.thefishhouse.net)* This extensive saltwater fishing operation runs more than 60 boats. They venture into beautiful Resurrection Bay in pursuit of two fabled fish: silver salmon and halibut. These trips often take passengers through Kenai Fjords National Park on the way.

Homer Ocean Charters *(P.O. Box 2543, Homer, AK 99603, tel 907/235-6212 or 800/426-6212, www.homerocean.com)* Homer bills itself as the halibut fishing capital of the world, and it just may rate that title. Anglers frequently pull "barn-door" (more than 200 pounds/91 kg) halibut out of these scenic waters, and Homer Ocean Charters has found more than its share of monster halibut for its clients. They also guide people to king and silver salmon.

Kenai National Wildlife Refuge

It started with moose. To protect these splendid beasts and their habitat, the federal government in 1941 designated a large tract of land as the Kenai National Moose Range. In 1980 the boundaries of this protected area were expanded and the name was changed to the Kenai National Wildlife Refuge. Today the refuge sprawls across nearly 2 million acres (0.8 million ha), encompassing more than half of the Kenai Peninsula.

The Kenai Peninsula's moose are fun to watch, but motorists should beware these big animals lumbering across the roads.

Kenai National Wildlife Refuge

 Map p. 117

✉ Headquarters & Visitor Center, Ski Hill Rd., Soldotna

☎ 907/262-7021

http://kenai.fws.gov

The 1980 changes reflected a sophisticated understanding of ecosystems and a recognition of the need to set aside entire landscapes to protect resident species. In habitats ranging from ice fields to alpine tundra to low-elevation lakes to rivers to spruce-birch forest, this refuge shelters not just moose but wolves, brown and black bears, Dall sheep, sandhill cranes, lynx, wolverines, and trumpeter swans.

Start your visit at the Soldotna **visitor center,** which can be hard to find. At Mile 96.1 of the Sterling Highway, turn onto Funny River Road and immediately turn right on Ski Hill Road, before you reach the RV park or building supply store. Drive 0.8 mile (1.3 km) and you're there. Browse the center's dioramas and wildlife films or take the 0.75-mile (1.2 km) **Keen Eye Trail,** which leads through spruce-birch forest to an observation platform at Headquarters Lake.

The refuge boasts some 4,000 lakes, and countless wetlands, rivers, and creeks. No wonder moose love it and anglers flock here. South of the Sterling Highway, which bisects the refuge, lies a scattering of small lakes amid two big lakes, **Skilak** and **Tustumena**—the latter one of Alaska's largest, at 117 square miles (303 sq km). But true lake country lies north of the highway. All this makes for great canoeing—so great that the **Kenai National Wildlife Refuge Canoe Trail System** has been dubbed a national recreation trail.

This trail consists of two subsystems: The 60-mile-long (97 km) **Swan Lake Canoe Route** links 30-some lakes and is perfect for day trips, while the 80-mile-long (129 km)

Swanson River Canoe Route, which connects 40 lakes and 50 miles (80 km) of river, is better suited to multiday adventures. Here, you'll pass shores lined by spruce and birch where moose feed in the shallows, swans glide by, and loons sound their plaintive calls. Perhaps you'll spot a coyote trotting through a meadow or a river otter snaking down a mudbank. Because this is true wilderness, even day trips require caution and experience. Guided trips are available.

Driving & Hiking

For a drier experience, drive east on the Sterling Highway to Mile 75.5 and the west entrance to the **Skilak Lake Road.** This 19-mile (30 km) gravel road branches off the highway and skirts Skilak Lake, passing through the **Skilak Wildlife Recreation Area,** before rejoining the highway at Mile 58. Views extend beyond the lake to the southern part of the refuge, where the husky Kenai Mountains dominate the horizon. Flowing from those peaks is the Skilak River, fed by the Skilak Glacier, which in turn stems from the Harding Icefield (see pp. 124–125).

Most of the refuge's maintained trails begin at the loop road. **Bear Mountain Trail** is a moderate 1.6 miles (2.5 km)

INSIDER TIP:

Autumn is short but spectacular in Alaska. The colors are a wonderful mosaic of bright colors. The air is clear and crisp, the mosquitoes are gone, and the berry picking wonderful—just watch out for bears!

—PAM GROVES
Professor, University of Alaska

with views of the Kenai Mountains and frequent wildlife sightings. **Hidden Creek Trail,** a fairly difficult 2.6-mile (4 km) round-trip excursion, winds through the scene of the 1996 Hidden Creek Fire; vistas open across Cook Inlet to the volcanoes of the Aleutian Range. ■

Berry Heaven

The Kenai Peninsula is blessed with soaring mountains, prolific salmon runs, sumptuous forests, and a lovely coastline, as well as a diverse abundance of edible berries. Pickers will find some old favorites, such as blueberries and raspberries. They'll find somewhat more exotic species, too, such as high-bush cranberries, currants, and salmonberries. And they'll find species few people have ever heard of, such as nagoonberries, watermelonberries, and cloudberries. To find out when and where to pick, and to make sure you know how to avoid poisonous berries, contact the University of Alaska, Fairbanks, Cooperative Extension Service office in Soldotna (*tel 907/262-5824*).

Kenai & Vicinity

Strategically situated on a bluff above the mouth of the Kenai River, Kenai has long attracted residents and visitors. For centuries the Dena'ina people lived in the area, subsisting as fishers, hunters, trappers, and farmers.

Characteristic onion domes atop the Holy Assumption of the Virgin Mary church testify to Kenai's Russian Orthodox roots, first put down in the late 18th century.

Kenai
🗺 Map p. 117

Visitor Information

✉ Kenai Visitors &
Cultural Center,
11471 Kenai
Spur Hwy. at
Main St.

☎ 907/283-1991

🕐 Closed
Sun. mid-Sept.–
mid-May

www.visitkenai.com

In 1791 Russian fur traders built a fort here, making it the second permanent Russian settlement in Alaska. Just six years later at the Battle of Kenai, the Dena'ina defeated the Russians, and the site declined to the status of a minor trading post.

The Americans built Fort Kenay here in 1869, two years after purchasing Alaska from the Russians. In the 1880s fish canneries put Kenai on the map, and the discovery of major oil and gas fields in Cook Inlet in the 1950s

consolidated Kenai as the largest and most industrial of the peninsula's cities. Still, its population is a mere 7,000, while its scenic setting befits a resort town more than an industrial city.

Visiting the Town
Start at the edge of Old Town Kenai at the **Kenai Visitors & Cultural Center.** The staff at this handsome complex will load you up with tourist information, and the center also serves as a museum. Take time to browse

its excellent collection of native artifacts and items from the Russian and American eras, as well as noteworthy temporary exhibits, such as wildlife art by major American painters.

The center offers a walking-tour map of **Old Town,** which comprises a few blocks between the highway and the mouth of the river. Steer toward the three robin's-egg-blue onion domes atop the **Holy Assumption of the Virgin Mary** Russian Orthodox church. The first church on this site was built by a Russian monk in 1845, the present church in 1894. Tours are available of this domed building, one of the state's oldest Orthodox churches and a national historic landmark. A block away is **St. Nicholas Chapel,** a traditional Orthodox chapel made of logs.

On the fringes of Old Town, off Mission and Riverview Roads, are viewpoints of the river, the canneries, the Kenai Mountains to the east, and Cook Inlet and the Aleutian Range to the west. One of the overlooks features an interpretive sign about beluga whales, which sometimes swim past. Blue-gray when born, belugas are bright white as adults, making them easier to spot. For a closer look at the water, head down Spruce Street to **Kenai Beach Dunes,** a fine beach backed by low sand dunes on the north side of the river mouth.

South of downtown are the **Kenai River Flats,** some 3,000 acres (1,214 ha) of marsh on either side of the Warren Ames Bridge. The flats offer great wildlife-watching, particularly in spring.

A great variety of waterfowl favor the area, notably thousands of snow geese that congregate here in April to feed during their migration to Siberia. In May and early June caribou arrive to calve, and visitors may spot baby caribou testing out their legs. In spring and summer, when the candlefish and salmon are running, harbor seals and belugas swim upriver to feed just off the flats.

INSIDER TIP:

Anchor Point, south of Kenai on the western side of the peninsula, has a great view across Cook Inlet that shows, on a rare clear day, four volcanoes.

—ROWLAND SHELLEY
National Geographic field researcher

Kenai Landing

To experience a fusion of past and present Kenai, drive to Kenai Landing *(2101 Bowpicker Lane, tel 800/478-0400, www .kenailanding.com),* at the end of Cannery Road. Here converted existing cannery buildings create a complex that includes a hotel, restaurant, galleries, theater, museum, indoor warehouse market with dozens of vendors, waterfront promenade, and nature trail. Developers even restored part of the cannery to process sockeye and coho salmon on a small scale, allowing visitors to watch this traditional process—and sample the tasty end product. ■

ear-watching

Ten people stand very quietly on a slope overlooking the river, all eyes on an approaching grizzly. Walking along on all fours, the huge male comes within 100 feet (30.5 m)—much closer than recommended in literature on bear safety, given that a bear can run 100 feet in less than three seconds. For a moment the grizzly pauses right below the group, and then, to the relief of its watchers, it wades into the river, a salmon dinner on its mind.

Before the salmon begin their runs in Alaska rivers, bears often graze on grass.

Other grizzlies (Ursus arctos) are already out in the water, fishing, and the two juveniles in this big male's path aren't about to tangle with him. They move aside. About 50 feet (15 m) from the bank, the dominant bear finds a spot to his liking atop the rim of a six-foot-high (1.8 m) rocky ridge that spans the river, creating a barrier over which migrating salmon must jump. He crouches at the edge of the cascade, facing downstream, and waits. Suddenly, a 10-pound (4.5 kg) coho launches itself over the barrier, but this salmon isn't destined to reach its spawning grounds. With unnerving quickness the grizzly pivots and snatches the fish out of the air. Ripping off strips of flesh, the bear devours the salmon rapidly and readies itself to catch the next unlucky fish.

For hours this group of people watches the big male and the 15 to 20 other grizzlies working this stretch of river. Some of the bears fish below the falls in the shallows, splashing around as they try to pin elusive salmon with their five-inch (13 cm) claws. A sow and her two small cubs lurk around the edges of the prime fishing grounds, looking for opportunities without exposing the cubs to attack. With so many bears in such a small area, disputes are inevitable. Every so often the bears woof and grunt, and occasionally things escalate to roars and bluff charges.

Because these folks are on a reputable, organized bear-watching trip, they aren't taking any greater risk than someone who goes rafting or flightseeing. Were they on their own, it would be foolhardy to get so close, but these excursions operate under tight safety restrictions laid down by the government agency that oversees the public land where the bear-watching takes place. The trips are led by experts who know how to behave around bears and who make sure tour participants follow the rules. And for that rare confrontation, these guides come prepared with guns, pepper spray, or flares, depending on the person and place.

Licensed guides typically schedule bear-watching trips around salmon runs in summer and early fall, when bears predictably congregate. Trips are available at many sites in the southern parts of coastal Alaska.

Homer is the most popular jumping-off point. Bear-watching is especially popular in **Katmai National Park, Tongass National Forest,** and the **McNeil River State Game Sanctuary** (run by the Alaska Department of Fish and Game). There's a lottery system at McNeil River, where reservations can be hard to get, so plan well in advance.

Information about most of the major bear-viewing sites is at *www.alaskacenters.gov;* click on "bear viewing." Be aware that these trips are expensive, but be aware, too, that watching an 800-pound (300 kg) grizzly from 100 feet (30.5 m) is an experience you won't soon forget.

EXPERIENCE: Taking Pictures You'll Be Proud Of

Picture this: You come home after two weeks in Alaska and invite family and friends over to see your photos. The first one is a blurry shot of something big, maybe Mount McKinley. The second shows a mammal but the glare is so bright that you can't tell if it's Uncle Harry or a grizzly bear. The third . . . well, it doesn't matter, because everyone has moved to the family room.

For your next trip to Alaska, you may want to consider going on a nature photography tour. They come in many shapes and sizes, but typically you would join a group of about ten people led by a professional photographer. You would travel through a region of Alaska for a week or so shooting images of moose, calving glaciers, wildflowers, snoozing sea otters, puffin colonies, and the other natural treasures of the Alaska wilds. Your professional guide provides advice ranging from the best shutter stop for capturing a breaching humpback whale to expert knowledge on the feeding habits

of grizzlies so you can nail that shot of a bear snagging a leaping salmon. Two photography guide companies are **Wilkinson Expeditions** *(www.alaskatrips.com)* and **Photo Safaris** *(www.photosafaris.com).* Others abound, but there's no single source for finding them. You'll have to browse the Web and contact local Alaska tourism offices.

Small groups size up the bears at Hallo Bay, in Katmai National Park and Preserve.

Homer

The Homer region has relatively sleepy origins. For millennia native peoples came here in search of shellfish. Russian fur traders also passed through. True settlement only began after the Americans bought Alaska, in 1867, when coal was discovered nearby and railroaded to ships at the end of the Homer Spit.

Fishing boats, water taxis, and tour boats throng the harbor on Homer Spit.

Homer

📍 Map p. 117

Visitor Information

✉ Homer Chamber of Commerce, 201 Sterling Hwy.

☎ 907/235-7740

🕐 Closed Sat.–Sun. Labor Day– Mem. Day

www.homer alaska.org

A community formed around the dock area, but was abandoned in 1907. The coal industry collapsed during the following decade. Homer remained a remote outpost until the Sterling Highway arrived in the early 1950s.

The road initiated Homer's modern phase. Not that a million people flocked here—even today the population is a mere 5,000— but newcomers kept trickling in, and a diverse lot at that: artists, charter boat captains, Russian Old Believers, '60s dropouts, restaurateurs, naturalists, and shopkeepers. Homer richly deserves its reputation as an eclectic town.

This outpost at the end of the road has also attracted travelers, drawn by the magnificent scenery—a gorgeous bay, glaciers, volcanoes, plentiful wildlife, forests, and an enchanting coastline. The town has become a jumping-off point for boat and plane travel into the wilds across Kachemak Bay (see pp. 139–145) and to the far side of Cook Inlet.

Alaska Islands & Ocean Visitor Center

One of Homer's newest and more impressive attractions, the Alaska Islands & Ocean Visitor Center, greets motorists as they enter town along the Sterling Highway. The term "visitor center" is misleading, though, as this elaborate high-tech facility is a natural history and cultural museum, not a place to find out where to get a good seafood dinner. Visitors enter through massive sculpted metal doors with handles shaped like kelp.

The center has a specific mission: to study the **Alaska Maritime National Wildlife Refuge** and share its findings with the public. This unusual refuge comprises a constellation of 2,500 far-flung islands that host marine mammals and some 40 million seabirds—more than in the rest of North America put together. Jump at any opportunity to boat out to one of the refuge islands.

If you miss a boating adventure, at least go to the **Seabird Theater,** near the visitor center entrance—the next best thing to observing a seabird nesting colony on one of the islands. Towering above theatergoers are realistic-looking, guano-stained artificial rocks, inhabited by more than 120 sculpted puffins, auklets, cormorants, and other birds. At the press of a button, the colony seems to spring to life, as huge screens overhead and amid the rocks erupt in a swirl of seabirds, real enough to make you duck. Shrill birdcalls fill the room and you may even catch a whiff of a seabird colony.

Other appealing, often interactive exhibits further explore the natural history of the islands, while several rooms are devoted to humans' ongoing relationship with the refuge. A full-size talking model of an Aleut trapper tells how foxes were introduced to the islands and ended up doing great harm to resident seabirds. In a re-created field biologist's tent, talking figures

INSIDER TIP:

Every port visited by a cruise ship has outfitters offering mountain bike, hiking, and kayak tours. They're often a much better deal than what the ship offers.

—EVERETT POTTER
Writer, National Geographic Traveler *magazine*

of Olaus Murie and other famed early naturalists share tales of their exploration of the refuge.

When you finally emerge from the center, consider a hike along the trails that run from there down through Beluga Slough to **Bishop's Beach,** a nice spot for a stroll during low tide. As you watch for shorebirds, don't neglect the stunning backdrop of mountains that frame the bay. Up the beach on the edge of town is the Bishop's Beach Picnic Area.

Galleries & Museums

In town, but still with a view over Kachemak Bay, is the **Bunnell Street Arts Center.** This nonprofit institution occupies Homer's largest and oldest

Alaska Islands & Ocean Visitor Center

✉ 95 Sterling Hwy.
☎ 907/235-6961
🕐 Closed Sun.– Mon. early Sept.–late May

www.islandsand ocean.org

Bunnell Street Arts Center

✉ 106 W. Bunnell St., Ste. A
☎ 907/235-2662
🕐 Closed Sun. in winter

www.bunnell streetgallery.org

commercial building, the Inlet Trading Post, which used to sell hardware to homesteaders. In the gallery's main room—an airy space with a grand piano—visitors can catch monthly shows, often of a single artist. The emphasis is on cutting-edge contemporary art. In the back room, browsers can contemplate the works of some 60 Alaska artists. The center also offers an array of concerts, workshops, readings, and other events.

work, from grand oil paintings to serigraphs to turn-of-the-20th-century-style engravings. Also look for the unusual, such as wildlife sculpture fashioned out of fossilized whale flipper finger bones and the popular, whimsical work of Don Henry, a local artist whose work is displayed in public venues around town. Henry creates figures, such as an eagle or tree, out of found metal objects—for the most part, old kitchen utensils.

Homer's Pratt Museum highlights the region's human and natural history.

Pioneer Avenue: While considered one of the state's finest galleries, the Bunnell Street gallery faces stiff competition from galleries along Pioneer Avenue, less than a mile uphill (Homer boasts one of the state's leading art communities). The cluster of three shops on East Pioneer between Svedlund Street and Kachemak Way is known as **Gallery Row.** In a light, bright space at 475 East Pioneer Ave., **Fireweed Gallery** (tel 907/235-3411, www.fireweedgallery.com, closed Sun. except in summer) features a wide range of high-end Alaska

Next door to Fireweed, at 471 East Pioneer, is **Ptarmigan Arts** (tel 907/235-5345, www.ptarmiganarts.com), a local artists' cooperative where the variety is dazzling: fiber art, paintings, hats, glass, and ceramics. Across the street, at 448 East Pioneer, is **Picture Alaska Art Gallery** (tel 907/235-2300, www.picture alaska.com), which displays fine art, top-notch crafts, and a collection of 350 vintage photos of Alaska. It also sells art supplies and women's clothing.

Gallery Row and several other galleries celebrate Homer's

passion for the arts on the first Friday evening of every month by opening their doors to showcase new works. Many of the artists are present to discuss their work and, like everyone else, to sample the drinks and hors d'oeuvres.

Pratt Museum: The Pioneer Avenue area is also home to the Pratt Museum, one of Alaska's best small museums, which specializes in the region's natural history, human history, and culture. Start outside in the native plant garden and at the Harrington Cabin.

Inside the museum, just behind the ticket counter, is a large space devoted to temporary exhibitions, which have included animals sculpted from willow twigs and plankton art. The main floor displays artifacts that evoke the lives of natives, homesteaders, and commercial fishers. A video shows native hunters in a kayak stalking a seal. Natural exhibits include a beaked whale skeleton, a beluga whale skeleton, and a summer feed from a live camera mounted on Gull Island. Visitors can pan and zoom the camera for a closer look at this bird colony out in Kachemak Bay. On Tuesdays and Fridays at 4 p.m. visitors can help feed fish and other intertidal critters in the Marine Gallery.

Outdoors Homer

For the best views in Homer, drive (or bike, if you've got strong legs) to the top of the plateau that rises more than 1,000 vertical feet (305 m) above town. To get there, head east on Pioneer Avenue, which soon turns into East End Road. Continue about a mile (1.6 km)

Pratt Museum

✉ 3779 Bartlett St.

☎ 907/235-8635

🕐 Closed Mon. mid-Sept.–mid-May, & Jan.

💲 $$

www.pratt museum.org

EXPERIENCE: An Abundance of Birds

Some visitors to Alaska will be happy if they see a few bald eagles, which are as common as crows in many parts of the state. Other visitors will move heaven and earth to spot a single bristle-thighed curlew, a species rarely seen on this continent and one that obsessed birders come to Alaska in hopes of adding to their North American life lists. Alaska, with some 470 bird species to its name, can satisfy bird-watchers of all levels.

Many tours incorporate bird-watching into their outings. For example, boats taking passengers across Kachemak Bay on the Kenai Peninsula often swing by Gull Island to admire the kittiwakes and puffins. Other tours revolve around birds, such as journeys out to the Pribilof Islands that focus on the millions of nesting seabirds—not that these bird-minded tours won't also check out the Pribilofs' raucous fur seal rookeries.

Alaska celebrates its avian riches with a number of festivals, such as the **Sandhill Crane Festival** every August in Fairbanks, the **Bald Eagle Festival** in Haines in November, and the **Copper River Delta Shorebird Festival** in Cordova in May.

The best single source of birding information in the state is **Audubon Alaska** (tel 907/276-7034, http://ak.audubon.org), in Anchorage. Their office can't accommodate visitors, but they're happy to help bird-seekers over the phone and via the website. They're brimming with avian info, such as birding maps, Listservs that note sightings of rare birds, and birding guidebooks.

Carl E. Wynn Nature Center

☎ Center for Alaskan Coastal Studies: 907/235-6667

🕒 Open daily mid-June–Labor Day; rest of year various days

💲 $$

www.akcoastal
studies.org

out of town to East Hill Road, turn left, and climb steeply until you intersect Skyline Drive. A left turn on the mostly paved road will take you past luxury homes and the magnificent views that lured those home-owners up here.

If you turn right on East Sky-line and drive 1.5 miles (2.4 km), you'll reach the **Carl E. Wynn Nature Center,** affiliated with the Center for Alaskan Coastal Stud-ies. Its 140 acres (57 ha) shelter wildflower meadows, spruce forest, and a migration corridor for moose and black bears. Visitors can solo hike the trails that crisscross the center or join a guided hike.

Finally, don't miss the **Homer Spit,** the literal and figurative end of the road (the Sterling Highway ends at the tip of the spit) where the town began. This legendary 4.5-mile (7 km) sand-and-gravel finger juts southeast midway

across Kachemak Bay. The spit is the heart of Homer, as close to a downtown as Homer comes. In summer it's jammed with cars, trucks, RVs, cyclists, and pedestrians. People come to stroll the beaches, browse the galleries, eat at the restaurants, fly kites, kayak in the bay, knock back a beer at the Salty Dawg, drop a hook in the Fishing Hole, get an ice cream cone, watch the sea otters, camp, or stay at the Land's End Resort.

Most of all, people come for boating, as this is the jumping-off point for commer-cial fishing boats and sportfishing boats are for hire; tour boats, water taxis, and the Alaska state ferry also stop here. Every day hundreds of anglers dreaming of beefy halibut and king salmon clamber aboard dozens of char-ter boats and motor out to the bay and Cook Inlet. Most come back smiling. ∎

Two Kenai Drives

Two especially scenic roads through the Kenai Peninsula showcase the region's spectacular beauty. They both begin along Route 1 in Anchorage, the Seward Highway. Forty miles (64 km) south, the road splits, with Route 1 becoming the Sterling Highway jogging west and south to Kenai, then Homer, and Route 9, maintaining the name Seward Highway, continuing south to Seward.

The **Seward Highway** cuts through the Chugach National Forest, with trails stemming from the road. Near the junc-tion itself is Tern Lake, a favorite for bird-ers. Five miles (8 km) south is Crater Lake Trail, where mountain goats are regularly seen. Farther on is Kenai Lake and beyond

that the placid backwaters of the Snow River, home to beavers and moose.

The **Sterling Highway** is 136 miles (219 km) from the junction and no less dramatic, some of its notables described in the section on the Kenai National Wildlife Refuge (see pp. 128–129). Hikes abound. A good family venture is the 4-mile (7 km) round-trip up the Russian Lakes Trail to the Russian River Falls; in summer you might see sockeye salmon attempting to leap the rapids. Once the highway reaches the Cook Inlet, eyes quickly turn to the mountains beyond, one being Redoubt Volcano, which erupted in 1989–1990. The mountain views, on clear days, last all the way to Homer.

Across Kachemak Bay

This alluring slice of Alaska doesn't have a name, so most people refer to it as "across Kachemak Bay," or simply "across the bay." Broadly, the area includes everything on the 20-by-60-mile (32 by 96 km) protrusion of land at the southwestern tip of the Kenai Peninsula, bounded by Kachemak Bay to the north and the Gulf of Alaska to the south.

The southern and western portions of this area are hard-core wilderness that few people reach, so typically "across Kachemak Bay" means the coastal areas nearer Homer and the closer parts of the Interior within 400,000-acre (162,000 ha) Kachemak Bay State Park.

Even the more accessible area is remote, reachable only by boat or small plane. Civilization is limited to two towns, Seldovia and Halibut Cove, and a sprinkling of houses, cabins, and lodges. Otherwise, the region is a realm of fjords and secluded coves backed by forests and icy mountains.

To reach your destination quickly, or for an overview of the bay, take a small plane. But for a closer look, take a boat. For more information on boat and plane service, contact the Homer Chamber of Commerce *(tel 907/235-7740, www.homeralaska.org)*.

The **Center for Alaskan Coastal Studies** *(tel 907/235-6667, www.akcoastalstudies.org)* offers excellent boat tours with land segments (see pp. 144–145). Several times a week in summer a **state ferry** *(tel 907/465-3941 or 800/642-0066, www.dot.state.ak.us/amhs)* makes the 75-minute run from Homer to **Seldovia,** stays there four hours, then returns to Homer. Several smaller water taxis based in Homer take people to points across the bay. A few

Seldovia's tiny commercial district consists of a handful of businesses, including Herring Bay Mercantile.

fit folks paddle across the bay in kayaks, but it's a long, sometimes rough trip. Far more people contact kayak outfitters across the bay and start from there, skimming along the shore or out to Gull Island for a look at this raucous seabird nesting site.

The most popular vessels are four boats out of Homer that make trips around and across the bay in summer. The **Danny J**

Kenai Peninsula Tourism Marketing Council

  35571 Kenai Spur Hwy., Ste. 205, Soldotna

☎ 907/262-5229 or 800/535-3624

www.kenaipeninsula.org

(tel 907/226-2424, www.halibut-cove-alaska.com, fare), a 29-passenger fishing boat, stops at Halibut Cove twice a day. The noon departure tours around Gull Island, and allows passengers three hours to wander around Halibut Cove. The 5 p.m. departure gives people three hours in town, half of which many folks spend at the famed Saltry restaurant. Central Charters (tel 907/235-7847, www.centralcharter.com) operates the Discovery (fare), which makes a six-hour run to Seldovia, touring the coast and spending about three

---

Wilderness Lodges

Alaska has more than its share of bears, cold, mosquitoes, rain, and other qualities that make camping tough. In other words, there's a market niche for wilderness lodges, and Alaska has hundreds of them. Some are basic, some are luxurious, and many fall in between, but they all provide safety and comfort deep in the wilds. Most also provide expertise, equipment, and guides for outings. A majority are geared mainly to anglers and hunters, but more and more lodges cater to guests who want to go hiking, watch wildlife, and savor the scenery. Several of the state's finest wilderness lodges lie across Kachemak Bay from Homer. Contact the **Homer Chamber of Commerce Visitor Information Center** (tel 907/235-7740, www.homeralaska.org).

---

hours in town. Rainbow Tours (tel 907/235-7272, www.rainbowtours.net) runs the **Rainbow Connection** (fare), a 97-passenger vessel that does a daily seven-hour excursion to Seldovia, taking the scenic and wildlife-rich route down and lingering in town for about three hours. The quickest trip to Seldovia is on the

150-passenger **Kachemak Voyager** (Seldovia Bay Ferry, tel 907/435-3299 or 877/703-3779, www.seldoviabayferry.com, fare), which scoots over from Homer at nearly 30 miles an hour (48 kph).

Halibut Cove

When visitors first cruise into Halibut Cove (population about 50), they quickly realize this is no ordinary remote Alaska village. Passengers can't help but notice that some of the town's dwellings are log mansions, not log cabins. Once ashore, they discover another odd feature: no roads. Not only are there no roads into town, but no roads, period. Residents get around by kayaking or taking a skiff across the lagoon on which the town is centered or by strolling the raised boardwalk that follows the shoreline. Visitors are welcome to wander the dozen blocks of private boardwalk between 1 p.m. and 9 p.m., provided they respect residents' privacy.

The first place most visitors encounter is **The Saltry** (see Travelwise p. 252)—one of Alaska's best restaurants. In the early 1900s three dozen herring salteries operated in Halibut Cove, swelling the town's population to around a thousand. Alas, the salteries overfished the herring, the fishery collapsed, and all the salteries shut down. By the mid-1900s the population could be counted on two hands, but the setting slowly drew artists and a smattering of others back to the cove. Today the town hosts several lodges, bed-and-breakfasts, and cabins; a boatbuilder; commercial fishers; and a Morgan horse farm.

Nearly half of the cove's residents are artists, some quite well known. Visitors can browse their work in the **Experience Fine Art Gallery** (*tel 907/296-2215*), a co-op that shows only local artists. The **Cove Gallery** (*tel 907/296-2207*) is owned by the family of

are only reachable by boat, water taxis often drop off and pick up hikers. A fairly easy, rewarding route is the **Grewingk Glacier Lake Trail,** 3 miles (4.8 km) one way from the Glacier Spit Trailhead to the shore of Grewingk Glacier Lake. You walk along the beach, through forest, and across rocky terrain to the

Kachemak Bay State Park
⛰ Map p. 117
☎ Dept. of Natural Resources: 907/262-5581
www.dnr.alaska.gov/ parks/units/kbay/ kbayl.htm

Wilderness lodges overlook Kachemak Bay's lushly forested south shore.

highly regarded artist Diana Tillion, a beloved Halibut Cove resident who died in 2010. The gallery still displays some of Tillion's innovative paintings, many created with octopus ink, drawn from the creatures with a hypodermic needle. No worries—the octopi weren't harmed and they could regenerate the ink.

Kachemak Bay State Park:
The town of Halibut Cove abuts Kachemak Bay State Park and dozens of miles of developed hiking trails. As most trailheads

lake for a grand view of the glacier. Bring a map and talk to park staffers before setting out. For a stiffer challenge, ask about the **Poot Peak Trail** to the lower summit (*only technical climbers should attempt upper summit*).

Seldovia

The town across Kachemak Bay is Seldovia, a fishing village of about 250 people with maybe another 100 outside of town. Seldovia actually has a few roads, even a paved **Main Street.** On a small hill above Main Street is

Seldovia
⛰ Map p. 117
Visitor Information
☎ 907/234-7612
www.seldovia.com

Black Kittiwake

Bald Eagle

Lynx

Wolves

Orca

Dall Porpoise

Sandhill Crane

Aleutian Tern

Tufted Puffin

Red-faced Cormorant

Common Murre

Sea Otter

Ancient Murrelet

Horned Puffin

Chinook Salmon

Eider Drake

Painted Anemone

Yellow Zoanthid

Painted Star

Orange Ochre Starfish

Sunflower Starfish

Pacific Herring

Residents of Kachemak Bay

Brown Bear

Moose

Harbor Seal

Western Sandpiper

the modest **St. Nicholas** Russian Orthodox church, built in 1891, a reminder that Russian fur traders settled here some 140 years ago. Also on Main Street, across from the harbor, are the small museum and visitor center of the **Seldovia Village Tribe.** At the southern end of Main on Seldovia Slough you can see a remaining section of the old boardwalk that used to rim much of the harbor; much of the town was destroyed by the 1964 earthquake. Along with the arrival of the highway in Homer, the quake knocked Seldovia from its position as the economic powerhouse of lower Cook Inlet, and it has remained sleepy ever since—much to the delight of most of its current residents and visitors.

Behind the school, off Vista Avenue, the well-marked **Otterbahn Trail** leads 1.2 miles (2 km) past a lagoon to **Outside Beach,** a great place to beachcomb while admiring Kachemak Bay and volcanoes across Cook Inlet. Check a tide table before leaving, as access from Outside Beach can be cut off at high tide.

If you have a vehicle, drive out the unpaved **Jakolof Bay Road,** a scenic route that curves east along Kachemak Bay for 13 miles (21 km) before becoming impassable. At Mile 7.5 steps lead down to **McDonald Spit,** a 1.5-mile-long (2.4 km) sandy finger that points into Kachemak Bay and is favored by marine life and birds. Over the last few miles of road you can clamber down to **Jakolof Bay,** known for its fine tide-pooling. ■

Boat Tour on Kachemak Bay

Kachemak Bay and the coastal lands on its south side are wild and vast—it would take a lifetime to know this region intimately. But the staffers at the Center for Alaskan Coastal Studies *(tel 907/235-6667, www.akcoastalstudies.org)* have spent cumulative lifetimes plumbing the mysteries of this place, and through their expertise, they can help day-trippers at least make the area's acquaintance.

Tours of the bay reveal its wildlife, striking scenery, and fascinating natural history.

In summer the center offers a daily tour, the most complete of which is the ten-hour guided combo tour *(fare)*, which includes a boat trip out of Homer, time at the center's field station, a hike, kayaking, and the boat ride back to Homer.

The journey begins in the **harbor** near the end of Homer Spit, amid the hundreds of commercial fishing and sportfishing boats. The no-frills vessels the center uses for its tours are just like the charter boats, only without anglers hankering for halibut. Watch for sea otters as the boat motors out the mouth of the harbor.

You'll reach **Gull Island ①** in just 30 minutes. The boat may spend an equal amount of time slowly circling these few acres of rock, because in the summertime Gull Island hosts thousands of nesting seabirds, including black-legged kittiwakes and common murres, as

NOT TO BE MISSED:

Gull Island • Peterson Bay field station • China Poot Bay

well as tufted and horned puffins, cormorants, guillemots, and gulls.

From Gull Island it's about a mile to the center's **Peterson Bay Coastal Science Field Station ②**, nestled amid spruce on a hill overlooking Peterson Bay. If weather allows, visitors sit on the deck of the log building for a briefing by the naturalist. As much of the hike will involve tide-pooling, the group first visits touch tanks, where you can see and handle such intertidal critters as a fish-eating sea star (starfish), a decorator crab, and a gumboot chiton. Watch for a little while and you'll see slo-mo action, perhaps a sunflower star chasing a sea urchin at a pace approaching that of dripping ketchup.

Hiking & Kayaking

As you begin the **forest hike** , notice yurts scattered around the grounds; some are available for overnight rental. The plant diversity along this trail is high since it marks a transition zone between coastal forest and interior boreal forest. As you near the water, the trail tiptoes through a ghost forest of dead spruce, killed off when the 1964 earthquake dropped the land six feet, allowing seawater to flow into the forest.

The trail emerges on the cobble shore of **China Poot Bay** ❹, where the retreating tide reveals a mysterious world of tide pools. For an hour or two the group peers into crevices and

under rocks, ferreting out such intertidal life as anemones, clams, limpets, yellow snail eggs, and an occasional octopus.

Back at the center, the group gathers for kayak lessons, and after 30 minutes of instruction everyone is ready for the guided paddle. Sometimes tours head out to Gull Island, other times deeper into **Peterson Bay** ❺, where you'll probably spot sea otters and an oyster farm that thrives in these clean, cold waters. After two to three hours, kayakers return to the center's dock, switch to a bigger vessel, and return to Homer.

> 🅰 See also area map p. 117
> ► Homer
> 🕐 10 hours
> ► Homer

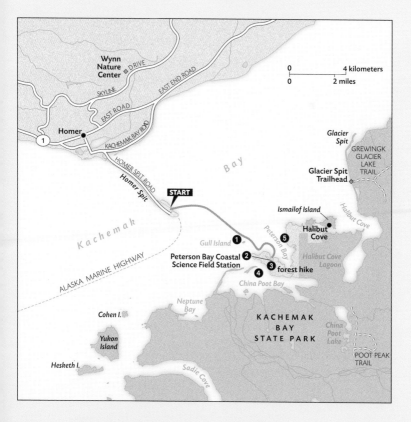

More Places to Visit on the Kenai Peninsula

Mount Iliamna looming over Ninilchik

Cooper Landing

Cooper Landing isn't so much a town as an area. Sure, you'll find lodges, cafés, and shops scattered for several miles along the Sterling Highway, about 10 miles (16 km) west of its junction with the Seward Highway. And you can visit the modest **Cooper Landing Museum,** which covers local human and natural history, and the **K'beq Footprints Heritage Site,** where local Kenaitze Dena'ina offer interpretive walks and display artifacts of their culture. But Cooper Landing is really about Kenai Lake, the upper Kenai River, and the Kenai's confluence with the Russian River, all close by.

Several outfits run guided rafts down the gentle (with a few Class II rapids) upper **Kenai.** Watch for moose, bald eagles, and grizzlies. One outfit offers sea kayak tours of **Kenai Lake.** And a lot of companies take anglers out on the river in drift boats, as its confluence with the **Russian River** is one of the world's great fishing hot spots during summer salmon runs.

This is combat fishing, where boats crowd in and anglers stand elbow to elbow. To reach the fiercest fighting, take the **Russian River Ferry** *(fare),* a cable ferry that crosses to the opposite bank of the Kenai River, world-renowned for its red (sockeye) salmon run.

www.cooperlandingchamber.com A Map p. 117

Visitor Information ✉ Cooper Landing Chamber of Commerce & Visitors Bureau ☎ 907/595-8888

Ninilchik

This small town (pop. 880) sits on the Sterling Highway, where the Ninilchik River flows into Cook Inlet. Anglers come to fish at **Deep Creek State Recreation Area,** where charter boats chase salmon and halibut. Others just poke around the weathered waterfront community, check out historic buildings, or grab seafood at a waterfront café. A highlight is the handsome **Russian Orthodox church,** built in 1900 on a high point above Ninilchik. *www.ninilchikchamber.com* A Map p. 117
Visitor Information ☎ 907/567-3571

INSIDER TIP:

Hike the Grewingk Glacier Lake Trail to the lake formed of glacier melt [see p. 141]. If you want something hardier, hike the ridge trail for a spectacular view of Kachemak Bay and Grewingk Glacier.

—GREGORY WILES
National Geographic field researcher

Resurrection Pass Trail

Running 38 miles (61 km) between Cooper Landing and Hope through part of **Chugach National Forest,** this trail is one of the region's best. Though a two- to four-day trek, it's a relatively easy grade on a well-maintained trail. You'll cross beautiful forest and alpine tundra and maybe see moose, bears, Dall sheep, and mountain goats. Lucky hikers will spot wolves and caribou. Along the way are rental cabins; reserve ahead in summer. *www.fs.usda.gov/chugach* A Map p. 117 ☎ 907/224-3374

A wild, nearly 1,500-mile (2,414 km) arc stretching southwest into the Pacific, home to abundant wildlife and a hardy, intriguing culture

Alaska Peninsula & the Aleutians

Salmon fillets drying in the open air near Lake Clark

a Peninsula & Aleutians

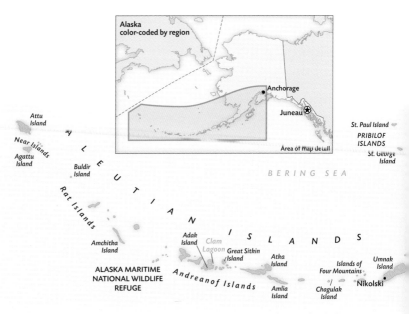

147

...est parts of this rugged, windswept area are just a couple hundred miles from Russia, nearer to Asia than the rest of Alaska. Even the areas closer to the state's more developed areas are, with a few exceptions, wild places rarely touched by human feet. Anyone willing to venture here will find a realm of stark, pristine beauty.

The Alaska Peninsula and the 1,100-mile-long (1,770 km) string of Aleutian Islands follow the westward curving Ring of Fire, a chain of volcanoes that frames most of the North Pacific. This northern arc—the spine of southwestern Alaska—contains more than 60 fire-breathing mountains, many still active. The subduction of the North Pacific plate beneath the North American plate along the 25,000-foot-deep (7,620 m) Aleutian Trench accounts for all the tectonic activity.

Despite the eruptions, earthquakes, and tsunamis generated by these volcanoes, not to mention the frequent cyclonic storms that

blast this region (bring your foul weather gear), life thrives here. Tens of millions of seabirds come to nest; more than half a million northern fulmars rear their young on Chagulak Island (the largest known colony in the world), and miniscule Kaligagan Island hosts more than 100,000 tufted puffins, the state's largest colony. Large mammals, including caribou, arctic foxes, moose, wolves, and, most famously, the huge brown bears of Kodiak Island and Katmai National Park and Preserve, roam the land. The waters host an abundance of large marine mammals, including humpback, beluga, bowhead, and gray

Alaska
color-coded by region

Anchorage

Juneau ✪

Area of map detail

Attu
Island

Near Islands

Agattu
Island

Buldir
Island

St. Paul Island

PRIBILOF
ISLANDS

St. George
Island

BERING SEA

Rat Islands

A L E U T I A N

Amchitka
Island

Adak
Island

Clam
Lagoon

Great Sitkin
Island

Atka
Island

Islands of
Four Mountains

Umnak
Island

ALASKA MARITIME
NATIONAL WILDLIFE
REFUGE

Andreanof Islands

Amlia
Island

Chagulak
Island

Nikolski

I S L A N D S

PACIFIC OCEAN

whales; orcas; northern sea lions; walrus; and sea otters. There are also vast numbers of fish.

The plethora of fish and wildlife long ago attracted the Unangan people, popularly known as Aleut, who settled most of the 200-plus Aleutian Islands, and the Alutiiq people, who mainly came to Kodiak Island and the Alaska Peninsula. They lived off this harsh but rich land for millennia until Russian fur hunters arrived in the 1700s. These trappers devastated both the sea otters and the Unangan, whose population plunged from perhaps 20,000 to maybe a few thousand. The sea otters have largely recovered but the Unangan have not. The number of Aleut stands at roughly 8,000 today and they live on only five islands. Yet the fascinating legacies of both the Unangan and the Alutiiq have survived and can be seen in southwestern Alaska today. The U.S. impact on this area has been felt mostly in two ways: the commercial fishing boom and the little-known but vital World War II battles that were fought in the Aleutians. ■

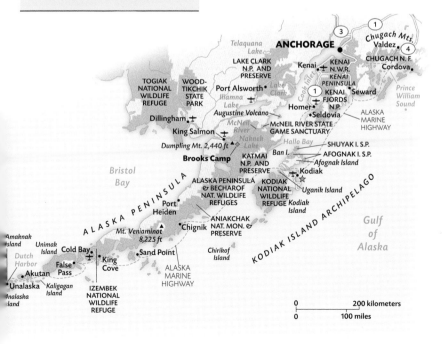

Lake Clark National Park & Preserve

At more than 4 million acres (1.6 million ha), Lake Clark National Park and Preserve is big. It encompasses tremendous diversity, from two 10,000-foot (3,048 m) volcanoes to a coastline dotted with seabirds to dense spruce forests, where wolves and bears roam, to 40-mile-long (64 km) Lake Clark to white-water rivers to an Arctic-tundra-like plateau favored by caribou.

Lake Clark National Park & Preserve

🅰 Map p. 149

✉ Field Head-
quarters,
1 Park Pl.,
Port Alsworth

☎ 907/644-3626
(headquarters)
or
907/781-2218
(Port Alsworth)

www.nps.gov/lacl

Access to the park is primar-ily by chartered aircraft. A few people boat to the coastal sec-tion, but most arrive via float-planes that land on the lakes or in wheeled planes that land on gravel bars or beaches. This wil-derness park demands respect; prepare thoroughly and be sure your skills and fitness are up to the challenging environment, or go with a guide.

Port Alsworth, the little settlement on Lake Clark, is home to the Park Service's field head-quarters. From here, the easy and maintained **Tanalian Falls Trail** passes through a forest of birch and spruce, skirts ponds and bogs,

paces the frothy Tanalian River to Kontrashibuna Lake, and ends 2.5 miles (4 km) later at the waterfall. Keep an eye out for Dall sheep on the high slopes, moose in the ponds, and bears every-where. The **Telaquana Trail** also

INSIDER TIP:

It is no exaggeration to say that you can experience all four of Alaska's seasons in one day, so be sure to pack and dress accordingly.

—EVERETT POTTER
Writer, National Geographic
Traveler *magazine*

A relaxing soak after a long day of hiking in Lake Clark National Park and Preserve

provides an undeveloped route from Lake Clark to Telaquana Lake. If you want to hike else-where, be ready to bushwhack and use a GPS instrument or a map and compass.

Many visitors navigate the park via the water, most often in inflat-able kayaks and canoes, which must be brought in. Paddling any of the long, large, unspoiled lakes—**Turquoise, Twin, Two,** and **Upper** and **Lower Tazimina** to name but a few—is a quintessential Alaska experience. ■

McNeil River State Game Sanctuary

McNeil River is arguably the best spot in the world to watch brown bears. Three factors account for what is possibly the greatest concentration of brown bears on Earth: good salmon runs, an excellent fishing area where low falls and rapids slow the migrating salmon, and the lack of other excellent fishing areas nearby.

Campers find refuge in their tents along the McNeil River.

McNeil River is very difficult to reach, however. Only about 250 permits a year are issued to the area; a lottery decides the winners. If you are one of the lucky few, you must pay several hundred dollars for the permit (for a guaranteed, guided, four-day outing), catch a plane to the sanctuary, bring your own camping gear, and hike 2 miles (3.2 km) to a 10-by-10-foot (3 m by 3 m) gravel pad. Here you stay with ten other visitors and an armed Fish and Game naturalist for six to eight hours, often in the rain and cold.

The rain and the expense are soon forgotten when a thousand-pound (454 kg) boar grizzly lumbers by maybe 75 feet (23 m)

away—and sometimes only a breathtaking 10 feet (3 m) from the pad. Or when a sow and her two rambunctious cubs show up to snag a few fish. You'll typically see several dozen bears in the course of a day. The record for the most in sight at one time is 74, most of them within 200 feet (61 m).

You also will appreciate the scenic sanctuary, lying in the shadow of Augustine Volcano. You'll probably see red foxes, harbor seals, and bald eagles, but the bears are the true attraction.

Incidentally, the safety record is perfect. Since restrictions were applied in the 1970s, no visitor has been mauled or killed and no bears have had to be shot. ■

McNeil River State Game Sanctuary

Map p. 149

Permits: Alaska Dept. of Fish & Game, Wildlife Conservation, McNeil River State Game Sanctuary, 333 Raspberry Rd., Anchorage, AK 99518

☎ 907/267-2189

💲 $$$$$ (non-resident permit) plus application-filing fee & air charter

www.adfg.alaska.gov

Katmai National Park & Preserve

Katmai's nearly 5 million acres (2 million ha) offer enough splendors, get-away-from-it-all tranquillity, and wildlife viewing to satisfy the most demanding lover of the outdoors. But this park has two additional special features: volcanoes and brown bears. Fifteen volcanoes rise in the park, some of them still steaming. In the lands below roam some 1,500 to 2,000 brown bears, one of the continent's largest protected populations of these storied predators.

The isolated beauty of Hallo Bay, on the Katmai coast, entices lovers of wildlife and pristine lands.

Katmai National Park & Preserve

🗺 Map p. 149

Visitor Information

✉ Headquarters, P.O. Box 7, King Salmon, AK 99613

☎ 907/246-3305

www.nps.gov/katm

The only way to reach Katmai is by plane or boat. Most people arrive on scheduled jets from Anchorage, which land in **King Salmon,** a bush town just outside the park's western border that houses park headquarters and a visitor center. From there you take a floatplane *(daily flights June–mid-Sept.)* to Brooks Camp.

Brooks Camp is the national park's hub and a busy place during the summer. It has a visitor center, a lodge (Brooks Lodge, see Travelwise p. 252), a campground, limited food service, equipment rentals, and guide services. Several nice day hikes start in the camp, but even these short hikes require standard wilderness precautions. The summer skies above Katmai are clear and sunny only about 20 percent of the time, and it can drizzle for days, so be prepared. And don't forget those 1,500 brown bears; travelers are strongly urged to attend the park's brief program on bear safety.

The moderate 4-mile (6.4 km) (one-way) trail to the 2,440-foot (744 m) summit of **Dumpling Mountain** starts in the Brooks Camp Campground. An overlook at the 1.5-mile (2.4 km) point provides excellent views of Naknek Lake and distant volcanoes. Forge ahead and you'll enjoy dense forest, alpine meadows, and even finer vistas from the top. Ranger naturalists also lead guided hikes out of Brooks Camp.

Three Forks Overlook

Every visitor to Katmai should take the eight-hour round-trip park bus tour along the 23-mile (37 km) dirt road to the **Three Forks Overlook** above the **Valley of Ten Thousand Smokes** (*reservations recommended July–Aug.*). This broad valley was devastated by the 1912 eruption of Novarupta Volcano (see sidebar this page), which buried the previously verdant landscape under as much as 700 feet (213.5 m) of

volcanic debris—ash, pumice, and rock. Robert Griggs, who stood above the valley in 1916 and beheld the innumerable steam vents, wrote "the whole

INSIDER TIP:

Pack a small pair of binoculars; you'll find yourself using them every day to spot wildlife.

—EVERETT POTTER
Writer, National Geographic Traveler *magazine*

valley as far as the eye could reach was full of hundreds, no thousands—literally tens of thousands—of smokes curling up from its fissured floor." Thus, the valley's name. The smoke is gone now, but the moonscape remains.

Hardy hikers can tackle the steep, strenuous 1.5-mile (2.4 km; one-way) **Ukak Falls Trail** from the overlook down to and across the valley floor, where the turbulent **Ukak River** network has carved deep gorges in the packed ash. The **Three**

A Rain of Ash

In June 1912, in an event that lasted several days, Novarupta Volcano exploded with a fury ten times more powerful than the 1980 eruption of Mount St. Helens. Gas, pumice, and ash belched from the belly of the earth and darkened the sky over most of the Northern Hemisphere. More chilling than any facts is the first-person account of an Aleut fisherman trapped in the vicinity: "We are waiting for death at any moment. We are covered with ashes, in some places ten feet and six feet deep. Night and day we light lamps. We cannot see the daylight . . . and we have no water. All the rivers are . . . just ashes mixed with water. Here are darkness and hell, thunder and noise. It is terrible. We are praying."

Forks Convergence area, where the Ukak and its tributaries meet, is particularly scenic.

Bear Viewing

No visitor to Katmai should miss watching brown bears snag migrating salmon at **Brooks Falls,** a half-mile (0.8 km) hike from Brooks Camp. Across a floating bridge, two elevated viewing platforms enable visitors to safely observe bears fishing from as close as

20 feet (6 m). During peak season—especially during the July sockeye run—space on the platform is at a premium; rangers limit each person to an hour, and visitors sometimes wait to get on the platforms. A third

viewing platform is located at the mouth of the Brooks River.

There's no crowd problem at **Hallo Bay** on Katmai's coast. Since 1994 **Hallo Bay Bear Camp** *(tel 907/235-2237 or 888/535-2237, www.hallobay.com,*

INSIDER TIP:

When coming to Katmai National Park and Preserve, make reservations first, then prepare. There is no cell phone or telephone service; bring water and food, and warm clothes because it can snow in July.

—KATHY SPANGLER
Former ranger, Katmai NP&P

5-hour to 7-day trips May–Sept., $$$$$) has brought eight to ten guests at a time to its remote camp to walk among the bears. No platforms, no shotguns. A guide simply takes four or five people out to mingle with the bears. Safety comes from the guide's long experience and understanding of bear behavior, the detailed instruction you receive, and the operation's scrupulous efforts to keep bears from becoming human oriented—and, as a last resort, flares. In 18 years there has never been a bear attack and flares have only been used four times. Seeing brown bears just 50 feet away in an utterly wild setting really is a sublime experience. ∎

EXPERIENCE: Alpine Flora

Alaska may be a land of mountains and glaciers, but in spring and early summer it is also a land of flowers. Many bloom in May, and blossoms abound in the fields and wetlands into July. Whole fields can be covered with wildflowers flouting their colors and swaying in the breezes. In their brilliant season they represent Alaska's vast vegetation that sustains the state's astounding animal life.

The state flower is the sky blue alpine forget-me-not, which grows to a foot high in alpine meadows, blooming mainly from late June to late July. Other notables are the wild iris, the late summer Douglas aster, and the bright pink salmonberry.

A good way to experience Alaska flora is to contact the **Alaska Botanical Garden** in Anchorage *(tel 907/770-3692, www.alaskabg.org).* It has numerous gardens and educational programs.

Birding on Attu Island

Eurasian siskin. Siberian blue robin. Oriental turtle dove. Asian brown flycatcher. The avid birder who sees that roll call of species immediately envisions a magical place: Attu, the westernmost island in the Aleutians, 1,000 miles (1,600 km) from mainland Alaska and continental North America.

The recognizable horned puffin, a frequent visitor to Attu, delights bird-watchers.

Attu is hallowed ground for birders: It is one of the best places to spot birds that can be added to a North American life list. In order for a bird to be placed on the list, it must be spotted in North America, and according to the boundaries drawn by the American Birding Association, Attu is in North America (but it's very close to Asia).

So, if a Eurasian siskin is spotted on Attu, it can go on the list. If the bird is spotted in Asia, where it is quite common, it can't go on the list. That's the primary reason people are willing to brave the often miserable weather and spend thousands of dollars to get to Attu to view bird species that they could much more easily and cheaply see in Asia. Between the storms that blow Asian species onto Attu and migration routes that pass over the island, 30 to 35 Asian species are often sighted in a typical two- to four-week season.

A few pioneering birders began going to Attu in 1977, and organized birding trips soon followed. They landed at an airstrip left over from World War II and set up camp on the southeastern part of the island. During the day, the birders would fan out to the coast, tundra, bay, freshwater marsh, and other habitats. Then they'd wait. When a rarity was spotted, word went out over the group's radios and other birders rushed to the site. From the years 1977 to 2000, more than a thousand birders made the trip to Attu.

Since 2000, Attu is only accessible by boat— and finding a boat to handle the stormy North Pacific isn't easy. Zugunruhe Birding Tours (*www.zbirdtours.com*) goes to Attu most years. You can also sign on to their Attu trips through Bird Treks (*tel 717/548-3303, www.birdtreks.com*) and Wildside Nature Tours (*tel 888/875-9453, www.wildsidenaturetours.com*).

Kodiak Island Archipelago

The 16 major islands and many smaller ones of the Kodiak Island archipelago sprawl across the Gulf of Alaska for 177 miles. Kodiak Island accounts for nearly three-quarters of the archipelago's dry land; it's the second largest island in the U.S. (Hawaii's Big Island is larger). Though this wild and windswept island realm is most famous for its numerous hulking brown bears, ironically it is also the most accessible and developed part of southwestern Alaska.

A thick understory of devil's club carpets the rain forest.

Kodiak Island

🄼 Map p. 149

Visitor Information

✉ Kodiak Island Convention & Visitors Bureau, 100 Marine Way, Suite 200, Kodiak

☎ 907/486-4782 or 800/789-4782

🕐 Open Mon.–Fri., occasional weekends

www.kodiak.org

Kodiak Island

The commercial fishing center of **Kodiak** (pop. 6,200) is by far the largest city in the archipelago (and the entire southwest of Alaska, for that matter); travelers can get here via jet flights or the state ferry. About 100 miles (160 km) of scenic gravel roads fan out from Kodiak, making up the only road system in the region.

Begin your tour down on the docks. The *Star of Kodiak,* the last Liberty Ship built during World War II, sits moored near the visitor center. After a 1964 tsunami wiped out much of downtown and several

canneries, the mothballed ship was towed up to Kodiak to serve as a fish-processing plant. It's now the home of a seafood corporation.

Kodiak's extensive Russian past is on display at the **Baranov Museum,** a bit down from the Liberty Ship. The oldest Russian building in the United States, it was built in 1808 by the Russian-American Company to store sea otter pelts. Inside is a wealth of artifacts from the Russian era, including some dazzling Easter eggs.

The Russian influence is further evident a block away at the **Holy Resurrection** Russian Orthodox church *(385 Kashavarof St., tel 907/ 486-3854, tours available),* the third Orthodox church built on this site; the first was in 1794. From the blue cupolas to the ornate interior, this 1945 structure is a visual feast. Continue northeast and you'll come to a lovely chapel and **St. Herman Theological Seminary** *(414 Mission Rd., tel 907/486-3524),* one of only three Russian Orthodox seminaries in the United States.

The new **Kodiak National Wildlife Refuge Visitor Center** is as much a museum as a place to ask questions about the refuge. Stand beside the model of a looming male brown bear and imagine bumping into a real one in the wild.

The history of native life in the archipelago is full and rich as well; the Alutiiq have lived here for more than 7,500 years. The **Alutiiq Museum and Archaeological Repository** *(215 Mission Rd., tel 907/486-7004)* houses more than 100,000 artifacts that evoke the lives of the Alutiiq and other Eskimos, though only a modest portion of the vast collection is displayed. Meander past seal-gut parkas, ceremonial masks, harpoons, fine woven baskets, and much more.

To sample some recent history, drive northeast on Rezanof Drive (which turns into Monashka Bay Road) and go almost 4 miles (6.4 km) to **Fort Abercrombie State Historical Park** *(1400 Abercrombie Dr., tel 907/486-6339).* The old concrete bunkers of this World War II–vintage artillery emplacement facing the ocean are interesting, but the views of the sea and the sightings of sea otters, puffins, whales, and other wildlife keep most people enthralled.

Kodiak National Wildlife Refuge

The 1.9 million roadless acres (800,000 ha) of Kodiak National Wildlife Refuge occupy the southwest two-thirds of Kodiak Island, all of **Uganik** and **Ban Islands,** and a chunk of **Afognak Island.** The 3,000-plus resident brown bears are a subspecies, Kodiak brown bears. Guides and air taxis take visitors to view bears on the refuge; they're easy to find in summer when the salmon runs are peaking. But look beyond the bears: The refuge is a scenic blend of mountains, tundra, deep fjords, and much more wildlife.

INSIDER TIP:

Kodiak Island is gorgeous. The town is nice and the fishing outstanding. If you rent a car, ask that yours be cleaned of fish remains.

—DAVID GRIMALDI
National Geographic field researcher

Shuyak Island & Afognak Island State Parks

The archipelago's outer islands include two stunning parks, 47,000-acre (19,000 ha) Shuyak Island State Park and 75,000-acre (30,000 ha) Afognak Island State Park. If you prefer the comforts of home, **Afognak Wilderness Lodge** *(tel 360/799-3250, www.afognaklodge.com)* is located in Afognak and affords great marine mammal sightings. ∎

Baranov Museum
- ✉ 101 Marine Way, Kodiak
- ☎ 907/486-5920
- 🕐 Closed Sun– Mon. except in summer & all Feb.
- 💲 $
- **www.baranov.us**

Kodiak National Wildlife Refuge Visitor Center
- ✉ 402 Center Ave., Kodiak
- ☎ 907/487-2626
- 🕐 Closed Sun.– Mon. except summer
- **www.fws.gov/ refuge/kodiak**

Kodiak National Wildlife Refuge
- 🅰 Map p. 149
- ✉ 1390 Buskin River Rd., Kodiak
- ☎ 907/487-2600
- **www.fws.gov/ refuge/kodiak**

Shuyak Island & Afognak Island State Parks
- 🅰 Map p. 149
- ✉ 1400 Abercrombie Dr., Kodiak
- ☎ 907/486-6339
- **www.dnr.alaska.gov/ parks/units/kodiak**

Kodiak's Chiniak Highway

This route traces the scenic northeastern shore of Kodiak Island, slaloming around three deep bays before swinging east to end at Cape Chiniak and Cape Greville. It passes through a variety of landscapes, including temperate rain forest, alpine meadows flush with wildflowers in the spring and summer, rolling tundra, stands of alder and cottonwood, and coastlines subject to pounding waves and turbulent tides.

The back roads of Kodiak beckon visitors to explore and experience the island's beauty.

Motorists also will encounter bits of rural Alaska amid the wilderness, such as a roadhouse, a winery, and, incongruously, some cattle and bison ranches. The first 12.8 miles (20.6 km) of the highway are paved; the last 30 (48 km) are decent gravel.

The drive begins at the corner of Marine Way and Rezanof Drive in **Kodiak ❶** *(visitor information, Kodiak Island Convention & Visitors Bureau; see p. 156)*. Head southwest on Rezanof, which soon turns into the Chiniak Highway. At Mile 2.4, enjoy the panorama that opens up at **Deadman's Curve** of Kodiak Harbor, Chiniak Bay, and some of the archipelago's many islands.

Back on the highway, turn left at Mile 4.4 into the **Buskin River State Recreation Site ❷** *(tel 907/486-6339, www.dnr.alaska.gov/parks/ units/kodiak/buskin.htm)*. This is the most popular fishing site on Kodiak Island's road system; big runs of sockeye and silver salmon migrate

up the river in summer. Beachcombers will see plenty of bald eagles, too, swooping down to get their share of the salmon.

INSIDER TIP:

When you stay on Kodiak Island, rise early and grab a harborside seat at the local coffee hangout. Sip leisurely and enjoy the comings and goings of the local fishing boats setting out for their day's work on the fishing grounds.

—SARAH ROESKE
National Geographic field researcher

About half a mile (0.8 km) farther down is the turnoff for **Anton Larsen Bay Road,** a 11.7-mile (18.8 km) spur that leads north past the island's golf course and along the western shore of **Anton Larsen Bay,** a pretty fjord with a large island at its mouth. At Mile 6.6 on the highway you'll see the largest U.S. Coast Guard station in America; more than a thousand people work here. A quarter mile (0.4 km) past the station's entrance the highway comes to **Womens Bay ❸,** which the road skirts for

---

NOT TO BE MISSED:

Kodiak town • Buskin River State Recreation Site • Pasagshak Bay Road

---

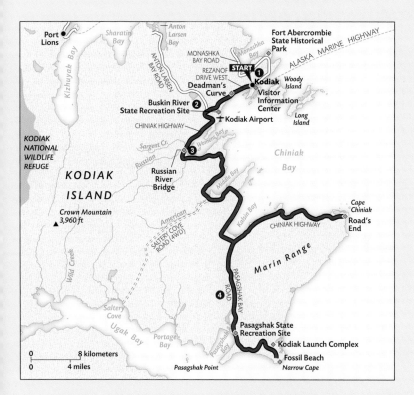

several miles. The bay was so named because Alutiiq women favored the location as a place to hunt, fish, and gather food.

At the head of the bay, near Mile 10, the highway bridges the mouth of **Sargent Creek,** where in the fall emperor geese fly in to spend their winter. A quarter mile (0.4 km) later, if in August and September, stand on the **Russian River Bridge** to watch spawning salmon. The wildlife theme continues from about Mile 19 to Mile 21.5, where eagles and the occasional eagle nest can be seen among the cottonwood trees along **Middle Bay.**

Rockets & Fossils

The route's major junction occurs at Mile 30.6, where the **Pasagshak Bay Road ❹** cuts due south for 16.5 miles (26.5 km). This road leads to two unusual sites for rural Alaska. First, the Kodiak Launch Complex, a

🅼	See also area map p. 149
▶	Kodiak
↔	85.6 miles (138 km), out and back, not counting spur roads
🕐	4 hours plus stops
▶	Kodiak

state-of-the-art private aerospace facility that launches rockets for commercial and military interests *(site closed to the general public).* Secondly you'll find **Fossil Beach,** where rocks contain fossilized seashells.

Retrace your route back north up to the junction with the Chiniak Highway. This time head east along the shore of Chiniak Bay. If the weather is clear, keep an eye out for commercial fishing vessels coming and going between Kodiak and the rich but dangerous fishing grounds in the Gulf of Alaska. The road ends at, well, Road's End.

Aleutian Islands

A submerged volcanic mountain range rises out of the North Pacific to form the Aleutian Islands, a string of more than 200 islands and tiny islets in a 1,100-mile (1,770 km) arc that curves west toward Russia and Japan from the tip of the Alaska Peninsula.

Standing near Unalaska's Russian Orthodox Church of the Holy Ascension, a crabber in seagoing gear shows off his catch.

Unalaska Island

🅜 Map p. 149

Visitor Information

✉ Unalaska/Port of Dutch Harbor Conv. & Visitors Bureau, 15 S. Fifth St.

☎ 907/581-2612 or 877/581-2612

🕐 Closed Sat.–Sun.

www.unalaska.info

The confluence of the mild Kuroshio, or Japan Current, and the frigid Bering Sea creates a great deal of rain, wind, and storms, which, along with the isolation, may account for the fact that only 8,000 people live in the Aleutians. More than half live on Unalaska Island.

The town of Unalaska on Unalaska Island is the hub of Aleutian life. Fewer than ten of the Aleutians are populated, even by tiny villages. Many islands are part of the **Alaska Maritime National Wildlife Refuge** (see pp. 162–163) and brim with seabirds and marine mammals.

From late April through September the state ferry makes a twice-monthly visit to Unalaska

and provides the least expensive way to get an extensive look at the Aleutians. Passengers can board in Kodiak (or from Homer or Seldovia on the Kenai Peninsula) and spend several days cruising down the Alaska Peninsula and out the Aleutians as far as Unalaska. You'll see sea otters, sea lions, harbor seals, porpoises, and whales. Scan the rocky coastline and islands for the dozens of species of seabirds. Or just sit back and drink in the misty headlands, barrel-chested cliffs, tundra-greened islands, and volcanic cones—assuming you're not awash in fog. Once in Unalaska you can look around town for about 5.5 hours before the ferry heads back north, or stay for a while and then fly out.

Unalaska Island

Many people refer to the town of **Unalaska** as "Dutch Harbor," but Dutch Harbor is actually only the name of the harbor. Though the town's permanent population is about 4,300, there are probably twice that many during the peak fishing season, roughly November to April, when transient fishermen and cannery workers arrive. The town actually straddles two islands: Unalaska and close neighbor Amaknak; they're connected by a 500-foot (152.4 m) span officially called the Bridge to the Other Side.

For an overview, start at the impressive **Museum of the Aleutians** on Salmon Way. This 9,250-square-foot (859 sq m) facility covers the islands' native culture, the Russian era, and the Aleutian campaign during World War II. There are 25 known Unangan prehistoric village sites within 3 miles (4.8 km) of the museum; the oldest, **Unalaska Bar,** dates back 9,000 years, making it one of the oldest sites in Alaska.

Unalaska's downtown national historic landmark and the outstanding symbol of the Russian era is the Russian Orthodox **Church of the Holy Ascension.** The current wooden church topped by two blue cupolas was completed in 1895, but the first church on this site dates to 1825. Inside is a superb collection of hundreds of significant icons, artworks, and artifacts.

More recent history is evident at the **Aleutian World War II National Historic Area.** It's a little-known fact that a bloody battle of the Pacific Theater was fought between Allied forces and the Japanese on Attu, the westernmost Aleutian island. A World War II–era building near the airport harbors a visitor center museum where you can learn about this year-long struggle that began with the bombing of Unalaska. Stroll the grounds of Fort Schwatka, the coastal defensive post on Amaknak Island, and note the **S.S. Northwestern,** which lies half submerged in nearby Captain's Bay.

Visiting Other Islands

The nearby islands offer an amazing wealth of birding, fishing, hiking, whale-watching, and other leisure opportunities. Contact the Unalaska visitors bureau for information on tour and charter-boat operators or how to get around on your own. ∎

Museum of the Aleutians

- ✉ 314 Salmon Way, Unalaska
- ☎ 907/581-5150
- 🕓 Closed Mon. in summer, & Sun.–Mon. rest of year
- 💲 $
- www.aleutians.org

Aleutian World War II National Historic Area

- ✉ Visitor center, near Unalaska airport
- ☎ 907/581-9944
- 🕓 Closed Sun.–Mon. except in summer
- www.nps.gov/aleu

Halibut Fever

Every summer halibut fever rages across Alaska. Small halibut are the tastiest, but many anglers lust for the trophy fish—a desire whose flame is fanned by halibut derbies, where the largest fish of the season earns thousands of dollars. The world-record specimen until 2010 was caught near Dutch Harbor and weighed 459 pounds (208 kg). And the previous record halibut before that was a 395-pounder (179 kg) also hooked around Dutch Harbor, but that angler, Mike Golat, almost lost the record. Rules declare that the halibut has to be gaffed—landed with a hook—not shot, but gaffing and hefting a fish that size into Golat's little skiff would have swamped it. So, quick-thinking Golat landed the fish by towing it to shore.

Alaska Maritime National Wildlife Refuge

The 3.4-million-acre (1.4 million ha) Alaska Maritime National Wildlife Refuge consists of more than 2,500 islands, reefs, islets, spires, and coastal stretches scattered all around Alaska. The bulk of the refuge, however, lies along the Alaska Peninsula and in the Kodiak archipelago, the Pribilof Islands, and, especially, the Aleutians.

Hundreds of thousands of fur seals breed on the Pribilof Islands.

Alaska Maritime National Wildlife Refuge

🄰 Map pp. 148–149

✉ Alaska Islands & Ocean Visitor Center, 95 Sterling Hwy., Homer

☎ 907/235-6961

🕐 Closed Sun.– Mon. early Sept.–late May

http://alaska maritime.fws.gov

www.islandsand ocean.org

Most of the units in the refuge are difficult and expensive to reach, involving the chartering of small planes and boats. But there are three sites in south-western Alaska where a relatively modest outlay of money can bring you face-to-face with this striking refuge. You'll be treated to breathtaking landscapes and an astonishing wealth of wildlife, notably millions of seabirds and many species of marine mammals.

Kodiak to Unalaska

The Alaska Marine Highway state ferry *Tustumena* (see Travelwise p. 235) departs Homer and Seldovia *(every two weeks April– Sept.)* for Kodiak and then heads out along the Alaska Peninsula and down the Aleutians as far as Unalaska, passing many refuge holdings on the way. During the summer, refuge naturalists travel on the *Tustumena;* they give pre-sentations and answer questions.

The voyage takes several days and the seas can be rough, but a passenger without a vehicle and no cabin can sometimes get a ticket from Homer to Unalaska for a few hundred dollars. You'll probably want to take a plane back, but it's still a bargain. Once in Unalaska you can go out to nearby parts of the refuge with one of the town's many tour operators *(contact Unalaska/Port of Dutch Harbor Convention & Visitors Bureau; see p. 160).*

Adak Island

Lying 350 miles (563 km) west of Unalaska, half of Adak Island is a wilderness section of the maritime refuge. This exceedingly remote place is accessible by twice-weekly flights from Anchorage and by roads and trails established when Adak was home to a big naval base and a city of 6,000 people. The base closed in 1997 and now maybe 80 people live there, giving it a ghost-town feel. Stop at the refuge headquarters in town to find out how to explore this starkly beautiful place, with its 2,000-foot (609 m) sea cliffs and mountains.

Don't miss the 6-mile (9.6 km) **wildlife drive** around pretty **Clam Lagoon,** where you should spot sea otters, seals, and all sorts of birds, including sought-after Asian rarities (see p. 155). At **Finger Bay,** a dramatic, fjord-like cut in the island, you can take an easy, 1-mile (1.6 km) hike up to and along **Lake Betty.** Right outside of town are the black sands of **Kuluk Bay beach,** a good place to watch seabirds and, if it's clear, to gaze 20 miles (32 km) across the water to the 5,704-foot (1,739 m) volcano that is Great Sitkin Island.

St. Paul Island

To go from remote to even more remote, head about 200 miles (321 km) north of the Aleutians into the Bering Sea to the **Pribilof Islands,** the biggest of which, **St. Paul,** is about 8 by 14 miles (13 by 22.5 km). PenAir *(tel 800/448-4226, www .penair.com)* flies from Anchorage to St. Paul four or five times a week. Almost all visitors go on a package tour through St. Paul Island Tours *(tel 877/424-5637, www.alaskabirding.com),* an outfit run by the Unangan (Aleut) people, who make up almost the entire population (a scant 700 or so) of the Pribilofs (the largest Aleut population in the world). All visitors stay at the King Eider Hotel; there are no other lodgings and no camping.

INSIDER TIP:

Planning on heading to the coast? The good news here is, there's less need for insect repellent; mosquitoes don't handle salty water well.

—SARAH ROESKE
National Geographic field researcher

The knowledgeable guides show you blue arctic foxes, reindeer, nesting puffins, and other seabirds, but most of all they take you to the fur seal rookeries. About 800,000 of these husky seals come to the Pribilofs every summer to breed—the largest such gathering in the world. From observation blinds you can watch mothers nursing pups, males fighting over females, and all the rest of this raucous scene. ∎

Adak Island

🅰 Map p. 148

✉ Aleutian Islands Unit NWR, 146B Seawall Rd., Adak

☎ 907/592-2406 (summer) or 907/235-6546 (rest of year)

http://alaska maritime.fws.gov

More Places to Visit on the Alaska Peninsula & the Aleutians

Alaska Peninsula & Becharof National Wildlife Refuges

These neighboring refuges on the Alaska Peninsula, administered as a single unit, more than live up to their status as a refuge for wildlife. Sea otters, falcons, moose, sea lions, wolves, waterfowl: The diversity and numbers are staggering. A 10,000-head barren-ground caribou herd spends much of its year in these refuges. Most of the salmon that constitute the Bristol Bay fishery, the richest salmon fishery in the world, spawn in streams that originate on refuge lands. And the numbers and size of the brown bears are legendary.

The combined 5.5 million acres (2.2 million ha) of these refuges also contain smoldering volcanoes, the second biggest lake in Alaska, rugged coastline, windswept tundra, and rushing rivers, as well as some unusual geological features. At **Gas Rocks,** near Mount Peulik, underground gases seep through cracks in the granite. About a mile away stand the otherworldly **Ukinrek Maars**—rounded craters created in 1977 during a series of eruptions. **Castle Cape Fjords** is a jumble of rock spires composed of light and dark layers so distinctive that sailors use them as a navigational aid.

Despite their myriad attractions, the refuges are little visited. They are challenging to reach, hard to get around in, completely undeveloped, and the weather is mercurial. Staff at the refuges' **King Salmon Visitor Center** can suggest ways to visit. **King Salmon,** though a town of only 400, offers a fair selection of lodging, stores, and restaurants (and several bars), as it's the main gateway to the Alaska Peninsula.
http://becharof.fws.gov or *http://alaskapeninsula.fws.gov* Map p. 149 King Salmon Visitor Center, King Salmon airport 907/246-4250 (visitor center)

Izembek National Wildlife Refuge

Izembek is indeed a haven for a lavish assortment of wildlife. Gray and minke whales cruise nearshore waters; sea otters, sea lions, and seals inhabit the coastline and nearby islands; salmon galore spawn in Izembek streams; caribou herds migrate through in fall, with hungry wolves in tow; and brown bears mass to gorge on the salmon. But Izembek is most famous for the enormous flocks of migrating waterfowl and other birds that come to feed on some of the world's largest eelgrass beds, found in 150-square-mile (388.5 sq km) **Izembek Lagoon.**

Izembek is reasonably accessible. Scheduled flights and the state ferry go to **Cold Bay,** a small town beside the refuge that has some visitor facilities and the refuge headquarters. If you rent or bring a car, you can bounce around the 40 miles (64 km) of gravel roads that fan out into parts of the 417,533-acre (169,000 ha) refuge.
http://izembek.fws.gov Map p. 149 907/532-2445 or 877/837-6332

Leftovers at Unimak's World War II airfield, the first for wheeled aircraft in the Aleutians

Sparsely settled, and renowned for two premier wild places—Prince William Sound and Wrangell–St. Elias National Park and Preserve

Prince William Sound & Around

Bush planes take visitors on flight-seeing excursions or drop them at wilderness campsites.

Prince William Sound & Around

This swath of south-central Alaska encompasses a striking blend of land and sea. The land is a vast and diverse expanse of spruce lowlands, rain forest, majestic rivers, and high country rife with towering peaks and massive glaciers; it supports plentiful wildlife.

Land meets sea at Prince William Sound, a roughly 30-by-70-mile (48 by 112 km) offshoot of the Gulf of Alaska. The sound is a wonderfully irregular world of lushly forested islands, fjords that slash deep into the mainland, jagged peninsulas, and deep waters teeming with life.

Humans have lived off the bounty of land and sea in this region for millennia. The 13.2 million acres (5.3 million ha) of Wrangell–

St. Elias National Park and Preserve were and still are home to the Ahtna, an interior Athabaskan people. Prince William Sound lies in the traditional territory of the Alutiiq, the coastal dwellers whose strongholds were on Kodiak Island and the Alaska Peninsula to the southwest. The Eyak, a small indigenous group, live around the Copper River Delta, with one foot in the Wrangell–St. Elias area and one in Prince William Sound.

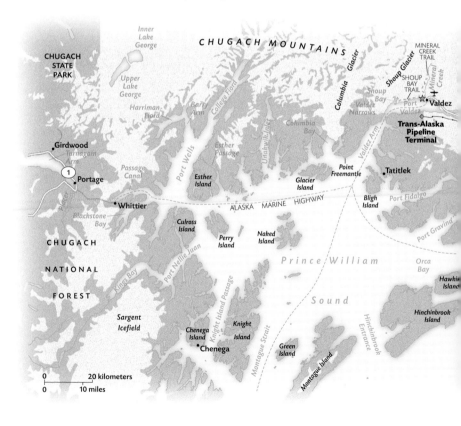

Recent History

Europeans arrived in 1778, when Captain Cook sailed into the sound, which he dubbed Sandwich Sound. By the time Cook's expedition got back to England the Earl of Sandwich (Cook's patron) had fallen into disrepute, and the editors of Cook's maps changed the name to honor the king's third son, who later became King William IV. The major influx of outsiders occurred in the late 1890s, when the Klondike gold rush brought fortune seekers into the Port of Valdez and north through what is now the Wrangell–St. Elias area. But copper had a more lasting impact on Wrangell–St. Elias. From 1906 to 1938 the Kennecott Mines Company operated in what is now the park; at one point it was the richest copper mine in the world.

Prince William Sound has also gained a place in history. The 1964 Good Friday

NOT TO BE MISSED:

The intricate walrus ivory carvings in the Whitney Museum **169**

Driving through the remote, wildlife-rich Copper River Delta **172–173**

Paddling a sea kayak on a trip out of Valdez and Cordova **174–175**

A boat ride amid the icebergs up to the Columbia Glacier **175**

Flightseeing over Wrangell–St. Elias National Park and Preserve **179**

Backcountry hiking and camping in Wrangell–St. Elias National Park and Preserve **179**

Touring the old copper mining compound at Kennecott Mines National Historic Landmark **185**

Hiking on the Root and Kennicott Glaciers **185**

earthquake, the most violent quake ever recorded in North America, had its epicenter here. The shock waves and tsunamis that followed pounded the area, leveling the city of Valdez, which was rebuilt later on higher ground 4 miles (6.4 km) from its original site. And on March 24, 1989, coincidentally also Good Friday, the oil tanker *Exxon Valdez* ran aground and spilled 10.8 million gallons (41 million liters) of crude into the sound. Cleanup efforts and the passing years have erased visible signs of the spill; restoration and environmental monitoring efforts continue today. ■

Alaska color-coded by region

Anchorage

Juneau

Area of map detail

Valdez

Historically, Valdez should be thought of as two cities—the one prior to the 1964 Good Friday earthquake and the one since then. Before 1897 Valdez amounted to little, but that year some 7,000 gold-crazed greenhorns inundated Valdez in a mostly doomed effort to reach the Klondike goldfields.

Commercial fishing boats crowd the mooring piers of Valdez harbor.

Valdez

🅰 Map p. 166

Visitor Information

✉ Valdez Convention & Visitors Bureau Visitor Information Center, 104 Chenega St.

☎ 907/835-4636

🕐 Closed Sat.–Sun. Labor Day– Mem. Day

www.valdez alaska.org

A modest town grew up in the ensuing decades, especially after the Richardson Highway linked the Port of Valdez to the Interior, but on Good Friday 1964 a massive earthquake and consequent tsunamis obliterated much of that Valdez.

Citizens rebuilt the town on higher, more stable ground 4 miles (6.4 km) to the west. Growth accelerated rapidly after the oil industry and the trans-Alaska pipeline came to Valdez in the 1970s. Today Valdez is a prosperous city of 4,000 that serves as a terminal for oil tankers and a recreation hub for sportfishing, kayaking, flightseeing, river rafting, hiking, winter sports, wildlife viewing, and

boat tours of the sumptuous eastern end of Prince William Sound.

Downtown & Beyond

Start your tour downtown at the **Valdez Museum,** a nicely organized facility on Egan Drive that displays a mix of native, gold rush, early settlement, and oil-industry artifacts. Check out the evocative photos of the stampeders struggling to the goldfields; then read the quotes from contemporaries, such as: "Think of a man hitching himself to a sled, putting on 150 pounds, and pulling that load from 7:00 a.m. till 2:00 p.m., eating frozen bread and beans and drinking snow water for lunch,

INSIDER TIP:

Don't fall for the high-test bug repellent, which can take the paint off a pencil and ruin plastic. The 28% deet is all the strength you need.

—SARAH ROESKE
National Geographic field researcher

then walking back the distance of 10 miles. If this is not turning yourself into a horse what is it?"

The history lesson continues at **Remembering Old Valdez,** which lies four blocks south of the museum and recalls pre-earthquake Valdez. A scale model faithfully details the town's appearance, right down to the window design on the Alaskan Hotel. Check for yourself: Carefully examine photos of Old Valdez on the walls and compare them with the model. Don't miss the harrowing video of the earthquake.

The trans-Alaska pipeline and its terminal can be seen across the bay from Valdez, but not visited; instead, check out the exhibits and information on the pipeline and its history at the Valdez Museum. For a real-life view of the oil tankers loading up, albeit from 3 miles (4.8 km) away, stroll out the **Dock Point Trail,** a three-quarter-mile (1.2 km) loop that starts at the east end of the small boat harbor.

If your taste runs to waterfalls and a dramatic canyon, go west on West Egan Drive to Mineral Creek Road. **Mineral Creek Trail** at the end of the road extends nearly a mile (1.4 km) to the

canyon's end and an abandoned gold stamp mill. For a very long day hike, cross Mineral Creek on West Egan and head out the 9-mile (14.4 km) **Shoup Bay Trail.** The first 3 miles (4.8 km) to Gold Creek are easy, but the next 6 miles (9.6 km) become steep and rugged. Those who reach the bay earn views of a nearby kittiwake rookery and Shoup Glacier.

In a new facility at Prince William Sound Community College, the superb **Maxine & Jesse Whitney Museum** is said to be the largest private collection of

native art and artifacts in Alaska. If the museum isn't too busy, a staff member may give you a personal tour. Don't miss the fantastic parkas, like the one made from 40 murre breasts with wolverine lining. The highlight of the museum, however, is the scrimshaw—birds, dolls, ships, whales, and other figures carved from walrus ivory. ∎

Going to Extremes

Arching over Prince William Sound, the Chugach Mountains stretch 300 miles (482 km) from the east, turning south into the Kenai Peninsula. Ocean storms crash against the peaks, helping to pile up an average annual snowfall of about 600 inches (15 m). Accordingly, extreme skiers and snowboarders favor these wild slopes; runs can measure 3,000 to 5,000 vertical feet (0.9 to 1.5 km) top to bottom.

Valdez Museum
- ✉ 217 Egan Dr.
- ☎ 907/835-2764
- 🕐 Closed Mon. early Sept.–mid-May
- 💲 $$

www.valdez museum.org

Remembering Old Valdez
- ✉ 436 Hazelet St.
- ☎ 907/835-5407
- 🕐 Open daily mid-May–early Sept., by appt. rest of year
- 💲 $$

Maxine & Jesse Whitney Museum
- ✉ 303 Lowe St.
- ☎ 907/834-1690
- 🕐 Open daily in summer, by appt. rest of year
- 💲 Donation

www.mjwhitney museum.org

Cordova & Copper River Delta

Nestled at the base of the temperate rain forest and glacier-clad mountains on Orca Inlet, Cordova is known for its famously tasty Copper River wild salmon. The town's population of 2,300 just about doubles in the spring and summer, when outsiders come to fish the rich fishing grounds at the mouth of the Copper River and work in the seafood-processing plants.

Angling for a prize catch, fishermen head upriver along a slow, smooth stretch of the Copper River.

Cordova

▲ Map p. 167

Visitor Information

✉ Cordova Chamber of Commerce, 401 1st St.

☎ 907/424-7260

http://cordova chamber.com

The Copper River Delta measures about 60 miles (96 km) wide at the mouth and includes 700,000 acres (203,300 ha) of mudflats, willow-lined sloughs, creeks, ponds, and grassy wetlands that moose, bears, and river otters call home. And up to five million shorebirds refuel here during spring and fall migrations, inspiring the annual renowned shorebird festival (see sidebar p. 172).

Cordova

In a fishing town like Cordova, the natural place to start a tour is the harbor. Begin a stroll at the **Prince William Sound Science Center** (300 Breakwater Ave., tel 907/424-5800, www .pwssc.org, closed Sat.–Sun.), which sits on the dock near the mouth

Cordova Bound

You can only reach Cordova by sea or air. The state ferry system runs a ship from Valdez several times a week, and jet airplanes make daily scheduled flights.

of the harbor. Its deck offers fine views of the harbor. In addition to all the fishing boats, you may get lucky and spot sea otters; hundreds of them live in Orca Inlet. Primarily a research and education facility, the center runs a limited community education program of field trips, lectures, and science projects open to the public.

From the center, stroll along Breakwater Avenue, which runs above the north side of the harbor. You'll pass the **Anchor Bar & Grill** (207 Breakwater Ave., tel 907/424-3262), a hard-core fisherman's hangout where you can soak up some serious local flavor. At the end of Breakwater, turn right on North Railroad Avenue, the harbor's east side. You'll pass a couple of canneries, where workers in white smocks and rubber boots may be taking a break outside.

After a long block, turn right on Nicholoff Way, which skirts the south side, of the harbor. Near the corner, stop at **Baja Taco** (tel 907/424-5599), a little joint with a view where locals and visitors alike gaze at the harbor while munching fish tacos. The whole café used to be in the red school bus that now houses the kitchen. A couple of buildings down from Baja Taco is the **Ilanka Cultural Center** (110 Nicholoff Way, tel 907/424-7903), which serves the area's native peoples. Its small but elegant museum displays, among other things, a purse made of swan's feet and one of the world's few complete killer whale skeletons.

Wild Salmon

Alaska is bullish on wild salmon. Its commercial wild salmon fishery is the largest in the world, hauling in more than 160 million salmon a year. The state currently doesn't allow fish farming, and it passionately promotes the health, economic, and conservation benefits of wild salmon. In fishing towns like Cordova, bumper stickers and signs in windows promote wild salmon. The **Alaska Seafood Marketing Institute** (tel 800/478-2903, www.alaskaseafood .org) is the source for all things salmon: a buyer's guide, recipes, a summary of the salmon's life cycle, and much more.

Downtown: Cordova's downtown consists of a few square blocks just east of the harbor; much of the action takes place on First Street. The **Orca Book & Sound Company** (507 1st St., tel 907/424-5305) is a good small book and music store; it also exhibits local art. Across the street is the **Killer Whale Café** (504 1st St., tel 907/424-7775), a local favorite known for its cheesecake and biscuits and gravy. Farther down the street two more hard-boiled bars sit side by side: the **Alaskan Hotel & Bar** (600 1st St., tel 907/424-3288) and the **Cordova Hotel & Bar** (604 1st St., tel 907/424-3388).

A couple of buildings down, browse through the **Cordova**

Cordova Historical Museum

 622 1st St.

☎ 907/424-6665

🕐 Closed Sun. Mem. Day– Labor Day, & Sun.–Mon. rest of year

💲 $

www.cordova museum.org

Historical Museum. It covers in depth the 196-mile (315 km) railroad that was miraculously built in the early 1900s from the copper mines in Wrangell–St. Elias through forbidding mountains to the Port of Cordova. A little bit of everything else Cordovan is also here: photos of the Iceworm Festival, an Eyak canoe, a small painting by Sydney Laurence (Alaska's most celebrated landscape artist), and commercial fishing gear. By

---

EXPERIENCE:
Shorebird Festival

The Copper River Delta is the largest continuous wetland on the Pacific coast of North America, and millions of shorebirds use it in May. They fly in here to rest and feed for the next leg of their spring migration north. Hundreds of thousands of birds are generally seen at any one time, including plovers, sandpipers, trumpeter swans, and northern pintails. The town of Cordova celebrates the migration with the **Copper River Delta Shorebird Festival,** usually in early May, with workshops, field trips, speakers, dinners, and parades. You can learn more at the website of the Cordova Chamber of Commerce *(http://cordovachamber.com).*

---

summer of 2014 the museum should be moved into the new Cordova Center, a literal stone's throw from the current museum.

A block east of the museum, housed in the historic courthouse, is the Cordova Ranger District Office of the Chugach National Forest, which oversees the Copper River Delta and provides a wealth of information. Some people flightsee over the delta and the mountains behind it—an exhilarating tour. But most take advantage of the amazing 48.8-mile (78.5 km) **Copper River Highway** that crosses the delta.

Copper River Highway

Mile 0 is at the state ferry terminal, on the north side of Cordova. Follow Ocean Dock Road, which turns into First Street, through town; First Street becomes the Copper River Highway as it leaves town. Around Mile 7 it goes through what locals call **"the gap,"** emerging from the mountains and forest into the open delta country, characterized by some spruce and hills but mostly flat wetlands greened by alder, willow, and grass. Moose, bears, beavers, and trumpeter swans— 5 to 10 percent of the world's trumpeters nest here, some 100 to 150 overwinter—populate the next few miles. At Mile 10.5, Forest Service interpretive signs describe the delta and forest. Three miles (4.8 km) later a 4-mile (6.4 km) spur road leads to the **Sheridan Glacier** and the **Sheridan Mountain Trail,** a strenuous hike that wends past waterfalls to a picturesque alpine basin.

Back on the highway, a side road at Mile 16.8 dead-ends at **Alaganik Slough,** a classic stretch of delta made accessible by an elevated and signed boardwalk. Bears, eagles, gulls, and other animals come to feed on the spawning candlefish in summer. The **Haystack Trail,** departing the highway at Mile 19.1, is another easy boardwalk trail. It curves 0.8 mile (1.3 km) through spruce

INSIDER TIP:

At the Million Dollar Bridge, crossing the Copper River, is a campground where you can sit on benches and watch Childs Glacier calving. You'll hear the glacier groan and watch the calves crash into the water.

—ROWLAND SHELLEY
National Geographic field researcher

forest to the top of a knoll that looks out over the delta and the Gulf of Alaska beyond, an excellent viewpoint for spotting wildlife.

Near Mile 27 the highway starts crossing the main channels of the Copper River on bridge after bridge. Unfortunately, in 2011 the Alaska Department of Transportation had to close the bridge at Mile 36 for safety reasons. They're building a new bridge, but it probably won't be finished until 2015. Interim plans include ferrying people (not vehicles) across the channel to awaiting vans, which would carry travelers along the remaining dozen miles to the end of the highway.

Beyond Mile 36 the road heads north through cottonwood forests along the east bank of the river and ends at Mile 48.1, at the **Million Dollar Bridge.** It actually cost $1.4 million in 1910 to build this 1,550-foot-long (472 m) bridge. It was part of the railroad between Cordova and the Kennecott Mines, but the 1964 quake destroyed it. Repairs made it passable, but it doesn't go anywhere.

Walk through the campground beside the bridge to the river bank. The **Childs Glacier** lies just on the other side. This glacier calves massive ice slabs, sometimes sending large waves rolling across the river to the bank where visitors stand. Stay on the high ground. ∎

Copper River Delta

⚑ Map p. 167

Visitor Information

✉ Cordova Ranger District, Chugach National Forest, 612 2nd St., Cordova

☎ 907/424-7661

www.fs.usda.gov/chugach

A maze of waterways and marshes, the vast Copper River Delta drains the expansive Wrangell and Chugach Mountains, emptying into the Gulf of Alaska.

Prince William Sound

Prince William Sound is one of the most beautiful bodies of water in the world. Its jumble of islands and 1,500 miles (2,414 km) of ragged coastline, with hundreds of coves, bays, lagoons, narrows, and deep fjords, provide plenty of opportunities to explore.

Sea kayaking is a popular activity in Prince William Sound, where new vistas open around each bend.

Prince William Sound

▲ Map p. 166

Visitor Information

✉ Valdez Convention & Visitors Bureau Visitor Information Center, 104 Chenega St.

☎ 907/835-4636

🕐 Closed Sat.–Sun. Labor Day– Mem. Day

www.valdezalaska.org

The surrounding land has been graced with thick rain forest, tidewater glaciers, and the craggy Chugach Mountains. Exploring the sound by ferry, tour boat, private charter, or kayak is an Alaska must-do.

Western Sound

The gateway to the western sound is **Whittier,** a truly odd town. To reach it by car, you travel through a tunnel shared by trains (see sidebar opposite), and almost all of the community's residents live in a couple of concrete high-rises built in the 1950s. But Whittier is only about 60 road miles (96 km) from Anchorage, so many people wishing to see Prince William Sound come here.

Numerous tour boat, charter-fishing, and kayaking operators stand ready to take visitors out for three hours or for the whole day. Ferry service is also very popular out of Whittier.

Large or small, most tours either head into **Blackstone Bay,** just south of Whittier, to watch several active tidewater glaciers calving great hunks of ice into the sea, or they head northeast up to **College Fiord, Barry Arm,** and **Harriman Fiord,** where dozens of glaciers await. Some tours ease through **Esther Passage,** which narrows to a few hundred yards at some points. Throughout this western region lofty glacier-fed waterfalls tumble into the sound, bears fish along the shores, mountain goats gambol on the upper mountain slopes, and orcas, humpback whales, sea otters, and sea lions swim the blue depths.

Tour vessels and itineraries vary widely. The Greater Whittier Chamber of Commerce *(www.whit tieralaskachamber.org)* lists outfitters operating out of Whittier.

Eastern Sound

Valdez (see pp. 168–169) is the gateway to the sound's eastern half. A full-day boat tour out of Valdez may cruise west through the upper reaches of **Valdez Arm,** staying about 200 yards (183 m) off the forested northern shore. Dozens of waterfalls course down slender channels through the green tundra on the steep mountain slopes, sometimes ending with a swan dive off a sheer cliff. A raft of about 40 sea otters floats by, cuddling their pups, and eating off their midsections while floating on their backs.

Just past Shoup Glacier, the boat enters the **Valdez Narrows,** a passage between two fingers of the mainland that squeezes down to 600 yards (548 m) across. The white heads of mature bald eagles dot the tops of shoreline spruces and you'll spy a couple of bulky

eagle nests. With binoculars you can see mountain goats near the snow line high on the slopes. Black bears often patrol the shores through here.

As the boat rounds Point Freemantle and steers northwest toward Columbia Bay, icebergs begin to appear, evidence that the boat is nearing its main quarry: the **Columbia Glacier.** Hundreds of square miles in area, almost 30 miles (48.4 km) long, and some 2,000 feet (610 m) thick, the Columbia is one of the largest and most active glaciers in the Northern Hemisphere. The boat slows as the captain picks a path through the glacial castoffs, some the size of houses and others ferrying harbor seals. The boat stays about half a mile (0.8 km) from the 3-mile-wide (4.8 km), 300-foot-tall (91.5 m) terminus so people can safely watch as giant slabs of ice calve with loud, gunshot-like cracks into the water.

On the return journey, you will see hundreds of raucous sea lions in a crowded colony, colorful tufted puffins diving for food, more waterfalls and icebergs, more mountain goats, humpback whales, and orcas. The list just goes on and on. ■

Anton Anderson Memorial Tunnel

To link by rail the military bases in Anchorage and Fairbanks to an ocean port (Whittier) during World War II, Army engineers blasted a 1-mile (1.6 km) tunnel through Begich Peak and a 2.5-mile (3.6 km) tunnel through Maynard Mountain. In 2000, the tunnel was then made passable for cars. Organized caravans of cars take turns with trains, easing over the recessed tracks at around 25 miles an hour (40 kph), passing dripping rock walls in the dimly lighted tunnel—definitely not a drive for nervous claustrophobics. Occasionally you will hear the roar of the giant fans that clear fumes from the massive tunnel. Try not to think about the signs that say "Evacuate to Safe House only when strobe light flashing."

Exploring the Richardson Highway

The scenic Richardson Highway connects Prince William Sound to points north. Tracing an old gold-rush route, the road follows a dramatic river up into the coastal mountains and then follows a succession of pretty rivers down the mountains to the flatlands of the Copper River Valley.

The view from Thompson Pass stretches for miles across the Chugach Mountains.

Known as Alaska's first road, the Richardson was initially called the Valdez to Eagle Trail. The highway eventually ends in Fairbanks; this drive ends at the Edgerton Highway.

Note that the mileposts along the Richardson were erected prior to the 1964 earthquake that leveled Old Valdez and forced the town to a new site 4 miles (6.4 km) farther away. So when you see, for example, the mile marker at Thompson Pass and it says "26," that means you're 26 miles (41.8 km) from Old Valdez but 30 miles (48.3 km) from New Valdez.

About 9 miles (14.5 km) out of Valdez, the Richardson comes alongside the **Lowe River** and paces this braided waterway east for several miles. Around Mile 13, the highway swings northeast and enters the narrow confines of **Keystone Canyon ❶**. Seemingly at every

NOT TO BE MISSED:

Keystone Canyon • Thompson Pass • Worthington Glacier

bend waterfalls cascade from towering cliffs into the Lowe. Turn out at Mile 13.4 to contemplate **Horsetail Falls** and about half a mile (0.8 km) later to savor **Bridal Veil Falls ❷**. At Bridal Veil stretch your legs along the 2.5-mile-long (4 km) **Valdez Goat Trail,** which traces an old native route that figured prominently in getting gold seekers and military personnel from the coast to the Interior. At Mile 16.4 there's an outfitter who runs raft trips through Keystone Canyon.

At Mile 18.8 the highway seriously starts climbing and after a few miles rises above tree line into the alpine tundra. At Mile 24 a 1-mile (1.6 km) dirt road leads to **Blueberry Lake State Recreation Site ❸**, which has a campground, picnic tables, and fine fishing. Scan the lake and ponds for trumpeter swans.

The Road's Highest Point & Beyond

Two miles (3.2 km) farther the road reaches its highest point, 2,678-foot (816 m) **Thompson Pass ❹**. It's one of the snowiest places in Alaska. It once got 62 inches (1.5 m) of snow in a day and almost 1,000 inches (25.4 m) one winter. Enjoy the grand views. At Mile 28.7 stop at the **Worthington Glacier State Recreation Site ❺**. There's a visitor center, interpretive panels, and a trail that leads to the face of the glacier.

For the next 40 miles (64 km) or so dozens of turnouts allow you to stop and gaze at the mountains, the rivers, and the waterfalls. Watch for wildlife, too, especially in the backwater areas from about Miles 53 to 58, where moose and beavers abound. At Mile 64 the trans-Alaska pipeline meets the highway and at Mile 64.7 you can pull off at **Pump Station No. 12** and read about the pipeline. The highway then runs along the **Little Tonsina** and **Tonsina Rivers.** Your drive ends at Mile 82.5, where the Edgerton Highway meets the Richardson.

🅝 See also area map p. 167
▶ Valdez
🔁 82.5 miles (from Old Valdez)
🕐 2 hours plus stops
▶ Edgerton Highway junction

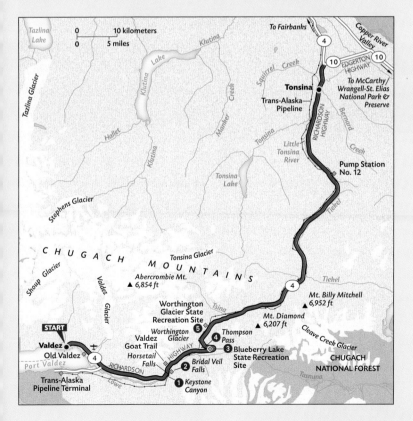

Wrangell–St. Elias National Park & Preserve

Hulking mountains, glaciers the size of Great Smoky Mountains National Park, abundant wildlife, active volcanoes, rugged Gulf of Alaska coastline, boreal forest, tundra, frothing rivers, and very little evidence of civilization: This park epitomizes wild Alaska. And Wrangell–St. Elias is big; by far the largest park in the United States, it could swallow six Yellowstones.

A boulder riding a glacier down from the Bagley Icefield

**Wrangell–
St. Elias National
Park & Preserve**

🅰 Map pp. 167
& 181

✉ Mile 106.8
Richardson Hwy.

☎ Visitor center:
907/822-7250

🕐 Visitor center
closed Sat.–
Sun. except
in summer

www.nps.gov/wrst

The park's **Headquarters Visitor Center** in the community of Copper Center on the western edge of the park is a good place to start your exploration, but don't let its familiar atmosphere mislead you into thinking this park is like national parks in the lower 48. Sure, the visitor center offers tidy displays on ecology, friendly rangers ready to answer questions, and a short film, "Crown of the Continent." But outside these walls lie 13.2 million acres (5.3 million ha) of wild Alaska. There is only one

developed campground and there are very few established trails. The one outpost of civilization deep in the park is the enclave of McCarthy/Kennicott (see pp. 184–185). One of those rare trails is the **paved path** behind the visitor center. This half-mile (0.8 km) loop along the lip of the ridge has many interpretive signs and affords great views of the park's spruce plain and the massive Wrangell Mountains beyond, including three volcanoes—Mounts Drum, Wrangell, and Blackburn.

Visiting the Backcountry

Only well-equipped backcountry veterans should bushwhack into Wrangell–St. Elias on their own, and even they should consult with rangers prior to slipping into the wilderness. Everyone else can venture in via the Nabesna and McCarthy Roads or with the help of the numerous guide services that operate out of McCarthy/Kennicott, the handful of tiny towns scattered along the highways that skirt Wrangell–St. Elias's western boundary, and Yakutat in the park's far southeast. The main gateway communities are Glennallen, Copper Center, and Chitina *(Copper Valley Chamber of Commerce, tel 907/822-5555, www.traveltoalaska.com).*

To taste that delicious backcountry without struggling across creeks and up mountains for days, take a plane. Air charters will drop small groups at remote sites, landing on riverside gravel bars, on

Getting to Wrangell–St. Elias

The primary airports that serve Wrangell–St. Elias are Gulkana, Chitina, and McCarthy; you can also fly into Tok in the north and Glennallen, Valdez, Cordova, and Yakutat in the south.

strips left behind by abandoned mining operations, on mountain slopes (the less vertical ones), and even on glaciers. You disembark with your gear and wave as the small plane takes off—the last

vestige of the outside world you'll see for a while. You might pitch your tent amid the wildflowers of the alpine tundra or beside a lake on which car-size icebergs bob. Some sites even have cabins. At

INSIDER TIP:

For a world-class wilderness experience, Wrangell–St. Elias is the place. But prepare for any kind of weather. Plus you'll need good map-reading skills and the proper equipment.

—TODD STOEBERL
Ranger, Wrangell–St. Elias NP&P

the appointed time the following day—or the following week, or whenever—the plane will return.

For those who want to wing it but not overnight in the park, **flightseeing** tours provide an overview of this rough-hewn landscape usually reserved for mountain climbers atop a summit. Four major ranges meet in Wrangell–St. Elias, producing an uplift that includes 9 of the nation's 16 highest peaks, led by 18,009-foot (5,489 m) Mount St. Elias. The plane might fly past the tendrils of steam that often rise from Mount Wrangell, one of North America's largest active volcanoes; or fly over glaciers, its shadow a speeding speck of black rippling across the gleaming whiteness of the snow and ice below; or maybe fly low along the broad, braided path of one of the big rivers that surge seaward from the high country.

Those rivers provide another avenue through the backcountry. Outfitters offer raft trips ranging from half a day to a couple of weeks down the **Copper, Kennicott, Chitina, Nabesna,** and **Nizina Rivers.** Some of these

---

Summer's the Best

The best time to visit Wrangell–St. Elias is, of course, summer. Lodges and guide services operate from mid-May to the end of September. June is best for wildflowers; berries ripen in August. July is usually the warmest month. Skies are often cloudy, though September can be clear and beautiful, with colorful fall foliage, no mosquitoes, and dustings of fresh snow on the mountains. For the hardier, March and April offer excellent cross-country skiing.

---

involve bucking-bronco rides through Class IV rapids. Others feature calm floating more oriented to fishing or watching for moose.

Some river runners cater to kayakers, too, though arguably the best kayaking awaits in the coastal waters of **Icy Bay** and **Yakutat Bay** in the extreme southeast corner of the park. Paddlers can poke around in the nooks and crannies of these bays and spot bald eagles, Dall porpoises, the pied plumage of a harlequin duck, and brawny

Steller sea lions, which can weigh as much as a Ford Escort.

Visitors who don't want to take on the backcountry by themselves or use a guide service still can penetrate the tough hide of the park by driving either the McCarthy Road (see pp. 184–185) or the Nabesna Road. Unpaved and rough in spots, even these roads present challenges—nothing about Wrangell–St. Elias is easy—but at least they give travelers a glimpse of the park's interior. And each road provides access to jumping-off points for further exploration.

Nabesna Road

The 42 miles (67.6 km) of the Nabesna Road start in the town of **Slana** on the northern boundary of the park *(Mile 59.8 on Glenn Hwy., aka Mile 65.2 on Tok Cutoff).* Be sure to ask about current road conditions at the Slana Ranger Station *(tel 907/822-7401, late May–late Sept.)*; sometimes weather makes this potholed byway impassable, particularly beyond Mile 29. And even people in 4WD, high-clearance vehicles may want to forego the last 4 miles (6.4 km).

The route begins in the black-spruce flats, home to numerous winged species, from mosquitoes to the northern hawk owl. Around Mile 7 **Rufus Creek** slides along the north side of the road while the gathering braids of the **Copper River** flow along the south side. These waterways herald the wet country soon to appear, a world of ponds and lakes backed by mountains on the north, south, and east. Watch for moose feeding on aquatic plants. These horse-size members of the deer family plunge their heads into the water and bite off submerged vegetation, then raise back up and chew as water drains off their faces and, if male, massive antlers.

There are primitive **campsites** at Miles 16.6 and 16.7 with picnic tables, but the real attraction is the sweeping view, which encompasses Kettle Lake, 14,163-foot (4,317 m) Mount Wrangell, 9,240-foot (2,816 m) Tanada Peak, and 16,237-foot (4,949 m) Mount Sanford. At Mile 29, often the turnaround point when the creeks are running high, stretch your legs by hiking along **Trail Creek.** There's no well-defined trail, but it isn't too hard to walk north along

the creek bed; you can go for days if you want. **Lost Creek,** at Mile 31, offers a similar opportunity and takes hikers to a few lakes and a spring.

During the last third of the drive the mountains start squeezing in; at this point the gravel road begins developing its own rugged topography, getting bumpier and dipping through creeks in imitation of the land around it. As the road veers south and grinds into the former mining settlement of **Nabesna** you are confronted by a sky full of mountains. This is the end of the road; for 200 miles (322 km) to the south sprawls the vast wilderness of Wrangell–St. Elias. ■

Retreat of the Glaciers

If Jane and John dig out the slides of their 1963 Inside Passage cruise, they could show you a striking shot of the terminus of the Mendenhall Glacier looming within 500 or 600 yards (457–549 m) of the visitor center. But if they visited the Mendenhall today, they'd be shocked to see that the glacier is now well over a mile (1.6 km) from the big viewing windows at the visitor center.

The weight of the Rainbow Glacier created a bowl-shaped depression.

Glaciers all over Alaska are receding. Occasionally a renegade surges forward, but Bruce Molnia, a research geologist with the U.S. Geological Survey, estimates that 99 percent of the state's glaciers below a mile (1.6 km) in elevation are in recession. These Alaska glaciers have been pulling back since the end of the little ice age, around 1850, but a major study published in *Science* in 2002 found that the melting has increased substantially over the past half century and accelerated greatly since the 1990s. In recent years the Mendenhall has been receding some 500 feet (152 m) annually, many times more than its average in decades past.

Glaciers advance and retreat for a variety of natural reasons, but scientists studying Alaska's glaciers think that climate change is a significant factor.

Glaciers are receding because they're melting. And the low-elevation portions of glaciers—which include about 80 percent of the state's total glacial ice—are melting all over, not just at the terminus; glaciologists talk about glaciers "thinning." In that 2002 study published in *Science*, the researchers tracked 67 Alaska glaciers. They discovered that from the mid-1950s to the mid-1990s, an estimated 480 cubic miles (2,000 cubic km) of ice melted off those glaciers and flowed into the ocean. It may be hard to visualize a cubic mile of water, but it's a lot. Now consider that Alaska contains about 50,000 to 100,000 glaciers (though some are quite small), that nearly all of the low-elevation glaciers are melting, and that many seem to be doing so

INSIDER TIP:
The Icefield Trail is a great way to see Exit Glacier near Seward. The moraines along the road show the extent of the relatively recent little ice age.

—GREGORY WILES
National Geographic field researcher

rapidly. The glaciers of coastal Alaska, the Yukon, and British Columbia could release more meltwater into the oceans than the glaciers of any other region on Earth outside the Poles.

Tourists admire the snout of Portage Glacier.

The *Science* paper notes that dwindling Alaska glaciers may contribute enough fresh water to the sea to raise the global sea level a fraction of an inch a year. Insignificant? Not when you consider that the rate may accelerate; that many glaciers and ice sheets around the world are likewise melting and may soon melt faster; and that even a rise of a few inches can cause widespread damage.

EXPERIENCE: Glacier Trekking

Moulins, kames, firn lines, bergschrunds, seracs, wave ogives; you're entering an exotic world when you step onto a glacier. A moulin, for example, is a narrow tube of ice through which water atop a glacier flows into a glacier. And a serac is a jagged ice tower.

You'll see some of these features and learn a bit about them if you take a glacier tour in Alaska. And unless you're an old hand at navigating glaciers, taking a guided trip is advisable; glaciers present many dangers to the uninitiated. Never mind crevasses and collapsing snow bridges; merely walking across an accommodatingly flat, firm stretch of glacial ice can be tricky.

Many tours begin by having participants don their crampons (a framework of spikes that fits over a boot) and

practice walking up and down a gentle slope of ice. From there the trekkers will learn about using other equipment, such as ice axes, and about the dos and don'ts of hiking across a frozen river of ice. Then they'll set out into that realm of radiant blue pools and glittering ice caves.

Tours can run from two to four hours, providing a taste of glacier trekking for rookies. Others last multiple days and combine glacier trekking with backpacking or climbing; participants may even camp on a glacier. Glacier-trekking hot spots include the **Matanuska Glacier** in the Mat-Su Valley (for a good glacier tour try MICA Guides, *www.micaguides.com*) and the **Mendenhall Glacier** near Juneau (try NorthStar Trekking, *www.northstar trekking.com*).

McCarthy/Kennicott

Long before people started coming to Wrangell–St. Elias National Park and Preserve to find wildness and scenic beauty, they came for copper. Between 1911 and 1938, 100 million to 200 million dollars worth of copper ore was dug out and processed in the Kennecott Mines, deep in the middle of what is now the national park. Today the site is preserved as Kennecott National Historic Landmark.

The generous front porch of the Kennicott Glacier Lodge provides far-reaching views.

McCarthy/ Kennicott

🏔 Map p. 181

Visitor Information

✉ Copper Valley Chamber of Commerce, Glennallen

☎ 907/822-5555

www.travelto alaska.com

Copper was discovered here in 1900. The settlement that grew up around the mine, Kennicott, is essentially a ghost town now. (The mining company misspelled the name of the explorer, Kennicott, after whom the mines—Kennecott with an "e"—were named.) Five miles (8 km) away, however, tiny McCarthy thrives. This was true even when the mine was producing lots of copper; the mining company kept Kennecott fairly clean for the miners, so the entertainment,

including bars and brothels, sprang up among the buildings of nearby McCarthy.

The McCarthy Road from Chitina, on the park's western boundary, is one of only two roads that penetrate into the Wrangell–St. Elias National Park (for the Nabesna Road, see pp. 180–181).

Probing 60 miles (96.5 km) into wilderness, the **McCarthy Road** is a legend in Alaska. It's narrow, it's rutted, it crosses 240 feet (73 m) above a river on an old one-way bridge, and it runs on top of an abandoned railroad bed from which old spikes and metal debris will surface to bite car tires. However, the road has been improved in recent years and isn't nearly the car graveyard it once was.

McCarthy

The McCarthy Road doesn't *quite* reach all the way to Mc-Carthy. It stops at the Kennicott River, where you must park *(fee)* and cross the channels of the river via two footbridges. Once across, walk the mile (1.6 km) into McCarthy proper, or wait and take one of the fairly frequent shuttle vans *($)*.

McCarthy developed as the supply and recreation center for

Getting to McCarthy

You can drive yourself to McCarthy; however, Kennicott Shuttle *(tel 907/822-5292, www.kennicottshuttle .com)* **runs shuttle vans from communities outside the park to the town. You can also fly into McCarthy.**

---

the miners, meaning it had a few stores and plenty of frontier fun. It's a far quieter place these days, but it welcomes tourists with restaurants, hostelries, and many historic buildings. Just as you enter town, you'll see the **McCarthy-Kennicott Historical Museum.** The collection focuses on the old mining days, and there are lots of displays about the miners' lives outside the mines.

Kennecott Mines

After you have found your bearings in McCarthy, catch a van *($)* up to the mill buildings of Kennecott Mines, preserved as a national historic landmark.

INSIDER TIP:

On the road to McCarthy, don't miss the town of Chitina. In July, drive out of town a bit and watch people using hand nets to catch fish in the Copper River.

—SARAH ROESKE
National Geographic field researcher

Here two prospectors spotted a green patch that might be good for their pack horses; it turned out to be copper ore.

A brochure for a self-guided tour is available at the Kennecott Visitor Center; however, the only way to see the interior of some of the mill buildings is with a guide on an organized tour.

The main bit of life left in Kennicott, beside the landmark, is the historic **Kennicott Glacier Lodge** *(tel 907/258-2350 or 800/582-5128, www.kennicott lodge.com, open in summer).* This is a fine place to stay, eat, or put up your feet on the 180-foot-long (54.8 m) front porch while savoring views of the Kennicott and Root Glaciers. If you'd like a closer look, the easy to moderate **Root Glacier Trail** runs alongside the glacier for about 1.5 miles (2.4 km). ■

Kennecott Mines National Historic Landmark

✉ Visitor center, Kennecott Mines

☎ 907/822-7476 (summer) or 907/822-7250 (winter)

⌚ Closed mid-Sept.–Mem. Day

www.nps.gov/wrst

More Places to Visit Around Prince William Sound

Copper Center

Founded in 1896, this town of about 320 souls on the western edge of Wrangell–St. Elias National Park and Preserve was the first non-native town in south-central Alaska. During the big gold rush around the turn of the 20th century, would-be miners heading for the Klondike via Valdez Glacier staggered into Copper Center when they came down out of the mountains.

Whether for a bed, a meal, or a drink, most of those stampeders eventually found their way to the Blix Roadhouse. The Blix was replaced in 1932 by the **Copper Center Lodge** (tel 907/822-3245 or 866/330-3245). The 1932 building was in turn replaced by a three-story lodge following a 2012 fire. The restaurant lives on, too. Order a halibut sandwich and you'll get what seems like a pound of fish.

Next door, the **George I. Ashby Memorial Museum** (contact lodge, open daily June–mid-Sept., donation) fills the rooms of two historic log buildings. The contents of the first building cover a little bit of everything: pioneer history, local Alaska native culture, and the outdoors. It is a pretty low-key place—note the drawer labeled "Rocks and Stuff"—but amid the traps, rifles, and old mining tools are some intriguing historic photos and letters. The second building is devoted to the 1898 Alaska gold rush. *www.traveltoalaska.com* Map p. 181 **Visitor Information** ✉ Copper Valley Chamber of Commerce, P.O. Box 469, Glennallen, AK 99588 ☎ 907/822-5555

Kayak Island

This long, slender island lies just southeast of Prince William Sound, outside its protective bosom and exposed to the open Pacific. Sticking out as it does, Kayak Island was the first place in the state that Vitus Bering encountered during his 1741 voyage of discovery for Russia. However, neither Bering nor the island deserve their reputations as the person and place for the first European contact with Alaska. A subordinate of Bering's, Aleksey Chirikov, commanding a second vessel that got separated from Bering in bad weather, reached Alaska a day or so earlier.

But even if its historical reputation drops a notch, Kayak Island remains an alluring hideaway with both scenic beauty and a wealth of wildlife. Few people visit, though it can be reached by plane from Cordova, 62 miles (100 km) away. (You can also travel by boat from Cordova, but the 16-hour journey can be rough.)

Walking the shoreline of Kayak Island can be a treasure hunt: All sorts of flotsam drifting on the Pacific—rubber duckies, running shoes, glass fisherman's floats, and even the classic messages in bottles—washes up on the island's southwest-facing beaches. *www.fs.usda.gov/chugach* Map p. 181 **Visitor Information** ✉ Cordova Ranger District, 612 Second St., Cordova, AK 99574 ☎ 907/424-7761

Tetlin National Wildlife Refuge

Most of the refuge's 683,000 acres (278,000 ha) are wet. During migration, its untold numbers of ponds and lakes host multitudes of waterfowl, as many as 200,000 sandhill cranes, and many other birds. Moose, grizzlies and black bears, caribou, wolves, and other wildlife also use the refuge. Tetlin is tough to penetrate, but starting about 30 miles (48 km) southeast of Tok the Alaska Highway skirts the refuge for about 65 miles (105 km). With seven pullouts featuring interpretive signs, this stretch of highway serves as an unofficial tour route. The refuge visitor center is located at Mile 1229. *http://tetlin.fws.gov* Map p. 181 **Visitor Information** ✉ Refuge headquarters, Tok ☎ 907/883-5312

The huge heart of Alaska, with both Fairbanks and Denali National Park and Preserve opening the interior to visitors

Interior

A Siberian husky, the ever resourceful sled dog

...r

...ns a raw wildland dotted by a few villages whose residents live ...It is this wildness that draws most visitors, whether to behold ...watch grizzly bears, camp in Denali National Park and Preserve, or canoe p... ...ers. Travelers want to see what the early Koyukon Athabaskan saw.

Along the Elliott Highway motorists often spot moose feeding in roadside ponds and lakes.

Bounded by ocean on three sides, with most of its population, economic activity, and visitors sticking close to salt water, Alaska in many ways feels like a coastal state. But far inland from the Pacific Ocean, the Arctic Ocean, and the Bering Sea, sprawls the interior—Alaska's heartland. It includes features reminiscent of the state's coastal areas, such as brawny mountains and massive glaciers, but also offers distinctive traits.

Taiga—subarctic boreal forest dominated by white spruce—covers much of the northern interior. Unlike southern Alaska's stately coastal forests, taiga is sparsely vegetated and consists of modest trees, mostly spruce, that top out between 30 and 40 feet (9–12 m)—half that in the poor soil of the so-called drunken forests. The interior also features enormous expanses of tundra—windswept slopes and soggy plains devoid of trees and blanketed by a complex blend of ground-hugging plants.

Humans have inhabited the interior for millennia. First came the Athabaskan, who led

NOT TO BE MISSED:

nomadic or seminomadic lives, following caribou herds and setting up summer fish camps by salmon rivers. Though to a lesser degree than coastal Alaska natives, Athabaskan did have contact with Russian fur traders, starting in the 1820s; many worked as contract trappers for the Russian-American Company.

Modern settlement of the interior didn't really get started until 1902, when a gold strike brought thousands of people to the Fairbanks area, quickly establishing that city as the region's hub. In 1923 completion of the

470-mile (755 km) Alaska Railroad, from Seward to Fairbanks, further opened the interior to development. A sizable military buildup began during World War II, and the Prudhoe Bay oil discovery and pipeline boom followed in the 1960s and 1970s. Between 1967 and 1969, the population of Fairbanks and environs alone grew from 40,000 to 65,000. ■

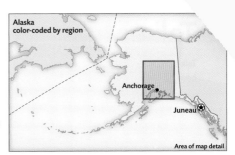

Alaska
color-coded by region

Anchorage

Juneau

Area of map detail

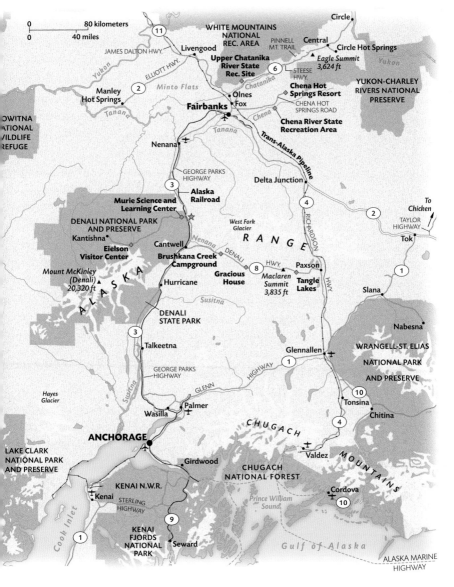

Talkeetna

...erfect antidote to the harried modern American lifestyle. This town of some 900 souls features log homes, cafés that serve musk ox burgers, an airstrip that calls to mind an unkempt gravel road, and a laid-back attitude. Folks often stroll around town instead of taking to their automobiles.

The West Rib Pub & Grill serves a delectable musk ox burger.

Talkeetna

 Map p. 189

Visitor Information

✉ Talkeetna Chamber of Commerce

☎ 907/733-2330

www.talkeetna chamber.org

Talkeetna's end-of-the-road character is enhanced by the fact that it indeed lies at the end of the road—a 14.3-mile (23 km) spur that branches off the Parks Highway at Mile 98.7. The spur emerges on Village Park at the head of **Main Street.** Here you'll find the historic **Talkeetna Roadhouse** (tel 907/733-1351, www.talkeetnaroadhouse.com),

where for decades travelers have stopped for a meal, a room, or one of its storied cinnamon rolls. Several art galleries also line Main Street; try **Talkeetna Air Taxi's Downtown Gallery** (tel 907/733-8282, summer only), which shows 60-plus Alaska artists.

Stroll the **Talkeetna Historic District** (Talkeetna Historical Society, tel 907/733-2487), which includes 16 buildings on the historical society's walking-tour map. Learn even more at the **Talkeetna Historical Society Museum** (alley south of Main & B Sts., tel 907/733-2487).

An outfitters' hub, Talkeetna is very busy in summer. Bush pilots offer **flightseeing trips** around Denali National Park (some even land on glaciers; see p. 194), while local **river trips** take in the scenery at the confluence of the Talkeetna, Susitna, and Chulitna Rivers. Or consider riding on the **Hurricane Turn,** a flag-stop train that ambles back and forth between Talkeetna and the Hurricane Gulch area. ■

Sheldon to the Rescue

In the mid-1900s, bush pilot and Talkeetna resident Don Sheldon ferried researchers and climbers to high-elevation glaciers on Mount McKinley, routinely making landings few other pilots would attempt. He shone in risky situations and rescued many a lost hiker and imperiled mountaineer. One story recounts the time a boat capsized in the Susitna River, leaving five passengers clinging to rocks in the rapids. Sheldon reportedly landed upriver in a floatplane, drifted down the rapids, grabbed one of the men, and delivered him to safety. He repeated the risky maneuver four more times, rescuing all five men.

Denali Highway

Travelers expecting the Denali Highway to run through Denali National Park and Preserve will be disappointed, as this road lies southeast of the park. But drivers who realize that and approach the highway for its own considerable charms will enjoy the ride.

Note that 112 of the highway's 134 miles (216 km) are unpaved, dusty, and potholed in sections. And no towns or service stations line this route—only a handful of traditional Alaska roadhouses and lodges. In a pinch, motorists can get a flat fixed or fuel up at one of the lodges, but be prepared for back-road driving conditions.

Highway Highlights

Starting from **Cantwell,** on the Parks Highway, motorists will enjoy a few miles of pavement before the road turns to gravel. After a few miles you'll come to the **Nenana River** and follow it upstream about 15 miles (24 km), with plenty of chances to canoe or kayak. For creekside camping, turn in at Mile 30 to Brushkana Creek Campground, which offers 18 sites. Pullouts along the next 10 miles (16 km) offer fine views of the West Fork Glacier and several prominent Alaska Range peaks.

At Mile 52.8 travelers come to **Gracious House** (tel 907/333-3148 or 907/259-1111 in summer—allow ten rings, www.alaskaone.com/gracious), a do-it-all Alaska lodge where you stride through the log doorway beneath a caribou rack to get a room, a meal, a flightseeing trip, a hunt, air taxi service, a tent site, a tow, and more.

Along much of the route, particularly between Miles 75 and 90,

wetlands invite travelers to break out the binoculars and look for trumpeter swans, moose, and river otters. Keep those binocs handy for the pullout near Mile 98, as well as the pullout atop 3,835-foot (1,169 m) **Maclaren Summit,** the second highest road pass in the state. When you've had your fill of sweeping views of the mountains and the Maclaren and Susitna River valleys, carefully scan the slopes for passing caribou and grizzlies.

INSIDER TIP:

For an inexpensive experience of the interior, rent a truck/camper/car fit for gravel roads. Drive the Denali Highway, stop anywhere, and just walk into the tundra: instant wilderness.

—SARAH ROESKE
National Geographic field researcher

If you'd like to venture into the surrounding wilds, there's no better place than the **Tangle Lakes,** around Mile 112. Try the **Tangle River Inn** for canoeing, fishing, bird-watching, or a jet-boat tour. Just past the lakes you'll return to pavement and cruise past more grand views to the end of the road at **Paxson,** on the Richardson Highway. ∎

Denali Highway
⊞ Map p. 189
Visitor Information
✉ Bureau of Land Management Glennallen Field Office, Mile 186.5 Glenn Hwy., Glennallen
☎ 907/822-3217
www.blm.gov/ak/st/en/fo/gdo/denali_hwy.html

Tangle River Inn
✉ Mile 115 Denali Hwy.
☎ 907/822-3790 (May–Sept.) or 907/895-4022 (winter)

EXPERIENCE: National Park Seminars

Much about travel in the Alaska outdoors is deliciously uncertain. Will a wolf cross your path? Will the snout of a tidewater glacier sheer off and belly flop into the sea? Will a trail take you through a meadow of blooming wildflowers? But at least one thing is certain: Visitors will have questions about the grand natural world around them. What do wolves eat? Why do glaciers split? How do those dainty wildflowers survive Alaska winters?

Denali National Park's Murie Science and Learning Center, among others, conducts seminars in the wild.

Travelers seeking in-depth answers to such questions should consider taking one of the smorgasbord of 20-odd field seminars offered annually by the Alaska Geographic Institute and its public lands partners, most of them during the summer. Nearly all of the courses are run out of Denali National Park's Murie Science and Learning Center, but several take place at other sites around Alaska.

Note the term "field" in "field seminars"; don't expect to be sitting behind a desk listening to a teacher at the blackboard. You and maybe ten others will be traipsing about outdoors, guided by a park scientist or some other expert. In fact, these classes are so far from the classroom that each has a rating that informs prospective participants of the required level of physical fitness.

Most of each seminar day will be spent hiking in search of animals, kneeling on the tundra identifying plants, peering through magnifying loupes at rocks, or otherwise getting up close and personal with the wilds. Typically, nights will be spent camping, perhaps with an evening discussion around a fire. For example, the Denali courses usually use a permanent camp on the Teklanika River about 30 miles (48 km) into the park. Family-style meals are served in the dining yurt and participants are assigned four to a tent cabin to get some sleep before the next day's outing.

A Wealth of Subjects

The range of courses reflects the range of natural wonders found in Alaska. Some new offerings crop up each year, but many old favorites return year after year. You might select a seminar on Denali's large mammals in which you'll learn about the ways of caribou, bears, moose, and other charismatic megafauna while hiking through their haunts. Visitors can make friends in high places in the alpine wildlife class. As part of the course on the ecology of migratory birds you'll venture out with a park ornithologist, peering through a spotting scope at some of the winged summer visitors that come to Alaska to nest. If you like getting to the bottom of things, you may enjoy the geology seminar, which explores the mountains, glaciers, rivers, and other building blocks that provide the ecosystem's foundation.

In addition to such bread-and-butter seminars, the institute usually offers a few unexpected courses, such as the science of fly-fishing, which includes studies in stream ecology and hydraulics, and field journaling, which encourages participants to write and sketch about their experiences in the wilds. Finally, the institute rounds out the 20-odd classes it serves up each year with seminars oriented to families with children, such as one on wildlife and one on dinosaurs.

To find out more, contact the **Alaska Geographic Association** (tel 907/274-8440 or 866-257-2757, www.alaska geographic.org). You also can contact the **Murie Science and Learning Center** (tel 907/683-1269, www.murieslc .org). Bear in mind that many of these courses are extremely popular and fill up months in advance. Make your reservation soon after the courses are announced, usually around the first of the year.

Denali National Park & Preserve

Denali is big, not only in the aggregate—at more than 6 million acres (2.4 million ha), it's larger than Vermont—but in its particulars. Glaciers dozens of miles long. Rivers a mile wide. Moose that stand seven feet (2.1 m) at the shoulder. And, above all, 20,320-foot (6,194 m) Mount McKinley, the continent's highest point.

Locals simply call it "the mountain." More than 2 million of its acres (0.8 million ha) are wilderness, and nearly all of the remaining 4.2 million acres (1.7 million ha) likewise show little evidence of human presence. It's no wonder grizzly bears and wolves thrive here.

The presence of bears, wolves, and big game animals such as caribou, Dall sheep, and moose was a key to establishment of the park. For thousands of years Athabaskan had hunted in the area but with a light touch that maintained healthy wildlife populations. Things changed in 1903, however, with the discovery of gold near the mountain. As gold seekers rushed in, market hunters followed and began killing game at an unsustainable pace to provide meat to the stampeders.

Charles Sheldon, a pal of Theodore Roosevelt's and an avid outdoorsman, came out to do some noncommercial hunting and was disgusted with the slaughter being perpetrated by the local market hunters. He worked tirelessly to create a national park that would protect the area's wildlife. Sheldon at last attained his goal in 1917, when President Woodrow Wilson signed a bill to set aside the region as Mount McKinley

Mount McKinley dominates this section of the Alaska Range.

National Park, handing the pen he used to one of the delighted onlookers—Sheldon himself.

Orientation

As Denali is so big and wild, the park is more difficult to tour than, say, Yellowstone or the Great Smoky Mountains, but with a little effort casual visitors can make Denali's acquaintance. The park comprises two main areas: the

In the high country, you carve out campsites in the snow.

Denali National Park & Preserve

⚑ See pp. 189 & 195

✉ Mile 237 Parks Hwy.

☎ 907/683-2294

💲 $$

www.nps.gov/dena

Greater Healy/ Denali Chamber of Commerce

☎ 907/683-4636

www.denali chamber.com

front country and the backcountry. Closed to private vehicles, the backcountry takes in most of the park. Just one road, the **Park Road** (see pp. 196–199), accesses this wilderness, and visitors must use shuttle buses. To fully experience Denali, travel this road at least halfway.

The front country holds its own charms, evident even amid the sprawl of roadside services near the entrance. Note the promenade above the rushing Nenana River and views from some of the restaurants and hotels. Several tour operators offer guided excursions into the park and surrounding wildlands.

Flightseeing trips are a popular, though pricey option. These small planes tour the park and, weather permitting, circle the mountain. Buzzing around Mount McKinley offers a visceral sense of its magnitude. At 20,320 feet (6,194 m), it's the champion of North America. While short 9,000 feet (2,743 m) of Mount Everest in elevation above sea level, McKinley looms 6,000 feet (1,829 m) taller than Everest when measured from its base.

Visitor Center

Travelers get their bearings 1.5 miles (2.4 km) into the park at the **Denali National Park Visitor Center,** which doubles as a natural history museum. Check out visually stunning films on the big screen in the spacious theater. Interpretive hikes and a shuttle bus to the park kennel leave from here. But don't expect to board Fido at this kennel; it's for the park's sled dogs, which rangers use to patrol Denali in the winter. In summer the rangers stage sled demonstrations three times a day.

The center also houses the **Murie Science and Learning Center** (tel 907/683-6432, www .murieslc.org). While many of its programs are aimed at school groups and teachers, a fair number are offered to casual visitors. The truly gung ho can sign up for three- to five-day field seminars on such topics as the wolves of Denali, high-country wildflowers, and glaciers of the Alaska Range.

Hiking

Though the backcountry offers few established trails, hikers can choose from a variety of well-maintained trails in the front country. Denali is so wild that even in the front country you need to watch out for wildlife—particularly bears and moose. If it's one of these two, watch from a safe distance—the Park Service recommends a minimum of 25 yards (23 m) for a moose (double that if it's a cow with calves) and 300 yards (275 m) for a bear. Rangers advise maintaining that 25-yard minimum even for large docile mammals, for their protection and comfort. Stretch that to at least 100 yards (90 m) for nesting raptors or in the proximity of large mammal dens.

While the **Savage River Loop Trail** (2 miles/3.2 km round-trip) begins at Mile 14.8 on the Park Road, all other trails start at or near the visitor center. One of the easiest is the **Taiga Trail** (2.6 miles/4.2 km round-trip), which winds through subarctic forest and connects with three other trails. Perhaps the most popular is the **Horseshoe Lake Trail** (1.4 miles/2.3 km round-trip), a gentle route that meanders past a river, creek, ponds, and the eponymous lake. All that water

hosts plenty of life, from tiny flowers to beaver, muskrat, and moose.

Those with strong legs and a lot of energy should consider the **Mount Healy Overlook Trail** (4.5 miles/7.2 km round-trip from Taiga Trail or 5.5 miles/8.9 km round-trip from the visitor center), which passes through the park's primary habitats and ends atop a ridge with views of the front country. To reach the trailhead from the visitor center, walk half a mile (0.8 km) on the Taiga Trail. From the overlook, watch for Dall sheep and eagles. The latest addition is the **McKinley Station Trail,** a 1.5-mile (2.4 km) path through spruce forest from the visitor center to Riley Creek. ■

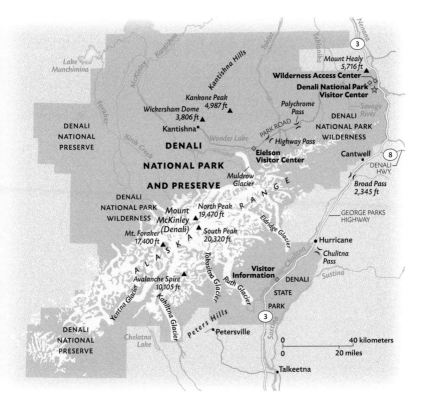

A Drive Through Denali National Park

The 92-mile (148 km) Park Road extends into Denali's otherwise wild heart. It slips through spruce and aspen forests, tightropes along mountainsides above broad river valleys, crosses vast expanses of alpine tundra, and provides ample opportunities to view the park's resident wildlife.

A park-operated shuttle bus rolls along the restricted road through Polychrome Pass.

So popular is this drive that when the George Parks Highway opened in 1972, the Park Service closed most of the Park Road to private vehicles to prevent traffic jams; access beyond the first 15 miles (24 km) is by shuttle bus only. Some visitors may chafe at the lack of freedom, but the restricted access protects the park. Passengers are free to hop off the bus at certain spots, see the sights, then (space permitting) take a different bus either farther into the park or back to the entrance. If you opt for a walkabout, prepare to spend at least an hour in the wilderness. At a minimum, carry rain gear and insect repellent and know the ABCs of dealing with bears.

NOT TO BE MISSED:

Views of Mount McKinley
• Polychrome Pass • Wonder Lake • Kantishna Roadhouse
• Grizzly sightings

For information and to catch a bus, head to the **Wilderness Access Center ❶**, a half mile from the park entrance. While travelers *can* make reservations at the WAC, in busy summer season it's best to make reservations weeks or even months ahead (*tel 907/272-7275 or 800/622-7275, www.reservedenali.com*).

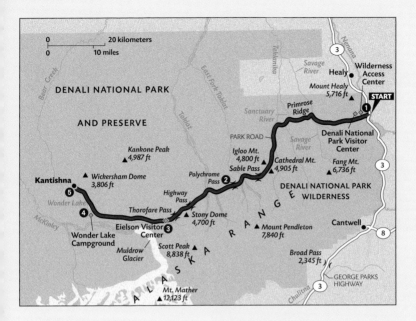

The park offers a range of travel options. First decide whether you want a tour bus or shuttle bus. Tour buses provide full service and popular itineraries. For example, the Tundra Wilderness Tour features a naturalist guide, a box lunch and drinks, pickup at places besides the WAC, and service to and from the Teklanika or Toklat Rivers (Mile 31.3 or Mile 53). That said, it costs much more than a round-trip shuttle to Toklat.

While shuttle buses are billed as no-frills transportation, most drivers are quite knowledgeable about the park and will share information about the land and wildlife. Visitors can choose from a list of half a dozen distances and destinations, ranging from a two-hour round-trip that turns around at Mile 15 to a 13-hour round-trip that goes to the end of the road, at Mile 92. For the best views, grab a window seat that will face south when the bus is on the road.

Toward Polychrome Pass

The first 15 miles (24 km) of road to Savage River is paved, skirting the base of **Healy Ridge** and threading two river valleys. At

M	See also area maps pp. 189 & 195
►	Wilderness Access Center
↔	106 to 184 miles (170 to 296 km) round-trip
⏱	5 to 13 hours
►	Wilderness Access Center

first, views are limited by trees as the bus passes through subarctic evergreen forest. But after a few miles the road climbs, and the predominant white spruce and accompanying aspen, paper birch, and balsam poplar diminish in both number and stature. Higher elevations bring successively harsher growing conditions and sparse vegetation. Watch for snowshoe hare; during spikes in their population cycle these rabbits can be spotted every few hundred yards. You also may glimpse their most notorious predator, the lynx. What's more, on a clear day near Mile 9 you may spot the tip of Mount McKinley peeking over closer mountains, though it's actually more than 70 miles (113 km) away!

At Mile 14.7 the **Savage River** marks the boundary between the park's front country and

Backpackers head toward Polychrome Pass.

better odds for spotting the park's charismatic megafauna. Soon after bridging the **Sanctuary River** at Mile 22, the road turns south and runs about 17 miles (27 km) along the Teklanika River to Sable Pass. Wolves sometimes roam this river valley, and people have spotted them near or even on the road. Moose favor ponds and willow thickets in the forested bottomland. Scan surrounding snowline slopes for Dall sheep; passengers often spot herds grazing on precipitous meadows as casually as cows feed on Wisconsin flatland. Though grizzlies range widely and unpredictably, sows and their cubs have been repeated visitors over the years around **Sable Pass** (Mile 39.1). Also favoring the pass at times is a wolf pack—one of about a dozen that roam the park.

Spectacular Scenery

While wildlife often vies with scenery for visitors' attention, the dramatic landscape takes center stage as the road rises to **Poly-chrome Pass ❷**. Passengers may feel the urge to flee their south-facing seats as the narrow road negotiates dizzying drop-offs, although the views usually keep even white-knuckled passengers riveted. Everyone can breathe easy and savor the vistas as buses linger at the Polychrome Pass rest stop. In addition to the mountains, sprawling river valleys, and glaciers, visitors are treated to an overlook of the orange-, yellow-, red-, purple-, black-, and white-banded Alaska Range foothills for which the pass is named.

Both wildlife and scenic beauty abound along the 20 miles (32 km) from Polychrome Pass to the Eielson Visitor Center. Amid open tundra the road crests **Highway Pass** at 3,980 feet (1,213 m) with a panorama to match its lofty status. Watch for soaring golden eagles and scan nearby rock piles for the pikas and marmots those eagles are hunting. Also scope out the ridgetops and remnant snowbanks, where caribou hide to escape swarming bugs.

The **Eielson Visitor Center ❸** is all about location, location, location. The new building opened in 2008 and features exhibits, a short

backcountry. Here, buses pass a checkpoint beyond which private vehicles (with some exceptions) are not permitted, and pavement gives way to gravel. For the next 8 miles (13 km) the road parallels **Primrose Ridge**, mostly above the tree line in the tundra. Passengers enjoy unobstructed views of the mighty Alaska Range, about 15 miles (24 km) to the south. Open views of the river valleys and tundra-covered slopes promise excellent wildlife-watching opportunities. Grizzlies may pop up just about anywhere. Both shuttle and tour buses always stop long enough to allow passengers to watch and photograph animals, though tour drivers may not bother if the critter is just a dot on a hillside a mile away.

The stretch from Savage River to Polychrome Pass, at Mile 45.9, offers even

interpretive trail, a ranger desk, and guided outings. From this perch, visitors get a top-to-bottom view of **Mount McKinley**—that is, if the weather cooperates. Summer showers account for most of the park's 16 inches (41 cm) of annual rainfall, and clouds often obscure all or part of the mountain, even on fairly clear days. But if you beat the one-in-three odds of seeing the summit, the view will knock your socks off.

From Eielson the road descends along the Thorofare River, past the Muldrow Glacier, then follows the McKinley River to **Wonder Lake ❹**. Watch for moose in the roadside ponds—not to mention beaver, muskrat, and waterfowl. At Mile 84.6 most buses take the short spur to **Wonder Lake Campground,** a beautiful spot to picnic. This is the closest (27 miles/43 km) the road comes to Mount McKinley.

A few buses continue to **Kantishna ❺** (Mile 91), a mile from road's end. This area was absorbed into the park in the 1980 expansion—along with some 4.2 million other acres (1.7 million ha). Several preexisting privately owned lodges remain here, deep in the

The Kantishna Roadhouse is one of five lodges at road's end in Denali.

otherwise lodgeless park. These provide a more comfortable alternative for visitors who long to be in the backcountry but prefer not to camp.

Backpacking

While driving along one of Alaska's few highways, surrounded by mountains, forest, or open tundra, it's hard not to wonder what lies beyond that thin strip of asphalt (or gravel). What would you discover if you simply got out of the car and started walking away from the road?

Enter backpacking. Load the essentials for a safe trip on your back and off you go. You can follow a trail or create your own route. However, the Alaska wilderness is a demanding place, so prepare carefully before you go wandering off.

The **Alaska Public Lands Information Centers** (see sidebar p. 10) are a great place to start. They can help with the most basic question—where to go? Do you want to explore the temperate rain forest? The tundra? The mountains? Do

you want to watch wildlife? Go fishing? See alpine flowers?

The APLIC also can help you with safety and comfort issues, such as cold, bears, bugs, and navigation. This line of thinking will lead you to another key decision—marked trail or cross-country hiking? Most of Alaska is trailless, but it certainly has some well-trodden paths that are well trodden because the scenery is spectacular, such as the Resurrection Pass Trail or the Chilkoot Pass Trail.

If you opt for trailless, it may be wise to also opt for a guided excursion, unless you and your companions are hardened backpacking veterans. No matter what, pack a compact pair of binoculars, you'll find yourself using them every day to spot wildlife.

Nenana

Nowadays most travelers zoom by Nenana (pop. about 400) as they drive the George Parks Highway (Rte. 3), but this small town has a history. A traditional Athabaskan gathering place, it served as a construction base for the Alaska Railroad in the early 1900s.

Nenana

△ Map p. 189

Visitor Information

✉ Parks Hwy., Nenana

☎ 907/832-5435

🕓 Closed Sat.–Sun. Labor Day– Mem. Day

Nenana City Office

☎ 907/832-5441

www.nenana.org

In 1923 President Warren G. Harding drove a golden spike here to celebrate the railroad's completion. The town still serves as a port for tugs and barges that ply the currents of the Tanana and Yukon Rivers, bringing supplies to remote villages during the brief warm-weather thaw. Though it offers no grand attractions, this sleepy old berg does claim a few inter-esting sites.

Just off the highway, motorists encounter the visitor center, in a beflowered, sod-roofed log cabin. Beside it sits the colorful *Taku Chief*, a tug that worked up and down the rivers for more than 30 years. Head down the five or six blocks of A Street, the main drag, and you'll find a nice variety of down-home businesses, such as the **Rough Woods Inn** (*2nd & A Sts., tel 907/832-5299*), a lodge and café known for its yummy pies.

Two Centers of History

At the junction of A and Front Streets lies the **Alaska State Railroad Museum** (aka Alaska Railroad Depot). This is a small affair housed in the 1922 rail-road station. In addition to the plethora of train artifacts, the museum displays items relating to native and gold rush history. Check out the photograph of Frank Bateau in harness pulling his own sled; he didn't let the fact that he couldn't afford dogs stop him.

Four blocks east is the **Alfred Starr Nenana Cultural Center** (*415 Riverfront, tel 907/832-5527, closed in winter*), built in 1998 to showcase local native history and culture. The center overlooks the Tanana River. Sit out on its deck for a while to watch the tugs and barges that travel as far as 1,400 miles (2,250 km) to provide a lifeline to remote villages. Just upriver, fish wheels scoop the day's catch from the current. ∎

Nenana Ice Classic

Since 1917 Alaskans have wagered on the exact time the icebound Tanana River at the town of Nenana will break up. Each winter, Nenana residents erect a large tripod on the frozen river and run a line from the tripod to a clock in a building on shore. When the ice breaks up—usually in late April or early May—the tripod falls and stops the clock, determining the time. Between February 1 and April 5, some 300,000 tickets are sold all over Alaska (*www.nenanaakice classic.com*). Each sells for $2.50. Half the money goes to the winner(s) and half goes to local nonprofits, minus administrative costs.

Fairbanks

Fairbanks serves as interior Alaska's hub, gateway, supply center, and de facto capital. But despite being the state's second largest city (roughly tied with Juneau), Fairbanks has a population of only about 30,000. Of course, that's relatively huge in this vast, sparsely settled region; thus, Fairbanks hosts the region's main university, major shopping centers, big festivals, and lion's share of cultural institutions.

In Golden Heart Park, a statue commemorates the first people to cross from Asia to Alaska.

Because the city is small in absolute terms and surrounded by thousands of square miles of near wilderness, residents have remained tied to the land in ways seldom found among urban dwellers in the lower 48.

Fairbanks is set along the Chena River near its confluence with the mighty Tanana. While this suggests careful site selection, truth is the location was an accident. City founder, mayor, and notorious wheeler-dealer (many say criminal) Capt. E. T. Barnette had planned to build a trading post farther up the Tanana, but the stern-wheeler carrying Barnette and his supplies couldn't make it any farther up the Chena. Barnette was stranded in the middle of nowhere—the site of present-day downtown Fairbanks. That was in 1901. Gold was discovered in the surrounding hills the following year, and the ensuing rush turned Barnette's accidental trading post into a thriving city of thousands by 1905, with electricity, schools, police and fire departments, a library, a three-story "skyscraper," and 33 saloons in the space of four blocks. The town diversified enough to weather the inevitable bust of the gold rush and has since held its position as the interior's leading city.

Fairbanks

⚑ Map p. 189

Visitor Information

✉ Morris Thompson Cultural and Visitors Center, 101 Dunkel St.

☎ 907/456-5774 or 800/327-5774

www.explore fairbanks.com

Morris Thompson Cultural and Visitors Center

✉ 101 Dunkel St.

☎ 907/459-3700

www.morris
thompsoncenter.org

Downtown & Around

Visitors should start downtown on the **Chena River** at the striking **Morris Thompson Cultural and Visitors Center.** Finished in 2009, this facility serves as the gateway to the land and peoples of interior Alaska. It includes the Fairbanks Convention and Visitors Bureau (and the main visitor center), Anchorages's Alaska Public Lands Information Center, the Tanana Chief Conference (which represents 42 interior tribes and villages), an artisans' workshop and demonstration

Park, take the footbridge across the Chena, or stroll the promenade that follows the river along First Avenue. Active travelers may opt to rent a canoe or kayak and paddle along the river through downtown.

Hundreds of visitors explore Fairbanks and the Chena aboard the *Discovery II* and *III*—that is, hundreds of passengers per three-hour trip on either of these stern-wheelers (*1975 Discovery Dr., two blocks north of airport, tel 866/479-6673, www.riverboatdiscovery.com, closed mid-Sept.–mid-May,*

Ice sculptures stay gloriously frozen through summer in the frigid Fairbanks Ice Museum.

area, a museum, a theater, and a restored pioneer cabin.

Though downtown isn't posh, it is a pleasant place for a walk or alfresco dining at a restaurant overlooking the river—assuming it's a typically sunny summer day and not a February afternoon when the high temperature is minus 30°F (-34°C). From the visitor center you can step over to neighboring Golden Heart

$$$$$). The ships paddle past the city and countryside, along the way taking in various Alaska traditions, including a sled dog demonstration, a bush plane show, and a guided walking tour of **Chena Indian Village.**

The coolest spot downtown is the **Fairbanks Ice Museum** (*500 2nd Ave., tel 907/451-8222, www.icemuseum.com*), which centers on a 20°F (-7°C) exhibition space

EXPERIENCE: Dashing With Sled Dogs

When most people in the lower 48 think of dog mushing—aka dogsledding—they think of the Iditarod, Alaska's annual 1,150-mile (1,850 km) race. This grueling test of musher and dog certainly makes for grand adventure, but it's not exactly suitable for casual visitors. However, Alaskans love their mushing and dozens of these sled dog enthusiasts offer visitors the opportunity to take a ride in a dog sled and even learn enough to take the helm.

The quintessential trip involves venturing into the wilderness behind a dog team, slicing across the snow among the mountains and snow-flocked forest. Less quintessential but loads of fun are the plentiful shorter options, some as brief as five minutes. Many mushers close to towns will take you and the family out for a spin, talk about the art and history of mushing, and provide a tour of their kennels—including a chance to play with the puppies, of course.

Naturally, dogsledding is primarily a winter sport, but during the summer some mushers put wheels on their sleds and offer rides. Others take their dog teams to glaciers and ice fields for the summer and visitors take helicopters to go up for a sled ride. For information on mushing contact tourism offices; the Alaska Dog Mushers Association (www.sleddog.org), in Fairbanks; various mushing associations in other towns; or go to the website of *Mushing* magazine (www.mushing.com), where you'll find a list of mushing tours.

---

filled with creative ice sculptures. Venture inside or admire pieces from the heated viewing area. Every March, the city hosts the **World Ice Art Championships** (www.icealaska.com), during which sculptors from around the globe fashion both realistic and abstract pieces, some more than 20 feet (6 m) tall. Some of these sculptors create pieces for the ice museum, too. A large-screen slide presentation shows the artists at work.

West of town on the south bank of the Chena lies **Pioneer Park** (2300 Airport Way, tel 907/459-1087, www.co.fairbanks.ak.us/parksandrecreation/pioneerpark). Known until 2001 as Alaskaland (and still called that by most locals), this 44-acre (18 ha) spread is a combination historical museum, theme park, community center, tourist trap, and city park. The Alaska Native Village & Museum explores the Athabaskan era, while the early days of settlement are presented in various ways at Pioneer Hall, Wickersham House (home of James Wickersham, Alaska's first territorial judge), a refurbished railroad car used by President Harding, the Pioneer Air Museum, the Alaska Native Museum, the Kitty Hensley House, and the Tanana Valley Railroad Museum. The historical highlight is the stern-wheeler *Nenana,* a massive, beautifully restored riverboat that steamed the Yukon from 1935 through the mid-fifties.

Creamer's Field Migratory Waterfowl Refuge

In the midst of Fairbanks, flanked by subdivisions and malls, sprawls an almost 2,000-acre (809 ha) oasis called Creamer's Field Migratory Waterfowl Refuge. During the

Creamer's Field Migratory Waterfowl Refuge

✉ Farmhouse Visitor Center, 1300 College Rd.

☎ 907/452-5162

www.creamers field.org

Museum of the North

✉ 907 Yukon Dr.
☎ 907/474-7505
💲 $$

www.uaf.edu/ museum

spring (April & May) and fall (Aug. & Sept.) migrations, ducks, geese, and swans rest and eat here before continuing their long flights. From the trails and raised platforms that overlook the field or through a spotting scope at

INSIDER TIP:

Rent a bike in Pioneer Park, then pedal through town. There are some great mountain bike trails at the university.

—SARAH ROESKE
National Geographic field researcher

the visitor center, you can watch waterfowl feeding and squab-bling. Migrating sandhill cranes also flock here, dipping their 4-foot-tall (1.2 m) frames to load up on grain, especially during the annual Tanana Valley Sandhill Crane Festival in August. Watch patiently and you may spot some of the predators that stalk water-fowl, including peregrine falcons and red foxes.

Five easy trails, ranging from a quarter mile (0.4 km) to 2 miles (3.2 km), lead deeper into the refuge. From the **Seasonal Wetlands Trail** hikers can spot shorebirds and wood frogs, while on the **Farm Road Trail** you may encounter basking woodchucks or hunting northern harriers and American kestrels. The **Boreal Forest Trail** *(brochure available at visitor center)* leads through taiga, a habitat that covers much of the interior. Look for hare, moose, and

a host of wildflowers, including wild roses, dwarf dogwood, white violets, and calypso orchids.

Creamer's Field also offers many events. For example, there's an "Owl Evening" for listening to those haunting nocturnal calls; "Life Under the Ice," in which you learn how muskrats and blackfish survive those fearsome interior winters; and, of course, the Mother's Day frog walk.

University of Alaska

The University of Alaska, Fair-banks, boasts several attractions, including the acclaimed Museum of the North, a botanical garden, and tours of research facilities.

Museum of the North: As you enter the museum, pause to admire the hilltop views; on a clear day the Alaska Range saws the horizon. While you're out there, study the shimmering white curves of the museum's exterior. Greatly expanded between 2002 and 2005, the museum is noted for stunning new architecture that echoes those jagged mountains, and suggests glaciers, the northern lights, and even the tail of a sounding whale.

The expanded interior enables display of long-stored treasures. Take, for example, the newly opened **Rose Berry Alaska Art Gallery,** with soaring ceilings and curved walls—it's like being inside a glacier. This gallery highlights native artwork and classic Alaska land-scapes that have been languishing in storage. Another new venue is the **Arnold Espe Auditorium,** which presents various multimedia programs. Past shows include *Dynamic Aurora*, about the northern lights, and *Northern Inua*, showcasing the remarkable athletes at the World Eskimo Indian Olympics.

While enjoying the new, don't neglect the old; the **Gallery of Alaska** holds the heart of the collection and is the best Alaska primer provided by any museum. See if you don't feel a shiver as you approach Otto, the 9-foot (2.7 m), 1,250-pound (560 kg) brown bear—stuffed, of course— that guards the entrance. Behind this awesome beast are five galleries, each of which presents the human and natural history, art, and contemporary life of one of the state's five geographic regions. Venture into the **Western & Arctic Coasts Gallery** for a gander at an Inupiat umiak—an open boat made of walrus hide—and watch a video of Eskimos in an umiak hunting whales amid icebergs. Circle the voluptuous sculpture of a polar bear, fashioned from bronze with a marbled patina.

Contemplate the "Dinosaurs of Alaska," the world's largest collection of high-latitude dinosaurs and related vertebrates. Then . . . well, just keep going and you'll end up with a rounded view of the western and Arctic Coasts.

Georgeson Botanical Garden:
While the Museum of the North is UA's big draw, the campus does hold other attractions, such as the Georgeson Botanical Garden. The expected floral fireworks certainly bring people to the garden, but more interesting is its position as the hemisphere's northernmost botanical garden. Learn how Alaska's plants adapt and thrive in the land of the midnight sun and frigid winter. Starting around mid-July visitors can gawk at 30-pound (14 kg) beets, cukes the size of third graders, 80-pound (36 kg) cabbages, and other monster veggies that 21 hours of sunlight a day can foster.

Georgeson Botanical Garden

✉ 117 W. Tanana Dr., at W end of UA campus

☎ 907/474-7222

🕐 Closed in winter

💲 $

www.georgeson bg.org

The riverboat *Discovery II* paddles along the Chena River past Fairbanks and environs.

Geophysical Institute
✉ 903 Koyukuk Dr., at W end of UA campus
☎ 907/474-7558
www.gi.alaska.edu

Large Animal Research Station
✉ 2220 Yankovich Rd., just N of UA campus
☎ 907/474-7207
$ $$
www.uaf.edu/lars

Alaskan Tails of the Trails
✉ Waldheim Dr., about 9 miles (14.5 km) N of the University of Alaska, Fairbanks
☎ 907/455-6469
$ $$$$$
www.mary shields.com

Geophysical Institute: In summer the university offers guided tours of three research facilities within the Geophysical Institute: the **Alaska Earthquake Information Center,** the **Alaska Satellite Facility,** and the **Alaska Volcano Observatory.** Usually given on Wednesdays, the three tours are arranged back to back to back, so you can gorge on science if you're a glutton for knowledge.

INSIDER TIP:

Musk oxen and caribou share the tundra regions of Alaska. Both species live at the Large Animal Research Station in Fairbanks, where you can learn about the similarities and differences of these animals.

—PAM GROVES
Professor, University of Alaska

Large Animal Research Station. The university's most popular tour takes visitors through LARS—the Large Animal Research Station. Expecting cows and horses? Remember, you're only 200 miles (320 km) from the Arctic Circle; the large animals at this facility are caribou, reindeer, and musk oxen.

Visitors get a wonderfully close look at these distinctive far-north critters. Among the things you learn from the guides: Caribou and reindeer are the same species, but

after 10,000 years of separation—caribou in North America and reindeer in Europe—they've developed slight differences (for example, caribou are a bit taller and reindeer sport more white patches). Caribou and reindeer have hollow hairs, which insulate them during the bitter northern winters. The clicking you hear from the legs of caribou and reindeer is a special tendon that helps propel their feet forward.

The station's musk ox bulls weigh up to 700 pounds (315 kg), are very aggressive, and sometimes even charge four-wheelers, so LARS staffers use a big tractor when they enter the pen. On the other hand, fuzzy little musk ox calves are cute as can be. Perhaps that explains why musk ox moms nurse their young even after they've grown into 200-pound (90 kg) yearlings. This practice does have its perils: These strapping young sometimes shove so hard to suckle that they lift mom's hindquarters clear off the ground.

Sled Dogs

Fairbanks visitors can also visit various outfits that care for sled dogs. One of the best tours features Mary Shields and her dogs in a program she calls **Alaskan Tails of the Trail.** Shields is the first woman to finish the Iditarod, the grueling 1,150-mile (1,850 km) sled dog race, and she has run dog teams all over Alaska and even in Siberia. She limits the size of each group and invites visitors not only into her kennels but also up to her log home to chat about sled dogs and her unusual profession. ∎

Chena Hot Springs Road

The 56.6 miles (91 km) of Chena Hot Springs Road brim with scenery and wildlife. That alone merits a drive along this route, a local favorite. But there are two additional reasons. One, as the name reveals, is the delightful hot springs at road's end and the elaborate resort that has grown up around the steaming waters.

Toasty hot springs await weary motorists at road's end.

The second attraction is the Chena River State Recreation Area—254,000 acres (102,870 ha) of forest, mountains, rivers, and tundra that flank the road for nearly half its length.

Chena Hot Springs Road branches east off the Steese Highway (see pp. 209–210) just north of Fairbanks. The first couple of dozen miles are pleasant but unremarkable: rural homes, farms, woods, a few streams. The reasons to stop and tarry start at Mile 26.1, when the road enters the **Chena River State Recreation Area.** A mile (1.6 km) later motorists approach Rosehip State Campground, the first of three

campgrounds in the recreation area. Even if you don't camp at this pretty riverside site, take the short **Rosehip Campground Nature Trail.** Signs along the path explain such things as forest succession and river erosion, and it's a good place to spot wildlife.

At Mile 38, just shy of First Bridge, you'll find a picnic table at a pullout that also provides river access for canoeing and kayaking, popular pastimes in the recreation area. The area offers many good access points, making it easy to plan just the right trip. While the upper reaches of the Chena include Class II rapids, this lower stretch is pretty smooth. Exercise

Chena River State Recreation Area

🗺 Map p. 189

✉ Mile 26.1 Chena Hot Springs Rd.

☎ 907/451-2705

💲 $$ (daily parking)

www.dnr.alaska.gov/ parks/units/chena

EXPERIENCE: Panning for Gold

Starting with the Klondike gold rush in 1898 and the Nome rush a year later, Alaska has a rich history of gold fever. You can get a feel for those days by going gold seeking too. These opportunities fall into three categories, ranging from touristy to serious.

One, do a little gold panning at tourist attractions. At a number of old gold mines or abandoned dredges (such as along the **Steese Highway;** see pp. 209–210), visitors are given pans and then set loose on some running water and gravel that has been salted with gold so that pretty much everyone will find some. Sorry, nobody gets to take home any nuggets.

Two, gold pan at one of several established claims. Perhaps the most popular is the **Crow Creek Mine** (see pp. 103–104). This was once south-central Alaska's most productive mine and gold continues to come out of them thar hills. For a modest fee you can rent a pan and go try your luck. And you may come away with the yellow stuff.

Three, eschew the established sites and go prospecting on your own on public lands. Contact Alaska Public Lands Information Centers (see sidebar p. 10) to learn about areas and regulations. One tip—don't quit your day job.

Chena Hot Springs Resort

- 🅰 Map p. 189
- ✉ Mile 56.6 Chena Hot Springs Rd.
- ☎ 907/451-8104
- 💲 $$

www.chenahot springs.com

reasonable caution, however, because the current can be swift, and the water is cold. The good news: Paddlers have excellent odds of seeing moose and beaver.

Around Mile 39, just beyond Second Bridge, is the Tors Trail State Campground. Riverside sites amid tall spruce and birch draw people here, but the main attraction is the **Granite Tors Trail.** Strong hikers can complete this moderate-to-difficult 15-mile (24 km) loop in a day, though many prefer to overnight. Starting in the forest, the trail soon strikes out across alpine tundra, wildflowers in the foreground, huge mountains in the background. The trail is indistinct in places, and hikers must navigate by rock cairns—a challenge in mist or rain. Midway through the hike you'll cross the **Plain of Monuments,** an expanse of tundra dotted with tors—granite outcrops that range from a few feet to 100 feet (30 m) high. Formed underground tens of millions of years ago, these pinnacles

were exposed as surface materials eroded away. Grizzlies roam the tundra, so watch out for them.

From the campground, Chena Hot Springs Road follows the river north, passing ponds and marshes. At Fourth Bridge, around Mile 49, a short side road leads to parking for the **Angel Rocks Trail,** a scenic 3.5-mile (5.6 km) loop past massive tors. Those seeking a strenuous trek can branch off about 2 miles (3 km) from the trailhead on the **Angel Rocks to Chena Hot Springs Trail.** This leads to a ridge and follows cairn after cairn. The 360-degree views are fantastic. So is the fact that the trail ends at **Chena Hot Springs Resort,** where relief awaits cold hands and tired legs.

A soak in Rock Lake is a must, but the resort also offers lodging, camping, a restaurant, dogsledding, fishing, gold panning, and tours of the **Aurora Ice Museum,** where everything—the furniture, drinking glasses, even the bar—is made of ice. Then visit the eponymous hot springs at Mile 56.6, road's end. ∎

Steese Highway

Scenery, wildlife, history, bush towns, hot springs—travelers have many options along the Steese, which runs from Fairbanks to Circle. The first 53 miles (85 km) of this 161-mile (260 km) road are paved, the next 73 (117 km) mostly gravel but wide and easygoing. But the remaining 35 miles (56 km) are narrow and winding. One 117-mile (188 km) stretch lacks gas stations, so fill up before you start, and then refill in Central or Circle before turning back.

The Steese is a beautiful drive through the hills and mountains in fall (late August–early September this far north), when the trees and tundra turn yellow and red. However, the first few miles pass bland development, so plan to scoot out of town. Just past Mile 8 is a pullout where visitors can walk right up to the **trans-Alaska pipeline.** A viewing center with information and souvenirs opens in summer.

A mile farther is the exit to **Gold Dredge No. 8.** To reach it, turn left on Goldstream Road, then left on the Old Steese Highway. From 1928 until its retirement in 1959, this 250-foot-long (76 m), five-story dredge crawled across this landscape, creating its own water channel and processing so many tons of rock that it produced more than 7.5 million ounces (212 million g) of gold. Visitors ride a narrow-gauge railroad a mile (1.6 km) to the dredge. You can try your hand at gold panning, too.

At mile 28 lies the **Chatanika Lodge** (tel 907/389-2164), a motel, store, restaurant, and saloon that's a lively gathering place for both locals and travelers; the entrance and walls brim with antlers and trophy heads.

Gold Dredge No. 8

✉ 1803 Old Steese Hwy. N
☎ 866/479-6673
$ $$$$
www.golddredge 8.com

The sun sets well after midnight in summer along the Steese Highway.

Upper Chatanika River State Recreation Site

🅼 Map p. 189

☎ 907/451-2705 (Alaska Dept. of Natural Resources PIC, Fairbanks) or 907/451-2695 (Northern Region Division of Parks and Outdoor Recreation)

Across the highway from the lodge, informal trails lead a few hundred feet to the hulking carcass of **Gold Dredge No. 3.** Rusting amid huge piles of tailings, this is no spruced-up tourist attraction. Like a dinosaur skeleton, the long-abandoned dredge bespeaks a bygone era when these iron behemoths chewed across the land, hungry for ore.

Here the road paces the pretty Chatanika River, a rapids-free

Trail Information

For information on Davidson Ditch, Nome Creek Valley Gold Panning, and the Pinnell Mountain National Recreation Trail, contact the **Alaska Bureau of Land Management** *(tel 907/474-2200, www.blm.gov/ak).*

Class II stream that's a favorite among canoeists. At Mile 39, the **Upper Chatanika River State Recreation Site** offers a good put-in point at the pleasant campground. For longer paddles, put in at any of several roadside sites farther upriver; check water levels with the Fairbanks office of the state Department of Natural Resources before setting out.

Ditches are not usually big tourist draws, but at Mile 57.3 you may want to stop at the **Davidson Ditch Historical Site.** Built in 1925 to provide water for the area's floating gold dredges, the 83-mile (134 km) channel carried up to 56,100 gallons (212,000 l) a minute. From this

same turnoff (U.S. Creek Road) motorists with 4WD vehicles can cross steep hills about 7 miles (11 km) to the **Nome Creek Valley Gold Panning Area,** one of several places along the Steese road that allow recreational panning.

At 3,190-foot (972 m) Twelvemile Summit Wayside (Mile 85.5), hikers have access to one of Alaska's finest trails: the **Pinnell Mountain National Recreation Trail.** For 27 miles (43 km) it passes through wildflower-strewn alpine tundra, along mountain ridges that yield views of the White Mountains and Alaska and Brooks Ranges, and through habitat favored by all sorts of animals from pikas to wolves. A day hike up just the first couple of miles is rewarded with alpine vistas. The trail emerges at the Eagle Summit Wayside at Mile 107.5 on the Steese. **Eagle Summit,** less than a mile from this parking lot, boasts gorgeous wildflowers in season.

Toward Road's End

At Mile 127.5 the road eases through charming **Central** (pop. 96), whose services cater to the busy mining district that surrounds this small town, as well as travelers. The **Circle District Historical Society Museum** *(tel 907/520-1893, www.cdhs.us)* covers both natural history and mining, past and present.

The Steese ends at **Circle** *(visitor information, HC Company Store, tel 907/773-1222),* about the same size as Central. On the Yukon's west bank, this town is a jumping-off point for summer river traffic, including riverboats and jet boats. And the store does sell gas. ■

Elliott Highway

The Elliott slips along hills and ridgetops, serving up views of boreal forest, mountains, rivers, and wildlife. Starting 11 miles (18 km) north of Fairbanks at the Steese Highway junction, near the town of Fox (mile posts calculate to here), this route runs 152 miles (245 km) into the wilds.

The first 73 miles (118 km), to the Dalton Highway junction, are paved, but the last 79 miles (127 km) are gravel and winding. Gas is available at Mile Fox 66 and at road's end, but there's little else on this remote road.

Just how remote is suggested at Mile Fox 9, where you'll spot the sign OLNES CITY (POP. 1). Olnes is the third largest town on the Elliott.

Caribou aren't the only species whose migratory route crosses interior Alaska.

INSIDER TIP:

From the Wickersham Dome Trailhead at Mile 27.7, take a short hike on the Summit Trail for spectacular views. The area is also a popular blueberry-picking spot for Fairbanksans in late July and August.

—TIM MOWRY
Outdoors editor, Fairbanks Daily News-Miner

For a short walk or weeklong backpack, pull off at Mile Fox 27.7 and the **Wickersham Dome Trailhead** *(contact Fairbanks BLM office, tel 907/474-2200).* This path leads to a network of trails in the **White Mountains National Recreation Area,** but even a 20-minute walk will take you above the tree line to wildflower meadows and marvelous vistas.

At Mile Fox 66 the road enters Livengood (pop. 13), an old mining settlement that offers services at the North Country Mercantile. Seven miles (11 km) farther the Dalton branches north, looking like the main highway; turn southwest to continue on the Elliott. Beyond Mile Fox 85 the views open up on the White Mountains, Tanana River, Minto Flats, and Alaska Range.

At road's end lies **Manley Hot Springs.** The old resort has shut down, but people still enjoy soaking in the springs, a short walk from the campground. The center of life in this village is the historic **Manley Roadhouse** *(tel 907/672-3161),* founded in 1906. Grab a bite, have a beer, or arrange for a cabin, and then talk it up with the miners, road crews, trappers, and other folks who live in the bush. ■

More Places to Visit in Alaska's Interior

Chicken

Hundreds of miles into Alaska's outback, Chicken is an eccentric hamlet of 7 people—several times that when miners hit town in summer. Legend has it the town was established as Ptarmigan in 1903—owing to the prevalence of this bird—but townsfolk changed the name to Chicken (a synonym for ptarmigan) because it was easier to spell. There are no phones (cell service is spotty) and no flush toilets, but there is a post office, which gets mail on Tuesdays and Fridays, weather permitting. You can stop by the **Chicken Mercantile** for some of Sue Wiren's mythic cinnamon rolls, homemade pie, and—yes—chicken soup. Be sure to check out **Pedro Dredge No. 4.** If all that driving seems a bit much, at least read the NSFAQ (not-so-frequently asked questions) on the colorful website *www.chickenalaska.com*. For information on a guided tour, go to the unofficial/official town website: *www.townofchicken.com.*

▲ Map p. 189

Denali State Park

Overshadowed by its celebrated neighbor to the north, this 325,240-acre (131,720 ha) state park also warrants attention. It is pierced by more than 30 miles (48 km) of the George Parks Highway (Rte. 3), the main road between Anchorage and Fairbanks, where, on clear days, pullouts reveal fabulous views of Mount McKinley and its Alaska Range entourage of snowcapped, jagged peaks. Many people argue that the vistas from pullouts at Mile 135.2 and Mile 162.4 of the Parks Highway are the finest roadside views, bar none, of the mountain and the range. But other pullouts here also offer excellent views.

A number of trails run through the park. Many are backpacking routes, though casual day-hikers can certainly hike a few miles up and back on these longer trails. You'll reach alpine meadows just 2 miles (3.2 km) up the **Little Coal Creek Trail,** which leaves from the parking lot at Mile 163.8 of the highway. One beautiful and easy day hike is the 4.8-mile (7.7 km) **Byers Lakeshore Loop,** which begins at Byers Lake Campground and circles the lake. A quarter mile (0.4 km) north of Byers Lake is the **Alaska Veterans Memorial/POW-MIA Rest Area** (*Mile 147.1 George Parks Hwy.*), where a small visitor center is staffed in the summer. The park also offers public cabins for rent. *www.dnr.alaska.gov/parks/units/denali1.htm*

▲ Map p. 189 ✉ Alaska State Parks, Mat-Su/CB Area, 7278 E. Bogard Rd., Wasilla AK 99654 ☎ 907/745-3975

White Mountains National Recreation Area

The White Mountains National Recreation Area (*www.blm.gov/ak/st/en/prog/nlcs/white_mtns.html*) offers a million acres (400,000 ha) of mountains, rivers, and trails. In warm months, visitors pan for gold, hike, raft, and fish. In winter they cross-country ski, dogsled, snowshoe, or skimobile. In fact, much of the area is more accessible in winter than in summer because then the trails are groomed whereas in summer they can be boggy and difficult to walk. Some trails are open to motorized vehicles, others not.

The White Mountains NRA offers a dozen remote cabins, one on the Elliott Highway but the others on trails from 7 to 40 miles (11–64 km) off the road, accessible only by foot, boat, mountain bike, 4WD vehicle, or plane. Reservations are required and visitors are limited to three-night stays, from as little as $20 to $25 a night. Cabins have a stove (for which the campers must bring their own propane), up to three bunk beds, a table, a lantern, and little else. There is no running water.

Beyond cities, beyond roads, beyond ferries—the part of Alaska most visitors never see

The Bush

A walrus skull rests amid tundra wildflowers in the lush, remote Pribilof Islands.

The Bush

Travelers can delve deep into the wilderness at Denali National Park and Preserve. They can get off the roads and ride the state ferry to distant communities in Southeast Alaska. They can jet 500 miles (800 km) from the mainland and land at an isolated Aleutian Islands town like Unalaska/Dutch Harbor.

Walruses congregate at the Walrus Islands State Game Sanctuary, in Bristol Bay off Dillingham.

By lower 48 standards, these places are indeed remote. But the Bush takes remoteness to a whole other level. It is what lies beyond those relatively accessible parts of Alaska.

Hogatza. Kilbuck Mountains. Kogoluktuk River. Flat. Sleetmute. Marys Igloo. Platinum. Thunder Mountain. Oliktok Point. Red Devil. Shaktoolik. Wild places and villages few travelers have heard of and fewer still have seen. Vast expanses where grizzlies, moose, and wolves outnumber people. Settlements inhabited by 200 to 300 natives and maybe a handful of non-native get-away-from-it-all types. This is the Bush.

Residents in most Bush villages lean heavily on subsistence lifestyles. They hunt moose, walruses, caribou, geese, beluga whales, bears, ducks, seals, and bowhead whales; trap beavers, mink, otters, wolverines, and hare; gather berries and wild onions; and fish for just about everything. Many also earn money as commercial fishers, hunting and fishing guides, summer firefighters, miners, and government workers, and by making and selling native crafts.

No hard-and-fast boundaries define the Bush. Roughly, it includes the western half of mainland Alaska and the northeastern quadrant—about three quarters of the state. This vast region encompasses a range of ecosystems, though most of it falls under the two broad categories of tundra or boreal forest, each laced with mountain ranges. It also features a long, complex coastline that fronts the Bering Sea, the Chukchi Sea, and the Beaufort Sea, a part of the Arctic Ocean.

Getting There

By definition the Bush is not connected to the rest of the state by road or railway, with the exception of the Dalton Highway, built to serve the Arctic oil fields at Prudhoe Bay. People travel by boat along the coast, up the rivers, and across the watery coastal plain of the Yukon-Kuskokwim Delta. To reach anywhere else, they take those small planes.

Casual visitors almost always travel to the region by plane, which generally makes the Bush an expensive destination. Daily jet service from Anchorage serves several larger towns. Flying into these few hubs (versus chartering a flight to more remote regions) or simply driving the Dalton Highway are the most practical least expensive means of transportation to Alaska's outback. Many areas are also accessible by boat.

The larger towns offer lodging, restaurants, grocery stores, and tour operators, mostly geared to anglers and hunters. Smaller villages usually lack such amenities, but sometimes let travelers sleep in their schools or other government buildings (possibly on the floor). ■

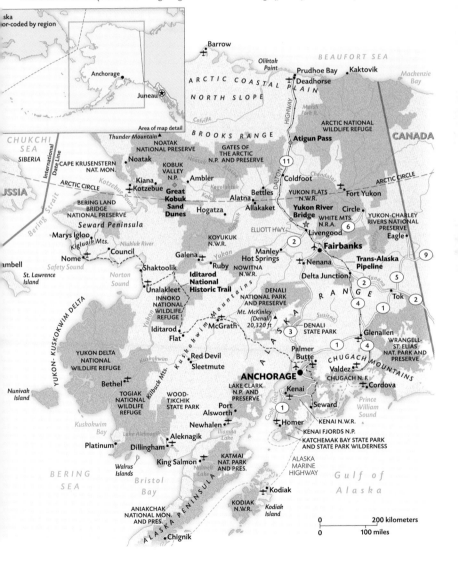

Dillingham & Vicinity

If you like fish, Dillingham is your town. This is the harbor for the Bristol Bay commercial sockeye salmon fishery, one of the world's most productive. Dillingham also offers outstanding sport-fishing opportunities: Guides, charter boats, and wilderness fishing lodges abound.

Dillingham derives its living from the sea, which accounts for the flotilla of fishing boats in its harbor.

The town has plenty to offer non-anglers, as well, serving as a jumping-off point to several prime wilderness and wildlife areas. Though a working town with a utilitarian ambience, Dillingham does offer basic services for travelers, such as hotels, restaurants, and stores.

Your first stop should be the library, at the corner of Seward and D Streets—not to check out a book but to stop at the visitor center and **Sam Fox Museum** (tel 907/842-4831, closed Sun.), which share a building with the library.

The small museum focuses on local history, particularly that of the Yupik Eskimos. It also serves as an art gallery. Visitors can buy carved ivory, masks, Eskimo dolls, and other arts and crafts at several stores in town.

For a look at present-day Dillingham, stroll down to the **harbor,** where hundreds of small fishing boats crowd the docks—when not out fishing, of course. To learn more about the industry, ask the visitor center about a tour of one of several **commercial salmon canneries.**

Wilderness Areas

If you want to explore outdoors, consider the **Togiak National Wildlife Refuge.** At 4.7 million acres (1.9 million ha), this wilderness of lakes, rivers, mountains, and coastline is huge; its eastern boundary lies just 3 miles (4.8 km) west of town but the western boundary is 130 miles (210 km) away. To navigate this expanse, almost all travelers enlist the help of guides. Rafting tours often start on headwater lakes and drift the waterways for several days. Most trips are geared to fishers or hunters, though sightseers and wildlife-watchers will also enjoy themselves. The refuge shelters moose, wolves, and otters. Nearly 30,000 caribou of nearby herds visit the refuge, while whales, sea lions, and seabirds frequent the 600-mile (965 km) coastline.

Winding north from Dillingham is one of the Bush's rare roads, a **scenic byway** that leads 25 miles (40 km) to the village of **Aleknagik** and the southern end of **Lake Aleknagik.** Ten miles (16 km) up the lake is the southern border of **Wood-Tikchik State Park**—at 1.6 million acres (647,500 ha), the country's biggest state park. Visitors can reach it via charter boat out of Aleknagik or from Dillingham via the Wood River, although most people fly to one of the big lakes and then take a guided raft, canoe, or kayak trip through the network of lakes connected by rivers. The park is a transition zone. To the east you'll find wooded and wet lowlands, while the western reaches feature tall peaks, alpine valleys, and fjord-like arms of lakes that reach deep into the mountains. The wildlife-watching is excellent, especially when the salmon are running and eagles, brown bears, river otters, kingfishers, foxes, and other critters gather along with the anglers to feast on the fish.

INSIDER TIP:

If you visit Dillingham or the nearby parks, bring a good fishing rod. There's great saltwater and freshwater fishing. Get a fishing license in Dillingham or on the Internet (www.adfg.alaska.gov).

—ANDY ADERMAN
Wildlife biologist, Togiak NWR

Round Island: Wildlife-watchers on the lookout for something different may want to take a floatplane or charter boat from Dillingham to Round Island, the heart of the **Walrus Islands State Game Sanctuary,** in northern Bristol Bay. Thousands of blubbery, tusked male walruses haul out on the beaches of this rugged little island each year. You'll also find some 250,000 seabirds, hundreds of Steller sea lions, and red foxes. Special permits are required, and conditions can be tough, so consult thoroughly with the Fish and Game folks before putting this trip on your itinerary. ∎

Dillingham
- Map p. 215

Visitor Information
- Seward & D Sts.
- ☎ 907/842-5115
- ⏱ Closed Sat.–Sun.

www.dillingham chamberof commerce.org

Togiak National Wildlife Refuge
- Map p. 215
- ✉ Information: 6 Main St., Kangiiqutaq Bldg.
- ☎ 907/842-1063

http://togiak .fws.gov

Wood-Tikchik State Park
- Map p. 215
- ☎ Dillingham Ranger Station: 907/842-2641

www.dnr.alaska.gov/ parks/units/wood tik.htm

Walrus Islands State Game Sanctuary
- ☎ 907/842-2334 (Alaska Dept. of Fish & Game, Div. of Wildlife Conservation)

Bethel & Vicinity

Visitors are often surprised at how big Bethel is. Its population ranges between 6,000 and 8,000, depending on the season. It also hosts one of the busiest airports in Alaska, with daily jet service from Anchorage and squadrons of small planes from dozens of nearby villages; the town is the transportation and supply hub for much of western Alaska.

Spectacled eiders nest at the Yukon Delta National Wildlife Refuge.

Bethel
🄰 Map p. 215
Visitor Information
✉ 192 Alex Hately St.
☎ 907/543-2911
**www.bethelak
chamber.org**

**Yupiit Piciryarait
Cultural Center &
Museum**
✉ 420 Chief Eddie
Hoffman Hwy.
☎ 907/543-4500
🕐 Closed Sun.–Mon.
💲 $

**Yukon Delta
National Wildlife
Refuge**
🄰 Map p. 215
☎ 907/543-3151
🕐 Closed Sun.
**http://yukondelta
.fws.gov**

However, Bethel retains the off-the-grid, ramshackle feel of a Bush community. Some residents of this predominantly Native town still wear traditional Yupik Eskimo clothing, such as caribou-skin parkas and sealskin mukluks. Yet Bethel definitely exists in the 21st century: You can get a latte in a dozen different places, and locals include Albanians, Filipinos, and Koreans who have come to work here, many as cab drivers—a surprising number for a place that only has a couple dozen miles of road. To learn about the history and contemporary culture of the Yupik/Cupik and Dene, drop by the **Yupiit Piciryarait Cultural Center & Museum.** One

of its three galleries houses a permanent collection of native art and artifacts, while the two others offer changing exhibits. The gift shop sells local native art and crafts.

Bethel's big attraction is the vast **Yukon Delta National Wildlife Refuge,** where glacial silt deposited over the millennia by the Yukon and Kuskokwim Rivers has created the second largest delta in the U.S., exceeded only by the Mississippi. Most of the refuge comprises wet tundra mixed with ponds, lakes, rivers, and creeks. Caribou, lynx, bears, wolves, polar bears (along the coast), and musk oxen (on Nunivak Island) roam the refuge, as do millions of birds. Call to arrange a guided tour. ∎

Nome & Vicinity

Unlike most Bush towns, Nome didn't start as a native settlement. Born abruptly after the discovery of gold in 1898, it was initially named Anvil City, after the gold strike in Anvil Creek. By the summer of 1900 some 20,000 people had arrived in this remote boomtown on the Seward Peninsula at the edge of the Bering Sea. Though gold mining remains big business around Nome, the rush is long past and the population now stands at about 3,700—still big enough to make this town the hub of northwestern Alaska.

INSIDER TIP:

If you are visiting in the winter, be sure to check the aurora forecast *(www.gedds .alaska.edu/AuroraFore cast)* **and go outside late at night to see the northern lights.**

—PAM GROVES
Professor, University of Alaska

Of all the Bush communities, Nome is the one most geared to travelers who aren't hunters or anglers. In fact, enough package tours come to town that sometimes all the hotels are filled, so reserve early. Nome is unique among Bush locales because about 300 miles (483 km) of decent gravel roads fan out along the coast and up into the tundra-covered mountains of the peninsula. Properly informed and prepared, visitors can rent a car and tour around on their own.

Start at the visitor center, on **Front Street,** the town's main drag, which runs along the Bering Sea. The center's resources and staff are exceptional and extend well beyond the usual help with lodging or restaurants. They can

hook you up with just the right tour guide or provide maps and handouts for you to go it alone, whether you're looking for historic gold dredges (or currently operating ones), good fishing holes, or rare birds. Pick up the walking-tour map, which emphasizes historic sites, though most gold-rush buildings have burned down or

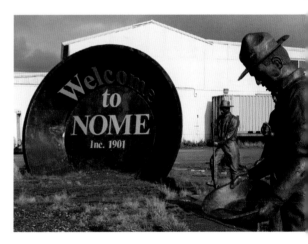

A giant gold pan welcomes visitors to Nome, Alaska.

been destroyed by storms.

Steps from the visitor center, in the basement of the library building, is the **Carrie M. McLain Memorial Museum,** which focuses on early Bering Strait–area Eskimo life, the gold rush, and the 1925 diphtheria epidemic. The

Nome
 Map p. 215
Visitor Information
✉ 301 Front St.
☎ 907/443-6555
🕐 Open daily late May–late Aug., closed Sat.–Sun. rest of year
www.visitnome alaska.com

Carrie M. McLain Memorial Museum
✉ 223 E. Front St.
☎ 907/443-6630
🕐 Closed Sun.– Mon. mid-Sept.–late May

Maruskiya's of Nome
- ✉ 247 Front St.
- ☎ 907/443-2955

Chukotka-Alaska Store
- ✉ 514 Lomen Ave.
- ☎ 907/443-4128

latter ended after the heroic delivery of serum to Nome by dogsled from Nenana, 650 miles (1,050 km) away—an event that inspired the renowned Iditarod Sled Dog Race, which starts in Anchorage and ends in Nome every March. Don't miss the museum's outstanding collection of historic photos.

Nome is an excellent place to buy native art and crafts, notably carved ivory, a specialty of northwestern villages. These sculptures aren't fashioned from elephant tusks; Alaska ivory comes from the tusks of the walruses that throng the coastal waters of northwestern Alaska. Try **Maruskiya's of Nome** and the **Chukotka-Alaska Store.** The Russian names serve as a reminder that Nome is only 161 miles (259 km) from Siberia.

Three Roads

Three main roads pierce the wilds of the Seward Peninsula: the Nome-Council, Nome-Taylor (Kougarok), and Nome-Teller. The 72-mile (116 km) **Council Road** heads east along the Bering Sea for about 30 miles (48 km), then veers inland northeast to the Niukluk River. In early summer, as ice melts, marine mammals and birds congregate in the leads (gaps in the ice); look for ringed seals, eiders, harlequin ducks, and loons. Twenty-two miles (35 km) from town is **Safety Sound,** a hot spot for waterfowl and seabirds, including the Mongolian plover. Gold-rush cabins in Council augur the end of the road.

The 86-mile (138 km) **Kougarok Road** runs north into the rugged **Kigluaik Mountains,** which invite hiking. Note the remains of the Wild Goose Pipeline, meant to supply water to the early gold mines (*refrain from disturbing the site*). Scan the roadside cliffs for nesting eagles, peregrine falcons, and gyrfalcons, and watch for grizzlies. Beyond Mile 80, the road can be rough.

Wending its way northwest to the village of Teller, the 72-mile (116 km) **Teller Road** is another good birding route and may yield glimpses of reindeer and their herders, as well as musk oxen. ∎

Polar Bears & Pack Ice

While visitors associate grizzlies and black bears with Alaska, fewer realize the state also harbors polar bears. That's because visitors rarely see one, which is just as well, as they are far more dangerous to humans than are the two other bear species. A few thousand polar bears spend some of the winter on the northwestern and northern Alaska coasts, ranging south as far the Yukon-Kuskokwim Delta, but during the summer—when most visitors are around—the bears are roaming the pack ice far to the north. Many scientists worry that polar bears may be among the early victims of global warming, as the ice pack on which they spend most of their lives is melting.

Kotzebue

Just as extreme weather shapes the tundra, forcing plants to hug the ground for dear life, so the harsh Arctic climate has shaped Kotzebue. Perched on the tip of a narrow, 3-mile-long (4.8 km) spit that juts into a sound on the Chukchi Sea, this town of some 3,300 hardy residents—a large majority of them Inupiat Eskimos—takes some serious weather hits.

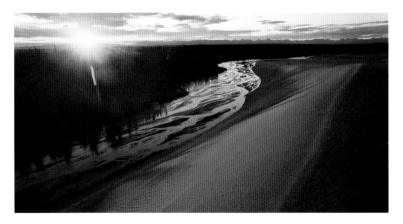

Kotzebue is a jumping-off point for visits to the dunes in Kobuk Valley National Park.

Accordingly, its buildings are low-lying and solidly built. Yet a close look at Kotzebue and its environs reveals much beauty in its people and their art.

The **Northwest Arctic Heritage Center** serves both as a museum covering the region's natural history and Inupiat Eskimo culture and as the National Park Service headquarters for the remote Kobuk Valley National Park (see p. 226), Noatak National Preserve, Cape Krusenstern National Monument, and Bering Land Bridge National Preserve (see p. 232). Visitors can see a stuffed polar bear, musk ox, and other, smaller critters as well as the harpoon, kayak, dogsled, and other artifacts of traditional Inupiat life.

Most of the few visitors to **Noatak National Preserve**

traverse its 6.3 million acres (2.5 million ha) by rafting down the Noatak, a wild and scenic river. Except for a few rough stretches, the long voyage—up to three weeks—is a gentle float, but its remoteness dictates using a guide. The tundra and mountains are home to grizzlies, wolves, and swans. Between April and August you may sight the huge Arctic caribou herd.

From Kotzebue it's only 10 miles (16 km) by plane or boat to **Cape Krusenstern National Monument.** While most folks venture here to look for rare birds blown in from Asia, look for musk oxen, or take in the otherworldly scenery. The monument's raison d'être is archaeological—more than 100 coastal sand-and-gravel ridges hold artifacts that speak to some 9,000 years of human activity. ∎

Kotzebue
Map p. 215

Visitor Information
✉ 258A 3rd Ave.
☎ 907/442-3401
**www.cityof
kotzebue.com**

**Northwest Arctic
Heritage Center**
✉ 154 2nd Ave.
☎ 907/442-3890
🕐 Closed Sun.
June–Sept.,
Sun.–Mon.
Oct.–May

**Noatak National
Preserve**
www.nps.gov/noat

**Cape Krusenstern
National
Monument**
www.nps.gov/cakr

Dalton Highway

Though in its strictest sense not the Bush, this road *is* wild and beautiful. It's also long and rough, mostly gravel, passing through boreal forest, across tundra, and beyond the Arctic Circle to the North Slope and the Arctic Ocean. Also known as the Haul Road, the Dalton Highway was built in the mid-1970s to provide construction access to the northern stretch of the trans-Alaska oil pipeline. It runs 414 miles (667 km), from Mile 73.1 on the Elliott Highway (84 miles/135 km north of Fairbanks) to Deadhorse.

After crossing the Arctic Circle, the Dalton runs 300 miles (480 km) north to the Arctic Ocean.

Dalton Highway
🅜 Map p. 215

Bureau of Land Management Northern Field Office
✉ 1150 University Ave., Fairbanks, AK 99709
☎ 907/474-2200 or 800/437-7021
www.blm.gov/ak/dalton

Big gravel-flinging trucks still service the oil fields along this highway. If you see one coming, pull over and pray for the safety of your windshield. Bring replacement headlights and belts, two full-size, mounted spare tires, coolant, plenty of food and water, blankets, and sleeping bags. Also carry extra gas, as service stations are scarce along this route. Always drive with your headlights on. Or, several companies run tours up

the Dalton *(visitor information, Fairbanks Convention & Visitors Bureau, tel 907/456-5774, www .explorefairbanks.com)*.

The route north begins along a stretch of forest where birders have happily logged more than a hundred species. At Mile 55.5 the road crosses the amazing 2,290-foot (698 m) **Yukon River Bridge**; to learn about the pipeline and Alaska's longest river, stop by the **Yukon Crossing Visitor Contact Station** *(closed early Sept.–late May)*.

Around Mile 95 the scenery shifts from varied spruce forest to wildflower-dotted tundra. Pause at the **Finger Mountain BLM Wayside** (Mile 98) to stroll the short interpretive nature trail.

The Dalton crosses the **Arctic Circle** at Mile 115; look for the interpretive sign. Sixteen miles (26 km) farther, **Gobblers Knob** offers a stellar view where the sun never sets at the summer solstice.

At Mile 175, **Coldfoot** (pop. 11) provides gas, lodging, tours, and flightseeing. Visit the **Arctic Interagency Visitor Center** for local information.

Above the tree line at Mile 244.7, the road crests the high point of the drive—4,800-foot (1,463 m) **Atigun Pass,** in the striking Brooks Range. Watch for Dall sheep and grizzlies as you descend to the tundra of the **North Slope.** Millions of birds nest here, including tundra swans and snowy owls.

The highway ends in the town of **Deadhorse.** Lodging in this oil patch town is in high demand, so reserve early. To venture the last miles over the oil fields to the Arctic Ocean, you must join a tour (see p. 222). ■

Arctic Interagency Visitor Center

✉ Mile 175 Dalton Hwy., Coldfoot

☎ 907/678-5209

🕐 Closed early Sept.–late May

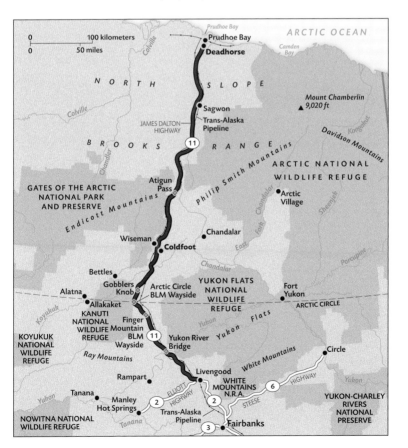

Winter in Alaska

Granted, sometimes the stereotype about the brutality of Alaska's winters is accurate. In the Interior occasional inversions shove thermometers deep below zero; it was once so cold in Fairbanks that an auto tire shattered on the ground after falling off a truck. Winter storms along the Gulf of Alaska and other coastal zones often lash the shoreline with gale-force winds and buckets of rain.

The otherworldly aurora borealis is a highlight for many winter visitors.

As for the far north, near the Arctic Ocean, well, let's just note that folks up there routinely leave their vehicles running in winter—their cars might not otherwise start. And then there's the darkness. Above the Arctic Circle, which encompasses about a third of Alaska, the sun never rises above the horizon in midwinter, while southern regions get a measly five to six hours of daylight per day.

That's the bad news. The good news for winter travelers is that the stereotype applies more to the extremes. For most of the winter in most of Alaska the weather is tolerable. Take Anchorage—in February the average high temperature is 25°F (-4°C). Not quite tropical, to be sure, but not much different from Minnesota or Montana. Anchorage also gets much less precipitation in the winter than in the summer. Ditto for the Interior. The Southeast does get drenched in winter, but its proximity to the Pacific moderates temperatures. Bottom line, winter in Alaska offers a lot for visitors, and they shouldn't be afraid of the weather.

That said, motorists should respect the winter weather. Use common sense and don't head into a storm along a back road in an '89 Yugo without adequate gas and provisions. Consider bringing a small bag of sand to pour onto the snow beneath your tires for traction should you get mired. If you are caught in a blizzard while driving, pull over and wait it out, running the engine and heater about ten minutes every hour, not continuously—and be sure to crack a downwind window and keep the exhaust pipe clear of snow so as to avoid carbon monoxide poisoning. For more safety tips, contact any of the Alaska Public Lands Information Centers (www.alaskacenters.gov).

Winter Activities

Now, to be honest, less-than-unbearable weather is hardly a big selling point. Why then *do* people visit Alaska in winter? Many come to catch the aurora borealis (aka northern lights), which shimmies across the night sky in colossal, ever shifting bands of light (see sidebar this page).

Others take part in winter activities, notably skiing. Some even try night skiing while watching the northern lights. The biggest downhill ski area is Mount Alyeska, about 40 miles (64 km)

Aurora Borealis

Auroras occur when solar flares send streams of charged particles into the Earth's magnetic field, where they react with atmospheric gases to create those radiant colors. Onlookers watch, mesmerized, as undulating yellow-green streamers suddenly swell to drape the whole sky. Sometimes blues, purples, and pinks dance into the picture. On rare occasions the aurora is wholly red. Among the state's accessible regions, the Fairbanks area offers the best northern lights viewing. Some lodges and tour operators cater to aurora-watchers with such amenities as heated, glassed-in rooms or hot tubs from which to soak up the lights.

---

south of Anchorage, near the town of Girdwood. Fairbanks and Juneau also host downhill ski areas. Cross-country skiing abounds, including maintained trails just outside cities and towns. Guides and heli-skiing operators will take you deep into the backcountry.

If you'd rather have someone else do the work, try a dogsledding tour. Mushers statewide maintain kennels full of frisky huskies.

Visitors can also watch dogsled races, from short runs on a track to the granddaddy of them all, the Iditarod, in which mushers and their teams cover some 1,150 miles (1,850 km) from Anchorage to Nome. It starts on the first Saturday in March.

Festivals: Alaskans engage in dozens of other activities to ward off cabin fever. Among them is Fairbanks' well-known **Festival of Native Arts,** in February or March, which draws dancers, musicians, and artisans from settlements throughout the state, as well as Russia, Canada, and Japan. Another must-see is Anchorage's celebrated **Fur Rendezvous,** a two-week-plus extravaganza that begins in late February and defies categorization. Among the many eclectic elements: dogsled races, a dog weight pull, snowshoe softball, bingo, ice bowling, curling, a snow sculpture contest, a carnival, an oyster-shucking contest, horse-drawn carriage rides, a motorcycle show, a masque ball, a chess tournament, an antique tractor show, a mutt show, a weiner-eating contest, and, of course, a fur auction.

This breadth of imagination to spice up winter spreads far beyond Anchorage. Small communities stage simple diversions that often morph into larger events as restless souls from neighboring towns attend. Cordova's **Iceworm Festival** kicks off on the first weekend in February with a parade led by a 100-foot (30 m) ice worm. The **Bering Sea Ice Golf Classic,** in Nome, is held on the third Saturday in March; using bright orange golf balls and old shotgun shells for tees, golfers trudge the frozen sea in boots and parkas to challenge the makeshift course. Seward celebrates the third weekend in January with the **Polar Bear Jump Off.** Though it includes such normal activities as a seafood feed and basketball, the Jump Off is defined by events such as a waiter/waitress contest, oyster slurping, the ugly fish toss, and the dog weight pull—winners haul well over a ton. The highlight, though, comes when a host of costumed lunatics plunge into Resurrection Bay, whose water is about one degree shy of being ice.

Kobuk Valley National Park

Sandwiched between two mountain ranges, Kobuk Valley National Park offers 1.8 million acres (730,000 ha) of roadless, trailless wilderness. Kobuk lies above the Arctic Circle at the northern boundary of the boreal forest, where scrawny spruces and birches survive amid the vast tundra. Though few visitors make it to this park, Alaska natives use it for subsistence fishing and hunting, so please be respectful of any cabins, camps, or nets you may find.

The Great Kobuk Sand Dunes rise amid the tundra and boreal forest of Kobuk Valley National Park.

**Kobuk Valley
National Park**
🗺 Map p. 215
☎ 907/442-3890
www.nps.gov/kova

To reach the park, either charter a plane in Kotzebue or Nome or take a scheduled flight into one of several Inupiat villages on the Kobuk River—say, Ambler or Kiana—and air taxi or boat in from there. Guided tours often raft a portion of the **Kobuk River,** the park's main artery. Closer to the headwaters the river offers serious white water, but the lower river is a relaxed drift. While floating down the river or hiking its margins, watch for grizzlies, caribou, and golden eagles. Anglers cherish the river for its arctic char, grayling, and spirited giant sheefish.

A 1.5-mile (2.4 km) hike from the river is the park's central feature, **Great Kobuk Sand Dunes,** a 25-square-mile (65 sq km) mini Sahara whose golden dunes rise to 100 feet/30 m (remote dunes to the south reach 500 feet/152 m). Millennia ago upriver glaciers ground parts of the Brooks Range into sand, which gradually tumbled down the Kobuk and blew into the dune fields you see today. ■

EXPERIENCE: Into the Wild, With or Without Guides

The little Cessna plane bumps along the relatively flat stretch of meadow that passes for a landing strip. Disembarked, standing at the edge of the makeshift runway, you and your companions feel both anxiety and excitement when the growl of the twin propellers intensifies and the six-seater accelerates for takeoff. Moments later the plane curves up into the gray sky, the pilot waggles the wings in farewell, and the plane disappears over a spruce-studded hill. The whine of the engine fades and is replaced by a whisper of wind, the whistle of a gray jay, and the slither of a creek sliding over rocks. And, until that Cessna returns, the sounds of nature are all that you will hear as you and your companions stay behind deep in that unpopulated Alaska wilderness.

On Your Own

Many visitors to the Great Land consider wilderness drop-offs to be the ultimate Alaska travel experience. You hire a plane to leave you in the middle of the bush, and for a day or a weekend or a week or however long you want, you live a backcountry existence. You can soften the sojourn by going to a remote lodge, most of which cater to anglers or hunters, some of which are quite luxurious (see Travelwise p. 239). But the purer experience involves a rustic cabin or a tent.

Okay, sounds great, but is it safe? Not entirely, so precautions should be taken. First, not everyone in Alaska who owns a plane should fly one, much less ferry passengers to remote locales. Choose your aviation company carefully (see Travelwise p. 234).

Safety concerns continue after you've landed. Bears, hypothermia, avalanches—all the usual outdoor-Alaska threats are present, but the danger is magnified by the remoteness. If you get injured or sick, you can't just dial 911 and wait five minutes for the paramedics.

Even the ultra-prepared visitor who brings a satellite phone or personal locator beacon has to realize that it will take quite a while for help to arrive. If you and your companions don't have

INSIDER TIP:

Go on a tundra tour (by ATV or trail) on the North Slope. But walking the tundra is tough: It's a bog, and you have to pick up your legs high to move across it.

—DAVID GRIMALDI
National Geographic field researcher

extensive backcountry experience, it's best to go with a guide—the choice made by most drop-off travelers.

With an Outfitter

Guiding outfits often provide both the flight and the person who stays with your party, so picking the right outfit covers all the safety

bases (see Guided Tours p. 29). Common sense and plenty of questions can go a long way toward helping you select a reputable guiding company. For additional assurance, you can stick to public lands; outfits operating on public lands are vetted. You can check out a company's records by contacting the government entity that manages the land you want to visit.

Outfitters also can help with the most difficult question of all: where to go. On public lands alone (which constitute more than half of Alaska), there are scores of millions of acres (tens of millions of hectares) of designated wilderness. And there are plenty of wild places that lack official designations. Do you want to see wildlife? Glaciers? Coastlines? Volcanoes? Do you want to fish, bird-watch, canoe, backpack, raft, beachcomb, or kayak? Or do you just want to lounge around and savor the incredible scenery? Whatever your choice, you can look forward to the time when your heart will be beating a little faster as you wave goodbye to your plane.

Gates of the Arctic National Park & Preserve

For travelers eager to explore Alaska's great northern wilderness but unready to delve into some totally unknown expanse of the Bush, Gates of the Arctic is a good solution. Far larger than Yellowstone and utterly undeveloped, the park comprises a huge expanse of wild Alaska. "It seemed as if time had dropped away a million years and we were back in a primordial world," wrote Robert Marshall, famed explorer and conservationist, in the 1930s.

Trees and other flora are sparse this far north.

Today you'll find the same sawtooth mountains, the same pure rivers, and the same array of wolves, grizzlies, eagles, beavers, caribou, and other animals. But thanks to its designation as a national park, Gates of the Arctic is more accessible than during Robert Marshall's time. However, don't mistake it for Yellowstone; Gates of the Arctic is a rough unpredictable wilderness and only fit, well-prepared, and experienced outdoorspeople should tackle it without a guide—and even with a guide visitors should be sure they're up to the trip they select.

Most people fly from Fairbanks or Coldfoot (on the Dalton Highway; see pp. 222–223) into small gateway communities, such as **Bettles,** which includes a handy Park Service visitor center and several outfitters. From there small planes make the short flight into the park. Some hardy souls fly to the gateway village of **Anaktuvuk Pass** and hike into the park.

Exploring by River

The prospect of trudging over mountains and tussocky tundra convinces most people to instead traverse the park down one of its many rivers via raft,

Avalanche Dangers

Avalanches occasionally strike high-country hikers or snowshoers, but the majority of victims are backcountry skiers and snowmobilers. There are two ways to avoid avalanches: Stay out of avalanche territory altogether or venture into it armed with ample knowledge, gear, and a commitment to testing the snow, measuring slopes, and taking other necessary precautions. And, no, loud noises rarely trigger avalanches.

You should also know how to survive avalanches. For example, you should fight to stay on top of the cascading snow and, if you get buried, you should clear an air space in front of your face. Vitally, if your companions get buried, work fast to rescue them because chances of survival dip below 50 percent after about 30 minutes. For information, contact the Alaska Avalanche Information Center *(tel 907/255-2242, www.alaskasnow.org).*

canoe, or kayak. The **North Fork Koyukuk** involves a few tricky obstacles, though no appreciable or dangerous rapids. A floatplane can drop you at **Summit Lake** (or other lakes

INSIDER TIP:

After they get dropped off in a remote wilderness like Gates of the Arctic for the first time and the drone of the bush plane's engine fades away, most people say it's a quiet beyond any they've experienced before.

—JAY JESPERSEN
Veteran Arctic Alaska bush pilot

near **Redstar Creek**), from which you'll drift lazily past waterfalls, glacial valleys, and gorgeous mountains. Enjoy a few day hikes along the way, but fan out instead of walking single file so you don't wear a rut in the fragile Arctic landscape.

After four or five days and 100 miles (160 km) you'll float right into Bettles.

A designated wild and scenic river, the **Alatna** descends the south slopes of the Brooks Range. The first couple of dozen miles below the headwaters involve rapids and sweepers (trees whose branches graze the river surface), so be sure to have experience or a guide at the helm. Gorgeous scenery is your reward. Put in farther downriver for a gentle float past lush tundra into the forested lowlands.

Because Gates of the Arctic is, in the words of one park ranger, a "black belt wilderness," and because park staff have no way to reliably assess visitors' backcountry capabilities, staff can't be responsible for detailed route planning. Visitors must do this themselves or in consultation with their guides. However, once visitors choose a route, whether by river or by foot, rangers are happy to share information about safety and things to do and see. The staff also can steer people to a list of outfitters and guides authorized to operate in Gates of the Arctic. ∎

Gates of the Arctic National Park & Preserve

🅜 Maps pp. 215 & 223

✉ Bettles Ranger Station/Visitor Center, Bettles

☎ 907/692-5495

www.nps.gov/gaar

Arctic Interagency Visitor Center

✉ Mile 175 Dalton Hwy., Coldfoot

☎ 907/678-5209

🕐 Closed early Sept.–late May

Arctic National Wildlife Refuge

Thanks to the long-running controversy over whether to drill for oil in the Arctic National Wildlife Refuge (ANWR), this 19.3-million-acre (7.8 million ha) hunk of northeast Alaska has become the nation's most famous wildlife refuge. Yet few people know much about it, and far fewer have ever been there.

Arctic National Wildlife Refuge

🏔 Maps pp. 215 & 223

Visitor Information

✉ U.S. Fish & Wildlife Service, 101 12th Ave., Room 236, Fairbanks

☎ 907/456-0250 or 800/362-4546

http://arctic.fws.gov

ANWR is a tough place to get to (think little charter planes landing on gravel bars), a tough place to get around in (think trailless hiking and wilderness river running), and a tough place to get along with (think mosquitoes, days of fog, and bears). Ah, but the payoff is as big as the place. The refuge boasts the greatest diversity of flora and fauna of any park or refuge in the circumpolar Arctic. Look for wolves, moose, musk oxen, and all three species of bear—grizzly, black, and polar. And the famous Porcupine caribou, all 125,000 of them, or the millions of birds representing 201 species.

The best hiking is in the **Brooks Range,** which reaches its widest point—110 miles (177 km) north to south—as it arcs through the refuge. Outfitters frequently drop off visiting trekkers on riverbanks or dry ridges, often in the company of guides.

River running is increasingly popular, particularly on the **Kongakut,** the **Canning,** the **Hulahula,** and the **Sheenjek.** The first three run north from the Brooks Range to the Arctic Ocean, though most trips stop short of the sea. Float down the Kongakut at the right time and you'll see herds of migrating caribou.

The Sheenjek flows south to the Porcupine River from the region's highest peaks, which top 9,000 feet (2,740 m). Mostly smooth with just a few Class II rapids, the river passes rocky pinnacles and forests; watch for grizzlies, moose, and beavers. Visits to the area in the 1950s inspired conservationists Olaus and Margaret "Mardy" Murie to lobby for establishment of the refuge, which happened in 1960. ∎

Caribou Herds

Many people know about the Porcupine caribou herd owing to the controversy over plans to drill for oil in the state's northeast Arctic National Wildlife Refuge and whether such operations would harm the herd. At about 125,000 strong, it's an impressive herd, too, though far from being Alaska's largest. That honor goes to the Western Arctic herd, made up of almost 325,000 caribou. Altogether about a million caribou spend at least some of their time in Alaska. Some cross into Canada for part of the year; such long migrations are typical for these footloose critters. One radio-collared caribou walked 3,000 miles (4,820 km) in a single year—the longest measured migration of any land mammal.

Barrow

Barrow may not be at the end of the Earth, but it is unquestionably at the northern end of the United States—on the Arctic Ocean 375 miles (600 km) north of the Arctic Circle. This is hard-core land of the midnight sun, with the sun remaining above the horizon from May 10 to August 2—82 days straight.

Watching the sun set over the Arctic Ocean

In such a remote place visitors find whale bones leaning against walls and seal meat drying on racks outside houses. Less expected are SUVs, racquetball courts, and the nearly $80 million high school. This town of about 4,300 people, most of whom are Inupiat Eskimos, maintains a balance between the modern and the traditional.

Begin your visit by simply strolling the beach fronted by Stevenson Street to gape at the **Arctic Ocean.** (The sea off Barrow remains frozen ten months out of the year, though global warming may soon lengthen the ice-free season.) On the west end stand remnants of ancestral whalebone-and-sod houses—the Inupiat have lived here for at least 1,500 years.

Next, stop by the excellent **Inupiat Heritage Center,** which displays artifacts and offers traditional craft demonstrations. Affiliated with the New Bedford Whaling National Historical Park in Massachusetts, the museum centers on whaling. In the 19th and 20th centuries New England whalers worked these waters with Inupiat help. The museum gift shop sells Inupiat crafts, including parkas and etched baleen.

Don't miss one of the **guided tours** of the town and vicinity, which feature historic sites, contemporary culture, and wildlife. Millions of birds, including snowy owls, nest and breed around Barrow, and polar bears roam the area. ■

Barrow
🅜 Map p. 215
Visitor Information
☎ 907/852-5211
www.cityof
barrow.org

Inupiat Heritage Center
✉ 5421 North Star St.
☎ 907/852-0422
🕓 Closed Sat.–Sun.
💲 $$
www.nps.gov/inup

The tundra at Woolley Lagoon, southwest of the Bering Land Bridge National Preserve

More Places to Visit in the Bush

Bering Land Bridge National Preserve

Between 10,000 and 30,000 years ago the peopling of the Western Hemisphere began here, on the western tip of the Seward Peninsula, just 55 miles (89 km) east of Siberia. With much of the world's water locked up in ice, the shallow stretch of the Bering Sea between these two points lay exposed. The theory has it that as large game animals wandered across, humans from Asia followed.

Most of the preserve's 2.8 million acres (1.1 million ha) are mosquito-infested tundra. Sane visitors will find the rolling hills of the Interior more conducive to hiking. Try the old lava flows around **Imuruk Lake** and the five *maar* (crater) lakes in the **Devil Mountains-Cape Espenberg** area.

To learn flight details to this preserve, stop by or contact the **visitor center** in Nome (see p. 219), which showcases woolly mammoth bones and a 7-foot (2.1 m) tusk. The most popular fly-in destination is **Serpentine Hot Springs,** which centers on a wooden tub in the steamy bathhouse and a bunkhouse-style public-use cabin that sleeps up to 20 people. Between soaks you can roam amid granite tors on the nearby ridges and watch for wildlife, including the occasional stray bird from Asia.

www.nps.gov/bela Map p. 215
☎ 907/442-3890

St. Lawrence Island

If you stand on the shore in the town of **Gambell** *(visitor information, Sivuqaq Native Corporation, tel 907/985-5826)* and stretch your hand west, you'll nearly penetrate Russian airspace. That's a slight exaggeration, but Gambell is much closer to Russia than to mainland Alaska. On a clear day you can see across the 38 miles (61 km) of the Bering Strait to Asia. No wonder nearly all of the island's 1,500 residents, half of whom live in Gambell, are of Siberian Yupik descent and speak Siberian Yupik as a first language (they speak English, too).

Subsistence living remains common on this 95-mile-long (153 km) island; residents use traditional walrus-hide umiak boats to hunt walruses, bowhead whales, and seals. They're also known for their intricate ivory carvings, which visitors can purchase. The other 700 people, who live 39 miles (63 km) away in the town of **Savoonga,** supplement their hunting, fishing, and carving by herding some 10,000 reindeer.

To meet these distinctive people and see the island's wildlife and striking scenery, catch a flight from Nome. Map p. 215

Travelwise

Kayaks beached at the mouth
of Reid Glacier

TRAVELWISE

PLANNING YOUR TRIP

When to Go

Conventional wisdom dictates traveling to Alaska in summer to avoid harsh winter weather. In addition, many hotels, restaurants, and attractions reduce their hours or close from mid-September to mid-May. That said, a growing number of visitors sing the praises of Alaska winters. They wax poetic about the peace and quiet, lack of crowds, and dazzling displays of the northern lights.

Peak season runs from mid-May to mid-September. However, weather and other factors vary widely from region to region. In Fairbanks, for instance, July and August are the wettest months, whereas those months are among the driest in the Southeast.

When you check on weather, also ask about mosquitoes and other biting bugs. In many areas the best combination of warm temperatures, low rainfall, and fewer biting bugs occurs from mid-May to early June and mid-August to early September.

If you plan to visit the Southeast, also factor in ships that cruise the Inside Passage, inundating small towns with passengers. Some travelers appreciate the company, but if you want to avoid the crowds, experience decent weather, and find most facilities open, visit the region between mid-May and early June or in early to mid-September.

What to Take

If you'll be trekking into the backcountry, you should largely know what you'll need—if not, reconsider going. Don't overlook a few nonstandard items, such as head nets or bear-proof food canisters. Consult with staff at a public lands office or your outfitter for more specifics.

Anyone planning to spend time outdoors should bring a light rainsuit, a waterproof cap or hat, sunglasses, and layers of warm, breathable, moisture-wicking clothing. If you're headed to the Arctic coast or the Aleutians or planning a winter visit, pack additional tops and bottoms, plus a heavy coat and gloves. If you're going to a wet region, consider bringing rubber boots or buying a pair when you arrive. Otherwise, take hiking boots or sturdy walking shoes.

Also bring protection against biting insects—repellent, head nets, mosquito jackets, or whatever the locals advise. If you plan to visit in winter, you can skip the repellent.

Alaska is arguably the most informal of states. In small towns don't be surprised if you see someone in a flannel shirt, jeans, and knee-high rubber boots seated at a fancy restaurant. However, a number of restaurants, hotels, bars, resorts, and clubs, especially in Anchorage, require spiffier attire, though very seldom does it rise to the level of a jacket and tie for men or the equivalent for women.

GETTING AROUND

Air Travel

Ted Stevens Anchorage International Airport is Alaska's air transportation hub (tel 907/266-2525, www.dot.state.ak.us/anc). It lies 3 miles (4.8 km) southwest of downtown. Other major airports include **Fairbanks International Airport** (tel 907/474-2500, www.dot.state.ak.us/faiiap), 3 miles (4.8 km) southwest of downtown, and **Juneau International Airport** (tel 907/789-7821, www.juneau.org/airport), 9 miles (14.5 km) northwest of downtown.

Because this state has so few roads relative to its size, airplanes of all sorts and sizes play a prominent role. Remote Arctic towns like Kotzebue offer daily jet service. More remote and smaller settlements, like Adak, in the Aleutians, welcome twice weekly Alaska Airlines flights. Smaller airlines with smaller planes regularly service many otherwise isolated communities. Check with a travel agent, local visitor center, or chamber of commerce about flight availability to your chosen destinations.

Bush Planes

Bush planes—commonly three- to six-passenger propeller planes, some on wheels or tundra tires, some on floats, and some on skis—offer scheduled flights or are available for charter. Bush planes can go almost anywhere, landing on lakes, riverbed gravel bars, beaches, and even glaciers. However, they are expensive—perhaps $200 to $600 an hour for the plane. Hours add up quickly.

Some travelers harbor concerns about small plane travel that are entirely appropriate. Crashes do occur now and then, usually from foul weather. While even experienced pilots with shipshape planes sometimes have accidents, more crashes stem from careless operators who are cavalier about dangerous weather or proper maintenance.

Choosing a reliable operator is more art than science, but you can take several steps to improve your odds. If the National Park Service, a cruise ship company, or other discerning entity regularly uses the operator, it's likely among the best. If the company is recommended by the local chamber of commerce and has been around for a decade or two and can demonstrate a good safety record, it's also a good bet. Don't be embarrassed to ask a company about its safety record or its pilots' levels of experience. Use your instincts and common sense, too. You can also search for an operator's safety record on the National Transportation Safety Board website (www.ntsb.gov).

As a passenger on a chartered flight, you also play an important safety role. First, urge your pilot to err on the side of caution if the weather seems risky. Pay attention to the safety lecture at the start of the flight and take note of the location of flotation devices, survival kit, and so on. Bring along survival gear of your own, such as clothing that will keep you warm and dry if the pilot has to make an emergency landing in the wilderness. If you're carrying bear spray or compressed gas for a backpacking stove, ask the pilot to store it safely. With regard to comfort and convenience: Bring earplugs in case the pilot doesn't supply ear protection and carry your gear in smaller soft bags, not big, hard-shelled suitcases. Small planes adhere to space and weight restrictions and cargo and passengers must properly balance.

Boat Travel

Alaska includes islands galore, more coastline than the lower 48 combined, and long navigable rivers that meander through vast expanses. Thus, boat travel is very popular. Large cruise ships account for the lion's share, each year hauling hundreds of thousands of people to and around Alaska. These 2,000- to 3,000-passenger behemoths are balanced by smaller cruise ships that accommodate up to 250 passengers.

Overseeing the state ferries, the **Alaska Marine Highway System** (P.O. Box 112505, 6858 Glacier Hwy, Juneau, AK 99811-2505, tel 907/272-7116 or 800-642-0066, www.ferry alaska.com) is the other big player, transporting tens of thousands of people along the southeastern and south-central coasts, even into the Aleutians. Providing access to dozens of Alaska communities, the AMHS is an essential resource for exploring the Inside Passage.

If you want to transport your vehicle from the lower 48 to Alaska, start on the Washington State or British Columbia ferries and cross to Prince Rupert, British Columbia, where you can pick up the Alaska Marine Highway.

Operating on a much smaller scale are water taxis, which can take travelers to places not served by the cruise ships or ferries. While a few water taxis operate on more or less regular schedules, nearly all are for hire. Weather and tide allowing, they'll drop you off at a little fishing village, a remote trailhead, or a public use cabin. Water taxis are especially common in the Southeast and in Kachemak Bay. To locate water taxis, contact the local visitor center or chamber of commerce. Be sure to ask questions to ensure your water taxi company is reliable.

Bus Travel

Public buses and shuttles are scarce in Alaska, though tour buses are common. Ask at visitor centers or browse the Alaska Travel Industry Association website (www.travelalaska.com) for a listing of bus-tour companies.

Car Travel

Most people who drive to Alaska cross over from Canada via the **Alaska Highway**—aka the Alcan. The Alaska Highway is paved and offers ample services, though it still passes through wilderness for most of its 1,390 miles (2,238 km) between Dawson Creek, British Columbia, and Delta Junction, Alaska. Travelers who'd like to drive the highway only one direction can take their vehicle one way on the ferry.

Driving Tips

Alaska has all the usual driving hazards, such as teenagers, but the state also presents motorists with some unusual issues.

Frost heaves, for example, turn some highway stretches into roller coasters. Caused by the freezing and thawing of the soil, these speed bumps on steroids are especially common in the interior.

Watch for moose. Much bigger and longer-legged than deer, moose stand taller than the front end of a typical passenger car, so if a sedan hits a moose the moose's body will often come right through the windshield.

The most prevalent concern while driving in Alaska is remoteness. While most of Alaska lacks roads, south-central and parts of the Interior include a handful—most of them paved, all of them scenic. However, scenery means you're driving in remote, wild country, so bring emergency gear, including ample clothing, food, water, spare tires, and tools in case you get stuck. To check road conditions and other driving information, dial 511 or visit http://511.alaska.gov.

Rental Cars

Alaska's major airports host car-rental agencies, though sometimes you can get better rates from agency offices outside the airport. In popular parts of Alaska, summer gets very busy, so book months in advance. Rental cars are often even available in towns that remain inaccessible by road. While a passenger car will suffice for most highways, you may need a 4WD, high-clearance vehicle on gravel highways and other roads.

Train Travel

Train travel in Alaska is limited, but the two existing options both follow scenic routes. In fact, the **White Pass & Yukon Route,** which runs between Skagway and Fraser, Bennett Lake, and Whitehorse, Canada, is primarily a tourist train (see pp. 86–87).

The main train service is run by the state-owned **Alaska Railroad** *(tel 907/265-2494 or 800/544-0552, www.alaskarailroad.com or www.akrr.com).* In summer it goes daily between **Anchorage, Fairbanks,** and **Seward;** a 7-mile (11 km) spur leads from Portage to Whittier.

Passengers can opt for first-class cars—offered by the railway and private companies. You can also take such unique trains as the **Hurricane Turn Train,** which runs between Talkeetna and Hurricane—55 miles (89 km) one way, most along the beautiful Susitna River. The Hurricane is one of the nation's last flag-stop trains.; you can flag it down and hop on board.

PRACTICAL ADVICE
Maps
State and city maps are available from local tourism offices and visitor centers. If you'd like more details of the entire state, try the *Alaska Atlas & Gazetteer* (by DeLorme Mapping). All public lands are plotted on map brochures or detailed topographic maps. Contact a Alaska Public Lands Information Center *(www.alaskacenters.gov)* for assistance.

Safety
Wild place that Alaska is, safety concerns revolve around the out doors. Bears, for example, top the list of worries for most people (see pp. 132–133).

Though 1,000-pound (454 kg) predators tend to grab one's attention, hypothermia is actually a greater menace. A day hike can turn deadly if you go out in shorts and a cotton sweatshirt in 50°F (10°C) weather and get soaked in a storm. Likewise, canoeing can quickly become a disaster if the wind comes up and you capsize in icy water. Be aware of weather-related concerns and prepare accordingly.

In an emergency, dial 911 to summon police, medical, or fire department help. (In some rural areas it is necessary to dial "0.") Some roads include emergency phones and contact stations.

Taxes & Tipping
Rules for tipping waitstaff, taxi drivers, hotel staff, and so on, follow those in the lower 48—15 to 20 percent for waitstaff, 10 to 15 percent for taxi drivers, and $1–$5 a day for hotel maids. Guidelines for tipping tour operators are less standardized, but if you're on a small, personalized trip, a tip for good service is appropriate—perhaps 10 percent of the tour's overall cost.

Shoppers will be happy to learn that Alaska has no state sales tax, though some boroughs impose their own taxes.

Time
Nearly all the state lies in the Alaska time zone, one hour earlier than Pacific time—except for the western two-thirds of the Aleutian Islands, which observe Hawaiian-Aleutian time, two hours earlier than Pacific time.

Travelers With Disabilities
Major tour companies and government operations generally offer reasonable access and appropriate facilities. But in small towns and remote villages travelers with disabilities will encounter many obstacles. For more information, contact Access Alaska *(tel 907/248-4777 in Anchorage, 907/479-7940 in Fairbanks, 907/262-4955 in Soldotna, or 907/357-2588 in Wasilla, www.accessalaska.org).*

Visitor Information
The main statewide tourism information entity is the **Alaska Travel Industry Association** *(2600 Cordova St., Ste. 201,*

Anchorage, AK 99503, tel 907/929-2842, www.travelalaska.com). Before leaving home, ask the association to mail you its vacation planner, which is full of useful information.

Other useful information can be gathered from the **Alaska Public Lands Information Centers** *(www.alaskacenters.gov).* There are centers located in Anchorage *(605 W. 4th Ave., Suite 105, Anchorage, AK 99501, tel 907/644-3661),* Fairbanks *(101 Dunkel St., Ste. 110, Fairbanks, AK 99701, tel 907/459-3730),* Ketchikan *(Southeast Alaska Discovery Center, 50 Main St, Ketchikan, AK 99901, tel 907/228-6220),* and Tok *(Milepost 1314 Alaska Hwy., Tok, AK 99780, tel 907/883-5667).* The interagency APLIC allows visitors one-stop shopping for information on state and federally managed public lands. Recreation permits and reservations for backcountry cabins may also be made at these centers. The **Alaska Natural History Association** has outlets in each of these locations, selling natural history books, maps, and guides to all areas of Alaska.

ANNUAL EVENTS
January
Kuskokwim 300 Bethel, mid- to late Jan., tel 907/545-3300, www.k300.org. Premier mid-distance sled-dog race.
Polar Bear Jump Off Seward, 3rd weekend, tel 907/224-5230. The main event is the plunge (Sat.) of costumed folks into icy Resurrection Bay. Other events include the ugly fish toss, ice bowling, and a sled-dog race.
Anchorage Folk Festival Anchorage, two weekends in mid- to late Jan., www.anchoragefolkfestival.org. More than 120 acts take to the stages.

February
Alaska Ski for Women Anchorage, Super Bowl Sunday, tel 907/276-7609, www.alaskaskiforwomen.org.

This benefit is the country's biggest cross-country ski event for women. Largely for laughs, with skiers dressed in hula skirts and old prom dresses.

Iceworm Festival Cordova, early Feb., tel 907/424-7260, www.cordovachamber.com. Features fireworks, musical performances, food, and the parade, led by a 140-foot (43 m) ice worm.

Tent City Days Wrangell, mid-Feb., tel 907/874-3699 or 800/367-9745, www.wrangell.com. Commemorates gold seekers who established a tent city in Wrangell around 1900. Features a long-john contest, Jell-O wrestling, bed races, and the telling of tall tales.

Yukon Quest International Sled Dog Race Fairbanks (even years) or Whitehorse, Yukon Territory (odd years), mid-Feb., tel 907/452-7954 or 867/668-4711 (Canada), www.yukonquest.com. A 1,000-mile (1,610 km) sled-dog race that follows gold rush trails.

Fur Rendezvous Anchorage, late Feb. to early March, tel 907/274-1177, www.furrondy.net. Alaska's biggest winter festival offers three weeks of diversions, from a fur auction to ice bowling.

March

World Ice Art Championships Fairbanks, end of Feb. through late March, tel 907/451-8250, www.icealaska.com. The finest ice artists create elaborate sculptures.

Festival of Native Arts Fairbanks, late Feb. or early March, tel 907/474-6528. Alaska natives convene to perform and to display their arts and crafts.

Iditarod Trail Sled Dog Race From Anchorage to Nome, starts 1st Sat., tel 907/376-5155, www.iditarod.com.

Bering Sea Ice Golf Classic Nome, 3rd Sat., tel 907/443-6624, www.nomealaska.org. A benefit tournament held on a makeshift six-hole course atop the frozen Bering Sea. Golfers use bright orange balls and

spent shotgun shells for tees.

Cama'i Dance Festival Bethel, late March, tel 907/543-2911, www.bethelarts.com. The festival attracts 400 to 500 dancers to revel in traditional dance. Many of the participants are Yupik Eskimo dancers.

April

Alaska Folk Festival Juneau, early to mid-April, tel 907/463-3316, www.akfolkfest.org. Week-long celebration of folk music draws about 450 musicians to Juneau from all over. Free.

May

Copper River Delta Shorebird Festival Cordova, early May, tel 907/424-7260, www.cordovachamber.com. Celebrates the arrival of millions of shorebirds at the Copper River Delta. Workshops and birding trips.

Kachemak Bay Shorebird Festival Homer, early May, tel 907/235-7740, www.homeralaska.org. Birders can spot a hundred species a day. Includes workshops, field trips, boat tours, and sea kayak trips.

Little Norway Festival Petersburg, weekend closest to May 17, tel 907/772-4636, www.petersburg.org/visitor/littlenorway.html. Locals commemorate their Norwegian roots, the start of spring, U.S. Armed Forces Day, and the opening of the commercial fishing season. You'll find food, music, and a big parade featuring Norwegian costumes.

Juneau Jazz & Classics Juneau, late May, tel 907/463-3378, www.jazzandclassics.org. World-class artists perform on Juneau stages during this two-week event, which includes blues, as well as jazz and classical.

Kodiak Crab Festival Kodiak, late May, tel 907/486-4782 or 800/789-4782, www.kodiak.org/crabfest.html. Five-day festival features crab fixed any way you

can imagine. Also offers tennis, fencing, and table tennis tournaments, as well as poetry, folk dancing, and a native arts bazaar.

June

Sitka Summer Music Festival Sitka, early June, tel 907/747-6774, www.sitkamusicfestival.org. Three-week chamber music series attracts world-class performers.

Colony Days Palmer, mid- to late June, tel 907/745-2880, www.palmerchamber.org. A parade, a street dance, wagon rides, and other events commemorate Palmer's beginnings as a farming colony.

Midnight Sun Baseball Game Fairbanks, June 20/21/22, tel 907/451-0095, www.goldpanners.com/midnight_sun_game.html. A tradition since 1906, the Fairbanks Goldpanners play a team from outside on the summer solstice. Using only natural light, the game goes from about 10:30 p.m. to 1:30 a.m. Though the Goldpanners are strictly amateur, the level of play is high and many players have gone on to play in the majors, including such stars as Tom Seaver, Jason Giambi, and Dave Winfield.

Yukon 800 Fairbanks, late June, tel 907/456-5774, www.yukon800.com. In this "toughest, roughest speedboat race in the world," contestants roar along 800 miles (1,287 km) of the Chena, Tanana, and Yukon Rivers for two days.

July

Mount Marathon Race Seward, July 4, tel 907/224-8051, www.sewardak.org. Since about 1915, runners starting at sea level in Seward have raced 1.5 miles (2.4 km) up this 3,000-foot (914 m) mountain and back. The race draws tens of thousands of onlookers.

World Eskimo-Indian Olympics Fairbanks, mid- to late July, tel 907/452-6646, www.weio.org. Alaska native athletes gather for four days of competition in traditional events that derive from survival skills. These demanding challenges include carrying four adult men (the record is well over 2,000 feet/610 m), a tug-of-war using one's ears, and the high kick, in which contestants leap up and kick one foot as high as 9 feet (2.7 m).

Golden Days Fairbanks, weekend closest to July 22, tel 907/452-1105, www.fairbankschamber.org. Five days of fun, including a huge parade, pancake breakfasts, a river regatta, the Rubber Duckie Race, and historical reenactments.

Southeast Alaska State Fair Haines, late July to mid-Aug., tel 907/766-2476, www.seakfair.org.

August

Tanana Valley State Fair Fairbanks, early Aug., tel 907/452-3750, www.tananavalleyfair.org.

Tanana Valley Sandhill Crane Festival Fairbanks, mid-Aug., tel 907/452-5162, www.creamers field.org. A celebration of the cranes that flock to Creamer's Field during fall migration.

Alaska State Fair Palmer, late Aug. through early Sept., tel 907/745-4827, www.alaskastatefair.org.

September

Kodiak Rodeo & State Fair Kodiak, Labor Day weekend, tel 907/487-4440, www.kodiakrodeo andstatefair.com.

Alaska Airlines' Autumn Classics Anchorage, mid- and late Sept., tel 907/263-2787, www.sitkamusic festival.org. Part of the Sitka Summer Music Festival, these two weekends of top chamber music take place in Anchorage.

October

Make It Alaskan Festival Anchorage, 1st weekend, tel 907/279-0618, www.makeitalaskanfestival .com. Alaska craftspeople gather to sell their wares.

Alaska Day Festival Sitka, mid-Oct., tel 907/747-5940,

www.sitka.org. Honors transfer of Alaska from Russia to the United States on October 18, 1867. Tours of historic sites and traditional Russian dancing.

Alaska Federation of Natives Convention Location varies, mid- to late Oct., tel 907/274-3611, www.nativefederation.org. This week-long event is the biggest Alaska native gathering of the year, hosting 4,000 to 5,000 delegates. Many events are open to the public.

November

WhaleFest Sitka, early Nov., tel 907/747-8878, www.sitka soundsciencecenter.org. As humpback whales congregate nearby, Sitka celebrates with whale-watching tours, slide shows, and workshops.

Alaska Bald Eagle Festival Haines, usually 2nd weekend, tel 907/766-3094, www.baldeagles .org/festival. Attracts bird experts, artists, and entertainers for several days of lectures, photography workshops, and guided eagle-viewing tours.

Athabaskan Fiddlers Festival Fairbanks, mid-Nov., tel 907/456-5774, www.explorefairbanks.com. Celebrating the many Athabaskan who took up fiddle playing and gave it a native twist. Fiddle music takes center stage at this foot-stomping festival.

December

Winterfest Talkeetna, each weekend, tel 907/733-2330, www .talkeetnachamber.org. Celebrates December with arts, food, music, and goofy contests, notably the Bachelor's Auction and Wilderness Women Contest.

Winter Solstice Celebration Fairbanks, Dec. 21, tel 907/452-8671. To lighten their spirits on this darkest day of the year, people go downtown to enjoy fireworks, music, a treasure hunt, and sled-dog puppies.

FURTHER READING

Updated annually, *The Milepost* is a hefty book describing what you'll find along every road in Alaska, including ads for lodges, outfitters, and more. *The Milepost* pinpoints locations to the tenth of a mile and offers practical information about road conditions, activities, and the like. From the same publisher, the *Alaska Wilderness Guide* covers remote villages and settlements, national and state parks, other public lands, attractions, and activities.

Classics about Alaska still merit a read, such as John Muir's 1915 *Travels in Alaska*. In 1944, naturalist Adolph Murie wrote *The Wolves of Mount McKinley*. He followed in 1961 with the broader study, *A Naturalist in Alaska*. Margaret Murie penned another classic, *Two in the Far North*, in 1968. Maybe the best-ever book on Alaska travel is John McPhee's 1977 *Coming into the Country*.

Alaska: Saga of a Bold Land (2003), by Walter Borneman, is a good general history, as is *Alaska: An American Colony* (2002), by Stephen Haycox. Many books focus on narrower aspects of Alaska's past, such as *Wager with the Wind: The Don Sheldon Story* (1982), by James Greiner, which shares tales of a pioneer bush pilot. Tappan Adney's *The Klondike Stampede* (1994) captures the adventure of the Klondike gold rush. One notable account of Alaska native history is *The Epic of Qayaq: The Longest Story Ever Told by My People* (1995), by Lela Kiana Oman, which includes traditional stories of the Inupiat.

Alaska native writers have produced fascinating chronicles of contemporary life, and resident authors also have used fiction to examine life in Alaska (see p. 44).

Hotels & Restaurants

Alaska's hotels and restaurants share a few traits that travelers should note. To begin with, they're generally more expensive than their counterparts in the lower 48. Many hotels and restaurants open only for the summer season—generally mid-May to mid-September.

Even those establishments that stay open year-round often close for long periods in winter. Smaller travel-oriented businesses—remote lodges, rafting outfits, tour boats—may keep unpredictable hours and often set their seasons based on weather, perhaps opening later in May or staying open later in September. Access for disabled travelers is decent in cities or popular tourist areas, but spotty in rural areas. Check access with your destination or check the Access Alaska website (*www.access alaska.org*).

Accommodations

Accommodations in Alaska range from posh urban hotels and luxurious wilderness lodges through mid-range local hotels and bed-and-breakfasts to hostels and public-use cabins. Be aware that harsh weather, high costs, and isolation pose a burden to hostelries in remote areas, so they may not be as tidy as you might expect, but they still may be wonderful places. The following accommodations lie close to attractions listed in this book or are destinations in themselves.

Reservations: It's best to make reservations early, particularly during peak season, because some places book months in advance. Reservations also are advised when traveling to remote areas that have few options.

Lodging Chains: Though major chains have made inroads, Alaska still has far fewer of these than in the rest of the United States. For the most part the local places are fine, even outstanding, and offer a richer experience. But

quality varies widely, so ask visitor centers for suggestions, especially out in the Bush.

Bed-and-breakfasts: Bed-and-breakfasts are prevalent. Related organizations include the **Bed & Breakfast Association of Alaska** (*www.alaskabba.com*), **Anchorage Alaska Bed & Breakfast Association** (*tel 907/272-5909 or 888/584-5147, www.anchorage-bnb .com*), **Fairbanks Association of Bed & Breakfasts** (*www.ptialaska .net/~fabb*), **Kenai Peninsula Bed & Breakfast Association** (*www .kenaipeninsulabba.com*), **Bed & Breakfast Association of Alaska** (*www.accommodations-alaska.com*), and **Mat-Su Bed & Breakfast Association** (*www.alaskabnbhosts.com*).

Hostels: Alaska boasts dozens of hostels where travelers of all ages and backgrounds can find rooms or bunks at bargain rates. Guests may have to deal with such restrictions as daytime closures, separate dorm rooms for men and women, and curfews. It's best to bring your own sleeping bag or linens, though bedding is often available for rent. To learn more about Alaska hostels, go to *www.hostels.com*.

Wilderness Lodges: Hundreds of lodges dot Alaska's backcountry, enabling non-backpackers to experience the wilds. Access to many of these lodgings is limited to plane or boat. While most are geared to fishers, a growing number offer a broader focus on ecology, wildlife-watching, and scenery, providing such activities as flightseeing, hiking, canoeing, rafting, and a host of winter activities. Because they're remote, often luxurious,

and provide gourmet cuisine, many wilderness lodges are extremely expensive, running perhaps $300 to $500 (and up) a day per person. That often includes meals, guides, and gear, and sometimes includes transportation to the lodge.

Camping: While backcountry camping opportunities are practically limitless, Alaska has relatively few developed campgrounds. In the lower 48, national parks, national forests, and state parks usually offer the best shot at developed sites, but in Alaska such lands include few or no campgrounds. For information on where to camp contact the Alaska Public Lands Information Centers (*www.alaskacenters.gov*). Ask about the hundreds of remote public use cabins, especially on Forest Service and Alaska State Park lands.

Restaurants

Alaska eateries vary widely. Often, they are quite informal, pitching together people in work boots or outdoor gear with those in suits and ties. Most provide huge servings. And they serve seafood, lots and lots of fresh seafood, even in the Interior. There doesn't seem to be any dish Alaskans won't add halibut to.

How to Use These Lists

The hotels and restaurants have been grouped first according to their region, then alphabetically within their price category. Prices, phone numbers, closing dates, and other data change often; check important information with the businesses in which you're interested. Reservations are advised.

The letter L is used for lunch, D for dinner.

Credit Cards

If a business accepts major credit cards, those cards are listed using these abbreviations: AE (American Express), D (Discover), MC (MasterCard), or V (Visa). If the business does not take cards, "Cash only" is indicated.

■ SOUTHEAST ALASKA

KETCHIKAN

🏨 ALASKAN NANTUCKET HOUSE
$$$

600 FRONT ST.
TEL 907/247-3490 OR
800/928-3308
**www.alaskanantucket
house.com**
High atop a hill in a residential neighborhood above downtown Ketchikan, this three-story house offers two spacious rooms with eagle's-eye views of the town, the Tongass Narrows, and the surrounding forests and mountains. A historic home, the interior has been updated into an airy, elegant space highlighted by expansive windows worthy of the views. The penthouse room occupies all 1,000 square feet (93 sq m) of the upper floor.
🛏 2 🚭 🐾 MC, V

🏨 CAPE FOX LODGE
🍴 **$$$**

800 VENETIA WAY
TEL 907/225-8001 OR
866/225-8001
FAX 907/225-8286
www.capefoxlodge.com
Ketchikan's most elegant hotel boldly announces its northwest native flavor out front with a circle of six totems. Inside is a large collection of Tlingit and Haida art and artifacts. Beneath massive beams in the lobby are overstuffed chairs, a library, and a stone fireplace. The rooms are

spacious, with hilltop views of either Tongass Narrows or Deer Mountain. Those seated in the **Heen Kahidi Dining Room** will take in floor-to-ceiling views of downtown and the marina while savoring seafood, steak, pasta, and exotic dishes like reindeer sausage.
🛏 72 rooms, 2 suites 🅿 🚭
🐾 All major cards

🍴 ANNABELLE'S KEG & CHOWDER HOUSE
$$

326 FRONT ST.
TEL 907/225-6009
On the ground floor of the historic Gilmore Hotel, Annabelle's has been on Ketchikan's waterfront since 1927. Annabelle herself is no longer with us, but her casual Victorian restaurant continues to serve several kinds of chowder and beer—as the name promises—plus fresh seafood (try the halibut Olympia or the crab cakes), steaks, prime rib, and chicken. The restaurant is split between the down-home lounge and somewhat fancier parlor. Both are local hangouts with a friendly atmosphere.
🛏 120 🚭 🐾 All major cards

WRANGELL

🏨 ALASKAN SOURDOUGH LODGE
$$–$$$

1104 PENINSULA AVE.
TEL 907/874-3613 OR
800/874-3613
FAX 907/874-3455
www.akgetaway.com
On the docks, this pretty lodge is made from hand-milled Alaska red cedar. The rooms aren't luxurious, but they're comfortable and offer touches like Alaska native art, handmade quilts, and harbor views. Guests can get three home-cooked squares, featuring, of course, sourdough bread.
🛏 16 🚭 🐾 MC, V

🏨 GRAND VIEW BED & BREAKFAST
$$

TEL 907/874-3225
www.grandviewbnb.com
This soaring house sits so close to Zimovia Strait that at high tide guests can practically skip rocks from their rooms. Generous windows invite visitors to gaze at the icy waters and the surrounding forest and mountains. Often people will spot passing ships or bald eagles and ravens perching on the driftwood piled on the beach. The driftwood logs also make a nice backrest for guests who build bonfires on the beach to warm themselves on a crisp evening. Check out the extensive collection of Alaska artifacts and books.
🛏 3 🅿 🚭 🐾 All major cards

PETERSBURG

🏨 SCANDIA HOUSE
$$–$$$

110 N. NORDIC DR.
TEL 907/772-4281 OR
800/722-5006

🏨 Hotel 🍴 Restaurant 🛏 No. of guest rooms ⊞ No. of Seats 🅿 Parking 🕐 Closed 🛗 Elevator

FAX 907/772-4301
www.scandiahousehotel.com
This European-style hotel is
immaculate. Though it has
been a fixture in downtown
Petersburg since 1905, it was
completely rebuilt following
a 1994 fire. The exterior
rosemaling reflects the town's
Norwegian roots. Ample
rooms have a bright, contemporary feel.

Ⓘ 33 Ⓟ Ⓢ ⊟
Ⓢ All major cards

🍴 COASTAL COLD STORAGE

$

306 N. NORDIC DR.
TEL 907/772-4177 OR
877/257-4746
(OUTSIDE ALASKA)
Petersburg is a fishing town,
and Coastal Cold Storage
gives visitors a chance to enjoy
the fruits of that industry.
Primarily a place for anglers
to bring their catch for
processing, this company runs
a retail shop where you can
buy fresh halibut beer bits, fish
chowder, scallops, crab, and
other seafood.

🕐 Closed Sun.
Ⓢ All major cards

SITKA

🏨 ROCKWELL LIGHTHOUSE

$$$

VIA 1315 HALIBUT POINT RD.
TEL/FAX 907/747-3056
This four-story home was built
in the shape of a lighthouse,
and, indeed, its rooftop light
meets Coast Guard specs.
It sits on an island in Sitka
Sound about a mile (1.6 km)
from town—the owner will
run guests out in a skiff, or
they can do it themselves.
The views are incredible, the
decor nautical (think wood
and brass), and it does have an
interior spiral staircase, just like
a real lighthouse. Up to eight
people can sleep in the four

rooms, but no matter the size
of your party, you must rent
the whole house. For summer
visits you may need to reserve
up to a year in advance.

Ⓘ 4 Ⓢ Ⓢ Cash only

🏨 ALASKA OCEAN VIEW BED & BREAKFAST INN

$$–$$$

1101 EDGECUMBE DR.
TEL 907/747-8310 OR
888/811-6870
FAX 907/747-3440
www.sitka-alaska-lodging.com
This elegant two-story shore-
line house commands views
of Sitka Sound and Mount
Edgecumbe. The airy rooms
with private baths include
such amenities as DVD/VCR
players and data ports. Some
rooms have sofas, fireplaces,
and whirlpool baths.

Ⓘ 3 Ⓢ Ⓢ All major cards

🏨 SITKA HOTEL
🍴

$$

118 LINCOLN ST.
TEL 907/747-3288 OR
888/757-3288
www.sitkahotel.net
Here since the late '30s, the
Sitka was recently renovated.
Rooms are modest, but they
and the lobby offer Victorian
charm. Some have private
baths; some share baths
down the hall. There's also a
restaurant and the nautically
named Bilge Bar.

Ⓘ 60 Ⓟ ⊟ Ⓢ
Ⓢ All major cards

SOMETHING SPECIAL

🍴 LUDVIG'S BISTRO

$$$–$$$$$

256 KATLIAN ST.
TEL 907/966-3663
www.ludvigsbistro.com
Ludvig's is hands-down the
best restaurant in Sitka and
one of the best in Alaska.
Though small and informal,
it turns out superb, imagina-
tive food, such as Alaska
paella mixta, which features

saffron rice, prawns, scallops,
clams, calamari, and chicken
and chorizo sausage mixed
with vegetables and spices.
Check out the daily specials;
the chefs continually invent
new dishes, taking advantage
of the fresh seafood. The
food's Mediterranean accent
is reflected in the warm
yellows and coppers that
brighten this amiable bistro.
Reservations recommended.
The bistro closes for long
periods in fall and winter. For
a simple but savory lunch in
summer, try Ludvig's chowder
cart, parked beside the Sitka
Sound Science Center.

🍴 25 Ⓢ 🕐 Closed Sun. in
summer, Sun.–Tues. in spring &
fall Ⓢ All major cards

🍴 BACK DOOR CAFÉ

$

104 BARRACKS ST.
TEL 907/747-8856
The official address is on Bar-
racks Street, but you actually
have to slip down an alley to
reach the Back Door's main
entrance—hence the name.
A favorite local hangout,
especially among the literary
and artistic set, this café is
loud and lively. It offers make-
your-own bagel sandwiches,
coffee drinks, and the claim to
fame: great baked goods. Try
the cranberry-walnut scones
or poppyseed cake.

Ⓘ 25 Ⓟ Ⓢ Ⓢ Cash only

JUNEAU

🏨 PEARSON'S POND LUXURY INN & ADVENTURE SPA

$$$–$$$$$

4541 SAWA CIRCLE
TEL 907/789-3772 OR
888/658-6328
FAX 866/451-0002
www.pearsonspond.com
This exquisite log house is
tucked into the woods on a
pond close to Mendenhall

Ⓢ Nonsmoking   Ⓢ Air-conditioning   🏊 Indoor Pool   🎽 Health Club   Ⓢ Credit Cards

Glacier, a few miles north of downtown. With fireplaces, whirlpool tubs for two, outdoor hot tubs, an indoor fountain, and flowers everywhere, the inn aims for a romantic mood. The "adventure spa" portion of the inn's name is manifested by massages, exercise equipment, and the many activities available on the property, such as mountain biking, paddling around the pond, an outdoor sauna, and winter sports and activities.

🛈 5 suites, 2 off-site condos
🅿 🚫 🎯 🏔 All major cards

SOMETHING SPECIAL

🏨 ALASKA'S CAPITAL INN
$$$$
113 W. 5TH ST.
TEL 907/586-6507 OR
888/588-6507
FAX 907/586-6508
www.alaskacapitalinn.com
This B&B is more than 100 years old and has never looked better, having been restored in 2003. Built in 1906 by gold rush pioneer John Olds, this four-story mansion perches atop a hillside with a grand waterfront view. The historic building is complemented by period antiques, notably the array of beds, including a carved king sleigh bed and an oak spindle bed. The inn also features elaborate breakfasts, high-speed Internet access, and an outdoor hot tub. The top floor has been converted into a single elegant room, the Governor's Suite. Reserve early for summer stays.

🛈 7 🚫 🏔 All major cards

🏨 WESTMARK BARANOF
🍴 HOTEL
$$$–$$$$
127 N. FRANKLIN ST.
TEL 907/586-2660 OR
800/544-0970
FAX 907/586-8315
www.westmarkhotels.com/
juneau.php

The understated rich woods, the embroidered chairs, and the old-money atmosphere in the grand lobby suggest power, and since its opening in 1939 this downtown landmark has indeed been a home away from home for legislators, lobbyists, and corporate execs. It offers a wide range of rooms. To escape street noise and for better views, ask for a room on the upper floors. The Baranof has two restaurants: one casual, the other a place to close big deals, aptly named the **Gold Room.**

🛈 196 🅿 🚫 🍴 🎯
🏔 All major cards

🏨 SENTINEL ISLAND
LIGHTHOUSE
$
TEL 907/586-5338
The accommodations may be rustic in this 34-foot (10 m) decommissioned lighthouse, but it has a great location—on a 6-acre (2.4 ha) island about 25 miles (40 km) northwest of downtown. Guests can watch breaching whales, wave at passing ferries, and stroll the island. There are six bunks, sites for tents, and basic cooking and bathroom facilities. The lighthouse is operated by the Gastineau Channel Historical Society, which rents it at a reasonable rate, but don't overlook the fact that you'll have to pay a bit to get out to the island by charter boat, helicopter, or sea kayak.

🛈 6 🏔 Cash only

SOMETHING SPECIAL

🍴 HANGAR ON
THE WHARF
$–$$$$
2 MARINE WAY, NO. 106
TEL 907/586-5018
http://hangar.hangaronthe
wharf.com
In a made-over hangar where Alaska Airlines got its start, the Hangar still roars on

---

PRICES

HOTELS
An indication of the cost of a double room in the high season is given by **$** signs.

$$$$$	Over $300
$$$$	$200–$300
$$$	$120–$200
$$	$80–$120
$	Under $80

RESTAURANTS
An indication of the cost of a three-course meal without drinks is given by $ signs.

$$$$$	Over $75
$$$$	$50–$75
$$$	$35–$50
$$	$20–$35
$	Under $20

occasion as floatplanes take off from the channel not 50 feet (15 m) from the front door. An energetic crowd often jams this place—perhaps for the extensive beer list. You'll find the expected pub fare, but the Hangar also serves finer dishes, such as pepper scallops, jambalaya, coconut prawns, and halibut macadamia. On a sunny day the patio overlooking the water is a pleasure.

🍴 175 🅿 🚫
🏔 All major cards

🍴 TWISTED FISH
COMPANY
$–$$$$
550 S. FRANKLIN ST.
TEL 907/463-5033
http://twistedfish.hangaron
thewharf.com
Appropriately, the Twisted Fish is located right on the water, down by the cruise ship docks. Appropriately because this lively restaurant with a view specializes in fresh seafood—their motto is "A wild place for wild fish." Naturally, you can order all sorts of the usual

---

🏨 Hotel 🍴 Restaurant 🛈 No. of guest rooms 🎯 No. of Seats 🅿 Parking 🕐 Closed 🛗 Elevator

seafood dinners, like a pound of Alaska king crab legs or a saucy slab of salmon. But the marine theme permeates pretty much every section of the menu: Consider the wild berry halibut burger or the salmon lox and caviar pizza. 150 P S Closed in winter All major cards

GOLD CREEK SALMON BAKE

$$$

1061 SALMON LN.

TEL 907/789-0052

Not only can visitors gorge on succulent salmon hot off the grill, but at times they can see salmon runs in the creek right outside the dining area. Hours vary according to cruise ship schedules, so it's best to make reservations. 400 P Closed mid-Sept.–mid-May All major cards

HISTORIC SILVERBOW INN

$

120 2ND ST.

TEL 907/586-4146 OR 800/586-4146

FAX 907/586-4242

www.silverbowinn.com

The Silverbow is one of Alaska's idiosyncratic gems. First, it's a bakery—Alaska's oldest, having baked its first loaf of sourdough bread in the 1890s. In addition to fresh breads, the bakery produces scrumptious chocolate cheesecakes, peanut butter mousse cakes, and honest-to-God New York bagels. Second, the Silverbow is an excellent breakfast and lunch place, featuring imaginative salads, sandwiches, and soups, mostly for takeout but also to munch at its few tables or in the outdoor beer garden. Third, the Silverbow is a downtown inn, with 11 small but nice rooms upstairs. Fourth, the Silverbow is a

social center, with a large room for live music and first-run independent and art films. 20 P S All major cards

PEL'MENI

$

2 MARINE WAY

TEL 907/586-0177

The menu at this tiny restaurant ranges from meat dumplings to potato dumplings. That's it. Well, okay, they do offer a few drinks and some good, stolid, Soviet-style brown bread to go with the dumplings (*pel'meni* is the Russian word for these items), but the unchanging choice of entrees truly runs from A to B. This offbeat establishment appeals to the 20-something crowd, which often throngs this place, especially in the wee hours when little else is open. Customers also can play actual vinyl records from the restaurant's quirky collection. 20 P S Cash only

GLACIER BAY/ GUSTAVUS

BEAR TRACK INN

$$$$$

255 RINK CREEK RD.

TEL 907/697-3017 OR 888/697-2284

FAX 907/697-2284

www.beartrackinn.com

This luxurious spruce-log inn sits on acres of wildflower meadows and forest facing Icy Strait. The lobby features a 30-foot (9 m) ceiling, a stone fireplace, and handcrafted furnishings throughout, including not one but two mooseantler chandeliers. The rooms are spacious and contain "rustic-fancy" appointments. The restaurant serves guests morning, noon, and night and nonguests for dinner, which features a range of fare, from steak and seafood to caribou and musk ox. The inn offers a

full menu of outings, as well. 14 P Closed in winter S All major cards

GLACIER BAY COUNTRY INN

$$$$$

TEL 907/697-2288 OR 800/628-0912 (BOTH SUMMER ONLY) OR 480/215-0244 (IN WINTER)

www.glacierbayalaska.com

The inn sits on 160 acres (65 ha) of rain forest and meadows 4 miles (6 km) from Gustavus on the road to Bartlett Cove. You can't miss this three-story log castle with dormers, cupolas, and porches. Around the main building are five cabins, a gazebo, and an organic vegetable garden serving the kitchen. Inside are five theme rooms, a library, and the dining room, where guests savor such simple treasures as wild berries picked from the adjacent forest, tea-smoked breast of duck, and salmon en croute with green peppercorn sauce. The inn can arrange a wide variety of excursions, including kayaking, hiking, whale watching, and fishing. Maybe you can hook dinner. 10 P Closed in winter S All major cards

SOMETHING SPECIAL

GUSTAVUS INN AT GLACIER BAY

$$$$$

MILE 1, GUSTAVUS RD.

TEL 907/697-2254 OR 800/649-5220

FAX 907/697-2255

www.gustavusinn.com

This might not be the swankiest lodge nor the fanciest restaurant in the Glacier Bay orbit, but many think it's the best. Personal and informal, the place bears the imprint of its owners, whose family has been running it for decades. They know the area and can tell guests where to pick wild strawberries or find the best spot to hook a Dolly Varden. Daily they drive people to Bartlett Cove and the national park visitor center to go on naturalist-led hikes. They also prepare notable food for their guests and, at fixed-price (*$$$*) family-style dinners, for the public. Much of that food comes from the inn's enormous garden or surrounding meadows and forest.

🛏 13 🅿 🕐 Closed in winter
🚫 🏦 All major cards

🏨 ANNIE MAE LODGE
$$$–$$$$$

ON THE GOOD RIVER
TEL 907/697-2346 OR
800/478-2346
www.anniemae.com

One of the few places in the Glacier Bay area that stays open year-round, this pretty, two-story lodge sits in a meadow on the Good River, a five-minute walk from the coast. The views from the veranda take in forest and mountains and the river. The price includes from one to three ample and tasty meals a day and ground transportation. The staff can arrange almost any outing.

🛏 11 🅿 🚫 🏦 All major cards

🏨 GLACIER BAY LODGE
$$$$

179 BARTLETT COVE RD.
TEL 907/264-4600 OR
888/229-8687
FAX 907/258-3668
www.visitglacierbay.com

This massive-timbered lodge boasts two unique privileges. One, it's the only lodging inside Glacier Bay National Park. Two, the park visitor center is in the lodge, so guests can take advantage of all the park's organized activities, notably guided hikes, kayak trips, and naturalist-led boat tours of the bay. But the lodge offers more than location. It is a comfortably rustic place virtually surrounded by

old-growth rain forest and offers guests and park visitors alike a good restaurant, a popular bar, mountain bike and fishing gear rentals, a gift shop with authentic Alaska native arts and crafts, and a large stone fireplace that holds great appeal after a day out amid the glaciers.

🛏 50 🅿 🕐 Closed in winter
🚫 🏦 All major cards

HAINES

🏨 HOTEL HÄLSINGLAND
🍴 $–$$

13 FORT SEWARD DR.
TEL 907/766-2000 OR
800/542-6363
FAX 907/766-2060
www.hotelhalsingland.com

Listed on the National Register of Historic Places, the Hälsingland once served as the commanding officer's quarters at Fort Seward—the historic military facility. The lovely old Victorian has been updated without losing any of its charm. The hotel also harbors one of the best eateries in Haines, the **Commander's Room Restaurant,** which relies on its cook's garden for herbs and greens and on the Chilkoot Inlet for fresh seafood. Dishes tend toward the innovative, such as seared wild Alaska salmon in a rhubarb-ginger chutney.

🛏 60 🅿 🕐 Closed mid-Oct.–early May (restaurant closes mid-Sept.) 🚫 🏦 All major cards

SKAGWAY

🏨 HISTORIC SKAGWAY INN
🍴 $$–$$$

655 BROADWAY AT 7TH
TEL 907/983-2289 OR
888/752-4929
FAX 907/983-2713
www.skagwayinn.com

This inn occupies one of the Klondike Gold Rush National Historical Park buildings. Built

PRICES

HOTELS

An indication of the cost of a double room in the high season is given by **$** signs.

$$$$$	Over $300
$$$$	$200–$300
$$$	$120–$200
$$	$80–$120
$	Under $80

RESTAURANTS

An indication of the cost of a three-course meal without drinks is given by $ signs.

$$$$$	Over $75
$$$$	$50–$75
$$$	$35–$50
$$	$20–$35
$	Under $20

in 1897, it began life as a brothel, and each room is named after one of the original working girls. In 2004 the owners remodeled the inn, restoring its Victorian glory with cast-iron beds and period antiques. Breakfast is served downstairs in **Olivia's Restaurant** (open to the public for lunch and dinner).

🛏 10 🅿 🕐 Closed in winter
🚫 🏦 All major cards

🏨 THE WHITE HOUSE
$$–$$$

475 8TH AVE. AT MAIN ST.
TEL 907/983-9000
FAX 907/983-9010
www.atthewhitehouse.com

Built in 1902 by a gambler and saloon owner, who apparently did well at both professions, this large, two-story white clapboard house is in a quiet residential neighborhood two blocks from Skagway's main drag. A Victorian beauty, it has aged well and still boasts much of the original woodwork. Rooms are furnished in antiques, and the beds are graced by fine handmade quilts.

🛏 11 🅿 🚫 🏦 All major cards

🏨 Hotel 🍴 Restaurant 🛏 No. of guest rooms 🪑 No. of Seats 🅿 Parking 🕐 Closed 🛗 Elevator

THE STOWAWAY CAFÉ
$$–$$$

205 CONGRESS WAY
TEL 907/983-3463
www.stowawaycafe.com
This dockside café fittingly serves a lot of fresh seafood. Try the hot scallop-and-bacon salad or the prawns with Gorgonzola. The café also offers landlubber dishes, such as steaks, Thai curry, or smoked ribs. The Stowaway is very popular with locals and travelers, so reservations are recommended.
⊞ 40 **P** ⊕ Closed in winter
⊠ **⊠** All major cards

■ ANCHORAGE & MAT-SU

ANCHORAGE

SOMETHING SPECIAL

HOTEL CAPTAIN COOK
$$$–$$$$$

939 W. 5TH AVE.
TEL 907/276-6000 OR
800/843-1950
FAX 907/343-2298
www.captaincook.com
Though national hotel chains have moved into Anchorage in force, the venerable Captain Cook remains at the top of the heap. The building encompasses an entire block with three skyscraping towers. In homage to its namesake explorer the hotel pursues a nautical theme in its several rooms. Amenities include a dozen shops, an athletic center, a business center, and four restaurants. The best of the latter is **Crow's Nest Restaurant,** also one of the city's finest places to eat. As the name implies, it nests atop one of the towers and commands grand views of the Chugach Mountains and, appropriately, Cook Inlet. It's especially noted for its 10,000-bottle wine cellar.
① 547 **P** **⊟** **⊠** **⊠**
⊠ All major cards

THE HISTORIC ANCHORAGE HOTEL
$$$$

330 E ST.
TEL 907/272-4553 OR
800/544-0988
FAX 907/277-4483
www.historicanchorage hotel.com
This small downtown hotel has a big history. Beloved humorist Will Rogers and pioneer aviator Wiley Post slept here two days before they died in a tragic plane crash near Barrow. Alaska's most renowned painter, Sydney Laurence, lived in the hotel for years and created many of his masterful landscapes in a studio in the lobby. This 1916 building has been nicely renovated, with dark cherrywood furnishings and contemporary amenities like free Wi-Fi and large-screen digital TVs.
① 26 **P** **⊠** **⊟** **⊡**
⊠ All major cards

COPPER WHALE INN
$$$–$$$$

440 L ST.
TEL 907/258-7999 OR
866/258-7999
FAX 907/258-6213
www.copperwhale.com
This tidy little inn sits on a hillside on the west end of downtown, from which it commands views of Cook Inlet, the Alaska Range, and the Mount Spurr volcano. Note the binoculars on the windowsill. They're for scanning the waters below for seals or beluga whales. The nearby Tony Knowles Coastal Trail begs to be biked, and it just so happens that during the summer Lifetime Adventures operates on the inn's premises. This big 1939 home has been well kept, from the brass-trimmed fireplace and original pine floors to the lush flower gardens.
① 14 **P** **⊠** **⊠** All major cards

INLET TOWER HOTEL & SUITES
$$$–$$$$

1200 L ST.
TEL 907/276-0110 OR
800/544-0786
FAX 907/258-4914
www.inlettower.com
Completed in 1951, this 14-story building on the edge of downtown was Alaska's first skyscraper, and its views of Cook Inlet and the Chugach Mountains remain wonderful. After a recent large-scale remodeling, the place has a light, clean, modern feel and many new amenities, including spacious suites, large-screen TVs, and top-end linens. It also houses the **Pubhouse,** a fine restaurant and bar with an elegant air.
① 180 **⊞** 100 **P** **⊟** **⊠** **⊠**
⊡ **⊠** All major cards

A WILDFLOWER INN
$$$

1239 I ST.
907/274-1239 OR
877/693-1239
FAX 907/222-3062
www.alaska-wildflower-inn .com
With its white picket fence, tidy landscaping, and abundant flowers (in summer), this B&B signals its immaculate nature before you even enter the two-story saltbox house. Inside the first impression is verified. The common rooms are finely furnished and the three guest rooms—two of them suites with sitting rooms— are replete with featherbed comforters, a reading and game library, writing desks, elaborate quilts, and all the other comforts of home—well, more than most homes.
① 3 **P** **⊠** **⊠** AE, MC, V

SOMETHING SPECIAL

MARX BROS. CAFÉ
$$$$–$$$$$

627 W. 3RD AVE.
TEL 907/278-2133

FAX 907/258-6279
www.marxcafe.com
The owners bill their renowned restaurant as serving "innovative contemporary cuisine." That phrase hardly captures the flavor of halibut baked in a macadamia-nut crust with a coconut curry sauce and mango chutney or wild Alaska salmon basted with sun-dried tomato butter. The desserts aren't bad, either—the white chocolate coffee tower, for instance, consists of chocolate cake topped with white chocolate espresso mousse with a chocolate glaze and amaretto crème anglaise. The remarkably high quality stems in part from an intimate focus—no lunch and only about 60 dinners a night, five nights a week, in this charming little 1916 wood frame house with inlet views.

🛈 46 🅿 🚫
🃏 All major cards

🍽 RISTORANTE ORSO
$$$–$$$$$
737 W. 5TH AVE. AT G ST.
TEL 907/222-3232
www.orsoalaska.com
Pass through the lively downstairs bar and step upstairs into a quiet realm of Oriental rugs, reddish walls, and a striking slate-framed fireplace. This Tuscan inn setting suits the osso buco (braised lamb) and the seafood fusilli, replete with clams, prawns, calamari, scallops, smoked salmon, whitefish, and crab. Orso serves many traditional Italian pasta dishes, and at times the Alaska influence emerges, as with the smoked salmon chowder. Reservations advised.

🛋 120 🅿 🚫
🃏 All major cards

🍽 SACKS CAFÉ &
RESTAURANT
$$$–$$$$
328 G ST.
TEL 907/276-3546 OR

907/274-4022
www.sackscafe.com
As soon as you set eyes on the coral-colored exterior and bright Southwestern interior, you'll sense that the food at Sacks will be creative, even playful. It doesn't fit into any standard category, but you won't care when you start your meal with a seared calamari spinach salad or crab and scallop cakes with pico de gallo and honey chipotle aioli. Then move on to an entrée of grilled king salmon in a sashimi marinade and soy maple glaze or the prawn linguine, highlighted by portobello mushrooms, poblano peppers, sweet onions, pistachios, and an herb butter wine sauce. A tapas bar serves those who wish to graze. Sacks is a popular lunch spot, too. Reservations recommended for lunch and dinner.

🛋 84 🚫 🃏 All major cards

🍽 MOOSE'S TOOTH PUB
& PIZZERIA
$–$$
3300 OLD SEWARD HWY.
TEL 907/258-2537
www.moosestooth.net
This midtown brew pub and pizza place ranks high in the hearts and stomachs of Anchorage residents. The pizza ranges from the ordinary to the odd, such as gyro sausage. Desserts include Moose Pie and Death by Peanut Butter. The repertoire of beers is impressive and includes local north country brews, such as Polar Pale Ale, Northern Light Amber, and Pipeline Stout.

🛋 180 🅿 🚫
🃏 All major cards

🍽 NEW SAGAYA'S CITY
MARKET/MIDTOWN
MARKET
$–$$
900 W. 13TH AVE.
TEL 907/274-6173
3700 OLD SEWARD HWY.

TEL 907/561-5173 OR
800/764-1001
FAX 907/561-2042
www.newsagaya.com
These two stores are primarily groceries that carry regular items but specialize in fresh seafood and ethnic foods, including Chinese, Korean, Thai, and Hispanic. The not-so-well-kept secret is that people looking for a ready meal can find all sorts of food that they can eat at the inside and outside tables or take-out counters. Among the choices on offer are Asian food, lattes, deli sandwiches, excellent baked goods, salads, and great fresh seafood. Try the king salmon candy.

🅿 🚫 🃏 All major cards

🍽 THAI KITCHEN
$–$$
3405 E. TUDOR
TEL 907/561-0082
FAX 907/563-6868
www.thaikitchenak.com
Though this Thai restaurant, Anchorage's first, is hidden in a strip mall, you will remember the food. Locals crowd into the dining room to eat

---

🏨 Hotel 🍽 Restaurant 🛈 No. of guest rooms 🛋 No. of Seats 🅿 Parking 🕐 Closed 🛗 Elevator authentic Thai classics, like pad Thai and green curries, as well as less typical dishes, like jungle beef. If you can't decide what to order off the long menu, try the Thai Kitchen Platter, a heaping sampler of appetizers. 🛏 60 🅿 🕒 Closed L Sat. & Sun. 🆂 All major cards

🍴 SNOW CITY CAFÉ

$

1034 W. 4TH AVE.
TEL 907/272-2489
www.snowcitycafe.com
This bright, welcoming downtown favorite offers fine lunches, but breakfast is king. Repeatedly voted best breakfast in Anchorage, they do regular fare irregularly well: blueberry pancakes, eggs Florentine, Black Forest ham omelets. But the menu brims with appealing Alaska twists, such as the reindeer sausage scramble, sockeye salmon cakes, and the Kodiak eggs benedict, which features king crab. They give free espresso drinks to everyone on the day of the first snowfall.
🛏 105 🆂 🆂 All major cards

TURNAGAIN ARM

SOMETHING SPECIAL

🏨 ALYESKA PRINCE
🍴 HOTEL
$$$$–$$$$$
1000 ARLBERG AVE., GIRDWOOD
TEL 907/754-1111 OR
800/880-3880
FAX 907/754-2200
www.alyeskaresort.com
This is Alaska's foremost large luxury resort. Every room has such top-drawer amenities as heated towel racks, fluffy robes, a refrigerator, and an in-room safe. Imagine the extras in the 1,275-square-foot (115 sq m) Royal Suite—a mere $1,500 per night. For a memorable dining experience, take the tram up to the Seven Glaciers Restaurant, atop the ski slopes. Along with the

views, which include seven hanging glaciers, diners can savor mustard-crusted ahi tuna or Alaska sable fish in a saffron orange sauce.
🚪 304 🅿 🆂 🛏 🛏 🆂
🆂 All major cards

🍴 DOUBLE MUSKY INN
$$$–$$$$
MILE 0.3 CROW CREEK RD.,
GIRDWOOD
TEL 907/783-2822
www.doublemuskyinn.com
This establishment is an idiosyncratic cross between a fine restaurant and a rowdy roadhouse, with a Cajun-Louisiana-meets-Alaska accent. The place gets crowded and the service slow, but it kind of works with the laid-back attitude. The Cajun-meets-Alaska blend leads to dishes that are mouthwatering and often eye watering (i.e., spicy). Try the authentic shrimp étouffée or the lobster kabobs. The Double Musky has also gained a national reputation for fine steaks, especially its pepper steak.
🛏 85 🅿 🕒 Closed Mon. & six weeks in late fall 🆂 🆂 All major cards

MAT-SU

🏨 COLONY INN
🍴 $$–$$$
325 E. ELMWOOD AVE., PALMER
TEL 907/745-3330
FAX 907/746-3330
Teachers who came to the region during the Great Depression used the Colony Inn building as their dorm. A good renovation has given the place a refined though not luxurious country-inn atmosphere, with such modern amenities as Wi-Fi and Jacuzzis. In summer a homey restaurant on the ground floor (famed for its blue-ribbon pies) serves lunch Monday through Friday and brunch on Sunday. Reservations and

check-ins are handled a few blocks away at the Valley Hotel (606 S. Alaska St.).
🚪 12 🅿 🆂 🆂 All major cards

🏨 HATCHER PASS LODGE
🍴 $$–$$$
MILE 17 HATCHER PASS RD.
(PALMER-FISHHOOK RD.)
TEL 907/745-1200
www.hatcherpasslodge.com
Near Hatcher Pass summit, this A-frame lodge and scattered cabins nestle amid alpine tundra and rugged mountains. Guests come to cross-country ski and admire the views or to hike and admire the views. The lodge sits at the entry road to Independence Mine State Historical Park. Cabins include chemical toilets and water, while the lodge provides showers. A decent restaurant in the lodge serves lunch and dinner, and breakfast for guests.
🚪 12 🅿 🆂 🆂 All major cards

🏨 PIONEER RIDGE BED
& BREAKFAST
$$–$$$
2221 YUKON DR., WASILLA
TEL 907/376-7472 OR
800/478-7472
FAX 907/376-7470
www.pioneerridge.com
Pioneer Ridge rises amid the wide-open rural spaces of the Mat-Su outside Wasilla; you'll need driving directions from the owners or website to find it. As you approach, watch for this 10,000-square-foot (900 sq m) colony barn. Once part of the Fairview Dairy, it has been converted into a bed-and-breakfast. This B&B augments its authentic old-Alaska character with such decor as a wall-mounted moose head and antler chandeliers. Each room reflects an Alaska theme, like the Iditarod Room, which features a prized vintage Iditarod sled.
🚪 7 🅿 🆂 🛏
🆂 All major cards

🆂 Nonsmoking 🆂 Air-conditioning 🛏 Indoor Pool 🛏 Health Club 🆂 Credit Cards

🍴 EVANGELO'S TRATTORIA
$$–$$$$
301 PARKS HWY. (MILE 40), WASILLA
TEL 907/376-1212
Evangelo's spacious, comely interior includes banquet and conference facilities. The food is a pleasant surprise, from the fine salad bar and good pizzas to such elaborate fare as pepper-crusted ahi tuna. Evangelo's also serves several enticing seafood combinations, such as prawns, crab, and lobster sauteed in Cajun spices.
ⓘ 200 🅿 🚫
♿ All major cards

🍴 COLONY KITCHEN/ NOISY GOOSE CAFÉ
$$–$$$
1890 GLENN HWY., PALMER
TEL 907/746-4600
Across from the Alaska state fairgrounds sits this beloved family restaurant, known for its goofy decorations, funny signs, friendly service, and American heartland-style food: meatloaf, prime rib, chicken friend steak, and so on. Locals also drive many miles for the homemade pies, such as the rhubarb and raspberry with walnut crumb topping.
✚ 80 🅿 🚫 ♿ D, MC, V

🍴 TURKEY RED
$$–$$$
550 S. ALASKA ST., PALMER
TEL 907/746-5544
www.turkeyredak.com
Mat-Su is Alaska's breadbasket and Turkey Red takes full advantage by serving up lots of dishes that rely on local, often organic ingredients. Choices include pasta, seafood, salads, pizza, steak, and a number of offerings with a Greek background, such as *gyrokopita*–ground beef with cinnamon and ginger in phyllo. Be sure to pick up some fresh bread from the acclaimed Turkey Red bakery.
✚ 55 🅿 🚫 ♿ D, MC, V

🍴 VAGABOND BLUES
$
642 S. ALASKA ST., PALMER
TEL 907/745-2233
www.vagblues.com
On the main drag in old downtown Palmer, this café seems like something you'd find on an urban corner in San Francisco. The healthful, vegetarian fare includes pasta salads, bagel sandwiches, and large portions of homemade soup served in hand-painted bowls created by a local artist. Another highlight is dessert. Local performers fill the place with live music some evenings.
✚ 70 🅿 🚫 ♿ MC, V

◼ KENAI PENINSULA

SEWARD

🏨 KENAI FJORDS WILDERNESS LODGE
$$$$$
TEL 877/777-4053
FAX 907/777-2888
www.kenaifjordslodge.com
This lodge is on Fox Island, near the mouth of Resurrection Bay, 14 miles (23 km) from Seward. To stay there, guests must sign on for a trip with Kenai Fjords Tours (see p. 263). Trips include the one-hour boat ride to the lodge, an overnight in a cabin on an island in a bay, and choices of meals and excursions, such as kayaking trips, Resurrection Bay tours, and guided hikes. Guests are welcome to extend their stays in the cabins.
ⓘ 8 🕐 Closed in winter
♿ All major cards

🏨 EDGEWATER HOTEL
$$$–$$$$
202 5TH AVE.
TEL 907/224-2700 OR 800/780-7234
FAX 907/224-2701
www.hoteledgewater.com
The new arrival among downtown Seward hotels

reflects its recent vintage with high-speed Internet, an up-to-date business center, and 32-inch flat-screen TVs and DVD players in all rooms. It retains at least one time-honored Alaska service, however—freezer space for guests' fish. Recently acquired by Best Western.
ⓘ 76 🅿 🕐 Closed in winter
🔀 🚫 📺 ♿ All major cards

🏨 HOTEL SEWARD
$$–$$$$
221 5TH AVE.
TEL 907/224-8001 OR 800/440-2444
FAX 907/224-3112
www.hotelsewardalaska.com
Guests may appreciate this hotel's historical gold-rush atmosphere or its nice rooms and many amenities, but above all this establishment offers a great location in Seward's comfy old downtown. Practically next door to the famous Alaska SeaLife Center, it's about a block from the waterfront and overlooks the mountains and lovely Resurrection Bay.
ⓘ 62 🅿 🔀 🚫 📺
♿ All major cards

🏨 VAN GILDER HOTEL
$$$

308 ADAMS ST.
TEL 800/478-0400
www.vangilderhotel.com

This 1916 hotel lacks some of the newer amenities, but it compensates with Victorian charm and good service. Except for the four suites, the rooms are small, but they're spotless and offer nice touches like brass beds and period antiques. The parlor features a player piano and a collection of Alaska-themed books. Throughout are historic photos with informative captions. Brave souls might like the Fanny's Ghost Suite.

🛏 24 🅿 🚭
🏧 All major cards

🍴 CHINOOKS KITCHEN AND BAR
$$$–$$$$

1404 4TH AVE.
TEL 907/224-2207
www.chinooksbar.com

The great views of the harbor remain the same, but Chinooks' new owners have changed the menu—and they will keep changing parts of it throughout the year as they make use of local, seasonal food. Seafood still rules. Look for salmon, halibut, king crab, black cod, oysters, and other fishy favorites, sometimes in surprising forms, such as smoked scallop mac and cheese. But many other dishes don't come from the sea, such as beef braciola, Cajun corn dogs, and pork carnitas sandwiches.

🍴 160 🅿 🚭
🏧 All major cards

🍴 CHRISTO'S PALACE
$$–$$$$

133 4TH AVE.
TEL 907/224-5255
www.christospalace.com

It's easy for travelers exploring downtown Seward to walk by the unprepossessing exterior of Christo's and wonder if the word "palace" is a joke, but step inside and you'll understand. The interior is elegant, almost opulent: dark polished wood, vaulted ceilings, fine furnishings, and a beautiful mahogany bar thought to date back to the 19th century. Incongruously, the restaurant is known especially for its pizza, but Christo's also serves a wide variety of other dishes, ranging from Greek to Italian, Mexican to burgers.

🍴 102 🅿 🚭
🏧 All major cards

🍴 RAY'S WATERFRONT
$$–$$$$

1316 4TH AVE.
TEL 907/224-5606
www.rayswaterfrontak.com

Ray's is a Seward landmark. For many years anglers have come to this harborside restaurant after a day on the water. Most likely it's the straightforward but top-notch seafood that packs them in (on busy days expect long waits). Ray's signature dish is its seafood chowder. Dining areas have appealing views of the harbor.

🍴 175 🅿 🕐 Closed Oct.–mid-April 🚭 🏧 All major cards

SOLDOTNA

🏨 ASPEN HOTEL
$$$

326 BINKLEY CIRCLE
TEL 907/260-7736
www.aspenhotelsak.com

This new hotel sits on a bluff overlooking the Kenai River in Soldotna, one of the world's most famous salmon-fishing areas. Part of a small Alaska chain, it lacks charm, but its rooms are spotless, bright, spacious, and well appointed (refrigerators, microwaves, DVD players, Wi-Fi). And there's ample freezer space for any salmon you may catch.

🛏 63 🅿 🚭 🚭 🏊 🎾
🏧 All major cards

🍴 DUCK INN
$–$$$

MILE 19.5 KALIFORNSKY BEACH RD.
TEL 907/262-1849

The Duck Inn offers just about everything but duck—from steaks to seafood, chicken to pizza. It's known for its creative hamburgers and for halibut fresh from Cook Inlet. If you've been out combat fishing all day, you'll appreciate the soft lighting and soothing music. The inn also provides a small hostelry and a lounge.

🍴 60 🅿 🚭
🏧 All major cards

KENAI

🏨 KENAI LANDING
🍴 **$$–$$$$**

2101 BOWPICKER LANE
TEL 907/335-2500 OR 800/478-0400
www.kenailanding.com

Built in the 1920s, this former cannery complex was recently transformed into a contemporary resort. Accommodations range from immaculate but smallish rooms, with bathrooms down the hall in the former women's quarters—called the "Hen House"—to remodeled former fishermen's bunkhouses turned into three-bedroom cottages. The resort includes docks, a theater, more than 25 shops, nature trails, a restaurant, and even a remnant of the seafood-processing plant.

🛏 44 🅿 🕐 Closed early Aug.–late June 🚭
🏧 All major cards

🍴 SAL'S KLONDIKE DINER
$–$$

44619 STERLING HWY.
TEL 907/262-2220

This classic roadside diner looks touristy but has a heart of gold. Locals frequent the joint as much as travelers. They come for the tasty food, generous portions, and fast, attentive service. The diner is open seven days a week and all night Friday and Saturday. The menu includes burgers, sandwiches, fish and chips, and the other usual suspects, plus halibut and salmon. The staff bakes fresh pies and bread every day.

🔲 100 🅿 🅂
🅂 All major cards

🍴 CHARLOTTE'S BAKERY
$

115 S. WILLOW ST.
TEL 907/283-2777
This is the kind of bakery that locals can't get enough of. The food is good and varied, the room bright and appealing, the service friendly, and the prices very reasonable. The bakery turns out berry pastries, cookies, and other sugary treats to have with tea or take home. It also produces the fragrant bread for Charlotte's excellent sandwiches. The eat-in section offers salads, soups, omelets, and sourdough pancakes.

🔲 70 🅿 🅂
🅂 All major cards

HOMER

SOMETHING SPECIAL

🏨 ALASKA ADVENTURE CABINS
$$$$–$$$$$

2525 STERLING HWY.
TEL 907/223-6681
www.alaskaadventurecabins
.com
This property sprawls atop Baycrest Hill—the high point north of Homer—and views of the Cook Inlet and far beyond are incredible, to say the least. The word "cabins" hardly captures the unique, elaborate nature of the eight structures visitors can rent. For example, the Moose Caboose is a 54-foot (16 m) Pullman

car that has been remade into a gorgeous, if long and skinny, two-level structure with amenities like kitchens, a fireplace, gleaming hardwood floors, satellite TVs, two full baths, a big picture window, and a 30-foot (9 m) deck. The Double Eagle is a former shrimp boat with a bright, polished interior, fine furnishings, two bedrooms, a kitchen, a living room, two and a half baths, and three decks.

🛈 8 🅿 🅂
🅂 All major cards

🏨 ALASKAN SUITES
$$$$

42485 STERLING HIGHWAY
TEL 907/235-1972 OR
888/239-1972
FAX 907/235-7641
www.alaskansuites.com
Fantastic views. That's the first thing you'll notice on this property high on a hillside just west of Homer. Should you spot soaring bald eagles, you'll probably be looking down on them. When you do finally notice the accommodations, you'll find stand-alone log cabins (plus a cottage that sleeps eight) with back decks about 30 feet (9 m) from the bluff. The interiors are spacious (they sleep five) and luxurious, with a long list of amenities, including tiled bathrooms, a small refrigerator, a satellite TV, a sofa, and a La-Z-Boy recliner chair.

🛈 6 🅿 🅂
🅂 All major cards

🏨 CHOCOLATE DROP LODGE
$$–$$$$

57745 TAKU AVE.
TEL 907/299-4730
www.chocolatedroplodge.com
Six miles (10 km) east of Homer, the Chocolate Drop sits on a slice of rural land that overlooks Kachemak Bay. Views encompass much of the expansive bay, the distant Kenai Mountains, four glaciers,

and the eponymous Chocolate Drop peak. The rooms are light, spacious, and well furnished. Guests can soak in a sauna or in a hot tub on the deck. The innkeepers are known for their breakfasts and treats, such as reindeer sausage and seafood omelets. Watch for moose wandering around the property.

🛈 6 🅿 🅂 🅂 MC, V

🏨 OLD TOWN BED & BREAKFAST
$$–$$$

106 W. BUNNELL ST.
TEL 907/235-7558
www.oldtownbedandbreak
fast.com
This B&B occupies the second floor of a building that dates back to 1936. It served for decades as Homer's trading post. (The first floor is home to the Bunnell Street Arts Center; see p. 261.) Near the beach, it offers one large apartment for four. Sea breezes and ocean views set the mood. Rooms include such amenities as a cherrywood four-poster bed, hardwood floors, a handmade Alaska

---

🏨 Hotel 🍴 Restaurant 🛈 No. of guest rooms 🔲 No. of Seats 🅿 Parking 🔘 Closed 🅂 Elevator

wildflower quilt, and antique chairs. Breakfast is catered by a neighboring café.

ℹ 3 🅿 🅢 🅰 MC, V

🍴 CAFÉ CUPS
$$–$$$$
162 W. PIONEER AVE.
TEL 907/235-8330
www.cafecupsofhomer.com
This eatery is nothing if not whimsical; look for the four mammoth teacups that adorn the exterior. The intimate interior features plants, flowers, and dark wood. The food is excellent. The chef produces a wide range of dishes, from simple and cheap to elaborate and expensive, with an emphasis on Alaska seafood. Ask about the specials.

🏠 30 🅿 🕐 Closed Sun.
🅢 🅰 MC, V

🍴 HOMESTEAD RESTAURANT
$$–$$$$
MILE 8.2 EAST END RD.
TEL 907/235-8723
www.homesteadrestaurant
.net
This former roadhouse has moved up in the world, serving elaborate cuisine in an art-filled room—though the walls are still those of a rustic log cabin. Enjoy seafood, steak, prime rib, or rack of lamb as you appreciate views of Kachemak Bay and distant mountains and glaciers. Reservations recommended.

🏠 60 🅿 🅢
🅰 All major cards

🍴 FAT OLIVES RESTAURANT
$–$$
276 OHLSON LANE
TEL 907/235-8488
Noisy, cheerful, and informal, Fat Olives is a welcoming place, just like an Italian bistro ought to be. The familiar, high-quality food is welcoming, too, with something for everybody: wood-fired pizzas,

fresh seafood, roasted chicken, calzones, salads, beef, and many appetizers.

🏠 60 🅿 🅢
🅰 All major cards

🍴 FRESH SOURDOUGH EXPRESS
$–$$
1316 OCEAN DR.
TEL 907/235-7571
www.freshsourdough
express.com
Offering one of the best values in Alaska, this pleasant dining room serves breakfast, lunch, and dinner consisting of savory, healthful (often organic) food. Portions are large and the price small (for Alaska). Try the reindeer grill, an outstanding pizza, or the halibut hoagie. The bakery creates all its own fresh items from original recipes, including carrot cake puffin muffins and fudge moose mounds, obscene brownies, and wonderful sourdough bread.

🏠 50 🅿 🅢 🅰 MC, V

ACROSS KACHEMAK BAY

SOMETHING SPECIAL

🏨 KACHEMAK BAY WILDERNESS LODGE
$$$$$
CHINA POOT BAY
TEL 907/235-8910
www.alaskawildernesslodge
.com
As one should expect at a lodge this expensive, the owners and staff provide luxury and personal attention—to a maximum of 12 guests. But it's the owners' strong conservation ethic that makes this a world-class wilderness hideaway. They'll whisk you by boat to watch sea otters, seals, and whales, lead hikes through rain forests and alpine meadows in the adjacent state park, guide tide-pooling excursions in their bay, lead kayaks

to seabird rookeries, and hire floatplanes to view brown bears. As for the rustic luxury ... the four cabins, some with two bedrooms, are simply gorgeous, and guests can relax in a sod-roof sauna, an outdoor hot tub, or a solarium. Sophisticated food rounds out the experience; often it comes fresh out of the bay or the lodge's garden. Reserve early.

ℹ 4 cabins 🕐 Closed Oct.–April 🅢 🅰 All major cards

🏨 TUTKA BAY WILDERNESS LODGE
$$$$$
TUTKA BAY
TEL 907/274-2710
http://withinthewild.com
This lodge defines rustic luxury: cabins with floor-to-ceiling windows and fine furnishings; fine food with an emphasis on Alaska seafood; and extras like a hot tub gazebo and a sauna. Still, the surroundings steal the show. The forest, the mountains, the bay, the sea otters outside your window—these things make a stay here truly memorable. The lodge leads or arranges all sorts of excursions, some of which cost extra. Access is by boat or plane from Homer. The huge deck doubles as a helipad. Reserve early.

ℹ 4 cabins, 1 suite 🕐 Closed mid-Sept.–mid-May 🅢
🅰 All major cards

🏨 CENTRAL SUITES OF SELDOVIA
$$$–$$$$
253 SELDOVIA ST., SELDOVIA
TEL 907/234-3700
www.centralsuitesof
seldovia.com
This place is aptly named; it's centrally located and the units are emphatically suites, not mere rooms. Besides one or two bedrooms, the light and bright suites offer roomy living rooms and full kitchens. The suites occupy the second

---

🅢 Nonsmoking 🅢 Air-conditioning 🏊 Indoor Pool 🏋 Health Club 🅰 Credit Cards

floor of the old Seldovia theater building, but these days the show is outside the windows, which look out on the downtown, the harbor, and the surrounding forest and mountains.

🛈 3 suites 🅿 🚫
🚭 D, MC, V

🏨 PETERSON BAY LODGE
$$$

PETERSON BAY
TEL 907/235-7156
www.petersonbaylodge.com
This pretty lodge features a full menu of ecotours, including kayaking, fishing, hiking, and wildlife-watching, but the highlight of a stay here is getting a feel for daily life in the Alaska wilderness. The owners live in the main building, run an oyster farm as well as the lodge, and are happy to chat about their lifestyle. Some guests volunteer to help with the oysters and enjoy that even more than the outings and fine dinners. Guests stay in eco-cabins—large log-and-canvas structures set on hillside platforms with great views. Reserve early.

🛈 4 cabins 🚫 🕐 Closed in winter 🚭 Cash only

🏨 ACROSS THE BAY TENT AND BREAKFAST ADVENTURE CO.
$–$$

KASITSNA BAY
TEL 907/235-3633 (SUMMER) OR 907/345-2571 (WINTER)
www.tentandbreakfast alaska.com
Tucked into a scenic cove on the uncivilized side of Kachemak Bay, this establishment offers its variation on the traditional bed-and-breakfast. (They have two cabins, as well.) However, there actually are beds inside the platform tents that adorn the beach and hillside above it—but bring your own sleeping bag. No bathrooms, but the two

outhouses are nice and even feature stained-glass windows. When you're hungry after hiking, biking, tide-pooling, or sea kayaking, head to the handsome main lodge for family-style meals. Check out the weekend workshops, like one on fish-skin basketry.

🛈 5 tents, 2 cabins 🕐 Closed in winter 🚫 🚭 MC, V

SOMETHING SPECIAL

🍴 THE SALTRY
$$$–$$$$

HALIBUT COVE
TEL 907/226-2424
www.thesaltry.com
The caught-that-morning fresh seafood, home-baked breads, greens right from the garden, intricate sushi, an array of microbrews, the artsy room, and the Callebaut chocolate cheesecake are all a marvel. Not to mention the poached sockeye salmon with a ginger-lemongrass broth. When the restaurant is full, the population nearly doubles in tiny Halibut Cove, where a boardwalk on pilings substitutes for main street and people use kayaks and rowboats instead of cars. Unless you're staying in town, you'll have to book passage on the M.V. *Danny J.*, and they'll make your lunch or dinner reservations.

🔲 50 🕐 Closed Labor Day–Memorial Day 🚫 🚭 MC, V

■ ALASKA PENINSULA & THE ALEUTIANS

KATMAI NATIONAL PARK & PRESERVE

🏨 BROOKS LODGE
$$$$$

TEL 907/243-5448 OR 800/544-0551
FAX 907/243-0649
www.katmailand.com
The hub of big, remote,

and supremely wild Katmai National Park and Preserve, Brooks Camp is also home to the main building and adjacent 16 cabins that make up Brooks Lodge. Most people come to watch the renowned brown bears fishing for salmon on the Brooks River; others come to do some fishing themselves or to see the Valley of Ten Thousand Smokes. The cabins aren't fancy, but they're modern and offer private toilets, heat, and electricity.

🛈 16 cabins 🚫 🕐 Closed mid-Sept.–May 🚭 MC, V

SOMETHING SPECIAL

🏨 HALLO BAY BEAR CAMP
$$$$$

TEL 907/235-2237 (HOMER)
FAX 907/235-9461
www.hallobay.com
Surrounded by Katmai National Park and Preserve, scenic Hallo Bay is one of Alaska's premier brown bear viewing spots, yet on a typical night only about a dozen people stay here. The owners of this remote enclave limit access to protect the bears.

Hallo Bay's approach to bear viewing depends on keeping the brown bears utterly wild and uninterested in the humans who walk into their midst. That's right, walk right among them. While Hallo Bay's safety record is perfect, this method isn't for everyone, and you should explore it further before going. Up to four guests sleep on cots in heated structures that resemble canvas Quonset huts.

🚹 5 🕒 Closed mid-Sept.–mid-May 🚭 🏦 All major cards

KODIAK

🏨 BEST WESTERN
🍴 KODIAK INN
$$–$$$
236 W. REZANOF DR.
TEL 907/486-5712 OR
888/563-4254
FAX 907/486-3430
www.kodiakinn.com
Yes, it's just a chain motel, but hostelries are few and expensive in Kodiak, and this one is newly refurbished and situated downtown with views of St. Paul Harbor. It hosts one of Kodiak's best eateries, the **Chart Room,** good for seafood and steaks.

🚹 80 🅿 🖨 🖥 🚭 🏦 All major cards

🍴 HENRY'S GREAT ALASKAN RESTAURANT
$$–$$$$
512 MARINE WAY
TEL 907/486-8844
www.henrysalaska.com
Henry's has been a local hangout since 1957. Situated a block from the harbor in this fishing town, Henry's naturally favors seafood. Much is straightforward fare, such as grilled tuna and a fish-prawns-scallops combo, but you'll encounter surprises, too, like the crawfish pie.

🚹 100 🅿 🚭 🏦 MC, V

🍴 THE OLD POWERHOUSE RESTAURANT
$$–$$$
516 E. MARINE WAY
TEL 907/481-1088
Situated in a historic powerhouse on the water, this restaurant possesses the kind of views—fishing boats passing, sea lions swimming below the windows—that often signal mediocre food. Not to worry; both eyes and stomach will savor this Japanese eatery, which specializes in sushi.

🚹 100 🅿 🚭 🏦 MC, V

🍴 KING'S DINER
$
1941 MILL BAY RD.
TEL 907/486-4100
A loud, busy, fun place where both local families and men wearing the commercial fisherman's uniform—rubber boots and hooded sweatshirts—load up at breakfast on sourdough pancakes, at lunch on cheeseburgers, and at dinner on seafood and prime rib.

🚹 50 🅿 🚭 🏦 MC, V

ALEUTIAN ISLANDS

🏨 GRAND ALEUTIAN
🍴 $$$–$$$$
498 SALMON WAY, UNALASKA
TEL 907/581-3844 OR
866/581-3844
FAX 907/581-7150
www.grandaleutian.com
This fairly luxurious, executive-style hotel seems out of place out here in the remote wilds of the Aleutians, as though it drifted in from Anchorage. It offers bright, spacious rooms decorated with local and regional art and amenities such as Internet hookups and an extra vanity and sink. The hotel includes a fine restaurant (see following entry), a café, a lounge, and a gift shop that sells local arts and crafts.

🚹 114 🅿 🚭 🖨
🏦 All major cards

🍴 CHART ROOM
$$–$$$
GRAND ALEUTIAN
498 SALMON WAY,
UNALASKA
TEL 907/581-3844 OR
800/891-1194
www.grandaleutian.com
Downright posh, the Grand Aleutian hotel's Chart Room serves cuisine that befits its views of the surrounding waters—among the world's best fishing grounds. Salmon, shrimp, crab, halibut, and other seafood figure in most dishes. Locals also frequent this restaurant, especially on lavish "special" nights: a Wednesday night seafood buffet, a Friday night barbecue on the deck (summer), and a Sunday brunch. Reservations recommended.

🚹 100 🅿 🕒 Closed L, except Sun. brunch 🚭 🖨
🏦 All major cards

▨ PRINCE WILLIAM SOUND & AROUND

VALDEZ

🏨 MOUNTAIN SKY HOTEL
$$$
1465 RICHARDSON HWY.
TEL 907/835-9130
www.brooksideinnbb.com
Tucked away just out of town, this handsome and exceptionally blue B&B sits on several forested acres. The rooms are well kept and the breakfasts tasty, but the setting steals the show. Snowy mountains rise several thousand feet behind the house and salmon spawn in the stream that crosses the property, attracting hungry bears and eagles.

🚹 5 🅿 🕒 Closed in winter
🚭 🏦 MC, V

🚭 Nonsmoking 🖥 Air-conditioning 🏊 Indoor Pool 🖥 Health Club 🏦 Credit Cards

🏨 WILD ROSES BY THE SEA B&B RETREAT

$$$

629 FIDDLEHEAD LANE
TEL 907/835-2930
www.alaskabytheseabnb.com
Rose's B&B sits at the edge of the forest atop Blueberry Hill, a mile (1.6 km) out of Valdez. Views of the sound, the mouth of Mineral Creek Canyon, and the Chugach Mountains are grand. One of the rooms is a suite with a Jacuzzi, while another is a one-room apartment with a private entrance. Best to reserve far ahead.

ℹ️ 3 🅿️ 🚭 ⬡ MC, V

🍴 T.H.C. OFF THE HOOK

$$–$$$$$

100 N. HARBOR DR.
TEL 907/835-8114
Much about T.H.C. Off the Hook is unexpected, starting with the fact that this fine restaurant lurks inside a Best Western motel and serves up sweeping views of the small-boat harbor and the bay. Now, the mainline seafood—king crab, seared ahi tuna—are not unexpected, but some of the seafood dishes are, such as the Thai shrimp ravioli. And then there's the surprising dishes, like the *lomo saltado* (a Peruvian beef stir fry)—utterly unexpected unless you know that the head chef is Peruvian.

🍴 100 🅿️ 🚭
⬡ All major cards

🍴 MIKE'S PALACE

$$–$$$$

201 N. HARBOR DR.
TEL 907/835-2365
www.mikespalace.com
With its harbor views, varied food, cheerful atmosphere, and good prices, Mike's is a local favorite. You can get lasagna, enchiladas, steak, seafood, Greek gyros, veal, and Mike's highly regarded pizza.

🍴 80 🚭 ⬡ All major cards

CORDOVA

🏨 CORDOVA ROSE LODGE

$$$

1315 WHITSHED RD.
TEL 907/424-7673
www.cordovarose.com
This lodge comes by its nautical theme honestly; it's built on an old barge anchored beside a lighthouse at the mouth of Odiak Slough. Guests can scan the slough for birds and otters or gaze across the harbor at the distant mountains and islands. Everyone has free run of a sauna and library, and some of the rooms have access to a kitchen and deck with a barbecue. Less than half a mile (0.8 km) from downtown.

ℹ️ 10 🅿️ 🕐 Closed in winter
🚭 ⬡ MC, V

🏨 ORCA ADVENTURE LODGE

$$$

2 MILES (3 KM) N OF TOWN
TEL 907/424-7249 OR
866/424-6722
FAX 907/424-3579
www.orcaadventurelodge.com
If you like to play outdoors, this is the place for you. At the head of Orca Inlet, the lodge provides easy access to the mountains, forest, and sea. Guided outings include a wildlife viewing tour of Orca Inlet, a Sheridan Glacier hike, sea kayaking, a brown bear photo safari, an excursion to Childs Glacier, and fresh- and saltwater fishing. Winter visitors can try heli-skiing and ice climbing. The rooms are set in a renovated and historic cannery.

🍴 40 🅿️ 🚭 ⬡ All major cards

🏨 NORTHERN NIGHTS INN

$$–$$$

500 3RD ST.
TEL 907/424-5356
FAX 907/424-3291
www.northernnightsinn.com
A great bargain, this grand, centrally located 1908 house

PRICES

HOTELS

An indication of the cost of a double room in the high season is given by **$** signs.

$$$$$	Over $300
$$$$	$200–$300
$$$	$120–$200
$$	$80–$120
$	Under $80

RESTAURANTS

An indication of the cost of a three-course meal without drinks is given by $ signs.

$$$$$	Over $75
$$$$	$50–$75
$$$	$35–$50
$$	$20–$35
$	Under $20

features spacious rooms furnished with antiques and such amenities as entertainment centers, kitchens, private entrances, and wonderful views of the waterside. You also receive the attention of the innkeeper, a friendly and knowledgeable dynamo.

ℹ️ 4 🅿️ 🚭 ⬡ All major cards

🍴 BAJA TACO

$

NICHOLOFF ST. AT THE HARBOR
TEL 907/424-5599
www.bajatacoak.com
For years this café's owners came north from Mexico in summer to run a popular food stand out of a small converted school bus. Success led to expansion into a small café with a pleasant deck—though they still use a converted bus (albeit a larger one) as the kitchen. Try the fish tacos—what could be better in a fishing town?

🍴 40 🅿️ 🕐 Closed Oct.–mid-April 🚭 ⬡ Cash only

🍴 KILLER WHALE CAFÉ

$

504 1ST ST.
TEL 907/424-7775

A busy gathering place, this café fills with locals clad in rain gear and rubber boots. Serves traditional breakfast and a good selection of soups, sandwiches, and salads for lunch. Locals are partial to the Killer Whale's cheesecake.

🍴 70 🚭 💳 All major cards

PRINCE WILLIAM SOUND

🏨 PRINCE WILLIAM SOUND LODGE
$$$$$
ELLAMAR
TEL 907/440-0909
www.princewilliamsound.us
This remote cluster of log buildings is tucked into a forested little bay in the Tatitlek Narrows, 25 floatplane miles (40 km) from Valdez. The lodge offers ocean fishing for halibut, hiking, native village visits, whale-watching, kayaking, bird-watching, and serious loafing. The rooms are handsome and the food excellent. How about seafood paella (with mussels right off the beach) followed by rhubarb-blueberry crisp using ingredients from the garden?

ℹ️ 5 🕐 Closed mid-Sept.–mid-May 🚭 💳 Cash only

WRANGELL–ST. ELIAS NATIONAL PARK

🏨 ULTIMA THULE LODGE
$$$$$
TEL 907/854-4500 (VOICE MAIL ONLY)
e-mail: info@ultimathule lodge.com
www.ultimathulelodge.com
This cozy lodge lies deep in the heart of Wrangell–St. Elias National Park and Preserve. Flown in for several nights at a time, guests spend their days exploring the wilds by flightseeing, hiking, fishing, glacier trekking, or wildlife-watching.

ℹ️ 6 🕐 Closed Oct.–mid-March 🚭 💳 Cash only

🏨 COPPER RIVER PRINCESS WILDERNESS LODGE
$$$
MILE 102 RICHARDSON HWY. (COPPER CENTER)
TEL 907/822-4000 (SUMMER) OR 800/426-0500
www.princesslodges.com
One of a chain of luxury lodges set in beautiful parts of Alaska, the Copper River Princess sits above the confluence of the Copper and Klutina Rivers. Overlooking Wrangell–St. Elias, with great views of towering peaks, the Princess assumes a ritzy hunting lodge theme and offers a lot of amenities.

ℹ️ 85 🅿️ 🕐 Closed mid-Sept.–mid-May 🚭 🍴 💳 All major cards

MCCARTHY/ KENNICOTT

🏨 KENNICOTT GLACIER LODGE
$$$–$$$$
KENNICOTT
TEL 907/258-2350 OR 800/582-5128
FAX 907/248-7975
www.kennicottlodge.com
In the middle of Wrangell–St. Elias, this reproduction of a historic mine building sits amid a ghost town—the site of the old Kennecott copper mill. This lovely wooden building features a full-length front porch for gazing at the surrounding mountains, woods, and glaciers. The restaurant serves fresh, hearty food and is open to the public as well as guests. Reservations are recommended.

ℹ️ 35 🕐 Closed mid-Sept.–mid-May 🚭 💳 All major cards

🏨 MCCARTHY LODGE
$$$
DOWNTOWN MCCARTHY
TEL 907/554-4402
FAX 907/554-4404
www.mccarthylodge.com

This lodge comprises two separate facilities: a backpacker hotel for budget travelers and, across the street, Ma Johnson's, a nicely restored 1916 building that blends historic elegance with a hint of funkiness. Extras include a restaurant, a bar, and a shuttle service that takes visitors to the mill site and the glacier.

ℹ️ 20 🕐 Closed in winter 🚭 💳 MC, V

▨ INTERIOR

TALKEETNA

🏨 TALKEETNA CABINS
$$$–$$$$$
N. C ST. & MAIN ST.
TEL 907/733-2227 OR 888/733-9933
www.talkeetnacabins.org
Hand built by the owners, these three new log cabins are pretty on the outside and spacious and well appointed inside. Each includes a kitchen, living room, and full bath. The cabins lie near the river on the edge of historic Talkeetna. The owners also rent a three-bedroom house.

ℹ️ 4 cabins, 1 house 🅿️ 🚭 💳 MC, V

🏨 MAIN STREET SUITES
$$$
NEAR MAIN ST. & D
TEL 907/733-1782
www.talkeetnasuites.com
As travelers amble through the historic downtown of tiny Talkeetna (pop. 850), they easily could pass right by Main Streets Suites and never notice it. They'd likely spot the comely, handcrafted log building. And the ground-floor Wildflower Café probably would catch their eye, especially if they smelled the chef's grilled sesame salmon or crab-stuffed halibut. But tucked away up on the second floor are two spacious, well-appointed suites. The North

Suite's sun room offers a tasty view of lively Main Street.

📱 2 🆂 🅐 MC, V

🍴 TWISTER CREEK RESTAURANT

$$–$$$

13605 E. MAIN ST.

TEL 907/733-2537

www.denalibrewing company.com

One of the liveliest spots in town, partly due to its excellent food, much of it sourced locally. The menu ranges from nachos, burgers, and salads to fine dishes like seared halibut with lemon caper sauce and Thai coconut shrimp curry. One patron said that he and his buddies "would fight like dogs over the smoked turkey sandwich." The other reason for Twister Creek's popularity lies next door: the Denali Brewing Company, owners of the restaurant—which accounts for the signature beer cheese soup.

🪑 150 🅿 🆂 🅐 All major cards

🍴 TALKEETNA ROADHOUSE

$–$$

MAIN ST. BETWEEN B & C STS.

TEL 907/733-1351

www.talkeetnaroadhouse.com

This café/bakery is classic Talkeetna, in a historic building where locals and visitors have gathered for hearty meals, strong coffee, and famed cinnamon rolls since 1944. Upstairs are eight basic rooms for rent.

🪑 50 🆂 🅐 MC, V

DENALI NATIONAL PARK & PRESERVE

SOMETHING SPECIAL

🏨 CAMP DENALI

$$$$$

TEL 907/683-2290

FAX 907/683-1568

www.campdenali.com

Deep in the heart of Denali National Park and Preserve, this lodge understands its priorities. Sure, the cabins scattered across the hillside are a cozy delight and the meals are excellent, but Camp Denali focuses on the national park, the grand wilderness that surrounds it. Guests can choose from among several naturalist-led outings on such topics as tundra wildflowers, glaciers, and wildlife, and each evening visiting authorities host presentations on various aspects of the park. Camp Denali is the only park lodge with views of the Great One.

📱 18 🕐 Closed mid-Sept.–early June 🆂 🅐 Cash only

🏨 DENALI GRIZZLY BEAR 🍴 RESORT

$$$–$$$$

MILE 231 PARKS HWY.

TEL 907/683-2696 (SUMMER) OR 866/583-2696

FAX 907/683-2323

www.denaligrizzlybear.com

Sited at the entrance to Denali National Park and Preserve—with shuttle service to the park visitor center—this resort sprawls along 17 acres (7 ha) of riverfront property above the rushing Nenana. Lodging choices range from rustic cabins to swanky cabins to rooms in the new Cedar Hotel, whose rooms all feature decks overlooking the river—and lots of gleaming cedar. Owned and operated by born-and-bred Alaskans.

📱 72 rooms, 28 cabins 🅿 🕐 Closed in winter 🆂 🅐 D, MC, V

🍴 THE PERCH

$$–$$$$

MILE 224 PARKS HWY.

TEL 907/683-2523 OR 888/322-2523

www.denaliperchresort.com

As its name suggests, the Perch is on a hill (actually, a

glacial moraine) amid the treetops. Customers sit back and enjoy the views as they dine on beef, seafood, vegetarian dishes, pasta, and game such as caribou medallions with portobello mushrooms. Famous for its bread, which it supplies to other restaurants, the Perch lies about 13 miles (21 km) south of the park.

🪑 50 🅿 🕐 Closed in winter 🆂 🅐 All major cards

🍴 MCKINLEY CREEKSIDE CAFÉ

$–$$

MILE 224 PARKS HWY.

TEL 907/683-2277 OR 888/533-6254

FAX 907/683-1558

www.mckinleycabins.com

A casual family dining spot that provides much better food than most such places, the Creekside is known for its varied and enormous breakfasts; try the Mount McKinley–size skillet dishes. The vast lunch and dinner menus range from chili to halibut, soups to sandwiches,

---

🏨 Hotel 🍴 Restaurant 📱 No. of guest rooms 🪑 No. of Seats 🅿 Parking 🕐 Closed 🔼 Elevator

and salmon to burgers, salads, steaks, and Cajun linguine.

🛏 40 🅿 Ⓢ 🕐 Closed in winter 🅰 All major cards

FAIRBANKS

🏨 RIVER'S EDGE RESORT
$$$–$$$$

4200 BOAT ST.
TEL 907/474-0286 OR
800/770-3343
www.riversedge.net

This beautifully landscaped resort sprawls along the Chena River, with the restaurant and many of the cottages situated right beside the meandering waterway. Guests often throw a fishing line into the Chena, hoping to hook a grayling for supper. No worries if you come up empty; the resort's fine restaurant serves all sorts of seafood dishes.

ⓘ 86 cottages, 8 suites 🅿 🕐 Closed Oct.–April Ⓢ 🅾 🅰 All major cards

🏨 WEDGEWOOD RESORT
🍴 **$$$–$$$$**

212 WEDGEWOOD DR.
TEL 907/452-1442 OR
800/528-4916
FAX 907/451-8184
www.fountainheadhotels.com

Bordering Creamer's Field Migratory Waterfowl Refuge, this large, in-town luxury resort feels more like a country place. The Wedgewood's one- and two-bedroom suites feature kitchens, living rooms, and dining rooms and are tastefully decorated. The resort houses the superb Fountainhead Antique Auto Museum. Also on the resort property is the summers-only **Bear Lodge** hotel, with 157 spacious rooms and the inviting **Golden Bear** restaurant.

ⓘ 306 🅿 Ⓢ 🅾 🅰 All major cards

🏨 AURORA EXPRESS
$$$

1540 CHENA RIDGE RD.

TEL 907/474-0949 OR
800/221-0073
www.fairbanksalaskabedand
breakfast.com

This bed-and-breakfast comprises seven railroad cars set permanently on 700 feet (213 m) of track amid a spruce forest on the property. Dating back as far as 1924, the cars have been converted into elegant lodgings that would befit an 1890s railroad magnate. One of the sleepers is divided into four suites, while each of the three other cars rents in its entirety. Breakfast is served in the dining car.

ⓘ 7 Ⓢ 🕐 Closed early Sept.– late May 🅰 MC, V

🏨 BRIDGEWATER HOTEL
$$$

723 1ST AVE.
TEL 907/452-6661 OR
800/528-4916
FAX 907/452-6126
www.fountainheadhotels.com

On the Chena River, in the midst of historic downtown Fairbanks, this quiet, refined boutique hotel offers a European feel. Generous service and the fact that the hotel is kept so shipshape place it among the town's finest. Try to reserve one of the corner rooms facing the river.

ⓘ 93 🅿 🕐 Closed in winter Ⓢ 🔁 🅰 All major cards

🍴 PIKE'S LANDING
$$–$$$$

4438 AIRPORT WAY
TEL 907/479-6500
www.pikeslodge.com

Another Fairbanks institution on the banks of the Chena, Pike's is noisy and crowded, just the way patrons like it. The luxurious fine-dining room will fill your steak and lobster needs, after which you can mingle with the masses on the enormous summertime deck, which serves about 400 people at a time and has its own dock. Pike's is known for its Sunday brunch and desserts.

🛏 530 🅿 Ⓢ 🅾 🅰 All major cards

🍴 THE PUMP HOUSE
$$–$$$$

796 CHENA PUMP RD. (MILE 2)
TEL 907/479-8452
www.pumphouse.com

A national historic monument, this favorite Fairbanks restaurant is a converted early 1900s mining pump station. The sprawling lawn and deck on the Chena River are traditional spots for basking in the warm Interior summer sun. Seafood is first among equals on the lengthy menu, which also features beef, pork, chicken, pasta, vegetarian, and game, like the elk meatloaf.

🛏 220 🅿 Ⓢ 🅾 🅰 All major cards

🍴 GAMBARDELLA'S PASTA BELLA
$$–$$$

706 2ND AVE.
TEL 907/457-4992
www.gambardellas.com

A warm, homey downtown restaurant beloved by locals, Gambardella's has a genuine Italian feel and menu. The Italian sausage and bread are made on the premises, and the lasagna boasts a nationwide reputation, with ten layers of fresh pasta, ricotta cheese, and that homemade sausage.

🛏 200 🅿 🕐 Closed L Sun. Ⓢ 🅰 All major cards

🍴 BUN ON THE RUN
$

3434 COLLEGE RD. (IN PARKING LOT BY BEAVER SPORTS)

This wildly popular white-and-pink trailer in a parking lot dishes out food that is fast but wonderful—as well as cheap. The cooks are especially adept at baking. Among the consistent winners are coconut bars, muffins, cinnamon rolls, brownies, and calzones.

🅿 🕐 Closed Sept.–May 🅰 Cash only

🅢 Nonsmoking   🅢 Air-conditioning   🖼 Indoor Pool   🎽 Health Club   🅰 Credit Cards

CHENA HOT SPRINGS ROAD

🏨 CHENA HOT SPRINGS RESORT
$–$$$$
MILE 56.6 CHENA HOT
SPRINGS RD.
TEL 907/451-8104
FAX 907/451-8151
www.chenahotsprings.com
The sprawling resort at the
end of this beautiful road
centers on outdoor and indoor
hot springs, but activities are
many and varied, including
hiking, disc golf, horseback
riding, mountain biking, and
flightseeing. Guests can also
take a geothermal energy tour,
go gold panning, ride in a cart
pulled by sled dogs, or visit the
ice museum and ice bar—not
to mention all the winter
activities. Accommodations
range from tents and yurts to
rustic/swanky lodge rooms.
ℹ️ 80 rooms, 7 yurts 🅿️ 🚭
♿ All major cards

🍴 TWO RIVERS LODGE
$$$–$$$$
MILE 16 CHENA HOT SPRINGS RD.
TEL 907/488-6815
FAX 907/488-9761
www.tworiverslodge.com
In this historic log building
superb contemporary dishes
abound. The menu leans
toward the classics: Alaska king
crab, New York pepper steak,
steamed clams, and chicken
marsala. On sunny days the
wood-fired oven on a deck
overlooking the lake bakes
excellent focaccia and pizza.
🪑 90 🅿️ 🕐 Closed L
🚭 ♿ All major cards

▨ THE BUSH

DILLINGHAM

🏨 THAI INN
$$$
119 E ST., W
TEL 907/842-7378

www.thai-inn.com
Accommodations in this
remote town are basic—except
for this incongruous B&B
that brings a little piece of
Thailand to the Alaska Bush.
Perched atop the highest
inhabited point in Dillingham,
it offers great views of the
bay and mountains. Rooms
feature hand-carved teak
furniture from Thailand,
Thai art, and other Thai
decor. The Royal Orchid
Suite is especially huge
and luxurious.
ℹ️ 5 🅿️ 🚭 🛗
♿ All major cards

BETHEL

🏨 ALLANIVIK HOTEL
$$$
1220 HOFFMAN HWY.
TEL 907/543-4305
FAX 907/543-3403
Allanivik offers quiet, modern
rooms (some with shared
baths) in three buildings.
Alaska native art beautifies
most of the rooms and
public spaces. A café in the
adjacent solarium serves
Korean barbecue and sushi.
ℹ️ 30 🅿️ 🚭
♿ All major cards

🏨 BENTLEY'S PORTER HOUSE BED & BREAKFAST
$$$
624 1ST AVE
TEL 907/543-3552
www.bentleysbnb.com
Rooms in this big, friendly
B&B in downtown Bethel
explore an eclectic array of
themes, including rural
English and African. Ask
for one overlooking the
Kuskokwim River. The
rooms share about half as
many baths.
ℹ️ 30 🅿️ 🚭
♿ All major cards

PRICES

HOTELS

An indication of the cost of
a double room in the high
season is given by **$** signs.

$$$$$	Over $300
$$$$	$200–$300
$$$	$120–$200
$$	$80–$120
$	Under $80

RESTAURANTS

An indication of the cost of
a three-course meal without
drinks is given by $ signs.

$$$$$	Over $75
$$$$	$50–$75
$$$	$35–$50
$$	$20–$35
$	Under $20

NOME

🏨 AURORA INN & SUITES
$$$–$$$$
302 E. FRONT ST.
TEL 907/443-3838 OR
800/354-4606
www.aurorainnome.com
While this attractive new
hotel may lack character, it
does boast many amenities.
Some rooms offer views of the
Bering Sea, while the executive
suites feature full kitchens and
bay windows. Go in search of
the sauna should things get a
bit chilly.
ℹ️ 54 🅿️ 🚭 🛗
♿ All major cards

🏨 NOME NUGGET INN
$$
FRONT ST. & BERING AVE.
TEL 907/443-4189 OR
877/443-2323
FAX 907/443-5966
Right on the Bering Sea, this
fun place is stuffed with gold
rush memorabilia and kitsch,
although the plain guest
rooms lack the spirit of the
public spaces. Just off the
lobby is one of Nome's most

🏨 Hotel 🍴 Restaurant ℹ️ No. of guest rooms 🪑 No. of Seats 🅿️ Parking 🕐 Closed 🛗 Elevator popular hangouts, the Gold Dust Lounge, where guests can mingle and chat with locals while warming up with a cup of coffee.

🛈 47 🅿 🚭
♠ All major cards

KOTZEBUE

🏨 NULLAGVIK HOTEL
🍴 $$$$
308 SHORE AVE.
TEL 907/442-3331
FAX 907/442-1630
www.nullagvik.com
To plant this modern hotel north of the Arctic Circle took some doing, such as erecting it on pilings. The decor reflects Kotzebue's predominant Inupiat Eskimo culture. Check out the Observation Room. In the hotel restaurant, guests can savor such dishes as reindeer sausage, steaks, and seafood. This is the town's tourism hub, so reserve early.

🛈 78 🚭 🎽
♠ All major cards

DALTON HIGHWAY/ DEADHORSE

🏨 PRUDHOE BAY HOTEL
🍴 $$$$
DEADHORSE
TEL 907/659-2449
FAX 907/659-2752
www.prudhoebayhotel.com
Think mobile home on steroids and you'll have an accurate picture of this hotel's style. Here close to the Arctic Ocean, near the end of the Dalton Highway, most of the clientele are oil-field workers. While some of the rooms are spartan, a few provide TVs and phones. Its cafeteria is among the few eateries in the rough and ready town of Deadhorse. Watch for polar bears, caribou, and other wildlife.

🛈 170 🅿 🚭 🎽
♠ All major cards

GATES OF THE ARCTIC NATIONAL PARK & PRESERVE

SOMETHING SPECIAL

🏨 INIAKUK LAKE WILDERNESS LODGE
$$$$$
INIAKUK LAKE
TEL 907/479-6354 OR
877/479-6354
FAX 907/474-2096
www.gofarnorth.com
This exclusive fly-in lodge provides rustic luxury 6 miles (10 km) from Gates of the Arctic National Park and Preserve, one of the world's wildest and most remote places. The hand-built log lodge is a spacious marvel that even has electricity and hot water, thanks to solar and wind power. You can canoe, hike, fish, and watch for the abundant wildlife, including caribou, grizzlies, moose, and wolves. If you want even more remoteness, the owners can fly you (and a guide) to either of two cabins deep within the park for day trips or overnight stays.

🛈 5 rooms, 2 cabins 🕐 Closed Sept.–Feb., May–mid-June
🚭 ♠ MC, V

🏨 PEACE OF SELBY WILDERNESS
$$$$$
SELBY LAKE
TEL 907/672-3206
www.alaskawilderness.net
This isolated lodge surrounded by Gates of the Arctic offers the chance to get really far away from it all. The handsome main lodge was crafted from local white spruce logs. The expansive and nicely furnished loft is rented as a single unit. When it's time to bathe, guests use the outdoor, wood-fired hot tub by the lake. The lodge's other units consist of four rustic cabins at far-flung sites.

Contact the lodge for winter opportunities.

🛈 1 room, 4 cabins 🚭
♠ Cash only

BARROW

🏨 TOP OF THE WORLD HOTEL
$$$$
1200 AGVIK ST.
TEL 907/852-3900
FAX 907/852-6752
www.tundratoursinc.com
A fixture in Barrow, this aptly named hotel is also the town's tourism hub. All the rooms are clean and decent, particularly those in the new wing; try for one with an ocean view. Ask about walking tours, sightseeing excursions, and Inupiat Eskimo cultural programs.

🛈 50 🅿 🚭 ♠ All major cards

🏨 KING EIDER INN
$$$–$$$$
1752 AHKOVAK ST.
TEL 907/852-4700
FAX 907/852-2025
www.kingeider.net
This contemporary hotel comes as a surprise. Rooms are spacious, bright with blond pine furniture, and replete with amenities; about half have kitchenettes. One suite features a stone fireplace, a kitchen, a pine-log four-poster bed, and a Jacuzzi.

🛈 19 🚭 ♠ All major cards

🍴 PEPE'S NORTH OF THE BORDER
$$–$$$
1204 AGVIK ST.
TEL 907/852-8200
North of the border, indeed. Next door to the Top of the World Hotel, Pepe's is a local gathering place that serves up Mexican and American food and plenty of conversation. There're flautas and soft tacos, and steak and lobster.

🕐 220 🅿 🚭
♠ All major cards

🚭 Nonsmoking 🆒 Air-conditioning 🏊 Indoor Pool 🎽 Health Club ♠ Credit Cards

Shopping in Alaska

Most Alaska artisans draw from a deep-seated intimacy with the outdoors when creating their arts and crafts. This bond with the natural world also influences such products as clothing, books, and food. Works by Alaska natives often carry on ancient traditions, sometimes with a modern twist.

■ SOUTHEAST ALASKA

Arts, Crafts, & Gifts

Alaska Indian Arts Historic 13 Fort Seward Dr., Haines, tel 907/766-2160. Carved totems, prints, and other traditional Northwest Coast native items.

Annie Kaill's 244 Front St., Juneau, tel 907/586-2880, www.anniekaills.com. Fine arts and crafts by Alaska artists. The diverse offerings include art glass, paintings, stoneware, jewelry, pottery, prints, and even artful wooden benches.

Juneau Artists Gallery 175 S. Franklin St., Juneau, tel 907/586-9891. Local artists operate this gallery, selling work that spans a wide range of media, including watercolors, fused art glass, ceramics, photography, and bead art.

Sea Wolf Gallery Fort Seward Parade Grounds, Haines, tel 907/766-2540, www.tresham.com. The gallery and studio of native son Tresham Gregg, whose diverse work includes totems, bronzes, and wall sculptures.

The Soho Coho 5 Creek St., Ketchikan, tel 907/225-5954. Owner Ray Troll exhibits and sells his fishy art, but he also designs funny T-shirts and calendars. The gallery also displays the work of other local artists.

Books & Maps

The Observatory 299 N. Franklin St., Juneau, tel 907/586-9676, www.observatorybooks.com. This bookstore specializes in maps and books about Alaska and other Arctic regions—more than 3,000 titles and other items all told.

Old Harbor Books 201 Lincoln St., Sitka, tel 907/747-8808. This local institution carries an impressive number of books that deal with Alaska topics.

Parnassus Books 105 Stedman St., Ketchikan, tel 907/225-7690. In the Creek Street district, this packed store offers fine collections of books on Alaska, art, and women.

Food

KetchiCandies 315 Mission St., Ketchikan, tel 907/225-0900 or 800/225-0970, www.ketchicandies.com. If you're yearning for a den of dietary iniquity, head for KetchiCandies. Handcrafted daily, its fare includes classics (nut clusters and caramels) and unexpected temptations (ginger root drenched in chocolate).

Taku Smokeries 550 S. Franklin St., Juneau, tel 800/582-5122, www.takustore.com. Taku smokes salmon, and visitors can watch the process and taste the results. Along with hot-smoked sockeye, you can buy smoked salmon spread and more.

■ ANCHORAGE & MAT-SU

Arts, Crafts, & Gifts

Anchorage Museum 625 C St., Anchorage, tel 907/929-9200, www.anchoragemuseum.org. This large, excellent downtown museum is arguably the finest in Alaska, and the gift shop shares that reputation. A great place to buy a souvenir.

Alaska Native Heritage Center 8800 Heritage Center Dr., Anchorage, tel 907/330-8000 or 800/315-6608, www.alaskanative.net. The state's premier institution devoted to Alaska natives. Its gift shop offers a diverse array of authentic items.

Alaska Native Medical Center 4315 Diplomacy Dr., Anchorage, tel 907/729-1122, www.anmc.org. Virtually unknown to visitors, this medical center's gift shop may be the best place in the city to get first-rate authentic Alaska native works.

Aurora Fine Art Gallery 737 W. 5th Ave., Anchorage, tel 907/274-0234. One of many fine downtown galleries, the Aurora features both traditional and contemporary works.

Books

Alaskana Books 564 S. Denali St., Palmer, tel 907/745-8695, www.alaskanabookshop.com. Offering a vast selection of books on Alaska, this bookstore carries some 25,000 rare and out-of-print books.

Title Wave Books 1360 W. Northern Lights Blvd., Anchorage, tel 907/278-9283 or 888/598-9283, www.wavebooks.com. The state's largest independent bookseller, this store boasts a half million titles.

Clothing

Octopus Ink Clothing 410 G St., Anchorage, tel 907/333-4657, www.octopusinkclothing.com. Elaborate hand-painted clothes, many with an octopus motif.

Oomingmak 604 H St., Anchorage, tel 907/272-9225 or 888/360-9665, www.qiviut.com. Some 250 Alaska native women belong to this co-op. They hand-knit expensive, luxurious qiviut into marvelous hats, scarves, and tunics.

General Merchandise

Saturday Market 3rd Ave. & E St., Anchorage, tel 907/272-5634. Name aside, this outdoor market is held on both Saturdays and Sundays in summer. Hundreds of vendors sell crafts, food, and more.

■ KENAI PENINSULA

Arts, Crafts, & Gifts

Bunnell Street Arts Center

106 W. Bunnell St., Ste. A, Homer, tel 907/235-2662. This nonprofit occupies the Inlet Trading Post, where browsers can view the works of some 60 artists, many of them local.

Experience Fine Art Gallery
On the boardwalk, Halibut Cove, tel 907/296-2215. This quaint space is literally a community of artists, most of whom also display their works, which range from pottery to paintings, jewelry, and other pieces.

Fireweed Gallery 475 E. Pioneer Ave., Homer, tel 235-3411. This gallery offers a variety of high-end Alaska art. Look for such unusual works as sculptures fashioned out of fossilized whale bones.

Inua—The Spirit of Alaska
Cannery Row Boardwalk, Homer, tel 907/235-6644. This shop sells fine Alaska native crafts, particularly from the Inupiat and Yupik Eskimo villages of western Alaska.

Kenai Fine Arts Center 816 Cook Ave., Kenai, tel 907/283-7040, www.kenaifinearts.com. This center houses several artist organizations and displays and sells paintings, pottery, sculptures, and other visual arts by central peninsula artists.

Resurrect Art Coffeehouse Gallery 320 3rd Ave., Seward, tel 907/224-7161. Set in a historic building was once a church, this favorite local hangout offers espresso, tasty pastries, and a healthy helping of local art, ranging from simple crafts to expensive paintings.

Clothing

Nomar 104 E. Pioneer Ave., Homer, tel 907/235-8363 or 800/478-8364, www.nomaralaska.com. Visitors who want Alaska-tough apparel should comes here. Much of its gear and clothing is perfect for the outdoors.

General Merchandise

Kenai Landing 2101 Bowpicker Lane, Kenai, tel 800/478-0400. This complex features galleries, a museum, and an indoor market

with some 40 vendors. Goods include pottery and specialty foods. Part of the historic cannery has been restored to process salmon on a modest scale. The delicious result is available for purchase.

North Wind Home Collection 173 W. Pioneer Ave., Homer, tel 907/235-0766. It's hard to say what you won't find in this eclectic home furnishings emporium. Predictably, there are sofas, beds, clocks, and tables, but there are also baby clothes, local art, polar bear figurines, and, on occasion, black swan baby tutus.

ALASKA PENINSULA

Arts, Crafts, & Gifts

Alutiiq Museum & Archaeological Repository 215 Mission Rd., Kodiak, tel 907/486-7004. In keeping with the repository's mission to explore and preserve Alutiiq culture, the gift shop sells consignment items—dolls, baskets, ivory carvings, masks—for native artists and craftspeople.

Baranov Museum 101 Marine Way, Kodiak, tel 907/486-5920. The gift shop in this museum naturally carries classic Russian pieces, including icons, samovars, painted Easter eggs, nesting dolls, and lacquerware.

PRINCE WILLIAM SOUND

Arts, Crafts, & Gifts

Spirit Mountain Artworks Mile 33 Edgerton Hwy., Chitina, tel 907/823-2222, www.spiritmountainalaska.com. Though perched on the edge of remote Wrangell–St. Elias National Park and Preserve, this is one of Alaska's best galleries, featuring more than a hundred Alaska artists.

Books

Orca Book & Sound Co 507 1st St., Cordova, tel 907/424-5305. This legendary local bookstore offers rare, out-of-print, and first-

edition books. It also serves as an art gallery; visitors can admire and buy.

INTERIOR

Arts, Crafts, & Gifts

Denali Images Art Gallery 22336 S. Talkeetna Spur Rd., Talkeetna, tel 808/333-7779, www.denaliimagesartgallery.com. A photo gallery full of lush images of the Alaska Range, the aurora borealis, and Alaska wildlife. Check out the owner's handcrafted jewelry, too.

Gallery 49 and Co-Op Arts Learning Center 535 2nd Ave, Ste. 103, Fairbanks, tel 907/452-2787, www.co-op-arts.com. This gallery features the work of Alaska artists, most of them from the Fairbanks area. The Learning Center offers classes, some designed for tourists.

Goose Lake Studio Mile 239 Parks Hwy. (Denali entrance), tel 907/683-2904. This gallery displays works by Alaska artists, including owner Donna Gates King. Pieces include paintings, quilts, and pottery.

Judie Gumm Designs 3600 Main St., Ester (Fairbanks area), tel 800/478-4568, www.judiegumm.com. Using silver and beads to make such items as a flying geese necklace and salmon earrings, Gumm creates jewelry that's more like sculpture.

Santa Claus House 101 St. Nicholas Dr., North Pole (Fairbanks area), tel 907/488-2200, www.santaclaushouse.com. It sells virtually everything connected to Christmas.

THE BUSH

Arts, Crafts, & Gifts

Chukotka-Alaska 514 Lomen St., Nome, tel 907/443-4128. This small shop celebrates the Russia-Alaska connection by selling art and crafts influenced by native cultures from both sides of the Bering Sea.

Maruskiya's of Nome 247 Front St., Nome, tel 907/443-2955. This store specializes in ivory sculptures carved from walrus tusks.

Entertainment

Summer or winter, Alaskans love events, and visitors are welcome to join the fun. In addition to transitory events, some cities and larger towns offer ongoing entertainment (often only in summer), such as music, theater, dance, comedy, and general carousing.

■ SOUTHEAST ALASKA

Days of '98 Show Eagles Hall, 6th & Broadway, Skagway, tel 907/983-2545, www.thedaysof98show.com. Chronicling the last days of 19th-century con man Soapy Smith's life, this musical comedy has been getting laughs for more than 70 years. Prior to the show, watch "The Vagabond of Verse," a tribute to famed Far North poet Robert Service.

New Archangel Dancers Harrigan Centennial Hall, Sitka harbor, tel 907/747-5516, www.newarchangeldancers.com. This all-female group performs traditional Russian dances and stages frequent programs in downtown Sitka. They are a blaze of colorful costumes and bounding energy as they do the Cossack Horsemen's Dance or the Beryozka gliding dance.

Perseverance Theatre 914 3rd St., Douglas (Juneau area), tel 907/364-2421, www.perseverancetheatre.org. Among the nation's finest regional theaters, PT mixes classics with innovative, often edgy works. The classics range from *Death of a Salesman* to a rendition of *MacBeth* set in Tlingit culture and featuring an all-native cast.

Sheet'ka Kwaan Naa Kahidi Native Dancers 200 Katlian St., Sitka, tel 907/747-7290 or 888/270-8687, www.sitkatours.com/dance.html. In a community center the local Tlingit built in downtown Sitka, the public can catch traditional performances, during which dancers wear resplendent Tlingit regalia.

■ ANCHORAGE & MAT-SU

Alaska Dance Theatre 550 E. 33rd Ave., Anchorage, tel 907/277-9591, www.alaskadancetheatre.org. Alaska's premier professional dance company and school performs both ballet and modern. It often collaborates with Alaska musical companies to bring in big-name dancers.

Anchorage Opera 1507 Spar Ave., Anchorage, tel 907/279-2557, www.anchorageopera.org. Alaska's only professional opera company is one of the nation's best regional companies. Each year the troupe graces the performing arts center with full-blown operas.

Anchorage Symphony Orchestra 400 D St., Anchorage, tel 907/274-8668, www.anchoragesymphony.org. An accomplished company of professional musicians, the Anchorage Symphony plays several annual concerts in the performing arts center, often with prominent guests. It also gives children's concerts and other miscellaneous performances.

Chilkoot Charlie's 2435 Spenard Rd., Anchorage, tel 907/272-1010, www.koots.com. Arguably Alaska's most famous and eclectic nightspot, Koot's comprises some 11 separate bars. Many of the bars sport a theme, such as the Russia Room, which strives for a tsarist ambience; the Soviet Walk, which aims to simulate the atmosphere of a Soviet-era subway (don't ask why); and the Swing Bar, an ironic take on the 1940s complete with dry martinis, fedoras, and black and white televisions.

■ KENAI PENINSULA

Pier One Theatre on Homer Spit, Homer, tel 907/235-7333, www.pieronetheatre.org. Consistently intriguing and unpredictable, this esteemed theater stages a spectrum of plays and musical events. Visitors might catch an Edward Albee drama, a remake of *The Beggar's Opera*, a jazz harp trio, or a musical comedy covering a century of women's music.

■ INTERIOR

Blue Loon Mile 353.5 Parks Hwy., 3 miles (4.8 km) south of Fairbanks, tel 907/457-5666, www.theblueloon.com. Fairbanks's one-of-a-kind, self-proclaimed "cultural epicenter," the Blue Loon offers excellent food, nationally known musical acts, comedy, dancing, and first-run movies (mainstream and art house). Special events have included Monday night football on the giant screen, a hip-hop music fest, a scholarly lecture series, and an ugly sweater holiday party that lived up to its name.

Fairbanks Goldpanners Tel 907/451-0095, www.goldpanners.com. This fabled amateur baseball team has been taking the field in Fairbanks for more than half a century. But don't think "amateur" is a synonym for bush league; the level of play is high. Renowned major leaguers, such as Tom Seaver, Jason Giambi, and Dave Winfield have graced this diamond. A highlight is the Midnight Sun game, played without lights from 10:30 p.m. to 1:30 a.m. on the summer solstice.

Palace Theatre Pioneer Park, at Airport Way & Peger Rd., Fairbanks, tel 800/354-7274, www.akvisit.com. Nightly venue of the Golden Heart Revue, a lighthearted, costumed look at some of the leading figures of Fairbanks's gold rush past. You'll get a kick out of the Alaska fashion show, which is big on rubber boots.

Activities

Alaska offers several hundred million acres of great outdoors to explore, not to mention a rich cultural legacy. Given all that raw material, it's not surprising that there are hundreds, perhaps thousands, of guides and tour companies willing and able to show you around. This section is a mere sampler of available operators. Most are good, and many are excellent, but don't hesitate to check out an outfit if you're unsure about its reliability. Stop in and ask at the nearest chamber of commerce, visitor center, or Alaska Public Lands Information Center.

■ SOUTHEAST ALASKA

Boat Tours

Breakaway Adventures P.O. Box 2107, Wrangell, AK 99929, tel 907/874-2488 or 888/385-2488, www.breakawayadventures.com. Breakaway has been taking small groups up the mighty Stikine River since 1989, showing them moose, glaciers, and bears, and stopping at the hot springs along the way. The new boats feature sliding windows on all sides for easy viewing and warmth when it's blustery. Breakaway also runs trips to LeConte Glacier and the Anan Bear Observatory.

Esther G Sea Taxi 215 Shotgun Alley, Sitka, tel 907/747-6481, www.puffinsandwhales.com. In Capt. Davey Lubin, passengers get a former commercial fisherman, experienced mariner, biologist, botanist, and conservation-minded educator who can share much about the wildlife and ecology of gorgeous Sitka Sound. He offers small, personal, customized tours to a maximum of six people.

Hiking, Backpacking, Sea Kayaking, & More

Above & Beyond Alaska PO Box 211202, Auke Bay, AK 99821 (Juneau), tel 907/364-2333, www.beyondak.com. This outfit offers adventures from easy hikes to ice climbing, but it's especially known for its sea kayaking trips and its ventures onto the Mendenhall Glacier—including overnight stays on the glacier. Some of the kayaking journeys go to prime bear-viewing sites and whale-watching areas.

Gastineau Guiding 1330 Eastaugh Way, Juneau, tel 907/586-8231, www.stepintoalaska.com. Leads a mix of active cruise ship passengers and independent travelers on hiking trips in the rain forest, across the alpine tundra, and to a glacier. Also offers sea kayaking and whale-watching excursions.

Scenic Flights

Southeast Aviation 1249 Tongass Ave., Ketchikan, tel 907/225-2900 or 888/359-6478, www.southeastaviation.com. The pilots of this small outfit will fly customers almost anywhere in Southeast Alaska; each has been flying the Inside Passage for more than 25 years. They specialize in flightseeing trips in six-passenger floatplanes to beautiful Misty Fiords National Monument; trips range from a 30-minute introduction to 2.5 hours above the glaciers and rain forest–cloaked mountains.

Tours & Excursions

Alaska Nature Tours P.O. Box 491, Haines, AK 99827 tel 907/766-2876, www.alaskanaturetours.net. This company's bus, van, boat, and hiking tours focus on the rich wildlife and fine scenery that envelop Haines, notably the Chilkat Bald Eagle Preserve, where more than 3,000 eagles gather in fall. Tours range from the shoreline, where you'll see whales, seals, and seabirds, to the alpine tundra, where you may spot bears, marmots, or mountain goats.

Chilkat Guides Ltd. P.O. Box 170, Haines, AK, 99827, tel 888/766-2491, www.raftalaska.com. For almost three decades, Chilkat has been leading raft trips through the Arctic National Wildlife Refuge and through the Tatshenshini-Alsek World Heritage Site. They do day trips, too.

■ ANCHORAGE & MAT-SU

Scenic Flights

Rust's Flying Service P.O. Box 190867, Anchorage, AK 99519, tel 907/243-1595 or 800/544-2299, www.flyrusts.com. Taking off from the world's busiest seaplane base, Lake Hood, this decades-old company offers a bird's-eye view of south-central Alaska. Also runs bear-viewing trips and drops off passengers for hunting, fishing, and rafting adventures.

Snowmobiling/ATV

Alaska Backcountry Adventure Tours P.O. Box 3820, Palmer, AK 99645, tel 907/745-2505 or 800/478-2506, www.youralaska vacation.com. This outfit specializes in motorized recreation: all-terrain vehicles (ATVs) in the summer and snowmobiles (most locals call them "snow machines") in the winter. They do rentals and guided tours, including multiday backcountry safaris.

■ KENAI PENINSULA

Boat Tours

Kenai Fjords Tours Seward tel 800/478-8068, www.alaskaheri tagetours.com. Offers more than a dozen different boat tours of Resurrection Bay and Kenai Fjords National Park. Watch for whales, seabird rookeries, and sea otters. And get ready to be wowed when a house-size chunk of glacier breaks loose with a gunshot-like boom and thunders into the sea.

Canoeing

Alaska Canoe & Campground 35292 Sterling Hwy., Sterling, tel 907/262-2331, www.alaska canoetrips.com. For boat and gear rental, shuttles, and other services. Adjacent to the nearly 2 million acres (810,000 ha) of the Kenai National Wildlife Refuge, including the renowned Canoe Lakes Trails System.

Hiking & Backpacking

Center for Alaskan Coastal Studies P.O. Box 2225, Homer, AK 99603, tel 907/235-6667, www.akcoastalstudies.org. This group educates visitors about Kachemak Bay and nearby. Its all-day natural history excursion begins with a boat tour across the bay, stops at a research center, takes a hike through the rain forest, and finishes with outstanding tide-pooling.

▥ ALASKA PENINSULA & THE ALEUTIANS

Backcountry Exploration

Alaska Alpine Adventures 4605 N. Wolverine Rd., Palmer, tel 877/525-2577 www.alaskaalpine adventures.com. Alaska Alpine Adventures specializes in trips exploring Lake Clark National Park and Preserve and other remote destinations.

Bear Viewing

Hallo Bay Camp Katmai National Park P.O. Box 2904, Homer, AK 99603, tel 907/235-2237, www.hallobay.com. Fewer than a dozen people at a time fly the 120 miles (190 km) from Homer to this utterly remote shoreline camp amid Katmai National Park. Guests spend from five hours to a week seeing the brown bears up close.

Sea Hawk Air 506 Trident Way, Kodiak, tel 907/486-8282 or 800/770-4295, www.seahawkair.com. Kodiak bears are said to be the nation's largest brown bear subspecies, and Sea Hawk takes people to view them—safely—in Kodiak National Wildlife Refuge and Katmai National Park.

▥ PRINCE WILLIAM SOUND & AROUND

Boat Tours

Stan Stephens Glacier & Wildlife Cruises 112 N. Harbor Dr., Valdez, tel 866/867-1297, www.stanstephenscruises.com. The Stephens family has run tour boats across Prince William Sound since 1971. During the signature day trip to the massive Columbia Glacier, visitors often spot sea otters, puffins, sea lions, and humpback whales.

Scenic Flights

Wrangell Mountain Air P.O. Box MXY, No. 25, McCarthy, AK 99588, tel 907/554-4411 or 800/478-1160, www.wrangell mountainair.com. Even the longest flights can't take in all of 13.2-million-acre (5.3 million ha) Wrangell–St. Elias National Park and Preserve, but starting from this enclave amid the park, pilots manage to cover quite a bit. You may see the Bagley Icefield, the peaks of the Wrangells, the Stairway Icefall, and all manner of wildlife.

▥ INTERIOR

Climbing Schools

Alaska Mountaineering School 13765 3rd St., Talkeetna, tel 907/733-1016, www.climbalaska.org. The school offers multiday climbing courses as well as organizes climbing expeditions in Denali and throughout Alaska.

Outdoor Adventures

1st Alaska Outdoor School 1800 College Rd., Fairbanks,

tel 907/590-5900, www.1stalaska outdoorschool.com. This outfit offers a vast range of tours, from puttering around Fairbanks to a three-day journey to the Arctic Ocean. They do winter, too, with dog mushing, ice fishing, aurora-watching, and other trips.

Denali Zipline Tours 13572 Main St., Talkeetna, tel 907/733-3988, www.denaliziplinetours.com. For a bird's-eye view of the boreal forest, try a three-hour tour gliding from platform to platform on cables strung high in the trees, punctuated by occasional walks across swaying suspension bridges. The zip line segments range from 40 to 700 feet long (12–213 m) and at times participants are 60 feet (18 m) above the ground. The guides combine environmental education with lots of fun.

Scenic Flights

Talkeetna Air Taxi 14212 E. 2nd St., Talkeetna, tel 907/733-2218 or 800/533-2219, www.talkeetna air.com. In small planes equipped with skis, you'll fly over the rugged Alaska Range on your way to circling the Great One—20,320-foot (6,194 m) Mount McKinley. You may spot climbers inching up its slopes. Some trips land on a glacier at the base of McKinley.

▥ THE BUSH

Scenic Tours

Northern Alaska Tour Company P.O. Box 882991W, Fairbanks, AK 99708, tel 907/474-8600 or 800/474-1986, www.northern alaska.com. Using the 414 rugged and remote miles (667 km) of the Dalton Highway as its lifeline, this company makes the Arctic accessible. In 10-passenger vans or 25-passenger buses, visitors can take a one-day run up to the Arctic Circle and back. The company also features trips to Barrow, Nome, and other Arctic sites.

INDEX

ILLUSTRATIONS CREDITS

All photos by Michael Melford, unless otherwise noted below:

27, Norbert Rosing/National Geographic Stock; 31, BeBa/Iberfoto/photoaisa; 32-3, Bettmann/CORBIS;
34, Library of Congress Prints & Photographs Division, LC-USZ62-37810; 37, Gary Braasch/CORBIS; 41, Bates
Littlehales/National Geographic Stock; 42, David Sanger Photography/Alamy; 60, Alaska Stock LLC/National
Geographic Stock; 83, DeborahMaxemow/iStockphoto; 94, Ken Graham/AccentAlaska.com; 125, George
Burba/Shutterstock; 142-3, Maltings Partnership, Derby, England; 151, Galen Rowell/CORBIS; 192, Didier
Lindsey/AccentAlaska.com; 218, Wolfgang Kaehler/CORBIS; 219, Gabriel Bouys/AFP/Getty Images; 226,
Hugh Rose/AccentAlaska.com; 231, Galen Rowell/CORBIS; 232, Matthias Breiter/AccentAlaska.com.

National Geographic

TRAVELER
Alaska

Published by the National Geographic Society

John M. Fahey, *Chairman of the Board
and Chief Executive Officer*
Declan Moore, *Executive Vice President;
President, Publishing and Travel*
Melina Gerosa Bellows, *Executive Vice President;
Chief Creative Officer, Books, Kids, and Family*
Lynn Cutter, *Executive Vice President, Travel*
Keith Bellows, *Senior Vice President and Editor in Chief,
National Geographic Travel Media*

Prepared by the Book Division

Hector Sierra, *Senior Vice President and General Manager*
Janet Goldstein, *Senior Vice President
and Editorial Director*
Jonathan Halling, *Design Director,
Books and Children's Publishing*
Marianne R. Koszorus, *Design Director, Books*
Barbara A. Noe, *Senior Editor,
National Geographic Travel Books*
R. Gary Colbert, *Production Director*
Jennifer A. Thornton, *Director of Managing Editorial*
Susan S. Blair, *Director of Photography*
Meredith C. Wilcox, *Director, Administration
and Rights Clearance*

Staff for This Book

Jane Sunderland, *Project Editor*
Elisa Gibson, *Art Director*
Ruth Ann Thompson, *Designer*
Carl Mehler, *Director of Maps*
Michael McNey and Mapping Specialists,
Map Production
Marshall Kiker, *Associate Managing Editor*
Galen Young, *Illustrations Specialist*
Katie Olsen, *Production Design Assistant*

Manufacturing and Quality Management

Phillip L. Schlosser, *Senior Vice President*
Chris Brown, *Vice President, NG Book Manufacturing*
George Bounelis, *Vice President, Production Services*
Nicole Elliott, *Manager*
Rachel Faulise, *Manager*
Robert L. Barr, *Manager*

The information in this book has been carefully
checked and to the best of our knowledge is accurate.
However, details are subject to change, and the
National Geographic Society cannot be responsible for
such changes, or for errors or omissions.

The National Geographic Society is one of the world's
largest nonprofit scientific and educational organizations. Founded in 1888 to "increase and diffuse
geographic knowledge," the Society works to inspire
people to care about the planet. National Geographic
reflects the world through its magazines, television
programs, films, music and radio, books, DVDs, maps,
exhibitions, live events, school publishing programs,
interactive media and merchandise. *National Geographic*
magazine, the Society's official journal, published in
English and 33 local-language editions, is read by more
than 60 million people each month. The National
Geographic Channel reaches 435 million households
in 37 languages in 173 countries. National Geographic
Digital Media receives more than 19 million visitors a
month. National Geographic has funded more than
10,000 scientific research, conservation and exploration projects and supports an education program
promoting geography literacy. For more information,
visit www.nationalgeographic.com.

For more information, please call 1-800-NGS LINE
(647-5463) or write to the following address:

National Geographic Society
1145 17th Street N.W.
Washington, D.C. 20036-4688 U.S.A.

For information about special discounts for bulk
purchases, please contact National Geographic Books
Special Sales: ngspecsales@ngs.org

For rights or permissions inquiries, please contact
National Geographic Books Subsidiary Rights:
ngbookrights@ngs.org

National Geographic Traveler: Alaska (Third edition)
ISBN: 978-1-4262-1162-1

Artwork by Maltings Partnership, Derby, England

Printed in Hong Kong

13/THK/1